trade SECRETS

trade SECRETS

Everything you will ever need to know about everything

Meg Sanders, Annie Ashworth,

Katherine Lapworth & Alexandra Fraser

ORION

First published in Great Britain in 2001 by Orion
An imprint of The Orion Publishing Group Ltd
Orion House,
5 Upper St Martin's Lane,
London
WC2H 9EA

A CIP catalogue record for this book is available
from the British Library.

Printed in Italy by Printers Trento srl

CONTENTS

FOREWORD

There has to be a way to do those little jobs in life more effectively and efficiently whether it's removing stains from clothing or sailing around the world, worming the cat or trying on a bra.

With shameless and unswerving determination, we have left no trade uncovered in our quest to ensure that this new edition is as thorough as possible. Between us we have begged, cajoled and issued veiled threats to people in businesses of all kinds to persuade them to reveal the secrets of their success.

Our conclusion seems to be that so long as you are well stocked with vinegar and bicarbonate of soda in your store cupboard and a lemon in your fruit bowl, you should be able to tackle most of the problems life throws your way. Though perhaps they may not help when buying a Picasso at auction.

To those who have parted with their hard-earned secrets, we thank you for your time and enthusiasm for the project. To friends we have hassled, we hope you will talk to us again. We have had great fun putting the book together, and now consider ourselves experts in almost every area under the sun. The problem is remembering the right tip in the right situation!

Meg Sanders
Annie Ashworth

ACCOUNTANTS

Sam Shone;
Derek Hayes, ACA

Don't get caught out by the tax man – self assessment means you have to keep a note of all your expenses (especially if you are self employed). Make up a file and be ruthless about keeping a note of everything.

Keep a notepad in your glove compartment and jot down your business mileage as soon as you complete a journey, rather than trying to remember it later.

Take a map of the UK and find the furthest point from where you live and work. That is where your tax office will be.

The Inland Revenue has heard all the excuses in the book and a few more besides. So before you try to be clever, remember that tax officials have undergone a triple humour, pity and empathy bypass.

If you are adding up two columns of numbers that are supposed to balance, and you have a difference that is exactly divisible by 9, it means you have transposed two numbers.

Don't take shortcuts. The longer and more tedious route to a final calculation will be the right one. A rushed one may be wrong and will need reworking.

As a rough guide it's worth keeping three times your monthly outgoings in an instant-access account.

Try to keep your tax arrangements simple so that any tax saving isn't lost by the cost of administrating them.

The Inland Revenue helpline (number on your tax return) can answer your questions and save you pounds (if you use it rather than asking your accountant).

ACTORS

Adrian McLoughlin;
Glynis Fletcher;
Victoria Pritchard

Learning Lines

Highlight your lines with a highlighter pen, so you can see clearly what you are learning – 85 per cent of learning is done visually rather than aurally. You can also see at a glance how big your part is!

For learning verse, recite your lines while exercising – something rhythmic like swimming or running is best. The rhythm of the action will help the lines go in, it makes exercise a lot less boring and you'll look fantastic for the opening night!

Learn your lines by recording the other lines on tape with appropriate gaps, then playing the tape and saying your own lines in the gaps.

Nerves & Relaxation

Nerves are a good thing! Keep reminding yourself of this on opening night. Nerves are adrenaline and adrenaline, when working well, gives you an energy and awareness that are hard to beat. Find a way to channel the nerves to your advantage. Use the concentration that the adrenaline gives you to focus on the character and the 'reality' of the scene. Lose yourself in that, not in the nerves themselves.

For stage fright or first night nerves, a few drops of Bach Flower Rescue Remedy on the tongue, or four drops in a glass of water, work a treat. Repeat as often as you like.

Always centre your breathing before going on stage. Breath is the thing that gives away our nerves. Ask yourself, 'What is the worst thing that can happen?' That usually results in a bit of a reality check.

A shoulder massage helps relieve tension. Get the cast to line up one in front of the other and get each member to give the person in front a shoulder massage. The director has to go at the back.

To dispel nerves, take several slow deep breaths before going on stage.

Remember that you are not usually alone on stage and it is good to exercise the trust and confidence you have in your fellow actors by reassuring yourself that if anything does go wrong there will be somebody there to help you out.

If all else fails, say to yourself, 'Okay then, go home! Nobody is making me do this, I could leave right now and not go through with it!' This should remind you of all the fantastic things that you love about the job!

Voice Warm-ups

Warm up your articulatory muscles by pretending you've got a large toffee in your mouth and it's sticking to your teeth. Make exaggerated chewing movements for a good five minutes. This is best done in the privacy of your dressing room.

To reduce laryngeal (voice box) tension, rotate your shoulders and keep them down and relaxed when you go on stage.

Tongue twisters will help to relax your tongue. They also sound so daft that they take your mind off your nerves.

'Peggy Babcock' repeated over and over makes an amusing tongue twister, as does, 'I'm not a pheasant plucker'!

Work on your vowels with a phrase that (almost) uses them all: 'Are they eating cakes? Are your shoes sore?'

'My Bonny lies over the ocean' is a favourite singing warm-up as it exercises the voice over a wide range.

Gilbert and Sullivan are to be thanked for the best 'patter song' articulation exercises to be found anywhere.

Vocal warm-ups are a dead give away as to where you trained. You can always spot a fellow LAMDA or RADA student by the warm-up exercises they do. If you want to remain a mystery, make up something new.

If all else fails, there is always the actor's favourite vowel exercise: 'Me, Me, Me, Me, Me'.

On Stage

Learn to recognise the heat from the strongest light sources on stage (practise during technical rehearsals) – you will then always be lit properly.

When expressing strong emotions, learn to face outwards and upwards. Our instinct is to look down and inwards which is not always helpful on stage.

When speaking to the audience, engage with individuals if they are visible. Only concentrate on one person for a second or two before moving on.

If hands are a problem, try performing with them in your pockets – eventually you will start to relax and your hands will come out naturally.

Specs and contact lens wearers. If you have poor normal vision always use your glasses or contact lenses on stage so you will be able to see the other actors' faces.

When playing comedy, expect laughs from the audience to come in completely different places to those in rehearsals – they always will.

Never stop for a laugh in comedy, until the audience response forces you to.

Develop sufficient breath control to have the choice of when to breathe on a line. Try always to have more breath than you need.

Actively listen to the other actors. They may change a line or use a different tone of voice, which will change your response. It will also stop you thinking solely about what you have to say next and your response will be more natural and instinctive.

Make your character real. Invent a potted biography of them, right down to their favourite colour. This may never be needed but will help your character to have depths beyond the lines.

When facing upstage, raise your voice or project it more strongly.

Never fill a cup or a glass to the brim on stage. If you're nervous it'll go everywhere.

Working with Children

Remember to be positive and always praise the children for what they are doing – something that you find second nature may be a real challenge to a child.

Encourage children to work at exploring their voices, their bodies and their imagination – at a young age they are all equally important tools.

Get children moving and 'doing' as soon as possible – they are 'doers' not talkers – and don't be too fussy or pedantic about what they do. Let them explore an idea freely and, with a bit of guidance, you will be amazed where they end up!

Make sure you have sweets with you, to act as a bribe, if necessary. You could pretend they are part of the story you're working on – magic jewels, space vitamins, shrinking medicine, pirate treats… They will spark their imaginations, bodies and voices into immediate action.

Be prepared for some screaming!

AGA & RAYBURN OWNERS

Aga-Rayburn;
Mary Berry;
Claire Macdonald
of Kinloch Lodge;
John Wilks & Son

Four- and two-door ovens are rather different – take care when adapting recipes.

Cook root vegetables (including potatoes) perfectly every time. Bring to the boil on the hotplate, boil for five minutes, drain, place in the simmering oven with a lid on until they're soft enough to poke a fork into them without undue resistance.

Make fabulous toasted cheese sandwiches. Make the sandwiches up as normal, place on the simmering plate and pull the lid down.

Get a timer! Agas are vented through a flue, so all the cooking smells – including the fragrance of burning buns – are drawn away. A timer will remind you that you have something in the oven, so you don't have a nasty surprise in a week's time.

Wipe the lids and the top of your Aga with a cloth wrung out in warm soapy water, and buff up with a duster. Do this after each use to keep the top as good as new.

Never hang towels or blankets over the air intake on the fire door. This will cause the Aga to stifle and put itself out.

Use the oven as much as possible. For example, start frying onions on the hotplate and then leave them to soften by placing the pan (metal handles only) into the roasting oven.

Eating Chinese? Heat the wok first on the floor of the roasting oven to get the best 'sizzle'. (Metal-handled woks only of course!)

Cook dry toast or toasted sandwiches by placing the bread directly on the floor of the roasting oven, and pressing it down slightly. Melba toast is great done this way too.

If you are having a baking session, plan the recipes that need higher temperatures first (scones for example) then move on to sponges and biscuits as the Aga temperature will have dropped.

When making drop scones on the coolest plate, lift the lid 20 minutes before you start cooking to take off the intense heat, rub the plate with butter and cook the scones or potato cakes. Delicious!

When you are batch baking, immerse the plain (or cooling) shelf in cold water between each use to keep the temperature of the oven low enough.

Prevent your kitchen turning into a sauna (and the Aga losing heat) by cooking your Christmas pudding in the simmering oven.

Stock can be brought to the boil on the boiling plate and then transferred to the simmering oven and left overnight. This will extract all the goodness and flavour. Leave yourself a note to remind you to take it out in the morning, and skim off the fat once the stock has cooled.

Trainers and damp shoes can be filled with newspaper and put in the coolest oven (of a four-door Aga) for a short time to dry out. Don't forget them or you'll have roast footwear.

Alternatively, tie them by the laces to the Aga rail.

Dry glued ornaments on the back of the Aga.

Cut down on ironing by taking towels, sheets, pillowcases and so on, out of the tumble dryer, folding them and pressing them on to the lid of the simmering plate (not the boiling plate, which will scorch).

Dry out bacon rinds on a baking sheet in the simmering oven. Then feed them to the birds.

When making meringues, the mixing bowl must be dry and grease free. Wash it in hot, soapy water, rinse and leave on the back of the Aga to dry out completely.

When making bread, you want everything to be warm, so warm the flour and the bowl before you start by standing them on the back of the Aga

To open closed fir cones for Christmas decorations, pop them into the warming oven (of a four-door Aga) and they will unfurl beautifully.

For perfect sliced citrus fruit for Christmas wreaths and decorations, place the slices on wire racks on the top of the Aga. If you can leave them for two or three days (perhaps while you are away for a weekend) so much the better. The heat is ideal and ensures that they will keep their colour perfectly as they dry.

Flowers can be dried for arrangements by hanging them above the Aga, as the gentle heat will dry them slowly.

'Seal' fresh flowers by dabbing the end of the stalks on to the hotplate instead of immersing them in boiling water.

Prevent an Aga from losing heat when cooking a Christmas turkey by wrapping the turkey in plenty of foil (breast-side down) and time the cooking so that the turkey is ready one and a half hours before you want to eat. It will keep its heat if you leave it wrapped in foil, and the Aga will be free for roasting potatoes and boiling vegetables.

Conkers can be hardened for battle by leaving them overnight in the warming oven.

Save time making your morning cup of tea by filling up the kettle the night before and leaving it on the back of the Aga. The mug or cup can be left to warm too.

Farmers have put weak lambs and puppies into the coolest oven (with the door open!) for generations. Use the same method for hatching eggs too.

When your feet are frozen, open the coolest oven (on a four-door Aga), pull up a chair and rest your feet on an up-turned oven-proof dish (not metal of course) to thaw them out.

AID WORKERS

Ready to Go

Alison Woodhead; Helen Palmer; Claire Lewis at Oxfam; Duncan Green; Tim Aldred; Matthew Carter; Neal Baker; Steve Alston; Patrick Nicholson; Monica Conme at CAFOD; Peter Bowbrick; Maggie Baker; John Sills

Take plastic carrier bags. They are very useful and often unavailable in out-of-the-way places.

Take baby wipes to clean hands, face, body, surfaces and so on.

Take a pocket multi-tool, and attach it to your belt. You won't want to lose it.

Make up a survival tin to include: snare wire, flint and wire wool for fire starting, waterproof matches, SILOOM glow stick, needle, purification tablets, fish hooks, fishing wire and nail cutters.

Carry spare underpants and ear-plugs at all times.

A small 'housewife set' (sewing kit) is essential for removing splinters and repairing clothes.

Always carry a Swiss army knife – great for cutting toe-nails and scooping soil away for 'communing with nature'.

Always take an inflatable globe for directions, a pillow and a football, a copy of *Don Quixote* for sanity, and a jar of olives for martinis.

When all else fails, try producing your British Library card. It can get you into and out of most places.

Take something to read before you go to sleep. Often you cannot buy books in English. Gibbon's *Decline and Fall of the Roman Empire*, gives the maximum (excellent) reading for the minimum weight. Crossword puzzle books are also good.

Razor blades, shaving cream, deodorant and insect repellents may not be available at your destination.

To reduce the weight of your suitcase, use a shaving brush and shaving soap (yes, you can still buy them).

A universal bath plug comes in handy, especially in the former Soviet Union.

No bottle opener? You can take the top off a bottle of beer by using the cap of another bottle. Grip the neck of the bottle you want to open, place the top of the other bottle under the cap and, using the fingers gripping the neck as a fulcrum, use it to lever off the cap. Don't throw away the cap – you'll have to replace it on the empty bottle to open the last one.

Cheap plastic suitcases are strong and survive many years of rough treatment. Unfortunately they are also heavy.

Buy lots of books from charity shops before you go, and abandon them as you finish them.

Take today's newspaper with you. Anybody who has been away from home for some time will be desperate for that kind of news.

Neck pillows and eye-shades are wonderful for long air trips. Ear-plugs are great for flights in propeller-driven or other noisy planes (in the former Soviet Union particularly).

It can be cold even in hot countries. You may want a sweater in the evening.

Take a hat and wear it. An Australian felt hat is practical and reasonably formal. A panama is collapsible.

In many countries people have feet that are smaller or narrower than in the UK. You may struggle to find shoes to fit so take sandals with you.

Plastic sandals or flip flops are invaluable.

A palm top wins hands down over a laptop for those who must record what they do. Send it all home via IBM net or some other international, if expensive, ISP (Internet Service Provider). Alternatively print it out and send a fax.

A pocket short-band radio is a 'must have', particularly if it doubles as an alarm and watch with time zones – and it's great company on long bus rides.

Traveller's cheques are not accepted everywhere (Albania, for example). In other countries one particular brand is not accepted, as it is commonly forged. In some countries credit cards are accepted in major banks in the capital city only. Check before you go.

Always take dollars when you are travelling in Third World countries. They are accepted pretty much everywhere.

Check that the dollars were printed recently – old notes are not accepted, as forgeries are common. Torn and marked notes are not accepted either.

Take one-dollar bills for tips, taxis, hire of trolley at the airport and so on.

Decide on your strategy: travel heavy, carrying everything you might possibly need, or just take hand luggage, and make do.

You may not be able to buy printer ink or paper. It is wise to take a computer start-up disk with you. Anti-virus software is a must: most viruses come from Russia or the Third World.

Get a free Yahoo or Hotmail e-mail address. You can access this address from any computer connected to the internet, at an office you are visiting, or at an internet cafe. You can set your home e-mail to automatically forward all messages, or selected messages, to this address. Alternatively, you can set Yahoo to read the messages on your home e-mail server.

Leave a copy of addresses, and numbers of credit cards, air tickets, insurance policies, passports and traveller's cheques with someone at home.

Medical Considerations

Reduce heat rash by applying talcum powder liberally on feet and crotch areas.

In hot, humid places, do not wear waterproof or synthetic fibres as they promote heat rash and trench foot.

You can get spectacles made up locally at a very low price indeed. Don't. They are so badly made and fitted that they can cause permanent damage to your eyes. Get glasses made by your usual home optician and sent out by courier if necessary. Always take spares with you.

Aspirin and other pain-killers are often not available: it was once Tanzania's objective to have aspirins available in every small town. People will be very grateful if you can supply them.

Prickly heat occurs when you develop an allergy to your own sweat. Shower twice a day and use an antiperspirant to prevent it, and use powders as well if you get it.

Diabetics can take their insulin in an unbreakable thermos, re-cooling it whenever possible.

To reduce the risk of infection, if you are in unhygienic surroundings don't smoke. It is a common way of transferring bacteria from hand to mouth.

Don't wear open-toed shoes in the tropics because of leeches and other creatures.

Never urinate whilst submerged in water as this attracts minute water-borne insects to enter your urinary tracts.

Stop creepy crawlies creeping into bed with you. Apply Vaseline or shaving gel around the legs of your bed.

Wash your hands before and after eating, and after going to the loo (before too, if you are fastidious). Do not rub or touch your eyes.

Take care at night – tuck your mosquito net in all round your bed. If there's a gap, they're sure to find their way in.

Avoid wearing black – it attracts mosquitoes.

Garlic pills assist in keeping mosquitoes away.

Jungle Gel or jungle formula insect repellent containing DEET is very effective, but it melts plastic (on cup handles for example) so be cautious.

To avoid problems with gut rot, always have a supply of purification tablets. Take electrolyte rehydration fluid or powders as well, just in case.

Always clean under your nails as bacteria forms very fast in hot, humid conditions.

Take a sheet sleeping bag – they're very useful and, if suitably immersed in insect repellent, far better than a mosquito net.

If malaria pills disagree with you, and even if they don't, prevent bites by wearing long-sleeved shirts, socks and roll-on repellents.

Mosquitoes are much easier to catch (and therefore kill) when your hands are wet or soapy – they stick like glue!

Take a needle and thread to mend your mosquito net, and use it.

Deter unwanted bedfellows in the tropics by using four large jam jar lids. Place them under the feet of your bed, top them up with water – the ants cannot climb up for their midnight feast!

Iron clothes that have been hanging outside to kill the eggs of the tumbo fly. The larvae burrow into the skin – excruciating.

Leeches – pour salt on to the leech and the surrounding skin or touch them with a cigarette to get them to withdraw so you can remove them safely. The salt disinfects the wound.

It's important to get the biting part of a tick out of your skin. If you just grasp the body and pull, it can be left behind and will cause infection. Either hold a lighted cigarette over the body or deprive it of air by placing a big blob of petroleum jelly on it. It should then let go and come away easily.

For a snake bite – take the body of the snake with you to hospital to help identify the correct serum to use.

Tarantulas are usually in pairs – so look for the other one too.

Scorpion bites are very painful, but the venom stays local. Try to get a shot of local anaesthetic as soon as you can.

Aid kits, containing needles, syringes, dressings and other sterile equipment are available from travel clinics and sometimes from pharmacies. Dentistry kits are also worth taking. The thing is to make sure you have them with you if you need them, and maybe a friend to make sure they're used on you.

For rehydration purposes, Coca-Cola is as good as anything, as it contains lots of sugar and some salts – just make sure it's not the diet variety. Pour it between two containers to make it flat before drinking.

If you need a doctor or dentist, go to a first class hotel and ask who they use. Or ask an aid project, World Bank, United Nations etc.

You will be able to buy antibiotics on the street or in a shop without prescription. Ask your doctor for the generic name of the medicine.

Never let anyone stick a needle into you unless you have seen the needle and the syringe removed from a sealed sterile package, and you have seen the seal broken on what is injected into you.

In Pakistan you can expect diarrhoea one day in three – more often in the desert areas where there are Epsom salts in the water. In Kathmandu, expect one day in two. These are mainly dramatic but short-lived infections. In these countries and in Russia you may also get long term infections like giardia and amoebic dysentry. These may be much less dramatic, but they are serious in the long term. British path labs are very bad at diagnosing them (it needs a fresh and steaming specimen). Doctors abroad treat the symptoms even if there is no diagnosis by the path lab. If you get chronic tiredness and exhaustion, at any time after working abroad, insist that you are checked for dysentry, giardia and schistosomiasis. If the results are negative, get treated for dysentry anyway – bully your doctor.

Diarrhoea – baby wipes are heaven, soft tissue is pleasant, paperbacks will do. Learn to use your left hand – and eat with the right hand as the locals do.

If you feel ill and have a stomach-ache, it may just be dehydration. If you feel thirsty, you are certainly dehydrated. If your urine is dark yellow or brown you are dehydrated. Drink lots: pints of water rather than a cup of tea.

Take sunscreen and hats, and use them. If you are blonde, fair skinned or Irish be particularly careful. Sunbathing for one week on a holiday is one thing; sunbathing most days when you live in the tropics is another. You can be seriously and permanently wrinkled at the age of 24.

Keep drinking. You can buy fairly safe water in plastic bottles in most countries. Town water supplies are not safe in the former Soviet Union. Otherwise use water purifying tablets: purify the water in one plastic bottle while you are drinking from another.

Do not eat raw fish in Asia, especially Siberia: it has tapeworms. In fact be careful of all fish in Asia.

Do not drink milk or eat cheese, yoghurt, curd and other dairy products in underdeveloped countries until a foreign dairy expert tells you it is safe. Brucellosis and TB are not funny.

Have your teeth checked. You will not fancy going to a dentist in a country where 20 per cent of the population are HIV positive.

Have your own first aid kit: disposable syringes, plasters, fungicide, antiseptic, plastic thermometer (the mercury ones can explode in the plane). It might be difficult to explain your needs to a chemist, even with an interpreter.

Rehydration salts (electrolyte) are absolutely essential. Virtually any diarrhoea can be treated by one Immodium followed by rehydration salts. Cholera is treated by rehydration salts taken for four days, after which you miraculously recover. It is the dehydration that kills you so drink lots of it. Rehydration salts can be expensive in the UK, but the same is available very cheaply in the Third World. In an emergency, try one teaspoon of salt and five teaspoons of sugar to 1 ¾ pints/1 litre of boiled water (boiled so that you do not re-infect yourself). Or add to the water in a 1 litre Coca-Cola bottle, one capful of salt and five of sugar. These proportions are important.

Embassies should have clean blood plasma, but do not rely on them letting you have it.

At Work

Take all your essentials with you as you won't be able to take a couple of hours off on your first or second day to buy them.

Clear interpreters' fees with them and with your employer at the very beginning. Often they want fees appropriate to the top rate for fully bilingual interpreters, while your employer will only pay the rate students charge for rough translations. Everyone feels cheated, and you are in the middle.

When you first meet your interpreters talk to them for an hour or more, before your first meeting. This gives them time to get used to your voice. It also gives you time to explain what you are trying to find out, and to explain the jargon you will be using.

If you are a man and you have a woman interpreter, check with several people before you travel with her and stay in hotels with her. In a Muslim country this may be a 'no no' whatever she says. She may be compromised by being with you.

Insist that your local colleagues conform to EU health and safety laws, wear seatbelts and so on. Say that your firm is bound by these laws. Do not be afraid that you are abusing your power. How will you feel if one of them is killed?

Get travel insurance and read the small print. Many policies do not cover you for business trips, for more than one trip a year or for trips of more than a month. Many expect you to be treated by the local health service, which may exist in theory but not in practice, and is precisely what you are trying to avoid. A few hours on the internet will enable you to compare offers and read the small print.

Get enough currency or dollar traveller's cheques to see you through the first month until the administration gets organised.

Never lend money to a consultancy company. They will always pay you cash in advance to cover travel and subsistence if you insist. They all suffer from chronic cash-flow problems, and many go bust, so you may well have to wait several months for your fee. It is adding insult to injury if you have to wait this time for your expenses too.

Before you go, contact the people you are going to work with, and ask what to bring. It may be light bulbs, it may be baby food or it may be Angostura bitters that they are desperate for.

Ask the people you are working with to explain cultural differences. Get them to warn you when you are doing it wrong. Tell them you certainly will put your foot in it. For example, in the West it is polite to admire your host's possessions. In the East, they may have to give you a present of anything you admire. (If you do make this blunder, say, 'Thank you very much, you keep it for me'.)

Your subsistence allowance is meant to cover food, drink, and possibly accommodation for colleagues (locals who may work for the organisation or aid workers visiting on a temporary basis).

Find out when to arrive for a meeting – five minutes early, exactly on time, or exactly half an hour late as is expected in some parts of the world.

Telephones may not work outside the capital city, even in the former Soviet Union.

Briefcases and computers are status symbols and are very likely to be stolen. This may mean you losing several months' work. Do not keep papers in an expensive briefcase. Instead use a cheap canvas bag or a basket from the market. Back up all your computer data.

Prepare a five-minute sales pitch: why you are there, who is paying, how the country may benefit, how they personally may benefit, and who in government is backing you. This is the start to all interviews.

In some countries you can get voltage stabilisers for your computer from the hotel. You may have to buy one, but they are cheap compared with the alternative.

If you are on a long-term mission, get your parents or a friend to video each night's television, then send you the month's television on 30 tapes.

Hotel pillows are very big. Russian pillows are bigger still, half the size of a duvet. Take a blow-up pillow, or stuff the towels into a pillowcase to get a normal-size pillow. The house-keeper at the hotel may give you a reasonable sized pillow.

Tip the chambermaid or room servant once a week. Certainly tip them the day before you leave, and not on a weekend. Why? The senior chambermaid does the room the day you leave, to collect the tip. Weekend staff get the tip at the weekend.

Get advice from people who have been there before. It is pointless to have five suits when you go to Dar es Salaam, where cotton trousers and short shirts are normal, and suits would be unbearably hot.

Beware of advice lists written by the Foreign Office, the UN resident representative or anyone else on the cocktail circuit. They inhabit a different world.

Short trousers are unacceptable in most of Africa – a reaction against colonialism rather than because knobbly knees are sexy. In many countries women have to wear long dresses and long-sleeved blouses for decency. This also protects them from the sun. It is dangerous to flout the decency regulations.

Expatriates' Contingent Tax insurance covers you against having to pay UK tax if you have to return home early, for a funeral or because of a coup. You can also get insured against kidnapping, deportation and so on.

Get tax advice. There is very different tax liability for a consultant and an employee. If you do not know what you are doing, you may come back for your mother's birthday and find it makes you liable for a full year's UK tax.

If you are letting your own home, it is essential to get advice from a solicitor as well as from your estate agent. Also consider the tax implications.

Don't run daft risks. If someone who ought to know advises you not to go somewhere dangerous – don't.

There is an Arabic proverb, 'Don't tell the truth unless you have one foot in the stirrup' which can be translated as, 'If you are writing a truthful report, post it to the client after you have left the country'.

If your wheels are spinning in sand, stop revving. Get out and put something just in front of the wheel so it can get some grip – a piece of thick card, or some wood usually does the trick.

AMBASSADORS & CONSULS

Foreign &
Commonwealth Office,
www.fco.gov.uk

Check that any prescription medication you need when you are abroad is legal in the country you're going to. Phone the Consulate of the country in question and ask them before you leave. Sometimes a doctor's letter may be required to confirm that you really need the medication and are taking it legitimately.

Don't cross land borders with people you don't know, and never carry a parcel or any luggage through customs for anyone else.

Don't drive a vehicle across a border for anyone, and be very careful about lending any-one your car.

Avoid using luggage that has external pockets unless you can padlock them.

Most British Consulates have an answer phone for out-of-hours callers. The message on the answer phone should give you an emergency contact number. Hotels, tour operators and the police usually have the number of the nearest British Consular Office.

If you're going abroad to pursue a hobby such as bird-watching, botany, or train, plane or ship spotting be vary careful about using binoculars and taking photographs, particularly near military sites. You could be mistaken for a spy.

Take enough money to pay for a flight home – just in case your ticket becomes invalid for some reason.

Victims of crime, make sure you are issued with a police report. You'll need it if you want to make an insurance or compensation claim.

The British Consul can:

issue emergency passports;
contact relatives and friends and ask them to help you with money or tickets;
advise on how to transfer funds;
at most Posts, in an emergency, advance money against a sterling cheque for up to £100 supported by a banker's card valid for the appropriate amount;
as a last resort, and providing that strict criteria are met, make a repayable loan in exceptional circumstances for repatriation to the UK or other country of nationality;
help you to get in touch with local lawyers, interpreters and doctors;
arrange for next of kin to be informed of an accident or a death and advise on procedures;
contact and visit you if you are under arrest or in prison;
give details of organisations experienced in tracing missing persons;
in certain circumstances, make representations on your behalf to the local authorities.

Consuls cannot:

intervene in court proceedings;
get you out of prison;
give legal advice or instigate court proceedings on your behalf;
get better treatment for you in hospital or prison than is provided for local nationals;
investigate a crime;
pay your hotel, legal, medical or any other bills;
pay for your travel tickets, except in very special circumstances;
obtain accommodation, work or a work permit for you;
undertake work more properly done by travel representatives, airlines, banks or motoring organisations.

ANGLERS

National Federation of Anglers: Bill Coe, Lenny Goulding, Geoff Bibby, Dr Terry Thomas, Maggie Vaux, Wendy Miller

Avoid accidents. Don't fish during a thunderstorm. Your rod is probably made from carbon fibre which is an excellent conductor of electricity.

To keep your line free from knots when sea fishing, simply punch a couple of holes 1 in/2.5 cm below the rim on either side of an ice-cream container. Push a small skewer through one of the holes, then through the spool and finally through the hole on the other side of the tub. Fill the tub with water up to the level of the holes. As it rotates, the line gets wet and you avoid getting in a tangle.

Stop your hook from corroding by placing a few grains of rice in the hook box.

To extract a small lump of meat from a tin, just poke in a straw. A little piece of meat will go up inside the straw. Blow down the straw to get it out. The meat will be the perfect size and shape for bait.

It's important to keep your maggots warm in winter so that they remain active and wriggly. If you glue polystyrene to the outside of their box they will keep warm and stay lively all day.

To add flavour to your maggots or luncheon meat, sprinkle some curry powder on them the night before. The fish love the flavour.

Attract different sorts of fish by dyeing your maggots with food colouring. For example, red maggots attract perch.

To encourage bream to bite, melt some molasses in hot water and then mix your groundbait into it. Bream have a sweet tooth and will love this.

To stop your worms from sinking in the weeds when fishing in a lake, inject them with air and they'll float nearer the surface.

To put together a cheap kit, remember to look through all the magazines for second-hand equipment.

To stop your canvas tackle bag getting wet, always put it inside a heavy-duty plastic bag when on the boat.

Don't harm the environment. Keep your unwanted nylon line and take it home with you; chop it up into pieces so if you do lose it there won't be too much damage done.

Protect your hands from the cold and wet by rubbing petroleum jelly into them before you start fishing.

To keep your feet really warm, wrap them in kitchen foil and then put a pair of thick socks over the top. Your feet will stay snug and dry all day.

Don't waste money on expensive moonboots. Just buy your wellies one size too big and line them with some polystyrene.

To catch a really good salmon, put an item of clothing that belongs to your wife or girl-friend in with the bait feathers. Salmon respond to female pheromones.

Waders will keep you dry… up to the knees and thighs at least. Make sure your bottom stays dry too. Cut some rubber trousers off just below the knees and tuck them inside your waders. You won't look like a fashion-plate but you will be more comfortable than your wet-bottomed friends.

Make sure you are safe when you go fly fishing. Put a life-jacket on, especially if you are wading – in deep water your waders can fill up very quickly.

To stop yourself from falling into the water when you are in a boat, always remember to sit down!

Always be prepared for the big catch! Take some black plastic bin liners with you and some bags of ice in a cool box. When the big moment comes, put your catch inside the bin liner and surround it with ice bags. The one that didn't get away will stay frozen for several hours until you can get back to your freezer.

When fishing for carp, try enticing them with luncheon meat, sweetcorn or potatoes.

Get rid of slugs – use them as bait for chub, dace, roach and rudd.

Freshwater catfish aren't fussy when it comes to bait – it seems anything goes. Anglers have been known to try soured clams, ripened chicken entrails, pig liver, coag-ulated blood and even bits of scented soap!

Try tempting a mullet with banana, bread, cheese, peas or pasta.

Some brown trout are partial to… other brown trout. You can tell a cannibal trout by its hooked lower jaw.

Rainbow trout in America have been known to reach 50 lb (22.7 kg) in weight; unfortunately, they're a bit weedier in Europe with the maximum weight being around 24 lbs (11 kg).

You are allowed to fish with a bow and arrow on many American waters. The arrow is tied to the end of the line and the reel is fixed on the bow.

Store fishing lines in a dark place because UV light damages them.

Clean fishing rods with white spirit.

Rinse and dry fishing nets after each use, otherwise they will rot.

When you have rinsed your waders, hang them up straight and upside down to prevent kinks that will make them fracture.

Also rub olive oil into your waders to prevent cracking.

The sooner you pare a fish after catching it, the less mess you'll make.

Use polish on fishing rods to make them water repellent.

To stop fishing hooks going rusty put a couple of drops of vegetable oil in the box with them.

Soak fishing lines after use in washing-up liquid to stop them going rusty.

ANIMAL WELFARE OFFICERS

RSPCA **If you're thinking of keeping an exotic animal as a pet –** please think again. The reality is that many of these animals will suffer and die needlessly, either during capture and transportation or because their owners don't have the specialist knowledge or equipment to take care of them.

Young birds out of their nests are best left on their own. Try going away and coming back after an hour – they'll usually be gone by then. Only move them if they are in immediate danger from, say, traffic or predators. Don't move them far though. The parents are usually near by.

If you see a young hedgehog out during the daytime, it may be sick or injured, in which case phone the RSPCA.

Always cut up rubber bands and plastic beer can rings before consigning them to the bin. They can seriously injure a wide variety of animals if left intact.

Discarded bottles can be death traps for small animals, like mice and voles, so please recycle them.

Always completely remove the lids of tin cans and drop them into the bottom of the empty cans. If you only partially open them, and then push the lid down inside, a small animal can stick its head inside, and be badly cut or unable to pull it out again. The same is true for yoghurt pots with the lids only part removed.

To avoid travel sickness, don't feed an animal for 12 hours before making a journey.

When moving to a new house, keep your cat indoors for a couple of days, to let it get used to its new surroundings.

When your cat goes out of the new house for the first time, give it only part of its normal feed to encourage it to come home.

Never stare at a dog – it will be read as a threat.

Delivery people tend to be bitten by dogs when they leave a house, not when they arrive. If in doubt, back away slowly from a dog rather than turning your back and running, which may tempt it to chase you.

On bonfire night, keep pets indoors and let them watch television or listen to the radio to help drown out the bangs.

Build bonfires as late as possible and turn them over just before lighting them to make sure there are no hedgehogs or other small animals trying to hibernate inside.

Caged rabbits and other small outdoor pets should be put in a garage or outbuilding on bonfire night.

School Pets

If school pets are used to living at school, it's really better to let them stay there over the holidays provided they can be kept warm enough and someone can come in daily to feed and water them.

Check with parents when children volunteer to look after school pets.

Ask parents to sign a form accepting responsibility for the animal.

Attach clear care instructions to each animal's cage before handing them over.

Provide the name and address of the usual vet, and make sure parents know how the vet's bills will be met if necessary.

Make sure small children don't carry food around when you have cats or dogs in the house – it isn't fair on the animal.

ANTIQUE DEALERS & RESTORERS

Jane Knapp, Bath; Purdy Mellor, Tamworth; Stephen Zacirelo, Worcester; Peter Hanlon, Crediton; Patrick Beetholm-Smith, Kingsley Gallery, Bath; Maggie Masters, Stow on the Wold

Furniture

To age a piece of furniture, simply mix some furniture varnish with soot, and apply.

To remove a scratch from a table, crack open a walnut and rub it along the scratch. Walnuts contain a natural resin that will conceal the scratch.

Make new oak look old – place three tea-bags in hot water and leave some wire wool in the solution overnight. Rub the wire wool over the wood to age it.

To get rid of rings or minor scratches cover them with petroleum jelly and leave for 24 hours. Then rub it into the wood, wipe off the excess and polish as normal.

To darken wood use paraffin wax.

Polish wood with metal polish instead of the normal wood kind and it should come up a treat.

To remove greasy stains from wood mix talcum powder and methylated spirits into a sloppy paste. Paint on to the stain and leave to dry. Brush off.

To get rid of ink stains from furniture soak a piece of cotton wool in water and cover the stain with it. The mark will be drawn out and into the cotton wool.

Nourish furniture wood using a mixture of turpentine, linseed oil and malt vinegar.

To prevent the spread of woodworm treat the wood in May. The woodworm larvae emerge in June and July so this should nip them in the bud!

Even out the legs of old chairs by measuring the length of the shortfall on a piece of wood. Use this as a measurement to cut the other legs down to the same length.

To check the originality of handles look inside the drawer. If there are extra holes, the handles will have been added later.

Ceramics & Metal

To clean a gilded ceramic plate, simply soak it overnight in fabric conditioner and water. If there is no gilding, then soak in a weak bleach solution.

To fill a crack in pottery heat the piece slowly to 110 °C/225 °F/ Gas Mark ¼. This should open the crack slightly, allowing you to fill it with glue. Wipe off any excess and allow the piece to cool.

For hairline cracks put the plate in a saucepan of milk and boil for 45 minutes. The cracks should disappear.

Clean brass handles with lemon juice.

Stop cast iron from rusting by wiping with olive oil or sunflower oil.

To remove the craze on ceramic ware, soak the piece in baby disinfectant.

If you want to impress coin collectors don't polish a coin: use an old toothbrush and scrub it with hot water.

An easy way to identify silver is simply to sniff it. Silver has a stronger smell than plate.

To read faded silver hallmarks, light a candle. Let the soot settle over the hallmark and then place a piece of sticky tape over the soot. Transfer the tape on to a piece of paper and read the hallmark. Or you could breathe on a hallmark. The condensation should make it stand out more clearly.

To polish silver effectively, use your fingers.

Plated silver should not be stored away – use it.

To realign the teeth of a fork, put them in a vice and close it over the four prongs until they have become straight.

Stop brass from tarnishing by spraying it with furniture polish and leaving it to dry. This covers the brass with a thin layer of wax which protects it.

Clean a copper kettle by covering it with brown sauce and leaving overnight. Wash it off next morning and admire your reflection in the shiny surface!

Books & Paper

Remove brown stains from an old print by rubbing the paper with breadcrumbs.

To clean the tops of old books, gently rub with breadcrumbs.

To restore a wet book, put sheets of blotting paper between the pages of the first half. Place an even weight on top and gently dry with a hair-dryer. Repeat the process for the other half of the book.

Clean valuable old books with vellum bindings by dipping cotton wool in milk and gently wiping over the covers. Finally, clean off with a soft, dry cloth.

To repair cracks in papier mâché, use a little Polyfilla and sand down carefully. Then paint to match, and varnish.

Jewellery, Glass & Stone

To carry your barometer correctly, always hold it at an angle of 95°.

To get the most out of your barometer, store or display it anywhere except under a radiator.

Broken beads on frames can be replaced using dried split peas or lentils.

To restore bead work, hand wash in lukewarm water and blow dry gently with a hair-dryer.

Bring a shine to tortoiseshell by rubbing it with almond oil.

To remove marks from tortoiseshell, rub talcum powder over the mark with a cotton rag.

To protect ivory, polish with a little almond oil on a soft cloth.

To clean coral, lightly sponge with a weak detergent solution.

To improve the lustre and colour of pearls wear them next to your skin as often as possible.

Clean artificial pearls by rubbing carefully with a chamois leather.

Costume jewellery can still be expensive. Look after yours by cleaning it with a little baking powder, then brushing off any residue with a soft toothbrush.

Next time you clean your watch, remove the scratches on the face too. Just spend five or ten minutes gently rubbing the glass with metal polish, then wipe it off with a soft duster.

To unstick a decanter stopper, place the decanter in the fridge for 24 hours. Eight times out of ten, the stopper should then come out! For the other two occasions when it doesn't…

Remove a stuck stopper from an antique bottle by mixing two parts alcohol to one part glycerine and one part salt. Paint on the join between the stopper and the bottle neck and leave for 24 hours.

To clean a narrow-necked vase, fill with water and pop in a couple of denture-cleaning tablets.

To age a new piece of stone, cover it in yoghurt. In a few weeks, it will have acquired an 'I've been here for ages' look.

Preserve the shine on a slate hearth by spraying with WD40.

Textiles, Paintings & Toys

To clean delicate oil paintings, there's no need for fancy fluids. Spit on to a cotton-wool bud and gently rub the surface of the painting. Test a small area first (in case your spit is too corrosive).

To remove any slack from an oil painting, gently tap the small wooden wedges at each corner of the stretcher with a hammer.

Surface dirt can be removed from an oil or acrylic painting by rubbing with a piece of old bread.

When cleaning the glass of a painting, spray the cleaner on to your duster before polishing, not directly on to the glass. This stops the moisture from damaging the frame.

Clean gilt picture frames with a mixture made from one egg and a teaspoon of bicarbonate of soda.

To clean antique luggage, use saddle soap.

Clean velour upholstery with a solution of warm water and washing-up liquid. Dip some muslin into the mixture and wipe over the fabric.

If you want to get an even, thin layer of adhesive, gently roll the glue around a cocktail stick and then apply to the surface.

To prevent Araldite from looking too yellow, add a small amount of titanium powder.

To preserve stuffed animals, conceal a few mothballs in their glass case.

Give a stuffed animal a brilliant smile – wipe its teeth with a wet wipe to whiten its fangs.

To clean dark fur, dry some bran in the oven, rub it into the fur and then cover with a warm blanket. Leave it for half an hour before shaking the bran out and then brushing the fur.

To clean light fur, rub cornflour into the fur and roll it up in a warm blanket. Leave it for 24 hours before shaking out and brushing.

To store textiles, cover them up in acid-free tissue paper and roll around a cardboard tube (either from inside your kitchen paper roll or bought from a post office).

To test if something really is silk, throw it against a brick wall. If it sticks to the brick then it is the real thing.

To clean unpainted wax items, wipe them down with softened butter.

To replace an antique doll's eyelashes, get some false eyelashes and trim them down to a suitable length. Stick in place with a colourless, soluble glue.

If your antique doll is having a bad hair day, put a dab of cold cream on a comb and gently separate a lock at a time from the base of the head until you have got it all under control and she looks respectable again.

If you have a treasured teddy... keep him looking pukka with carpet shampoo and then just fluff him up afterwards.

Buying & Selling

When attending car boot sales, arrive early. The dealers will be out in force then and any bargains will get snapped up early.

The best time for sales is early spring and midsummer because that's when people tend to have clear outs, getting rid of 'rubbish' from their homes.

Don't be afraid to haggle – it's part of the fun and most people expect it.

If you are going to be selling at a car boot sale, you should take some loose change, a large umbrella, plastic sheeting (in case it rains) and something to sit on.

Take someone with you so that you can take it in turns to get drinks, keep an eye on the stall and deal with the rush… if there is one!

Don't put everything out at once – keep some good bits and pieces back so that you are not left with a lot of old rubbish.

Make sure that friends and family turn up and hang around your stall. If you've got a crowd there, it will attract other people.

Look out for people who offer quite a bit of money for a large number of items – they are often professional dealers or collectors who have spotted something they want on your stall.

ARBITRATORS

Citizens Advice Bureau

Keep a file of receipts, whatever the value of the product you have bought. Receipts are essential proof of purchase if you need to return an item for whatever reason.

If you buy faulty goods you should return them to the shop, with the receipt. You will be entitled to some or all of your money back.

Decided you don't like it after all? You will only be able to change it, or have a credit note or refund if this was agreed at the time of the sale with the seller. Check before you buy if you're not sure.

Beware when buying goods on extended credit. If you want to cancel the agreement (for example because you can no longer afford the goods), you will only be able to change your mind about keeping them if:

the goods were bought at the customer's home and the order is cancelled within a short period; or the seller agrees to cancel the sale – some sellers do this, others may provide a credit note instead of a cash refund; or the agreement contains cancellation clauses – these will set out whether and when cancellation is allowed and may also set out any charges payable on cancellation.

You may be able to claim compensation if you told the seller you needed goods delivered by a certain date and they were not delivered on time. If no date was given, then you must give the seller a date by which you expect the goods to be delivered before taking any further action.

That irritating parcel that you didn't ask for arrives. You do not have pay for these goods or send them back. Either:write to the sender saying that you did not order the goods. Give your name and the address at which the goods can be collected and, if necessary, say how collection can be arranged. The sender then has 30 days to collect the goods. If the sender does not collect within this period, the goods become your property; or do nothing, but keep the goods safe for six months. If the sender fails to collect them within this time, they become your property.

If you receive an invoice or letter asking for payment for goods that were not ordered, either ignore it or report the matter to the local trading standards as the sender may have committed a criminal offence. Try writing to the sender to complain too.

Buying second-hand? You cannot expect second-hand goods to be in the same condition as when they were new, unless the seller says that this is the case.

The basic statutory rights apply to second-hand goods bought from a seller: the goods must be of satisfactory quality and must match their description, but take into account the price and the age of the goods when assessing the quality.

If the seller has already pointed out stains, chips, cracks and so on, you cannot complain about defects afterwards.

It is a good idea to take someone along when buying second-hand goods especially if they are expensive. The other person can take notes of what the seller says about the condition of the goods. This is particularly useful in private sales, where not all the basic statutory rights apply.

Bull in a china shop? You are liable to pay for goods or property of the shop that become damaged by you or your children. If the goods are damaged by accident, it may be the shop's responsibility, since the seller has a duty to take care to protect goods from foreseeable accidents.

ARCHAEOLOGISTS

Andrew Townsend; Jonathan Erskine; Ian Ferris; Richard Hobbs

Treasure is defined as any item found that is made of more than ten per cent gold or silver which is over 300 years old, and in the case of coins, two or more such pieces. It also includes ten or more bronze coins more than 300 years old found in the same locality.

Objects found in association with treasure also count as treasure, for instance a pottery container with a hoard of Roman coins.

Single coins found on their own are not treasure and groups of coins lost one by one over a period of time (for example, those found on settlement or fair sites) will not normally be treasure.

All treasure finds must be reported to your local coroner within 14 days. Your local police station or museum will be able to tell you who to contact if you are unsure.

Send for a copy of the *Treasure Act Handbook* which has a full list of all relevant coroners in England and Wales. This can be obtained free of charge from the Department of Culture, Media and Sport (tel: 0207 211 6200).

The coroner will instruct you as to which museum or archaeological body you should take the find to. If the museum decides that the find is treasure they will inform the British Museum or the National Museum of Wales. If they or a local museum wish to acquire the find, the coroner will hold an inquest to decide whether it is treasure.

If your find is declared treasure, it will be valued by the Treasure Valuation Committee and you will be awarded the full market value for the find. If at any stage the find is not considered treasure it will be disclaimed and returned to you.

Before using a metal detector, always obtain permission from the landowner.

Detecting on scheduled ancient monuments is strictly forbidden unless permission has been obtained from English Heritage in England or Cadw in Wales.

Common land owned by your local councils may have by-laws relating to metal detecting.

All underwater finds of any date must be reported to the Receiver of Wreck, whose job it is to decide ownership. For more information contact the Receiver of Wreck at: Maritime and Coastguard Agency, Spring Place, 105 Commercial Road, Southampton SO15 1FG (tel: 01703 329474, fax: 01703 329477, e-mail: robbins@mcagency.org.uk).

All non-treasure finds (for example medieval bronze buckles, single coin finds, rehistoric flints) can be recorded voluntarily under the Portable Antiquities Scheme. A leaflet about the scheme with a full list of contacts can obtained from the Richard Hobbs, Museums & Galleries Commission Outreach Officer, c/o Department of Coins & Medals, British Museum, London WC1B 3DG (tel: 0207 323 8611). Alternatively visit the Portable Antiquities website at: www.finds.org.uk

Never try to excavate a site if you don't know what you're doing. Archaeology is essentially destructive, and once a site has been tampered with, its historical value is depleted or even destroyed.

To excavate a site you need permission from the landowner, or if the site is an ancient monument site, you need permission from English Heritage. You will also probably need support from your County Archaeologist, especially if you are an amateur.

If you plan to donate your finds to a museum, make sure you've contacted the museum first. You might discover that they don't actually need what you find.

It is a moral obligation for you to know what you're doing, to make meticulous notes, to wash, bag and catalogue your finds, and to study your finds afterwards.

If you are digging a deep trench, you will need to fulfil health and safety requirements.

Never lend your trowel or hand tape measure to anybody, however friendly. It's unlikely you'll get it back, whatever their good intentions.

The easiest way to avoid problems in excavation is to mark everything in indelible marker before you start to work. This includes bags, boxes, trays, labels and tools. You will never have enough time to do this once you have started work.

All beginners should find a real dig to work on as a volunteer or learner before committing themselves. Most archaeological work is very hard, tiring, wet, cold or sometimes hot.

If you go on any archaeological expedition outside Britain, learn how to fix basic problems in trucks, jeeps or minibuses. Take a lot of tools and insulating tape. Archaeological vehicles always break down – they're usually relics themselves.

A good toolbox should contain knicker elastic (for demarcating pegged-out areas), lollipop sticks, cocktail sticks, flour scoops and a perforated spoon.

You can never have enough string, nails and pencil erasers on an archaeological site. Find a friendly dentist and beg for old dental picks. They are invaluable.

ARCHITECTS

Royal Institute of British Architects, Roger Abbott RIBA

There are two types of architect: Chartered architects are members of the Royal Institute of British Architects (RIBA), which has a code of conduct and disciplinary measures. Registered Architects are just as qualified but are not members of the RIBA, perhaps because they are sole practitioners and the benefits of being members do not justify the professional membership fees.

Beware of people advertising themselves as Architectural Services, Designers or Technicians. The name 'architect' is protected and these people are not qualified architects.

If you need to find an architect, visit the RIBA website at www.architecture.com It has a list of all RIBA members, where they are based around the country and what projects they specialise in.

The RIBA also has a Clients' Advisory Service (tel: 0207 307 3700). Describe the project you have in mind and they can recommend a member in your area who specialises in that sort of work.

Fees vary depending on the type of job. Most architects will make a first visit free of charge, so get a number of quotes.

As a rule of thumb, architects' fees should come to between eight and 15 per cent of the total building costs.

Make a list of what it is you want to achieve in your proposed conversion, or extension. Do you need more space, storage, special features, light? This will help your architect to design the best plan for you.

When briefing your architect, have an idea of your budget and tell him or her. Otherwise you are wasting their time and your money.

The worst thing you can say to an architect is 'I know what I want. I just want you to do the drawings'. Why waste your money? You pay an architect to use his imagination and they will know what is achievable.

Don't forget! Building costs and architects fees are always quoted without VAT added. Remember to include VAT in your calculations.

The most critical part of any building work is employing a builder you like and trust. An architect can help you to find one from firms he has worked with.

AROMATHERAPISTS
Buying & Storing Oils

Mary Lapworth; Jenny Steel

Store essential oils in dark amber glass bottles. Your oils, some of which are expensive, will deteriorate in about eight weeks in a clear or plastic bottle.

Oils should be stored away from direct sunlight, in the cool and dark.

Oils will last for about a year if stored properly.

Citrus oils don't last for very long, so only buy small amounts at any one time.

To preserve the label, paint with clear nail varnish. This works for medicine bottles too.

Never buy cheap oils. They should be expensive in order to be effective.

Avoid buying fake oils. Learn the Latin names, which should appear on the packaging or bottle.

To keep oil fresh, never put new oil in an old bottle.

When an oil has gone bad, it will appear cloudy and give off an unpleasant smell. Essential oils should be clear.

Mixing Oils

Develop your sense of smell. Start with just four essential oils. Find a quiet, undisturbed place and take time to get to know and recognise these smells. Sniff each one separately; see what emotions, memories and feelings they evoke.

Carrier oils are used to dilute the essential oil. They allow the essential oil to be spread over the body and to be absorbed into the skin properly. They are ideal for dry or sensitive skins. Cold-pressed oils are the best. Sweet almond oil is most commonly used: it's non-allergenic, neutral and can be used for massaging babies.

Choose the right carrier oil. Sesame oil is great for stretch marks, walnut balances the nervous system, apricot and peach kernel as well as evening primrose oil are best for cell regeneration. For menstrual problems, use walnut or evening primrose oil.

To make your carrier oils go further, add five to ten per cent of wheatgerm oil, which helps to preserve the mixture.

To mix your essential oils with the carrier oil, use a toothpick.

Never put an undiluted essential oil directly on to your skin – except for one drop of tea tree or lavender oil.

Don't take oils internally.

When making up your mixture, add each essential oil a drop at a time.

To store small amounts of mixed oils for a short period, put them in an egg cup and cover with cling film.

To increase the life of the scent from your oils, add some sandalwood oil, which acts as a fixative.

Oils for Massage

Always do a patch test before applying oils to check that you, or whoever you are intending to use the oils on, are not allergic to any of them.

To mix enough oil for a body massage, mix ten drops of essential oil with two teaspoons of carrier oil. You will need more carrier oil for a person with a lot of body hair.

When giving a massage, ensure that the room is warm and that you have a suitable, comfortable area to work in. Make sure there are no distractions: take the phone off the hook and send the children round to friends.

Always warm your hands before giving a massage!

Avoid harsh overhead lighting when giving a massage. Candles give a wonderful light and create the right sort of atmosphere.

When you have prepared your oil for massage, make sure it is held in something sturdy that you won't knock over.

Always wash your hands after massaging the feet.

Oils at Home

At bedtime, you can put a couple of drops of lavender oil on your pillow to relax you. Ylang ylang is an alternative choice – it's a great aphrodisiac.

Smelly feet? A couple of drops of pine or parsley oil should help dispel the pong. And you could try some lemongrass oil in your wardrobe.

Make wonderful scented drawer liners by adding a couple of drops of essential oil to some pretty wrapping paper.

Put a couple of drops of your favourite oil on your handkerchief. This is a great idea if you've got a cold.

For a good mouthwash, add three drops of oil to one teaspoon of brandy. Benzoin, camomile, lavender or lemongrass is most effective.

To disinfect a dirty floor, add some bergamot, juniper and eucalyptus oils to the final rinsing water.

To make your own inexpensive room spray, add ten drops of your favourite essential oil to a plant spray filled with seven tablespoons of warm water. One tablespoon of vodka or pure alcohol acts as a preservative.

To get the most from your fire, put a couple of drops of pine, sandalwood or cedarwood oil on to the wood that you are going to burn. Leave it for an hour before lighting the fire. When the fire is burning, the heat releases the smell into the room.

To help your parties go with a swing, add a few drops of clary sage or jasmine to a vaporiser. At Christmas use frankincense (of course), cinnamon, orange, cedarwood or sandalwood.

Insects hate the smell of lemongrass, melissa, eucalyptus, tea tree or citronella oil. Use them when you're eating outside in the summer.

Soothe insect bites with a direct application of lavender or tea tree oil.

Repel biting insects with a blend of citronella, lemon, eucalyptus or tea tree oil in a carrier.

Get rid of fleas by adding a couple of drops of tea tree oil to some water and sponging your dog's coat.

Oils in the Bath

To get the most benefit from essential oils in your bath, don't put them straight under the hot water tap because they will evaporate too quickly. Instead, put your oils (five to ten drops) into the filled bath and mix around. Keep the door closed so that the vapours don't escape.

If you have sensitive skin, mix the essential oil with a base oil, such as sweet almond or apricot oil, before pouring into the bath.

Before you get into the bath it's a good idea to wash first. This way, you let the oils do their stuff without interference from soap or bubble bath.

Oils are lovely in a bath but can make things slippery. To avoid slip-sliding away, mix the oil with some full-fat milk or dairy cream before adding to the water.

Always wipe the bath down after use. Some essential oils can mark plastic baths if they are left on the surface.

If you are in the sauna, add two drops of eucalyptus or pine oil to ½ pint/300 ml of water and throw it over the coals. The smell is lovely and the oils are wonderful cleansers and detoxifiers.

For a wonderful foot bath, quarter-fill a washing-up bowl with warm water and add five drops of your favourite essential oil diluted in a cup of vodka (or pure alcohol). Lavender soothes the feet while a mixture of four or five drops of peppermint, thyme and rosemary (in whatever balance you prefer) acts as a pick-me-up for tired feet.

Chapped hands will benefit from a soak in some warm water into which you have added three or four drops of patchouli or comfrey oil.

When using essential oils in a vaporiser, use two to three drops for a small room and six to ten drops for a larger room.

If you don't have a vaporiser, put five drops of essential oil in a small bowl of water and place it on a radiator.

Take Care

Don't overdo it. Avoid essential oils for 48 hours every week.

Large amounts of clary sage oil can cause drowsiness, so don't use it before driving or operating machinery.

Avoid clary sage if you are on Hormone Replacement Therapy (HRT).

Avoid peppermint oil close to bedtime because it can cause insomnia.

Don't use aromatherapy to treat serious medical conditions. It's a great way to treat things such as stress, emotional problems or minor injuries but it's not the answer to every problem. Don't use aromatherapy to treat cancer, heart conditions, bad varicose veins, very high blood pressure, epilepsy or progressive neural disorders.

If you are pregnant, you must be very careful which oils you use. Some oils have strong diuretic properties while others are potentially toxic to an unborn foetus. The recommended oils for pregnancy are: lavender, lemon, neroli, orange, rose, sandalwood, camomile and geranium (in small quantities). Avoid camomile and lavender in the first few months if you have a history of miscarriage. If in doubt, talk to a qualified aromatherapist.

ART DEALERS

Sarah Von Holstein

Buying

When you are buying a piece of art, do not buy for investment. Buy what you will enjoy living with.

Contemporary art is an especially bad buy for investment purposes. Who can tell if the artist will become or remain valuable?

Only buy from a gallery if the dealers can spend time talking to you about the work. Don't buy if you are feeling pressurised or belittled. The atmosphere can be intimidating.

Spend time walking around as many galleries as possible. Some have access only by security buzzer, but don't be put off. They are not there to stop you going in, but to stop valuable paintings going out!

Opening nights of exhibitions are not a good time to buy. The gallery owner will not have time to talk to you. Go back the next day.

Be brave and ask for a discount. Young contemporary artists' work may have no margin for discount, and a ten or 15 per cent discount is the most one can probably expect. But it's worth a try.

Ask the dealer if he or she is the artist's representative and where else the artist exhibits. An exhibition history will show how established a particular artist is becoming.

If you want to buy the work of a well established (or dead) artist, consult a

Catalogue Raisonné, available from good art shops, to ensure the work you are interested in is genuine. The catalogue will list and illustrate the artist's work. If your painting isn't listed, it is not by that artist.

A dealer or gallery will be taking around 60 per cent of the price.

Exhibition catalogues can be a good investment in themselves – they can accrue value – and are a good way to start a collection of art books.

Keep a look out for exhibitions locally. You can often buy interesting work at reasonable prices.

Prints are an affordable way to start and amass an art collection. Limited editions and artists' proofs are especially collectable, but ask how big an edition is – large editions are less valuable.

Buy prints unframed. It's cheaper to have them framed yourself.

Don't put a piece of art you have paid a lot of money for on your household insurance. Have it covered by a specialist art insurer.

An increasing number of galleries are showing works on the internet. The sale, however, might have to be in person or by phone.

If you are buying on the internet, without viewing the piece, ask first how long you have to return it should you not be happy for any reason.

Paintings

A frame should not be the most noticeable part of a painting.

Art school shows are a good source of contemporary paintings, though they may not necessarily be cheap. Nor are they necessarily a good investment. You can spend the same amount of money on an established artist through a gallery, and the gallery will be actively promoting their work which will help to enhance its value.

Heavy oil paintings will take years to dry, so make sure the canvas is never folded.

Ask for a storage case for a valuable painting – it will come in useful if you ever move house.

Sculpture

Bronzes will be sold as part of an edition.

If an artists' work is made in an unusual medium (wax, hair, dough for example) enquire how long it is expected to last or you may end up having paid for a piece which will melt, decay or go mouldy!

Auctions

View at the sale preview as early as possible. Talk to the department specialists who will give you information and an explanation about the condition of the piece you are interested in bidding for.

Ask for a photograph or transparency, and provenance (details of the artist and history of the work) for more valuable pieces. You will have to return the images, but it is a useful way to consider your potential purchase before auction day.

An image also gives you the opportunity to get a second opinion from a dealer who specialises in this style of artist or medium. He may know when it was last up for sale and the price it went for.

Galleries, libraries and auction houses should have an At Sales Index/ADEC (Art

Dealers' Exhibition Catalogue), which lists artists who have sold works at auction, where, when and the sale price.

When you are bidding, decide how much you can afford, plus one bid, and do not get swept along by the tension and a persuasive auctioneer.

ARTISTS

Equipment

Francis Hatch, Sherbourne; Antony Whishaw, London; Dave Triffit, Oxford; Thomsin Smith, Hereford; Mary Jackson, Hampshire; David Peart, Chester; Arnold Shuttleworth

Make your own paint holders by placing empty yoghurt pots into a Tupperware container. When you have finished, simply snap the lid back on. This is especially useful if you are painting outdoors.

Create a paint-brush holder from a cardboard tube (from a post office). Plastic holders tend to make the brushes go mouldy.

Keep your paint-brushes in an empty chocolate box.

Store sable brushes in a container – to keep them away from moths.

To make your brushes last longer, wrap them in newspaper while they are still damp.

Store paint-brushes wrapped in brown paper with a rubber band round them.

Keep your brushes in good condition by putting a drop of linseed oil on each one and rubbing it into the bristles.

Don't spend money buying expensive art fixative, use hair-spray instead.

Masking tape makes a good, fine white line. Don't get it from art shops (it's too expensive); go to your local DIY shop instead.

Wash and squeeze water-colour brushes to a point. A little soapy water will help keep them in shape, then simply rinse again before you use them.

When painting with water-colours, dry your paint-brushes flat on a piece of kitchen roll.

Cheap, effective charcoal sticks can be made from wrapping willow tree branches in tin foil and baking them in the oven.

Keep brushes standing upright. A Pringles tube is ideal for large oil brushes – provided you've eaten the Pringles first!

To clean brushes in the great outdoors, fill empty camera film containers with white spirit.

Clean erasers by rubbing them on a scrap of cartridge paper.

Sharpen the wooden part of pencils and Conte pastels using a blade with snap-off segments so the blade is always sharp. Then you can sharpen the lead or pastel point on medium glass paper.

Don't waste paint. Cover your palette with cling film if you're taking a break from painting. This will keep the paint fresh for up to two weeks until you are ready to start again.

Don't waste oil paints on a palette. Scrape each individual colour into a blob, place the whole palette in a bowl and cover with a little water. To reuse, tip the water off and blow gently. Your paints will still be fresh and usable.

To clean your palette, use a mixture of white spirit and soap.

If you can't afford canvas, you can paint in oils on hardboard off-cuts primed with any matt household paint.

Keep white spirit in a jam jar with a lid to stop any evaporation.

If the top on a paint tube is stuck on with gunge, simply place the tube in a bowl of hot water for a few minutes and the top will then come off easily.

To get the last squeeze of paint from a tube, cut the tube in half.

Wear waterproof trousers so you can sit anywhere and not get covered in paint.

Wear surgeon's gloves to keep your hands clean.

Techniques

Save on the cost of paint by planning what you are going to do in a scrap-book.

Map out the picture you are going to paint using oil pastels, then paint over this template.

To kill the stark whiteness of paper stir a tea-bag into some water and paint the solution on to the paper to create a gentle, yellowish colour. Use the paper within four days otherwise fungus will start to grow! But don't worry, the paint will inhibit the mould once you start your picture.

When painting water-colours, use a water-soluble pencil to draw the outline; it will disappear when you paint over it.

Remove oil marks from paper by covering with talcum powder, leaving overnight and then brushing off.

If you make a mistake on your oil painting, just scrape it off with a razor blade and start again.

Using ordinary water-based paint is cheaper than a conventional primer.

Don't use ready-made blacks because nothing in nature is totally black. Instead, mix blues and browns together to make a more interesting black.

Create your own brown colour by sieving soil and then cooking it in a saucepan. Mix with acrylic to get a lovely deep colour.

Use an old box on its side for still life. If you cut along the sides, you can lift the lid to adjust the light that is shed on to the still life. This is very good for composition.

Get a really good splatter paint effect by using matchsticks or old toothbrushes.

Create a rust effect by using salt or coffee mixed with the paint.

To get a good, rough texture to your paint, simply throw loads of sand into the paint, mix it up and away you go.

Create texture across your canvas by using a garden plant spray filled with liquid paint.

Smooth down highly textured paint with a cheese-grater.

Discourage models from closing their eyes while you are working – it makes a big difference to the way the muscles of their face lie.

Don't even bother asking children to sit still. As soon as you ask them, all they can think about is moving.

Let children watch television as you draw them. It's the best way of keeping them still.

To paint a large canvas all one colour attach a paint-brush to a broomstick. This saves you from grubbing around on your hands and knees.

Prime paper with white spirit first – this provides an ideal base for oil paint.

Move large canvases around your studio by placing them on roller skates.

To view your painting from another perspective, look at it in a mirror.

The Finished Product

Store paintings face to face to protect the surfaces.

Pastels pictures can be stored covered with tissue paper fixed at the corners with bits of masking tape to prevent it slipping.

When framing pastels, always have a mount so that the glass doesn't touch the colours – it will stick to oil pastels and attract the particles of chalk pastels.

Stain wooden picture frames using shoe polish.

To dry paintings in a confined space, string them up on a washing line. This leaves the floor clear.

Hang pictures using heavy-duty fishing line.

Not all plaster walls are as solid as they seem, so spread the load by placing two hooks in the wall at a distance of half the width of the picture.

To restore old black enamel paintings, apply some black shoe polish and then buff off.

Keep oil paintings out of the kitchen because cooking fumes can destroy the paint.

A good way to get airflow in a frame is to use a buffer. Sliced up bits of cork work well.

When cleaning the glass of a painting spray the cleaner on to your duster first before polishing. This stops the moisture from damaging the frame.

Surface dirt can be removed from an oil or acrylic painting using a piece of old bread.

When hanging a painting, make sure that its centre is at eye-level.

AUCTIONEERS

Be Prepared

Roger Hollest, Phillips Son & Neal Ltd, www.phillips-auctions.com; Steven B Bruce Ltd, stevenbbruce@hotmail.com

Attend auctions to get the feel of what happens, particularly at the saleroom where you are likely to buy. No two auctions are quite the same.

Some auctions are 'admittance by catalogue only', and that can be expensive but the catalogue is a useful reference, particularly if you make a note of the successful bids.

Adverts in the paper notifying auctions should be read carefully. They may specify details such as 'no reserves'.

Subscribe to the *Antiques Trade Gazette* **–** it has a diary of fairs and auctions, and lots of other interesting information. Write to 115 Shaftsbury Avenue, London WC2H 8AD.

Read catalogues to understand the terminology.

Pay particular attention to the 'terms and conditions of sale' that should be printed in the catalogue. These are the rules of the particular auction house.

Read any 'glossary of terms' as these give further explanation of what the catalogue description actually means, particularly for pictures. For example, 'style of…', 'circle of…' and 'after…' all mean very different things.

Check what any symbols mean against a lot number. These can vary between auction houses. In Phillips, an * against a lot number means that VAT is payable on the hammer price for that lot – and 17.5 per cent is a significant extra charge!

Check what per cent is payable as buyers' premium, if any, at a given saleroom and remember that VAT is payable on the premium.

Don't feel embarrassed to ask questions of the auction staff. They are there to help.

If you can't make the whole auction, ask about how many lots per hour will be sold, and work out when the lot you're interested in will come up – but don't cut it too fine.

Find out in advance what you need to do about payment. For example are cheques or credit cards accepted?

Find out what the arrangements are for clearing (taking away) purchases.

When you know which sale you want to attend, you must view the sale carefully and examine each lot that might be of interest. Remember that the catalogue description may not make any mention of damage and it is your responsibility to satisfy yourself as to actual condition.

Feel free to turn things upside down, pull out the drawers and so on. A good saleroom will be happy to give unbiased advice on pieces, but if you're intending to spend a lot of money or hope to start a collection, you'd be well advised to take a dealer with you.

Don't turn up at the last minute for viewing – they sometimes close the doors early because it can take a while to get people out. It is very disappointing if you've come a long way and you can't even get in.

If you have to come a long way, it's worth phoning the day before to make sure that the sale is going ahead as planned and that any lots that you are interested in are still included.

Catalogues usually make things look better than they really are. If you can't view, most auctions houses will provide a written condition report to make things clearer.

Buyers' premium is sometimes on a sliding scale – more expensive items may attract a lower level of buyers' premium than cheaper items. The catalogue will contain such details.

Houses vary, but some consistently give low catalogue estimates. Don't assume you'll be able to buy the items at anywhere near that price.

If there's another auction in the locality on the same day, you may pick up bargains, because the competition will be halved.

Bidding

You may strike up a useful friendship with a porter or other member of staff who could bid for you if you cannot or would rather not be there in person. They may even be able to give you a clue as to reserve prices. Remember to show your appreciation.

Set the maximum amount you want to bid (remembering buyers' premium and any other charges).

Arrive in good time at the sale before your lot comes up.

You will probably be asked to register (give your name and address and show some form of identification) and be given a bidding number to show to the auctioneer when you buy a lot. (This may be called a 'paddle' number – a strange word, but first used in the USA where the system started!)

If you're known at an auction house, particularly at local sales, you might want to be inconspicuous. Personal feelings can come into play and rivals may enter the bidding just to push the price up. By standing at the back, you can see the whole room and see who's doing what.

If you can't be at the auction, you can leave a bid, but make sure you write clearly. Some houses accept e-mail bids, but make sure you leave a bid well in advance. On the day of the sale, it could well be overlooked in the rush of other things that have to be done.

If you are making a phone bid, you generally fill in a form and the auction house will give you an idea of when your lot will come up so you can stay by the phone and wait for their call. Again, give plenty of notice.

Play it cool when your lot comes up, allow bidding to proceed in the room. The auctioneer should take bids alternately from two people; then when one drops out, look for any further bidders.

If you want to bid, make a clear signal to the auctioneer. A raised eyebrow or flick of a finger may be sufficient for the seasoned professional but not for the beginner.

Once you start bidding, *do not exceed your maximum* in the heat of the moment. Once the hammer falls, you have entered a legally binding contract and will have to pay up.

If you're bidding in a foreign currency, make sure you know what exchange rate is to be used and any extra charges that might be incurred for conversion.

If your bid is successful, note the price you paid and show your bidding number to the auctioneer. Make sure your number is recorded correctly.

Follow instructions about payment and clearance. You will not make a good start to your relationship with the saleroom if you pay late or do not clear your purchase promptly.

It happens in comedy films, but not in real life. If you sneeze or scratch your head, you will not end up with an unwanted purchase. A good auctioneer will always ask you if you are bidding if they are in any doubt. However, it is not a good idea to wave to a friend across the saleroom.

Buyers beware – not all salerooms have a good reputation, sadly. The beginner should try to get a personal recommendation from an existing buyer before starting.

Running an Auction

If you ever find yourself in the position of having to run a fundraising auction (say an auction of promises), go to some auctions to watch the professional at work.

Make sure you have someone really good doing the accounts side. You'll have enough to worry about yourself.

Be aware of reserves and, if you're organising the catalogue, get people to be as specific as possible when describing what they are offering. For instance, if someone is offering to make a cake, what size will it be, can the buyer choose the decoration and how much notice does the baker need?

Make sure you look all round the room, and try not to be distracted by anyone in bright colours, or moving around. If you're not sure if someone has entered the bidding, just ask. Professionals sometimes do.

BACKPACKERS

Preparing to Leave

Phil Martin; Stephen Russel; Daniella Graziani

Sounds obvious, but ensure your passport is valid for the whole time you'll be away.

Check weather cycles when planning your intinerary so as to miss the rainy or hurricane seasons.

If you're a first-time traveller, you may find it less of a culture shock to travel in developed countries first. Leave the harrowing stuff until last if you're a bit shockable.

Pack light but include a padlock with a combination to keep your belongings safe.

Small plastic bags with a seal come in handy for lots of things.

Take a bulldog clip so you can hang anything wet (towel, socks, T-shirt) safely from your backpack as you walk along.

Pack a few extra passport photos for visas, permits and so on.

Before you buy a sleeping bag, make sure what the temperature is like at night. Even very hot climates can turn chilly once the sun goes down.

A drawstring bag made of synthetic fabric (like a gym bag) is useful for stashing dirty or wet clothes, and for day trips.

If you wear contact lenses, make sure you have enough cleaning solution for the trip, but take specs as well, just in case.

Condoms, apart from the obvious use, can make sterile wound dressings and can be used for carrying water!

It can be difficult to get good quality condoms abroad, and impossible in some places. Take your own – they don't take up much space in your rucksack.

Get photocopies of essential documents – passports, flight tickets, visas, credit cards, traveller's cheques, your doctor's address, medical insurance documents. Leave a set with your parents and take a set or two with you, stashed in different places.

Find out the phone numbers and addresses of the British Consulates in all the countries you're going to. Take a note of them yourself, and leave a copy with your parents. They almost certainly won't need them, but it'll make them think you're being sensible.

A tubular bandage is useful in case of a sprain, but you can also tuck cash inside one worn at the top of your arm or leg.

Make sure you have a small quantity of the local currency before you arrive. It will save time and hassle looking for a currency exchange straight away.

When buying shoes, forget quality. Leather will rot in humid conditions. Get some cheap pumps and replace them frequently. If desperate, wear flip flops, which are very useful in grubby shower blocks.

Lots of travellers lose weight for one reason or another! Drawstring waists will shrink with you.

If your nearest and dearest want to write to you, addressing letters to poste restante at large post offices, buy them some brightly coloured envelopes so their letters are easy to pick out.

Get an e-mail account that can be accessed from any machine. It's by far the best way to stay in touch.

Be Healthy and Safe

If you have any allergies or special medical requirements, make sure your travelling companions know about it, and carry some documentation about your person in case of an accident.

Carry an Aid kit. You can buy them at pharmacies or at some health centres and they contain sterile equipment that could save your life in an emergency.

If you get diarrhoea, flat Coke will help to rehydrate you. Don't add any ice cubes, and make sure you open the can yourself.

If you need to carry medication with you, make sure you have a doctor's note explaining exactly what it is. This should solve any problems with customs but also help if you lose your supply and need a local doctor to prescribe some more.

Make sure your doctor knows the conditions in which you will be travelling. The medication may not survive extremes of heat or humidity.

If you fall ill in the weeks following your return, make sure you tell your doctor where you've been. It could help with a correct diagnosis, and protect those you come into contact with at home.

In hostels, make sure you know where the emergency exits are and that there are locks on your doors. If there aren't any, go somewhere else.

Don't let your documents out of your sight, even if authority figures ask for them. Sometimes money will be demanded for their return.

Girly Concerns

Girls should pack a sarong. There are lots of places where shorts will get you unwanted attention.

Pack a wedding ring. It can help you fake your way out of lots of tricky situations.

Blondes – be prepared for unwanted attention in many parts of Africa, India, SE Asia and the Middle East.

Tampons are hard to find in many countries. Pack plenty. Even if you don't usually use the applicator type, they can be more practical if you can't get to wash your hands as often as you'd like.

Tight clothes are hot and uncomfortable and will attract unwanted attention. Go baggy.

In some cultures, making eye contact with a man is seen as a direct invitation. Try to get out of the habit.

Shout and make a fuss if you're groped. Make it clear that this is unacceptable – you may be doing a favour to the next woman to come along.

BAKERS

Bread & Yeast

Geoff Capper, Allen's Pies, Bolton; Stephen Hallam, Old Pie Shop, Melton Mowbray; Lawrie Finch; George Charman; Ron Gardiner; Dean Simpole-Clarke

The secret of fantastic bread is always to keep a little bit of dough back from the previous day's batch to add to the new mixture.

If you can't remember whether you've added yeast to your dough, here's a simple test. Take out a small piece of the dough – about gob-stopper size – and put it in a cup of hot water. If you didn't put in any yeast, it will immediately sink to the bottom. Dough with yeast in it will rise to the top.

To make authentic-tasting naan or pitta bread, gently warm the flour in a microwave first.

The longer you knead dough, the longer you should leave the dough to develop.

To prevent bread from drying out when baking, cover it with a cake tin while it's in the oven.

Don't throw day-old bread away, just brush it with olive oil and toast it in the oven.

It's easier to cut pizza with scissors than with a knife.

Dried out, stale bread can be revived if you wrap it in kitchen foil and leave on a low heat in the oven for about ten minutes.

To keep bread moist while baking, add a little honey to the dough.

To keep home-baked bread fresh for longer, add a couple of teaspoons of vegetable oil to the dough.

To stop garlic bread going soggy during cooking, wrap it in tin foil.

When kneading dough, stop every two or three minutes to let the dough 'rest'. After resting for a couple of minutes, the dough will be easier to knead.

Flour compacts during storage. Fluff it up before measuring out an amount for a recipe or you'll get too much flour.

If, when heating or baking bread at home, the bread burns and/or has burnt spots on it, cut the spots off and patch up the scars with beaten egg brushed on to the exposed areas. Then keep heating the bread.

To revitalise stale bread plunge the loaf or rolls into cold water for a moment and then bake on a low heat for ten minutes.

To remove crusts from bread try using a pizza cutter; it will give you a nice neat edge and waste less.

To test whether a loaf of home-made bread is baked properly tap it on top. A hollow sound means that it is baked.

Place a wet towel over your dough, when making bread, to make it rise more quickly.

To stop frozen pizzas sticking to the tray or foil during cooking and to make them taste nicer, brush the base with olive oil.

Make sweet pizzas – use fruit as a topping and even jam instead of tomato paste.

Never run out of breadcrumbs for stuffings and toppings – keep all your bread ends, pop into a food processor to make crumbs and then freeze in bags.

Try using a packet of stuffing instead of breadcrumbs on scotch eggs for a tasty change.

Who Ate All the Pies?

For a great rolling pin fill a claret bottle with warm water and replace the cork securely.

Stop gaping air pockets developing during baking, by soaking some breadcrumbs in water and sprinkling them into your meat pies.

If you haven't got a pastry cutter, use the thoroughly cleaned lid of an aerosol can instead.

When rolling pastry, put it between two sheets of cling film. You won't need to use extra flour to stop it sticking to the surfaces and it is easier to turn over, too.

Don't turn your body at an angle when rolling pastry. Turn the pastry around so that you don't hurt your back.

Have a couple of small freezer bags ready when baking so that you can pop them over your floury hands if the phone rings.

Always let pie pastry dry thoroughly before adding the filling. A skin forms which prevents the filling from seeping in during cooking.

Put sugar in a pie, not on it. This gives a much more even flavour, and sugar on a pie often burns.

When slicing apples for pies, put the slices in water and add a little salt to stop them discolouring: it has the same effect as adding lemon but it's cheaper.

When trimming pie edges, cut the pastry outwards on the dish, not inwards. This makes the pastry grip the edge of the dish.

For better-tasting apple pies, add cloves to the pastry, not the filling. Once the pie is baked, it is much easier to remove the cloves than when they are mixed into the filling.

For savoury pies, add a little pesto to flavour the pastry – delicious!

Before putting puff pastry on a baking tray, run ice cold water over the tray. When it is in the oven, the steam rising from the tray will really help the pastry to puff.

When cooking vol-au-vents, don't put them in straight lines on your baking tray. Instead, place them randomly but close together and they will lift each other up while cooking.

To store vol-au-vents, sprinkle a thin layer of salt on the bottom of a cake tin, cover with a tea towel and place your vol-au-vents on the cloth. They will stay fresh for ages.

Ensure a uniform thickness in pastry by placing two pieces of wood on either side of the pastry and running the rolling pin across the top of the wood.

Stop mice or mites getting to your flour – put a bay leaf in the packet.

Keep flour in the freezer to keep it for longer.

Make a quiche without the hassle or calories of pastry – simply bake the mixture in a lightly oiled, shallow casserole dish.

To prevent soggy quiche bases, brush the pastry with lemon juice and bake blind for three minutes before putting the filling in and cooking fully.

To stop the base and crust of fruit pies going soggy during cooking, sprinkle the pastry with flour before putting in the filling.

To stop pastry sticking to your rolling pin, put the pin in the freezer or fridge so that it's cold before you use it.

When you've cooked berries for pie fillings, save any left-over juice for topping pancakes and ice-cream.

To prevent jam tarts from bubbling over whilst cooking, sprinkle a few drops of cold water on to them.

To avoid a soggy pie crust, sprinkle a layer of breadcrumbs over it before cooking.

If, midway through cooking a fruit pie, you notice that the fruit is seeping out, sprinkle salt over the leaking fruit and put it back in the oven. The fruit will become crisp and can easily be removed.

Left-over mashed potato is wonderful in pastry dishes, adding a lovely flavour and texture.

Sweet Treats

Save time when making biscuits – instead of cutting lots of individual round shapes, just roll the dough into a sausage and cut slices off it.

For really crispy biscuits, use half flour and half cornflour.

When making custard, gently heat the sugar in the pan before adding the milk – your custard will never boil over.

To make shortbread with that delicious luxury taste, add a tablespoon of custard powder to the raw mixture.

Don't rush to get your scones in the oven. Resting them allows the baking powder to become active.

If you only have very cold butter to hand when baking, try grating it into a warm metal bowl. It will soon become softer and reach the right temperature.

To weigh golden syrup with minimal mess, just put the whole tin on the scales and keep spooning the sticky stuff out until the tin has gone down in weight by the amount you need.

To create an impressive chocolate bowl, brush or pipe lukewarm melted chocolate on to half of an inflated balloon until it's about 3 in/7 cm deep. Allow to cool thoroughly, then carefully burst the balloon.

Make your own piping bag by twisting some foil into a cone and snipping off the bottom.

To tell whether an egg is absolutely fresh, put it in a bowl of water. If it is really fresh, it will sink. Older eggs will float.

To remove the stones from cherries, use a hair grip stuck into a cork.

Don't waste orange or lemon peel from inside a grater; use a small, clean toothbrush to get it out.

A pinch of salt added to margarine makes whisking quicker.

Store castor sugar with rose petals, lemon zest or cinnamon sticks for extra flavour.

To soften hard brown sugar, leave it in a bowl covered with a damp tea towel overnight.

When making meringues, you must keep the bowl completely free of grease. Rub the bowl with salt and wash it thoroughly.

To give your meringues a toffee flavour, use brown sugar.

A quick way to mark out squares for toffee or fudge is to lightly press a wire cooling tray on to a tin of the mixture. The grid marks left behind will be a clear guide to perfect little pieces.

To light a Christmas pudding, put brandy in a saucepan and heat gently. Place the warm brandy in a metal soup ladle over a lighted candle until it bursts into flames. Carefully pour over the pudding.

To refresh dried out mincemeat, (for mince pies) add brandy or sherry.

To warm bowls that can't go in the oven, fill them with boiling water and leave to stand for five minutes. Then pour away the water, dry the bowl and serve.

If you're baking shortbread cookies, try substituting half of your plain flour with cornflour for a really rich taste.

Try using tea cakes or hot cross buns for a tastier bread-and-butter pudding.

To make chocolate cookies for parties, add a ¼ cup of beer. Or even better, some sherry.

To check the quality of baking powder, put a teaspoon of it into a cup of hot water. If the water bubbles a lot, the baking powder is good. If it doesn't bubble, throw it away.

For a delicious pudding, add some elderberries to your apple pie.

If your custard goes lumpy, quickly put the base of the pan into some cold water and keep whisking until things are going smoothly again.

To bring out the taste of chocolate in most recipes, add a few coffee granules.

Avoid mess and waste – cut the required amounts of frozen gateaux and cakes while they're still frozen.

If sugar goes hard and lumpy, pop it into your bread bin with a loaf and it will go soft.

If you have trouble slicing lemon meringue pies, try dipping your knife into some hot water before cutting.

Left-over chocolates can be transformed. Melt them in a bowl over hot water, and add nuts and raisins. Cool the mixture, make it into balls and chill. Delicious 'home-made' chocs!

Alternatively, spoon the hot mixture over ice-cream for an indulgent dessert.

To avoid sticky fingers when pressing down the base for a cheesecake use a potato masher or the bottom of a mug.

Improve home-made bread-and-butter pudding by adding finely grated carrot – it's a natural sweetener and adds extra texture and colour.

To make individual pavlovas, drop the meringue mix on to the baking sheet in large dollops – they are lovely to serve at a dinner party and they also take less time to cook.

Melt your favourite chocolate bar in the microwave, then pour over ice-cream for a delicious treat.

Substitute yoghurt for milk to make lighter scones.

For a crunchy topping for fruit crumbles and sweet tarts, grate some bread, then put it in a dish and bake. Mix with demerara sugar to taste and use as required.

To make pretty chocolate curls, microwave a chocolate bar for ten seconds and then use a cheese slice to create the curls.

If custard 'scrambles' during cooking, put it in a liquidiser with a tablespoon of milk and spin it until it goes smooth again.

If your meringue crust cracks as it cools, spoon cream over it.

Keep brown sugar soft by leaving a slice of apple in the jar.

For firm meringues, add a teaspoon of cornflour to the sugar before beating into the egg whites.

To slice baked meringue easily, grease the knife with butter before cutting.

To make your mousses more decorative, make two: one with white chocolate and one with dark. Put each in a separate, small, piping bag. Then, put both bags in one large piping bag. Squeeze into a dish and, as the mousse comes out, it will be a beautiful swirl of the two colours. The taste combination of the sweet white chocolate and the bitter dark is lovely too.

To prevent ice crystals forming on ice-cream when stored in the freezer, stretch some cling film over the top and press the film on to the surface of the ice-cream. Put the lid on the top and pop it back into the freezer.

For a spicy version of bread-and-butter pudding, use malt loaf layered with dates and bananas.

To make more meringue with the same number of eggs, add one tablespoon of water per egg.

To get the best taste out of nuts in baking, toast them first on a baking tray before adding to the mix.

To prevent mould growing on the surface of jam, moisten the waxed circle on top of the jar with whisky.

BEAUTICIANS

Skin Deep

Cathy Bradley, Hydro Springs; Theresa Cook; Clarins

Before putting on any face mask, cover your skin with a thin layer of gauze and apply the mask over it. You'll get the benefits of the ingredients seeping through and, when it's time to take the mask off, you can simply peel the gauze away. It's much quicker and you don't damage your skin by scrubbing at stubborn bits of mask.

Give tired skin a boost – use a honey facial. Apply honey to clean skin, leave on for one hour, then rinse off with warm water.

A good emergency face mask can be made from porridge oats mixed with honey.

Cucumber and yoghurt make a great face mask. Blend some mashed cucumber with natural yoghurt and apply to your face. Leave for about 15 minutes, then rinse off with warm water. Cucumber cools and tones while yoghurt acts as a pick-me-up for tired skin.

Make your own facial scrub – use two tablespoons of honey, four or five tablespoons of cornmeal and a tablespoon of ground almonds. Mix them together and then apply to your face. Leave for five minutes before rinsing off with warm water and a flannel.

Save your expensive toner – apply it using wet cotton wool. If you use dry, the cotton wool absorbs most of the toner and your skin doesn't get the benefit.

Don't waste cleanser by putting it on to cotton wool that just soaks up most of the cream. Use your finger tips instead and then rinse the cleanser off.

Make sure you take your make-up off even when you come in really late after partying the night away. Have a small plastic storage box of ready dampened cotton wool pads by your bed to make the task as easy and quick as possible.

To cleanse the skin effectively, squeeze an amount of cleanser the size of a small walnut into one hand, warm between both palms and apply to the skin. To increase effectiveness and prevent over-stimulation, place the hands flat, without pressing, over the entire face and then lift briskly away to create a suction effect. This literally draws out and lifts make-up and grime as gently as possible. Repeat this movement five or six times, then rinse skin thoroughly with tepid water.

Get help! A series of facials by a professional beautician can help to clean out pores so you have a good starting point for a fresh-looking complexion.

Need a simple make-up remover? Petroleum jelly removes eye make-up, lipstick and blusher.

Open your pores by putting your face over a bowl of hot steamy water. Cover your head with a towel to keep the steam in. If you've got oily skin, stay there for at least five minutes.

Remove warts with a solution of one part cider vinegar to one part glycerine. Apply this every day until the warts disappear.

Remove blackheads easily. Mix one tablespoon of Epsom salts with three drops of white iodine and one cup of boiling water. Leave the mixture to cool until warm, and then apply it.

Alternatively, dab neat lemon juice on the blackheads before going to bed. Wash off in the morning with cool water. Repeat for a few nights.

A great way to dry up any pimples is to smear toothpaste on them.

Don't waste money on expensive facial water sprays – just use a regular plant spray bottle filled with some mineral water. It's great for hot days and sets make-up a treat.

Face flannels can be thoroughly sterilised by 'cooking' them damp in a microwave oven for five minutes.

Remove dead skin and beat facial blackheads by adding a teaspoon of sugar to your soap.

To remove blackheads, apply gentle pressure to the affected area with the rounded end of a hair grip.

To get rid of spots, mix three teaspoons of honey with one teaspoon of cinnamon and dab the mixture on to your face nightly. In two weeks you'll have really clear skin.

For a cheap moisturiser, blend a banana with a little milk and smooth on to your face and leave for 20 minutes.

There's no need to buy expensive make-up removers – baby oil does the job brilliantly.

Cold milk removes make-up too.

Legs, Feet & Hands

Give your feet a treat – a cup of baking soda or Epsom salts dissolved in a bowl of warm water makes a wonderful foot bath.

Smelly feet? Try rubbing in a little eucalyptus oil.

Sprinkle some talc inside your socks or shoes to keep them dry and smelling sweet.

After having your legs waxed allow them to breathe. If you put tight trousers or stockings back on immediately you are encouraging infections.

Strengthen your ankles while watching television. Keep moving them in a circular motion.

Here's a fruity way to get rid of ugly verrucas: wrap a banana skin around your foot, with the inside of the banana skin against your foot and leave it on overnight. You could hold it in place with a sock over the top. Repeat nightly for four weeks and the offending verruca will disappear.

Fingers that have become superglued together can be unstuck by rolling a pencil gently between them.

To exfoliate and soften hands, work a mixture of olive oil and granulated sugar into them, then rinse off.

If you have excess moisturiser on your hands, don't rinse it off. Run your fingers through your hair – the cream will prevent frizz and makes a good conditioner.

Teeth

Run out of toothpaste? A little bit of bicarbonate of soda does the trick.

Nobody likes bad breath... chew on a little garden mint.

Try cleansing your mouth with fennel or aniseed seeds available from health food shops. Chew after meals to get the best results.

To stop flecks of toothpaste getting on your clothes while cleaning your teeth – wrap a towel around your shoulders to cover your front.

Save water – clean your teeth using a mug rather than have the water running constantly.

Eye Eye

If you are unfortunate enough to have superglued your eyelids together, don't despair. A damp cotton-wool pad held over the eye should do the trick.

To keep spectacles clean, rinse them in clear water every morning.

If your eyelids are sticky in the morning, dip a cotton bud in baby shampoo (which doesn't sting) and use it to clean the roots of your lashes. Then wash your eyes in clear, cool water.

When using eye cream at night, never put it too close to your eyes or they'll look puffy in the morning.

If you do suffer from puffy eyes first thing in the morning, simply lie down again for five minutes with used tea-bags over your eyes.

If your eyes are puffy after washing, apply the pulp of a roasted apple to your eyelids.

Make your own eye make-up remover using one part baby shampoo to 20 parts boiled and cooled water.

Avoid putting moisturiser around the eyes. Not only does it pull the delicate skin as you apply it, but your mascara will slip off if your lashes are greasy.

All Over

After peeling an avocado, rub the inside of the skin over your knees and elbows – or anywhere else that needs softening.

A handful of dry sea salt rubbed over the body before a bath helps to slough off dead skin.

Oatmeal makes a good alternative to soap – put a handful in a muslin bag and use it in the bath as a body scrub.

Salt baths help to heal any wounds or scratches on the skin. Add a cup of salt to the bath water.

Milk baths soften skin – add 1 pint/600 ml of milk to your bath water and pretend you are Cleopatra.

Dry skin? Add a drop or two of good-quality olive oil to your bath.

Don't throw old fruit away. Pop any fruit that's gone too soft into the blender. Use the mixture as an all-over body mask and nutrient. Once you shower it off, your skin will feel really soft and you'll smell good enough to eat.

If you suffer from bad circulation, try alternating hot and cold showers to get your system moving.

For baby smooth skin, add a cupful of milk granules to your bath and enjoy a long soak.

For a sensuous bath mix a few drops of your favourite perfume with some good olive oil and add it to the running water.

To give yourself a good back scrub, place a bar of soap inside the middle of a stocking or chopped off tights' leg. Knot the stocking on each side of the soap. Hold one end of the stocking in each hand and, with a see-sawing motion, scrub your back. For a more vigorous scrub use grainy exfoliating soap.

Save water – replace one bath with a shower each week.

BIRD BREEDERS

Ron Willcocks

Cages & Aviaries

Make sure the cage is large enough. The bigger the cage, the better. By law, birds should be kept in cages that are wider than their wingspan. Shape is important – don't just go for tall and narrow. Budgies, for example, should be kept in a space at least 12 x 24 x 24 in/30 x 60 x 60 cm.

For greenery that looks good all year, chop up fake Christmas trees.

Cockatiels are ground feeders in the wild so spend a lot of time on the cage floor. It's best to get a wide cage rather than a tall one (at least 14 in/35 cm square).

Square cages are better than round ones – birds like the security of having a corner to hide in.

Bamboo cages may look pretty, but they are impossible to keep clean and some birds can peck them to bits in minutes. Go for a plain metal wire cage.

When you get a new metal wire cage for your bird, wipe it down with vinegar and water to get rid of any excess zinc.

If your bird has a long tail, make sure you have a tall cage to accommodate its shape.

Keep the cage away from draughts or too much sunlight. Make sure that other pets (such as cats) can't get to it.

Paper is the best medium to line the bottom of the cage because it is more difficult for bacteria to grow on it. It's also easy to keep an eye on the state of your bird's poo.

Birds will sleep better if their cages are covered. During the day it's a good idea to cover one corner of the cage so that the bird can retire there if it wants a rest in the middle of the day.

Get the perfect perch. Don't just stick in a bit of dowelling and be done with it. Birds need different shapes and diameters of perch in order to exercise their feet. Sticks such as bamboo or willow that have varying diameters are best.

Never put sandpaper on the perch because the particles can get stuck in a bird's foot and cause infection.

Don't use cherry tree branches for perches – they are toxic, as are the resins in unmilled pine. Most hardwoods (not oak) and some fruitwoods (like apple) are safe.

Natural perches allow birds to chew on them, which is good for keeping beaks in tip-top condition.

African Greys' perches should be placed low enough to stop the birds looking down on people. This stops them behaving in an aggressive manner.

Never cover a parrot's cage with a towel or knitted blanket. The bird might get its claws caught up in the material and end up hanging itself. Use an old sheet instead.

When choosing a bird, decide what you want from such a pet. If you want a pet to talk to and entertain you, you will probably want to keep it indoors, so a cage is fine. If you want to breed and show birds, you will need to build an aviary.

Budgerigars are popular pets and can be kept inside or as aviary birds.

Canaries are wonderful songsters and live quite happily in an aviary with other birds.

Parakeets are quite happy in an aviary and will often nest successfully. Generally, they are better in a crowd than as sole pets.

Napoleon weavers are members of the finch family. To encourage them to nest, grow bamboo in their aviary.

If you're going to build an aviary, check its position carefully. Position it away from the road, so the birds won't be disturbed by noise, passers-by or headlights. It should be near the house, where you can see it, but not so that it will disturb your neighbours. Don't position an aviary under trees or branches, which could damage the structure.

When building an aviary, make sure the floor is easy to clean. Concrete slabs or concrete are ideal.

At Play

If your bird is bored, you could try introducing a mate. However, certain types of love-birds won't accept a new mate after the old one has died.

Two's company especially if you're out of the house a lot. Two cock birds get on better than two hens.

But canaries are not social birds. They are quite happy to be kept on their own. Two males will always fight, as will a male and female (except during the nesting season obviously!).

Cock birds are usually easier to tame, teach to talk and so make better pets. Hens can be a bit destructive when the breeding season starts.

Parrots make good pets and can be great mimics, if taught from a young age. Mind you, they can also be extremely noisy and harbour vandalistic tendencies!

Cockatiels can learn to talk and whistle. They make good pets because they're generally cheerful, gentle birds.

If you want to teach your bird to talk, you will have to be patient – you won't get results overnight. Just keep repeating the lessons over and over again. Birds find it easier to mimic women's and children's voices. Keep the sentences short.

Cockatiels can be great screamers. Sometimes this is because of boredom or loneliness, or because the owner rewards the screaming with attention. Don't get into bad habits. If your bird is a screamer, try dropping a cover over the cage when it starts. Remove it as soon as the bird is quiet.

Keep them amused. If you've got only one bird, you could give it a mirror for company. Birds like listening to the radio too – the choice of station is up to you.

Make a cheap playstand – fill a bucket with sand and stand some branches in it.

A fir cone makes a cheap and effective toy.

Parrots enjoy climbing hardwoods such as beech or ash. Scrub with soap first to remove any dirt or parasites.

Put strips of willow bark in the nesting boxes of lovebirds.

Parrots like to dig, so place a pot filled with earth in their cage and let them root around to their heart's delight.

When you let birds out to fly round the house, make sure that you keep the toilet lid down, cover up the fireplace and cover any windows with an old bed sheet. Large expanses of glass can confuse birds and they may fly into a window and stun themselves.

Don't leave hot drinks around while your bird is out of its cage.

Some plants are poisonous to birds so keep them out of the birds' way when they are flying around the house.

If you need to catch your bird, use a duster to cover him carefully before putting him back in his cage.

If you can't get your bird back into the cage, darken the room as much as possible. Birds are more subdued in dark conditions.

Don't rush around after your bird. You can literally scare them to death. If you are approaching a bird, do so slowly and deliberately.

Health & Cleanliness

When choosing a bird, check it for any signs of poor health. It should have bright eyes with no discharge, a good plump breast, no wheezy breathing, and no deformed bill or malformed claws.

Make provision in your will for your parrot – they often outlive their owners.

Bengalese finches make good foster parents.

You can tell the sex of a budgie by looking at the area above its beak (called the cere): purple or blue means it's a cock, brown means it's a hen.

Older budgies have a white iris, while younger birds (under 12 weeks) don't. Young budgies also have fine black bars on their foreheads, which disappear with their first moult.

Finches enjoy life in an aviary, but may need a bit of extra heating in the winter. Grow plants in and around the aviary to act as a windbreak.

Mynah birds are quite hardy, but aren't keen on damp weather and so are happiest indoors.

If you're having difficulty getting your African Greys to nest, place a pair of smaller, quieter, prolific birds in sight. Cockatiels and lovebirds are the best choice.

An African Grey parrot benefits from a bit of rain and fresh air now and again.

Budgies are quite happy with a saucer of water for bathing. Always clean out the saucer and replace the water – birds are like us: they won't bathe in dirty water.

Some breeders add a dash of raspberry cordial to their budgies' water – they swear it kills bacteria and keeps their birds healthy.

The floor of a bird's cage must be cleaned each day. Once a week give the cage a thorough clean, remembering to take out the bird first.

You can change the colour of your canary by adding paprika, cayenne or red pepper to its food.

If your parrot is feather-picking too much, try a mixture of water and aloe gel (one tablespoon of aloe to 2 pints/1.2 litres water). Spray the mixture on to him at bath time.

Gaps in the wing feathers of young birds and dried blood on the feather shafts of older birds can be signs of French moult, which is a viral disease. Take your bird to the vet immediately.

To spot a sick bird, look out for fluffed out feathers, closed eyes, dull and listless behaviour, and excessive sleeping.

If you think your bird is sick, turn the heating up. They can often lose a lot of body heat when they're not feeling well.

Birds can deteriorate rapidly when ill. Contact your vet straight away.

To examine a poorly bird, wrap him quite firmly in a warm towel.

Parrots need their beauty sleep – around 10 to 12 hours a night.

During cold weather make sure that there is enough humidity for your parrots. When the central heating goes on, the air gets drier.

Avoid accidents when clipping birds' claws – hold the bird up to the light so that you can see where the vein in the bird's claw ends and not cut into it.

It's easy to clean your bird's cage if you keep it lined with newspaper. Just take out each dirty sheet and replace it with a clean one.

If a bird's egg is cracked, a thin layer of clear nail varnish will preserve it.

Spruce up your parrot – spray him once a week with lukewarm water, first thing in the morning.

If your parrot doesn't like being sprayed, place a container of water in the cage and let him bathe when he feels like it.

What's the difference between the sexes? Hens' plumage tends to be paler and not as bright as the males'.

Be careful when handling the plumage of a water bird. It's a good idea to avoid touching it with your hands, especially if you're a bit sweaty. Wrap the bird in a clean cloth or bit of sacking to secure the wings.

To hold a small bird safely, place your hand over the bird. Its neck should be between your first and second fingers, its wings safely tucked in the palm of your hand. Remember not to squeeze too hard.

Alternatively, you can hold a small bird between your two hands, but this isn't as effective as the first method if your bird is a biter.

Diet

Parrots grow tired of bird seed. Spice up their diet with the occasional hot chilli as a treat.

Add a bit of variety to a parrot's diet. Hard dog chews with a small hole bored in the top are fun for them to peck at.

Collect berries in the autumn and then freeze them to keep for treats all year round.

Millet is a great treat for birds but be very sparing with it otherwise they'll end up eating it to the exclusion of everything else.

Birds need grit to help them digest seeds.

Fruit is ideal for birds. The fruit shouldn't have any marks and must be washed thoroughly before being given to birds. Peel oranges, and remove any large pips or stones. Give them a piece of fruit every day.

Another good source of vitamins is vegetables. Parrots go for cabbage leaves or stalks, sprouting seeds (like alfalfa) and sprouts. Freeze corn-on-the-cob so you've got some handy when it's out of season.

Food on the move. Some birds, like softbills and finches, rather enjoy eating live food. Mealworms are the most popular, but you could go into cricket or locust production to liven up your bird's diet.

Finches also enjoy dandelions and spinach. Chop them up finely before feeding your finch.

Budgerigars will tuck into the odd carrot now and again, but be prepared for some orange stains around their bills.

Canaries will enjoy a bit of hard-boiled egg as well as canned corn. Small pieces of whole-wheat bread are also greatly appreciated.

Cuttlefish bone is a good source of calcium. The softer side of the bone should be facing the bird.

Parrots also enjoy seeds with a high oil content.

Don't let your parrot out of its cage during mealtimes – they can be adept at stealing food from your plate, which is annoying, and they can get hold of food that is bad for them.

Soak seeds in hot water for 24 hours. This boosts the protein content and makes the seeds easier for chicks or sick birds to eat.

Plastic containers are cheap and easy to keep clean; they will suit most birds. Parrots, however, need metal bowls.

Fresh water should always be available. Don't place the water beneath a perch. If your birds are in an aviary, check for ice during cold weather.

BODYGUARDS & PERSONAL SAFETY ADVISORS

Out & About

John Chase; The Suzy Lamplugh Trust

Stick to well lit places, especially if you are a woman alone at night.

Trust your instincts and never assume it won't happen.

Always plan your journey home in advance.

Let someone know where you are and when you plan to be home – and remember to alert people if you change your plans.

Carry your keys, travel card and phone card in your pocket.

Don't wear a Walkman or Discman – it will stop you being able to hear what's going on around you.

Give up your bag or wallet if you are attacked – it is worth much less than your safety.

At a train or underground station, position yourself on the platform so that you can see which carriages have people on them and which are empty.

If you are accosted yell 'fire' – people are selfish and more likely to respond to a situation that might affect their own safety.

If you suspect you are being followed, don't be afraid to knock on the door of a house, shop, fire station or police station.

Stalkers are very rare but persistent: inform the police as soon as an incident occurs (even if it is an unpleasant phone call from a stalker) and tell them again every time it happens. Quote previous crime reference numbers each time because, even if no action is taken at that time, a record of your calls will be on the crime sheet.

If possible photograph or video an incident – especially if you see someone attempting to break into a house or car in your street. Then call the police.

If you witness an incident try to make notes. They will be useful to jog your memory when you talk to the police or make a witness statement.

If the worst happens, your first priority is to get away from a difficult situation as quickly as possible.

Travelling Abroad

Your best defence in an unfamiliar place or situation is common sense. Don't do anything foolish.

Don't wear flashy jewellery or anything that is likely to draw attention to you.

Walking down the street carrying a map means you will have tourist written all over your face, and be prey to people who will know you are on strange ground.

Avoid advertising the country you come from – don't sew the flag of your country on your bags.

Stick to the main tourist tracks – wandering off to discover the 'real country' could land you in serious trouble.

Seems obvious but make sure your money, passports and so on are kept in a bumbag around your waist and hidden under your clothes. Don't carry them in a shoulder bag.

Be observant of what is going on around you and look like you know what you're doing. Walk with purpose.

BRA FITTERS

Jill Kenton, Rigby and Peller, www. rigbyandpeller.co.uk; Bravissimo (tel: 020 8742 8882 or www.bravissimo.com)

At least 75 per cent of women are in the wrong size of bra, so the chances are you're one of them.

If a bra is properly fitted, you shouldn't be aware that you're wearing it. If you can't wait to get it off, you're in the wrong size.

Some shops that offer bra fitting don't carry a large enough range of cup sizes, so they'll sell you a larger back size to compensate, but it won't fit up front.

You only want to have two breasts. If it looks as if you have four, your cup size is too small.

Wrinkling all over the cup, especially at the top and sides, means the cup size is too big. The breasts should be enclosed in the cups with a smooth silhouette.

The front and back of a bra should be at the same level and shouldn't budge. If the bra rides up at the back, it can't be supporting you properly and it is probably too big. Choose one with a smaller back and a bigger cup size.

Underwired bras give better separation, support and lift, and give a better line under clothes. Soft cup bras are fine for maternity, breast-feeding, sports and mastectomy bras. All others are best underwired.

If underwired bras dig in at the side of the breast or stick out, the cup size is too small. Many women complain of this, but once they've been properly fitted, they're converted.

If you have marks on your shoulders from your bra straps, the bra is not giving your breasts enough support.

Pure cotton is not the best fabric for a bra as it stretches. You should aim for a maximum of 30 to 40 per cent cotton, and always have a bit of elastene.

A bra will last six months to a year, depending on how you treat it. If little bits of elastic start appearing at the back, it's high time to chuck it.

Handwash bras, rinse well, don't wring underwires, and always drip dry.

Bras hate heat, so don't wash them in a machine, never put them in a tumble dryer and never hang them over radiators.

Wearing a correctly fitted bra from the first protects delicate breast tissue and helps to prevent your boobs starting the long journey south.

Bra size does not necessarily carry across from make to make, so try on different sizes. If you are, say, a 36C, go down a back size and up a cup size to 34D, then up a back size and down a cup size to 38B to find the best fit in other makes.

When you get a new bra, do it up on then loosest catch, then if it stretches you can tighten it by moving along a catch at a time.

The adjuster straps over the shoulders need tightening with wear too. It's very hard to get these even yourself, so ask a trusted friend.

Big girls look smaller in a well fitting bra. Underwires show off the shape of your breasts and separate well. If your bra gives you one indistinct lump across your chest, it makes you look much bigger.

Stick to smooth bras for wearing under fitted or sheer tops.

For bigger boobs, wear fitted or streamlined shapes, as these are much more flattering than baggy clothes. Look for fitted tops with seams or darts under the bust as these will define your waist.

Round, scooped or V-necklines tend to be more flattering for bigger boobs than high necklines.

Wear plain colours to minimise a big bust – avoid busy patterns, large prints and patch pockets.

Keep tops light and bottoms dark to emphasise boobs, and darker tops and lighter bottoms to draw the attention away.

Wear jewellery away from your bust – it's more flattering around your neck than on your boobs.

For small girls, the technology has never been better. There are all kinds of little extras in bras nowadays – so a cleavage can be yours.

Wear a good sports bra. There are no muscles in the breasts and once you stretch the ligaments and they become damaged there is nothing you can do short of surgery.

Make sure a sports bra is smooth so seams and bindings will not rub. The straps should be fairly rigid to minimise bounce and be wide enough to sit comfortably without digging in. The jump test in the changing room is the best way to check out its efficacy!

Getting married? Make sure you try on your wedding lingerie under your dress to you avoid a last minute panic.

Make sure you find a good basque or strapless bra before you committ yourself to a strapless dress, especially if you have a big bust.

Lacy bras are sexy, but aren't so good under a very fitted evening or wedding dress.

To put on your bra, do it up with the catch turned round to the front, then rotate it so that it's at the back, slip your arms through the straps, lean forward and lower your breasts into the cups (your nipple should be on the seam and in the middle), slide the straps on to your shoulders and stand up.

Front fastening should be restricted to nursing bras – it just doesn't work for every-day use.

Get your breasts re-measured every six to eight months, and monthly when you're pregnant. Get fitted for a nursing bra as close to your due date as possible.

If your breasts enlarge before your period, get measured then too, and have a couple of larger bras so you're comfy all month. PMT and a tight bra – definitely something to be avoided!

Every woman needs between four and eight bras. They must be washed every day, like knickers, and be worn in rotation to ensure a long and supportive life.

BUILDERS

A Screw Loose?

Neil Harris, Tim Hobbs & Brian Harris, H S Hamilton & Sons; Godfrey Rawlings, Basement Construction; Phil Sheehan

When screwing soft metal such as brass into hard wood, there is a danger of snapping the head off the screw. Greasing the screw with a little tallow, soap or something similar will ease the friction and make it much easier to screw in.

Drill a pilot hole into wood (particularly MDF) so that it will accept a screw. A pilot hole is smaller than the actual screw.

Drill holes without leaving a mess behind by vacuuming up the dust as you drill.

When drilling above your head, push the drill bit through a yoghurt pot to stop the dust from falling into your face. It also saves you having to clear up afterwards.

To catch the dust when you are drilling, attach an envelope to the wall using masking tape, just beneath where you intend to drill. The dust will collect in the envelope and not on the floor.

Stop screws and nails rusting by storing them in an empty cold-cream jar.

Unscrew stubborn screws using a long-handled screwdriver.

Sticking Together

Make a glue brush using the tube of an old ball-point pen and some coarse string. Push the string all the way through the tube, then tease the ends out to make bristles. When you've finished using the brush, cut off the sticky end and pull a new bit through for the next job.

Unsticking a vinyl floor tile is easy. Cover the tile you want to remove with aluminium foil, put your iron on maximum heat and move it slowly over the tile. You should be able to lift the tile after a minute or so.

Concrete is easier to work with if you put some washing-up liquid into the mixture.

Straight Lines

To mark a straight line on a wall for a shelf, mark two points at either end of the shelf length. Rub chalk along a piece of string and then fix (or hold) the string at these points. Ping the string and the chalk is transferred onto the wall in a perfect straight line.

To build a level brick wall, place a brick at either end of the wall as you start each layer. Stretch a piece of string from one end to the other (securing the string with more bricks), and use the string as a guide.

To cut wood in a straight line, use another piece of wood to guide you.

Make your own spirit level – use a milk bottle with a little bit of water in it.

When hanging a door, put a wedge under the end farthest away from the hinges to keep the whole door balanced upright.

Measure twice and cut once – most people measure once and cut twice.

Getting Plastered

Plaster will set much quicker if mixed with warm water. Some plasterers find that weeing into their plaster has the same effect!

When plastering a brick wall, coat it first with a PVC-type glue. This prevents the surface from absorbing too much water and from drying out the plaster too quickly and making it crack.

Seal cracks effectively by wetting your finger and using it to spread the sealant.

If you need to fill a small hole in an emergency, use some toothpaste. Let it dry before painting the wall.

Protection

Protect your fingers when hammering nails. Push the nail through a piece of stiff paper or cardboard and use this to hold the nail in place. Tear the paper away before the nail is hammered into place.

To prevent wood from splitting, blunt the end of the nail.

Stop plywood from splitting when you use a saw on it – apply masking tape to the area you intend to cut.

Prevent birds from eating window putty – they're after the linseed oil – by mixing black pepper into the putty.

Store unused putty by rolling it tightly into a ball and wrapping it carefully in aluminium foil before replacing in a tub. The putty should keep for several months like this.

Put a damp-proof membrane between a new window or door-frame where it meets the wall to stop moisture getting in and rotting the wood. Heavy-duty plastic works well.

Finishing Off

When sanding floorboards, knock the ends of nails down into the floor. Exposed nail heads wear down sandpaper much more quickly than a flat surface.

Stop stairs and floorboards from squeaking – use a wax-based furniture polish.

Stop hinges squeaking with petroleum jelly rather than oil, which will run and spoil the paintwork and floor.

To age new bricks, brush them with milk.

To get stains off bricks, rub or grate the marked brick with another similar brick.

Before varnishing a floor, sweep all the debris up and then wipe it down with a damp cloth to pick up every last bit of dust.

Pick up metal objects with a magnet in a plastic bag. Then turn the bag inside out so that all the objects end up inside the bag.

Dirty hammers are actually dangerous – the head will keep slipping if it gets really grimy. Try banging it on a piece of wood covered with sandpaper a few times or, alternatively, rub the head over some coarse sand.

BUTCHERS

Frank Lee

Keep your wooden chopping block clean. Wash it down when you've finished butchering and then cover it with sawdust. This soaks up the damp while the resin in the block kills off any bacteria.

To sharpen a serrated-edged knife, use a steel on just the serrated side (not both sides).

Keep a carbon steel knife clean by dipping a cork in scouring powder and running it along the side of the blade. Rinse the knife, dry it and wipe it down with vegetable oil.

To make cocktail sausages, don't bother to buy the expensive ones in the shops. Just warm your hands and pinch a chipolata in the middle, forming two small cocktail sausages.

To make pork crackling, rub the fat with vinegar and then sprinkle with salt. The acidity will make the crackling. Pigs are much leaner nowadays so it's more difficult to get good crackling.

Score pork skin with a Stanley knife before putting it into the oven.

Gammon can be too salty – when boiling ham, put some lemon juice on it to reduce the saltiness. This also keeps the meat nice and pink.

Don't bother to pluck a pheasant – skin it instead. The skin comes off like a sock!

If you get blood on a sheepskin coat, just sprinkle potting compost on it. It works like blotting paper. Leave it overnight and brush it off in the morning.

BUTLERS

Breakfast

John Thomas, John Thomas International School of Butlers; Ivor Spencer; Don Weedon; Peter Greenhill; Boris Roberts; Robert Marshal

Freshen bread rolls for breakfast by covering them with a damp towel and placing them in a hot oven for a short while.

Warm a teapot by holding it over the spout of the kettle as it boils.

Always use boiling water when making tea – the air in the water helps the tea to brew properly.

Dinner is Served

For a truly professional-looking dinner table use a ruler, and line everything up 1 in/2.5 cm from the edge of the table.

Always lay the cutlery from the outside in, according to the sequence of courses.

Place the white-wine glass at the top of the first-course knife because that is usually what people will drink first.

Thirteen guests for dinner can be unlucky so put a teddy bear on a fourteenth chair!

When seating someone at the dinner table, pull the chair back and manoeuvre your guest in front. Very gently tap the back of their knee with the edge of the seat; their knee will automatically buckle and they will sit down.

The correct way to eat caviare is not with a silver spoon but from the back of your hand. It's even better if you use somebody else's hand!

To tell the difference between Oscietra and Beluga caviare, put a few eggs on a piece of paper and then crush them. If the oil is yellow, then it's Oscietra, but if it's grey then the caviare is Beluga.

Serve your best wine first. By the time you get to the cheaper stuff your guests will probably be incapable of noticing the drop in quality.

Don't wear strong aftershave when serving vintage wine because it will completely swamp the bouquet.

When picnicking, make an instant wine cooler by wrapping a wet newspaper around a bottle of wine. Ask someone to hold the bottle out of the sunroof or window as you drive to your chosen site.

When making coffee, don't pour boiling water on to the grounds as you will scald the coffee. Use water when it's just off the boil.

If you want the cream to float on your coffee rather than sink without trace, stir some sugar into the coffee first.

Burning Questions

Don't use a gas lighter to light a cigar – it will ruin the taste. Always use a match but keep it away from the end of the cigar until the sulphur has burnt away.

When relighting a cigar, always get rid of the stale fumes by blowing through it first and then lighting it.

Keep cigars in cool, dark places. You could keep them in the fridge for a while to condition them.

Silver Service

To keep silver clean, use lemon and salt.

Be careful when washing silver cutlery. Take care it doesn't rub together too much. Silver is a soft metal and picks up scratches easily.

Remove wax easily from silver candlesticks. Place them in the fridge overnight and it's then easy to pick off the wax.

If you are packing silver away for any length of time, wrap it in a clean T-shirt away from the light.

Prevent tarnish by storing silver wrapped in cling film.

Spit & Polish

If a crystal wineglass has a tiny nick in the rim, you can file it gently with the fine side of an emery board and make it usable again.

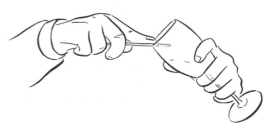

Pick up tiny fragments of broken glass with a pad of damp cotton wool.

Bone china should not be a museum piece. Take it out and clean it every year.

Rotate your best cutlery. Take it from the left-hand side of the drawer and put it back on the right-hand side.

For really clean glasses, wash in hot soapy water and then rinse in warm water with a couple of tablespoons of vinegar in it.

Polish glasses with a dry cloth. A damp cloth might grip the glass and break it.

Never store wineglasses upside down. They will absorb the smells of the cupboard they're in and this could affect the taste of the wine. Just clean glasses before use to get rid of any dust.

To dry a decanter, use a hair-dryer.

If you don't have a bottle brush, half fill the vase or bottle with warm soapy water and a handful of small pebbles. Shake vigorously. If the glass is delicate, use split-peas or dried lentils instead of pebbles.

To clean a smelly vase or glass, half fill it with water and add a tablespoon of mustard. Shake the mixture and then leave for an hour.

Keeping up Appearances

To avoid creasing, use tissue paper in between the folds when packing a case.

To avoid wrinkly trouser legs, pack the top of the trousers first, followed by the rest of the clothes. Then fold the trouser legs over the top.

Place shoes in plastic bags to prevent shoe polish getting all over the clothes.

Always pack silk inside out.

Hang a wet, clean white shirt outside on a cold morning and it will come up bright white.

CABBIES

John Godfrey,
Knowledge School;
Jonathon Jackson

Please don't do that whistling thing, or shout 'Oi!'. It's much better to raise your arm, even wave it about a bit. If you're holding a paper, so much the better. And stay in one place – you'll be much easier to spot.

You can hail a cab whichever side of the road you're on, and whichever direction it's travelling – as long as you can make yourself seen, it doesn't matter.

The best place from which to hail a cab is the busiest junction you can find.

If you want to tip a cab driver, the usual practice is rounding the fare up to the nearest pound.

If you drive a black cab, you can pay to be a member of a radio circuit, which means you are tracked by satellite and can be allocated the jobs nearest to your location.

If a passenger makes a regular journey, they might want to request the same driver on a regular basis. Lots of cabbies carry mobile phones to take personal bookings for satisfied customers.

If your destination is outside of your driver's area, he might be able to take you part of the way, or you could agree a fare rather than using the meter.

If you're interested in becoming a black cab driver in London, bear in mind that it takes about three to three and a half years of full-time study to learn The Knowledge which means learning 400 basic routes between destinations in a six-mile radius from Charing Cross Station. This includes having a detailed knowledge of 25,000 streets, and for each run you must know all the buildings and places of interest within a quarter mile radius of the start and finish point of the run. Taxi drivers should be able to give you quite a bit of information, if you ask them nicely.

To acquire the depth of knowledge required to pass the cab drivers' test, you will need to hire or buy a moped or motorbike to travel around London, and are likely to have to travel about 20,000 miles in the process. So please believe that we know the way better than you do.

On a busy Saturday night, cabs don't need to wait in a rank, but often drive a circuit round the busiest places. That way, they won't have to take the grottiest, drunkest punters when it comes to their turn on the rank, but can just pick up the passengers who don't look like they'll cause trouble.

Remember a cabby can refuse to carry a passenger. A good avoidance tactic if you don't like the look of someone is to gesture to your mobile phone, to indicate that you're already on a call. Don't take offence if a cabbie does that to you. Sometimes it's true.

If a passenger is causing trouble in a cab, the driver can radio other cars for assistance, or even drive to a police station if a passenger is refusing to pay.

CAKE MAKERS & DECORATORS

Making & Baking

Jane Asher Party Cakes; Carolyn Bruce-Moore, Top Tier, Stratford-upon-Avon; Julie Weiner

To give a cake a wonderful golden glow, try adding custard powder to a basic sponge mixture.

When making cakes, leave the eggs and fat out overnight so that they will be at the same temperature.

If you don't have a cake tin with a removable base, don't worry. Grease your tin as normal. Cut a long strip of kitchen foil and put it into the bottom of the tin so that each end of the foil strip goes up the side and hangs over the edge. Put a circle of greaseproof paper in the bottom of the tin and fill with the cake mixture. When you need to get the cake out, gently lift it using the foil tabs.

Make sure any essence you use adds flavour to the whole cake – mix it into one of the eggs before adding to the mixture.

Your cakes will never stick if you use olive oil to grease the tins.

Before using a new baking tin, grease it and bake it in a very hot oven for at least ten minutes. Wash as normal in soapy water and you'll find your tin stays as good as new for ages.

Do your cakes always sink? It's not necessarily the opening of the oven door that causes it but the closing. Unless you do it very gently, the sudden movement can cause the cake to sink.

If you want your cake to have a flat top for decorating, spoon out a bit of the mixture from the middle of the tin before baking.

To stop the fruit in cakes from sinking, first wash the fruit, then coat in glycerine.

To stop glacé cherries from sinking, coat them lightly in flour before using.

For a really moist fruit cake, use marmalade instead of candied peel.

Always soak dried fruit overnight – for extra flavour, soak the fruit in apple or orange juice.

For a special-occasion cake, marinate the fruit in your favourite liqueur for a week.

If your cakes always come out cracked, put a dish of cold water in the bottom of the oven before baking.

Do your cakes crumble when cut? After cooling and before cutting, pop them into the freezer for 20 minutes.

To improve the flavour and texture of cakes and to reduce fat at the same time, substitute one-third of the butter with a mashed banana.

To make fluffier, lighter cakes, whip the egg whites separately before adding to the recipe.

To give chocolate cakes an added kick and to give them a rich, brown colour, add a teaspoon of instant coffee granules to the mix.

Cakes are completely baked when you can stick a skewer in and it comes out clean.

To make beating brown sugar into a cake mix easier, put it through a food processor first – it makes it softer.

To prevent nuts sinking, coat them lightly with flour before adding to the cake mixture.

For an extra rich, tasty fruit cake, use cold coffee instead of milk.

For a moist fruit cake with extra flavour, grate a cooking apple into the mixture.

Blanch your own almonds by pouring boiling water over them in a bowl. After a few minutes, drain off the water – the skins will come off easily.

Before measuring out treacle or golden syrup, sprinkle the dish of the scales with flour. The syrup will come out easily.

Peel citrus fruits with a potato peeler before squeezing. Drop the rind into a jar containing golden syrup for a tasty addition to cakes.

Place pared orange peel in a low oven until it dries out. Crush and keep in a jar then add to cakes with dry ingredients.

Chop dates in a food processor or mincer before adding to a loaf mix. The resulting cake will be much moister.

For a moister fruit cake in electric ovens or Agas, place a dish of water on the floor of the oven when baking.

When dividing cake mix between two (or more) tins, check that you have split the mix evenly by weighing the tins before you put them in the oven. Even up the mixture as necessary.

Dried fruit for a Christmas cake is far tastier if soaked in brandy for three days before you bake it. Stir every 12 hours.

For an extra-light sponge cake, beat a tablespoon of hot water into the mixture just before baking.

It sounds obvious, but the best cakes are baked in warm kitchens, so turn on the central heating before you begin baking.

To stop cakes and pastries sticking to the inside of shaped cutters, brush the insides with a little oil.

Finishing Touches

Jam spreads more easily if you warm it first.

For firmer whipped cream, beat it with honey rather than sugar.

Before sandwiching your cake together with jam, spread a little butter on each sponge surface. This will stop the cake absorbing all the jam.

To cut a sponge cake horizontally, take two pieces of wood of equal thickness and of half the depth of the cake, and lie them either side of the cake. Slide the knife in a sawing action across the top of the wood and through the cake.

Use muslin instead of a sieve when dusting icing sugar through a doily. It is much finer and the effect is so much prettier.

To dry a cake out, put it under an anglepoise desk lamp.

Before icing a cake, sprinkle the top with some flour; this will stop the icing running down over the edges.

For a deceptively clever effect, put two colours of icing in a bag and then pipe out. The two-tone effect is stunning.

If you don't have a turntable for decorating a cake, don't worry. Take two plates, sandwich them together back to back with a little cooking oil and place on a damp tea towel to stop the bottom plate slipping. Placed on top, your cake will turn round beautifully.

Royal icing is notoriously difficult to beat with a food mixer. Try fixing the whisk attachment to a variable speed drill instead.

Glacé icings can be horribly sweet. Substituting milk for some of the water gives a creamy texture and reduces the sweetness.

To keep cakes fresh in the tin, throw in half an apple.

For a neat finish, make sure you cover and edge your cake board.

For a tasty, colourful cake topping, mix a little strawberry jam and boiling water into icing sugar.

Decorate your cakes with real flowers. To stop the flowers wilting cut a 3 in/7.5 cm piece of plastic drinking straw. Bend the end of the straw upwards and tape it. Fill the straw three-quarters full with water and insert the flower stem inside it.

Always sketch out your design in advance and make sure you have all the necessary equipment that you require.

Plan well in advance if you are making any pastillage models or flowers, to allow for items to dry out properly.

Simple cakes are often the most stunning, so always work and design to your own capabilities.

Roll marzipan out between two sheets of cling film or aluminium foil.

You can keep butter cream for two or three weeks in a covered container in the fridge, so save time by making more than you need and add flavours to suit each cake you make.

Don't be scared of fondant icing – it's really just like using Plasticine. If what you're doing goes horribly wrong, just squidge it back together and start again.

If you're rolling out coloured fondant icing, don't dust the board with icing sugar – it makes the colour paler. Instead, rub good old Trex (or similar) over the rolling surface and put the icing directly on that. It never sticks.

Fondant icing is best worked at room temperature. In the heat of summer this means getting up early to do your rolling and moulding.

Store fondant icing in the fridge in thin polythene bags or carefully wrapped in cling film. The important thing is to exclude air or it will dry out.

To make grass or hair out of fondant icing, press the icing through the mesh of a fine sieve. For a small quantitiy you can use a garlic press – but make sure you wash it thoroughly first.

Piping is easier if the cake is raised. If you don't have a turntable, place the cake on an inverted cake tin.

Use a small spirit level to make sure the dowelling is even on fondant-covered tiered cakes.

Make sure cutters are completely dry after washing, or they'll go rusty and you'll have to throw them away. The best way is to place them in the oven as it's cooling down after a baking session.

To avoid streaks when adding paste colour to fondant icing, add the colour to a small quantity of icing first, then blend that into the rest of the icing.

Colouring fondant icing evenly takes ages. Give yourself plenty of time or, alternatively, decide on a marbled effect and make a virtue of the streaks!

Sugar sprays can be lifted off a cake and kept for years provided you store them in a dry atmosphere and out of sunlight. A glass display dome is ideal.

Keep the top tier of a wedding cake in a box in a dry, dust-free room where there are no extremes of temperature. A spare bedroom is usually the best environment. And once you've used the top tier, you probably won't have a spare room!

Don't throw away cake boards. You can re-cover them with silver or gold paper for another time and even if one side gets scored by knife cuts, you can turn it over and use the other. You should get four goes out of a board, at the least. If you're careful with your knife, they'll go on for ages.

For adding tiny amounts of food colouring and flavouring, use an eye-dropper bought from the chemist.

To stop cake mix sticking to your spoon when you're transferring it to a tin, try dipping the spoon in milk beforehand.

Left-over royal icing? Just add a little more icing sugar and a few drops of peppermint essence, then roll out and cut shapes to make peppermint creams.

Icing sets more quickly if made up with boiling water.

To prevent breaking icing when cutting a cake, dip the knife blade in boiling water first.

To fill an icing bag with no mess, put it inside a tall glass or a jug, fold the top of the bag over the rim, then fill.

CAMERAMEN

Justin Quinnell; Duncan Elson; Ray Lowe; Nik Mather; Maddie Attenborough

Warm your batteries in your hand before use – you'll get more power out of them.

Always get your nickel/cadmium (nicad) batteries to discharge fully before recharging them.

To save batteries, don't keep zooming in and out while filming. And turn the camera off between shots.

Instead of zooming into a close-up of an object, stop recording and move physically closer to the object. Then film it in close-up. It will be a much more stable shot.

If you don't have a tripod, use a home-made monopod. Something along the lines of a ski-stick turned upside down would do.

Alternatively, lean on a wall, a gate, a car bonnet, anything that comes to hand that will give you a stable shot.

Make sure you get the colour right – always do a white balance, using some white paper, before filming.

If you're filming something on the move that's low to the ground (such as a cat or dog), take a plastic bag with handles, and cut a lens-sized hole in it. Put the camera inside and carry the bag around in pursuit of your subject. This avoids you crouching down all the time.

Vary your camera angles – for example, if you're taking shots of children, get down to their level and take your shots from a kneeling position.

If you need to shoot through a window, shoot at an angle so you don't get your reflection in shot as well.

Protect your camera. Put cling film around it in wet or sandy conditions and put some insulating tape around the gap in the tape compartment so that dust or moisture won't get in.

Think sound as well as picture when shooting a home video. If you are 20 ft/6 m from your subject, then so is the microphone.

Microphones don't select what they hear; they suck up every available bit of noise. So reduce ambient noise by closing curtains or windows to cut out interference caused by traffic, children playing, aeroplanes going overhead and so on.

Always wear headphones to monitor noise and to make sure you can hear the sound properly.

Tape down incoming leads and cables so that they don't get pulled. This reduces the risk of damaging your equipment.

To tidy up the cables running from your camera, take two 4 in/10 cm Velcro strips and glue them back to back. Use them as a strap for wrapping your cables together.

If your recording is important to you, remember to snap off or close the recording tabs at the side of the tape. This will prevent you or anyone else from accidentally re-recording over it.

CAMPERS & CARAVANNERS

Campers:
Hazel Constance;
David Wood;
Jean Anthony;
Mary Matthews;
Christine Green;
Robin Hamer
Caravanners:
The Caravan Club;
The Camping and
Caravanning Club;
Mr Chris Smith,
Bedfordshire Centre of
the Caravan Club;
Mr B Clarke;

When camping for the first time, don't go miles away from home just in case you forget something important – or you discover you loathe the great outdoors.

Preparation is everything. Try putting your tent up in good conditions and in your own back garden in order to check that it goes together smoothly and that all the pieces are there.

Weather your tent in preparation for all climates. Wet it before you leave or keep spraying it with water when it is erect then wait for it to dry thoroughly before packing it up again.

Don't camp in a hollow because cold air sinks and you will find the temperature drops substantially at night.

Avoid camping in a dried stream bed. If it rains, the stream may suddenly reappear!

You can never have too many safety pins. They have lots of emergency uses and don't take up too much room.

Mr B E J Hall, Devon &
Cornwall Caravan Club;
Mrs Worsell, Dorset
Caravan Club;
Mrs Moore, Dorset
Caravan Club

When erecting your tent, use thick rubber bands to attach the guy ropes to the pegs. The bands will take up any slack that develops and will prevent your tent from sagging.

Sitting on the ground can be wet and cold. Make your own insulated cushion from a sheet of kitchen foil sandwiched between two pieces of foam.

When you pack up your tent make sure it's dry and clean. Any remaining grass or leaves will rot in the tent when it's stored away.

Keeping toilet paper dry can be difficult. Cut the end off a large plastic bottle and cut a thin slit down one side. Put the loo roll inside and thread the end of the roll through the slit; you can then tear off nice, dry sheets of loo paper at your convenience.

Toothbrushes soon get mucky so cut one down and keep it in a film canister.

Keep your toothbrush clean by covering the head with some foil when not in use.

Keep your soap clean – store it in the foot of some tights slung over a nearby tree.

If you have a night out away from the campsite, tie a white plastic bag to the top of your tent so that you can find it when you get back later in the dark.

Keep your specs safe – use a safety pin to fasten the bridge of your glasses to the tent fabric when you're not wearing them.

No fly spray? Try hair-spray instead. Flies hate it because it sticks their wings together – they'll soon get the message and leave.

Avoid wearing too much yellow. Flies love the colour and can mistake you for a large flower.

Midges and flies can be a real problem. Cut a sock length off a pair of sheer tights and stretch over a baseball cap and down over your face for stylish protection!

Don't drink too much before you go to bed – there's nothing worse than having to wriggle out of your sleeping bag in the middle of the night to go to the loo.

When going to the loo in the great outdoors, you must dig a hole no deeper than 9 in/23 cm. Do your business and then bury it. All the bacteria that break down human waste are found in the top 9 in/23 cm of the soil.

If you need to evacuate someone who cannot walk from a hillside, lay a rucksack on the ground and sit the injured person down on it. Get two people to grasp the handles of the rucksack and carry the person down. Do not, however, attempt to move someone who has injured their back or neck.

Clothing

To keep warm, wear lots of thin layers rather than a few bulky ones. You can take layers off as you wish.

It's more hygienic if the layer next to your skin is cotton.

Colour code your stuff sacks so you know which is dirty washing, where your clean clothes are, which bag holds your smalls or wet-weather gear and so on.

When walking to the top of a steep or high hill, you will get very sweaty, so take a dry, clean T-shirt to change into for the journey down.

Make a snug neck loop out of a strip of fleece, secured by Velcro or poppers. It's better than having a scarf flapping around and much warmer, too.

Damp walking boots can be uncomfortable and cause blisters. Keep yours dry by banging a couple of sticks into the ground and then hanging the boots upside down on them.

Don't put wet boots in front of the fire because this makes them really stiff and they may even shrink. Stuff them with newspaper instead and leave them in a well-ventilated spot to dry out.

Don't take your shoes off in very hot weather. Your feet will expand and your shoes won't fit when you come to put them on again.

When packing your rucksack, work out what you will need last and put it in the bottom of the rucksack. Then keep packing things in the reverse order in which you will need them. There's nothing worse than having to unpack absolutely everything as soon as you arrive.

Keep clothes dry by packing them inside plastic carrier bags before putting them in your rucksack.

Bulky towels take up valuable room. Pack a square terry towel instead. They're pretty small but highly absorbent.

If you don't have a terry towel, a beer towel is good and compact, too.

J-cloths make good towels. They dry out quickly and can double up as flannels.

Leave clothes pegs behind. Just double up a long piece of rope and twist it. You can then tuck your wet clothes in between the twisted rope and leave them to dry.

Dry clothes on an old umbrella. Tear off the fabric and string fishing line between the spokes. Hang small items of clothing from the spokes.

A wire shelf from a fridge makes an excellent clothes horse. Tie it between two branches and thread your wet clothes through the shelf to dry.

Sleeping

Avoid washing your sleeping bag too often; make a liner for it out of a cotton sheet or duvet cover. You can wash that as often as you like.

No room to pack a pillow? Just button up your coat and stuff it with some clothes.

Make a comfy, emergency pillow by blowing up the bladder from a wine box.

Create a hot-water bottle. Collect some warm stones from around the fire and pop them in a sock. Don't use any that are too hot!

Alternatively, fill your metal water bottle with hot water and put that down your sleeping bag.

To keep warm during the night, lay a piece of foam insulation roll under your air bed. One underneath is worth two on top! If you don't have any insulating foam, a length of old carpet underneath your sleeping bag will keep you snug too.

If you have cold feet, wear a hat – you lose most of your body heat through your head.

No one can sleep if they are cold so make a draught excluder by rolling up a towel and placing it in front of any cracks.

Does the zip on your sleeping bag stick? Try rubbing some petroleum jelly or vapour rub along the teeth and it will be as good as new.

Fill your kettle before going to bed. You'll be so pleased that you don't have to walk down to the toilet block for water first thing in the morning that you'll enjoy that cup of tea much more.

Cooking

To get the best use from your small camp stove, shove it up your jumper – before you've lit it, of course! This warms the gas up and it will last for longer.

Avoid as much washing-up as possible: take boil-in-the-bag food.

If you need a grate over your fire, a boot scraper is a useful alternative.

Make your own frying pan – a flat stone left in the embers will heat up and can be used to cook food on.

Don't give up the luxuries of life. Take some service station sachets of salt, pepper, mustard and ketchup to spice up your food.

Secure your gas stove by putting a couple of spare tent pegs through the base.

Forgotten the corkscrew? All you have to do is hit the bottom of the bottle sharply several times with a book or rubber-soled shoe. The cork will gradually rise up through the neck of the bottle.

Keep matches dry – store them in a film canister.

Waterproof your matches by dipping the heads in melted wax.

Make the washing-up easier – coat the base of your pan with diluted soapy liquid before you begin cooking. If you don't have soapy liquid, try a generous coating of mud.

For stubborn food deposits, try rubbing with a clump of grass.

Scrunched up kitchen foil makes a good pot scourer.

Take small, easily stored amounts of washing-up liquid in eye-drop containers or film canisters.

Make baking easy – if the urge takes you, simply line a biscuit tin with foil, put it on the fire and you've got an effective little oven.

You can cook eggs in their shells on an open fire – just prick the shells first.

Wrap eggs in orange peel and put them in the embers of the fire to bake.

Keep pans and bowls of food safe from insects by covering them with cheap plastic shower caps.

Create a fly-free larder – hang up a net curtain around the food.

Attract ants away from your food – put a white piece of paper on the ground. The ants will make a beeline for that instead.

The best instant food is a banana.

To get rid of stale, nasty smells from a water carrier, fill it with water and drop a denture-cleaning tablet in to it. Leave for a couple of hours and then rinse out thoroughly.

To make thermos flask tea taste that little bit fresher, put half a teaspoon of lemon juice in the tea.

Get rid of smells from your thermos flask using a denture-cleaning tablet and some water. Leave to soak for 20 minutes.

Freshen your thermos flask by filling it with water and one tablespoon of bicarbonate of soda. Leave to soak. Rinse and drain.

Keep a thermos flask fresh by leaving a couple of sugar lumps in it when not in use.

Replace the stopper of your thermos flask so it's tilted to one side, allowing air to circulate. This will prevent it from smelling musty when you come to use it again.

Children & Camping

Children love to draw but paper can quickly get damp outdoors. Try laminating a piece of paper and take some chinagraph pencils or wipeable felt pens with you for happy children… and parents.

Don't bother with alarm clocks when camping with children. You'll never be up later than 6 am!

Keep your dog (or toddler!) away from the fire by attaching the animal or child to a length of guy rope which you then fix to the ground with a tent peg. Make sure the rope can't reach the fire.

CAR MECHANICS

John Gleeson; Derek James; A M Carter; Douglas Coker; Mervyn Dove; Tim Shallcross; N James; Jo Moss; David Shearman

Weather the Storm

When the car window steams up on a cold morning, smear a cut potato on the inside and then wipe off the excess moisture. This helps to stop condensation.

To avoid damp electrics, park the car's front end away from the wind, up against a hedge or a wall.

If the lock has frozen, try heating the key with a flame before trying the lock; do this several times but never force the key – you could break it.

Alternatively, soak a cloth in some warm water and hold it to the outside of the lock. If it is really stuck, you can try holding your hand over the lock for a couple of minutes, but keep changing hands so you don't freeze yourself!

The tubes of screen-wash bottles often freeze in the winter. Replace the bottle's hose with a longer length of hose and wrap this around something warm, such as the radiator. It won't freeze up again.

Antifreeze in your screen-wash bottle will damage the paintwork. Dilute some methylated spirits in the water instead.

To check your antifreeze, take an eggcup of coolant from the car and put it in the freezer. If it freezes, you definitely need more antifreeze!

Remove ice from your windscreen with a phone card if you don't have a proper scraper.

Stuck in mud? Take the rubber foot mats out of the car and lay them down in front of the tyres. Gently rock the car backwards and forwards until it gets a grip on the mats. You should then be able to drive away.

If it's really muddy, don't forget to tie your mats to the bumper before you start rocking the car backwards and forwards. When you finally get the car going, you won't have to stop and go back for the mats.

Cold engines use more fuel. Avoid unnecessary short trips, and remove excess heavy luggage and roof racks when they are not needed.

Quick Repairs

If you have to jack up the car on a soft surface, such as grass, put the jack on a board to stop it sinking under the car's weight.

If the casing on your rear light gets smashed, cover the light with some red plastic from a carrier bag until you can get it fixed.

If your indicator light goes, use the bulb from your fog light as an emergency bulb.

Patch up a leaking hose in an emergency with insulating tape or a belt from a plastic raincoat. But you must remember to leave the cap off the radiator so that the pressure doesn't build up. This will allow you to drive a short distance to the nearest garage.

Radiators often spring a leak. Chew up a bit of gum and stick it over the hole to keep you going!

Replace a broken fan belt with a pair of stockings.

If your exhaust is blowing, stay calm. Just secure a baked bean tin or any old can over the pipe with some string, wire or jubilee clips.

To charge up a battery really quickly, just drive around in third gear for a while. The high revs will do the job for you.

If you lose a set of bolts down a hole or drain whilst changing a tyre, don't panic. You can drive with three nuts on each wheel perfectly safely for a short while.

To free rusty bolts, pour on a small amount of Coke. The acids in the drink eat away at the rust. Wait until the bolt is dry before trying to release it. You may have to repeat this several times.

Left your lights on? If the battery is likely to be flat, don't even try to start the car. Just be patient, turn the lights off and wait for 15 minutes. If the battery is any good, it will recharge itself.

If the wiper blade on the driver's side disintegrates, take the blade off the passenger's side or use the rear wiper blade until you can replace it.

You can make a good waterproof repair for almost anything that needs to be protected from the damp using a bit of bin liner and a hair-dryer. Use the hair-dryer to melt a thin layer of bin liner across the hole or crack for a safe, interim measure.

If you need to do an emergency repair and your spanner is too big for the bolt, use a small coin or screwdriver to fill the gap.

Keep long hair, jewellery and clothing tucked away when doing any work on the engine. You don't want to get anything caught up in the moving parts.

Keep it Clean

Mop up oil spills with cat litter. Pour a thick layer over the spill and leave for about 24 hours. Just sweep it up when the oil has been absorbed.

To remove grease or oil stains, which tend to get on your clothes far too easily, coat the stain with lard. This will soften the stain and make it easier to treat.

If you don't use the ashtray for smoking, put your loose change in there. You'll always have something for parking meters and other emergencies.

An easy, accessible place to keep your rubbish is in a plastic bag hung over the gear stick.

Leaks in your engine are a lot easier to spot and fix if the engine is free of grease and grime.

While you're cleaning under your bonnet, it's a great time to look at all hoses, wires, belts and so on. Check the hoses for cracks, or spongy or soft spots.

Back tyres and brake locks wear down much more quickly than the front. When they start to wear, change the back to the front to get twice as much wear from them.

To keep your hands clean when you have to do any minor repairs, always have a supply of hand wipes from fast-food outlets and plastic gloves from petrol stations.

The Professionals

If the garage says parts need changing, ask them to give the old ones back to you in the box the new parts came in. That way they can't pretend they changed parts they haven't, and they can't use second-hand parts.

When having an oil change, ask what oil they need and provide your own. This will avoid their huge mark-up.

Where it says 'miscellaneous items' on the bill, ask what they mean. You may find you are being charged for use of tools, or for oil they have disposed of.

Always check your service book has been stamped. This is essential when you come to sell the vehicle.

Big-named tyre and break specialists aren't always the cheapest. Check with the dealership that sells your make of car. They may have the parts cheaper.

Make sure the garage working on your car is a member of the Retail Motor Industry Federation, or similar body. It will avoid duff repairs and rip-offs.

Many cars fail their MOTs for minor defects like faulty lights or blown bulbs. Check the car before submitting it for its test, to save it having to be retested.

Check your oil level and tyre pressure after a service. If these aren't right, mention it to the garage and consider using another garage next time.

CARPENTERS

Steven Powell

Nails, Screws & Drills

Always put a start-hole in the wood before you drill. This will stop the wood from splitting. Use a bradawl to make the hole.

Don't put screws in a row along the wood grain because this can split the wood.

To screw in awkward places, stick the screw to the screwdriver with a bit of wax.

Disguise small holes with a mixture of sawdust and glue.

If you want to disguise nail heads, use a second nail to drive the first nail a little deeper than the surface level. Remove the second nail and fill in the little hole with some sawdust and glue or a blob of paint.

When hammering, hold the hammer near the head, not at the other end. Make sure that you use several short sharp knocks rather than one almighty blow – this will prevent the nail from bending.

To make a nail go into hard wood more easily, run it through your hair before you hammer it in. The natural grease coats the nail, allowing it to slip into the wood more easily.

To stop your hammer slipping off the head of a nail, rub some emery paper over the hammer head.

To avoid damaging a wooden surface, don't hammer a nail in all the way. Stop just above the surface and sink the nail in using a nail punch and hammer.

When hanging a dado rail, bang a nail into the middle and then even the rail up and check straightness with a spirit level – this is much easier to do if the rail is attached to the wall.

To remove a nail from a wooden surface, slip a piece of thin hardwood under the claw of the hammer to prevent it from damaging the wood.

People often make small holes bigger by fiddling around trying to find the right size of wall plug. Push some broken matchsticks into the hole until it's filled instead.

It's quite hard to drill into thin wood because it often splits. Put a thicker piece of wood behind the thin piece and let the drill go into this thicker piece as well.

If the head of a round-headed screw has become damaged, use a file to make a new slot for your screwdriver.

Don't be too forceful – if you use too much strength when driving a screw home you could end up splitting the wood.

If you want to remove a stubborn screw, try putting a little oil on the screw head and leaving it for a while before trying to release it.

Make a feature of concealed screw heads by plugging the counterboard with a dowel, glued to the screw head. Once the glue has dried, plane the dowel and sand it flush with the surface.

Remember that screws (as well as most taps and lids) should be turned to the right to make them tight.

When drilling through metal, keep the speed of the drill down to stop it overheating. Surround the hole you are drilling with a small piece of putty and pour in a few drops of white spirit to act as a lubricant.

When drilling a deep hole with an auger bit, withdraw it every now and then to get rid of the waste or the drill will jam.

When you don't have a nail punch, file back the point on another nail, place it over the nail that needs sinking and tap it carefully with a hammer.

If you haven't got a small twist drill, nip off the head of a nail with pinchers and insert it into the grip of a drill. Drill slowly and steadily.

Hammering in tiny moulding pins can be very fiddly. Push the pin through a strip of paper and hold the paper, not the pin, while you tap it down.

Don't use a chisel-pointed bradawl as a screwdriver. Its end is not hardened and it will damage very easily.

Saw Points

For a smoother sawing action, rub the teeth of the saw with some candle wax.

Before you start to saw, make a small V-shaped cut with a knife and insert the saw. Start with a backward motion before pushing the saw forward.

When using a jigsaw, always put the 'good' side of the wood underneath and cut with the 'back' of the wood facing you. The jigsaw cuts on the upstroke so this won't spoil the surface of the wood.

Rub a candle over the sides of saws and shoes of planes. The wax will reduce the friction and make sawing or planing easier, especially if the wood you are sawing is full of resin.

When you are rip sawing (sawing in the same direction as the grain) tension can cause the saw cut to close up, trapping the saw. To prevent this happening, wedge the cut open by tapping in a small wooden wedge.

Eliminate splintering when sawing wood across the grain by marking the saw line with a sharp trimming knife and straight edge. Remember to make the saw cut on the waste side of the line.

A Great Finish

Always lift a power sander off the surface before switching it off.

It is much easier to use sandpaper if you glue a sheet on to a small block of wood.

Don't bother to take a sticking door off its hinges. Simply open and shut it several times over a piece of rough sandpaper.

If you have gaps left between doors when fitting units, cover the space with a length of thin beading.

Beading can give character to flat, boring doors. Arrange it in such a way as to give the impression of panels.

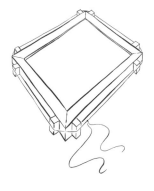

Tongue and groove panelling is attractive but expensive. Cut some grooves into hardboard and then paint it… no one will know the difference.

Making a picture frame? The mitred edges can be kept in place while they are drying by wrapping a piece of string around the frame, and inserting small blocks of wood, two on each of the four sides, under the string. Make sure the string is tight.

If a tube of filler or sealant is hard in cold weather, dunk it into a bucket of warm water for about half an hour before you want to use it.

If you are working away from your workbench, and don't have an oilstone, improvise by sticking a piece of fine silicon carbide paper to a wood off-cut.

Use light machine oil, not vegetable oil, on an oilstone to sharpen tools. The vegetable oil, combined with ground-off metal particles will gum up the stone and create a slippery surface so that the stone is no longer abrasive.

No plumb line? Just hang a bunch of keys from some string instead.

If you've mislaid your dustpan, wet the edge of a newspaper, brush the dirt over the edge and roll up the paper.

Measure it Up

Near enough isn't right, but right is near enough.

Set a wooden rule up on its edge when you are using it to mark measurements on a piece of wood. The gradations on the face of the rule mean you can mark out the measurements more accurately than if the rule was lying flat.

To mark a perfect circle on MDF, bore a hole at one end of a baton and push in a pencil. Measure the exact radius of the circle along the baton from the centre of the hole and drive a nail through it at that point. The baton can then be pivoted on the nail to mark the circle.

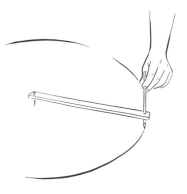

Forget your imperial measurements! Always measure in metric, because that is how timber is sold in shops. Don't mix the two.

CAR VALETS

Windows & Mirrors

Blue Chip Executive Car Valeting Service; Darren Bates

Stop your windows steaming up by putting glycerine or a little washing-up liquid in water and wiping the solution over the glass.

To clean your car windows, partly roll them down, first clean the top edges and next to the rubber gaskets. As these are the dirtiest parts of the window, clean them with a separate cloth before you tackle the main part of the glass.

Don't forget to wind the windows down slightly when you have finished washing them and wipe off any excess water and soap from the top.

Always wipe parallel to heated rear window lines. If you rub vigorously in the wrong direction, you risk snagging any cuts in the film and tearing it.

Spray glass cleaner on your cloth and not on the glass itself. This avoids over-spray on the vehicle's painted surfaces.

Buff up the windows with newspaper and a mixture of water and vinegar.

Keep a jar of bicarbonate of soda and a soft cloth in the car. When it rains, dampen the cloth and put loads of baking soda on it, then wipe the car windows inside and out – the rain will run straight off the windscreen.

If your rear wiper is either missing or a bit dodgy, rub the windscreen with a potato cut in half. The water will run away far more easily.

If your windscreen wipers judder or leave smears, use a good quality glass or window cleaner and some extremely fine wire wool. Rub the glass cleaner over the screen very gently using the wire wool, then polish with a clean cloth. Finally, spray some glass cleaner on to a cloth and clean the rubber on the wipers.

Don't apply vinyl and rubber protectants to your windscreen-wiper blades. It stops their effectiveness.

Bodywork

To avoid scratches on paintwork when cleaning car windows, get rid of chunky belt buckles and don't wear jeans with rivets or studs.

When polishing or buffing your paintwork, use a big piece of cloth and polish in large oval sweeps – using a small cloth and rubbing with your fingertips is very tiring.

If you have scratches on your paint, never use an abrasive polish. To remove a scratch you actually have to remove the paint around it, so go very carefully.

A high-quality synthetic leather is much easier to use than a real leather – it's much easier to wring out.

Keep your flunky (imitation chamois) in a sealable plastic bag to stop it drying out.

Never use yellow dusters – if the car is wet, the yellow can seep out on to the paintwork, and the synthetic fibres can scratch the car.

Always rinse loose dust off the bodywork before washing. This avoids scratching the paintwork with loose particles.

Don't clean your car with rags like old shirts, or anything with buttons. Use mutton cloth from a butcher, stockinette, or high quality 100 per cent cotton.

Take care of your chamois leather. Wash it in warm, soapy water and rinse it out after use. Let the leather dry away from direct heat so that the cloth keeps its natural oils.

Use steam cleaners for the vents, grills and engine, and they'll come up like new.

Never steam clean a Jag engine – you'll damage the electrics.

Never steam clean a Metro engine, as the distributor cap is attached with four bolts, which make it difficult to remove and you might end up with rusty bolts, which would make it impossible!

Before steam cleaning an engine, first spray the distributor and alarm system with WD40 and then cover them with a plastic bag.

If you use chemical cleaners for load dirt and brake dust, make sure you wash them off thoroughly or they will eat into the metal or lacquer.

If there is poor quality water in your area, wash the car in sections so you can leather the water off before it dries, preventing lime-scale damage.

Wash your car in sections, rinsing the soap off one part before going on to the next, to prevent the soap drying on the car and leaving dull streaks.

If the car is only mildly dirty, just leather it off rather than washing it. It saves time and effort and keeps the car looking its best.

If it has rained on your car, leather it off – this prevents the car looking dirty from the rain, and also gives the car a quick clean at the same time.

Don't try to remove dead insects or dried bird poo from your paintwork by scratching them off, even with your fingernail. Always spray it to make it soft, and then wipe it off.

To remove tree sap from your car, use mineral spirits, paint thinner or baby oil on a rag or paper towel. Hold it against the sap for a moment, then dab and rub it gently, turning the rag from side to side. Repeat until all the sap is removed, then wash and wax your car as normal.

If you have not polished your car for a long time, use tar remover or white spirit on the paintwork first before polishing.

For the heater vents on old cars, use a soft-bristled paint-brush, with masking tape wrapped around the steel join. Apply silicone spray to the bristles and wipe the excess on a rag. You'll be able to reach all the parts you can't reach with your fingers.

Don't use washing-up liquid to wash your car – it contains salt, which can cause rust to form.

If you get polish stains on your bumpers, remove them with alcohol or glass cleaner and a toothbrush or some rough towelling cloth.

To remove rust spots from chrome bumpers, use kitchen foil dipped in Coke.

Keep chrome bumpers looking as good as new – wipe them over with some petrol and then clean with black boot polish for a really shiny finish.

Use a nylon scrub brush to remove dirt from heavily grained vinyl soft tops. Be careful not to get the brush or the cleaner on the vehicle's paint.

To make a car look good in a short space of time, give it a wash and leather, then use rubber cleaner – not rubber paint – on the tyres and black plastic parts, like the bumper and the trim.

For total perfection, and if you're entering a *concours d'elegance*, clean up the exhaust pipe with cotton buds.

Wash your car from the top down, leaving the wheels (usually the dirtiest bit) until last.

Wheels & Tyres

Clean one wheel at a time. Don't run around the vehicle trying to keep each wheel at the same stage of cleaning because cleaners shouldn't be allowed to dry or remain on the wheels any longer than the instructions state.

To avoid any over-spray of cleaning products from tyre to wheel, cut out a cardboard disc the same size as the wheel with two horizontal slots for your finger and thumb. For extra strength cover the disc with tape to stop any liquid from seeping through the cardboard. Place the disc over the wheel to protect it when you're cleaning your tyres.

Always clean alloy wheels by hand. Clean the wheel in one position, then move the car slightly to clean from another angle.

To clean your chrome wheels, use lemonade. It works a treat.

Do a good job on the wheels – a car with well turned-out tyres looks like it has had a full valet.

For spoked wheels, use an acid cleaner, then brush and wash it off, then use an alkali cleaner (for example a household cleaner) to neutralise the acid, then wash the whole lot off.

Use a tent peg, or something hook-shaped to remove sludge from the edge of the wheel arches.

Upholstery, Carpets & Trim

Remember, cleaning your car is just like cleaning your home. Tidy up first, then vacuum, followed by carpet cleaning, upholstery cleaning, dashboard cleaning and any small interior detailing you care to do such as glass and chrome surfaces.

Before using either shop-bought or home-made stain remover, or upholstery or carpet shampoo on your vehicle's interior, first test it on an inconspicuous area, such as under the seat, to make sure it won't remove the colour from the material.

To remove dog hairs from the upholstery, use rubber gloves.

When cleaning the limousine, use boot polish on the rubber trim in the interior.

Use a damp cloth to remove fluff – it works better than a vacuum cleaner and it's so quick and easy you can do it every day, rather than waiting until your car is dirty enough to get the vacuum out.

Damp upholstery down slightly before vacuuming it.

Scrub over the carpet with a brush dipped in clear water to bring up the dirt before vacuuming, and to lift the pile.

Take carpets out to shampoo and vacuum them for a really thorough clean.

Use leather cream or hide food on leather seats, then buff it. It also smells gorgeous.

To remove woven-in pet hairs, wind masking tape round your hand, or use a dry car sponge, and use it like a brush.

To remove sticky sweets or chocolate from car upholstery, use a cloth soaked in lukewarm water, then blot and wipe until the stain is removed.

Crayon, oil or grease can be removed from car seats by scraping off any excess with a dull knife blade first, then blotting with a paper towel. If necessary, a stain remover can be used afterwards.

Coffee, fruit, ice-cream and milk stains can be rubbed with a cloth soaked in cold water, but don't use soap as this may set the stain.

Sponge urine stains with lukewarm mild soapsuds. Rinse with a cloth soaked in cold water, then soak a cloth in a solution of one part ammonia to five parts water. Hold it on the stain for one minute and then rinse with a clean, wet cloth.

Sponge vomit with a clean cloth dipped in cold water. Wash lightly with lukewarm water and mild soap. If the odour persists, treat it with a solution of one teaspoon of baking soda in one cup of warm water.

To remove cigarette stains from the upholstery, pour a small amount of milk on the stain and let it soak in. This dilutes the colour and stops it browning. Then rub with a raw potato and wash as normal.

If your car smells, use a cleaner containing bactericide. It is usually the bacteria that smells, so the cleaner needs to kill the germs to get rid of the smell.

When shampooing the interior of the car, shampoo and rinse one side at a time. Once the shampoo dried out, it is harder to remove.

Don't use polish or cleaners on steering wheels and floor pedals. They'll make surfaces slippery, which could lead to accidents.

Use a toothbrush to clean around the gear lever and in the switches on the dashboard.

To speed up the drying process after cleaning your car, leave the doors open, but make sure you shut off the interior lights by sticking something in the door jamb that keeps the buttons closed or by disconnecting the battery.

CAT BREEDERS

Choosing a Cat

Lyn Ingledew, Cat Naps; John Saxton, Towerwood Vet Group; Cath Chard, Bynkethyn Cat Protection League Shelter; Ann Cummins; Eileen Welsh; Dawn Teague

Choose a pedigree cat if you are intending to show or breed from it. Like all pedigree animals, they take a lot of time and money. Go to a specialist breeder. If you are going to show your cat, you will have to register it with the correct cat authority.

Choose a moggy if you just want a pet. They're cheaper (often free) and usually friendlier than the pedigree breeds.

Female cats are generally more affectionate and playful than male cats.

Animal sanctuaries are a good place to go to find a cat. Cats are only there because they are lost or unwanted.

Cats are quite happy to spend time alone so they make good pets if you're out of the house for quite long stretches. They are also ideal if you live in a flat or a busy city centre because they can adapt to living inside. They make good pets for people who can't get about too easily because they'll exercise themselves.

Tortoiseshell cats are nearly always female. On the rare occasion that a male tortoise-shell appears in a litter he is invariably sterile. But it's a myth that gingers are always toms.

Tortoiseshell cats are sometimes called calico cats in this country.

Manx cats don't have tails – just a hollow at the base of the spine, but they do have very long hind legs, which give them great speed.

When choosing a kitten, watch its behaviour with its littermates. You will be able to get an idea of its personality from the way it interacts with the others.

Check your kitten for signs of good health before you take it home. Its rear end should be free of diarrhoea or discharge. Its ears should be clean and dry (excessive scratching and dark wax could mean mites). Its nose should be slightly moist and feel velvety. The gums should be pink and there shouldn't be any bad breath. Check its coat for signs of fleas.

Kittens are more of a handful than adult cats because of having to train them and keep an eye on them. However, they're more adaptable than older cats.

Don't separate kittens from their mothers until they are fully weaned. This is usually at around eight weeks of age.

When you bring your kitten home, you should make it feel secure. Make a 'nest' out of a cardboard box. Wrap a jumper around a hot-water bottle and place it in the box with your kitten.

Take your kitten to a vet as soon as you can. You will have to get it vaccinated against feline enteritis and feline influenza (both of which can be fatal).

When holding a kitten, make sure you are supporting its whole body.

When introducing your kitten to other pets, always be on hand to supervise the meeting. If you already have a dog, keep it on its lead or put your kitten in a travelling case while they get used to each other. Don't leave them alone until they've got to know each other.

Cleanliness & Grooming

Cats are naturally clean so toilet training isn't too much of a struggle. Start off with a litter tray – you can use an old baking tray if you don't want to buy a proper plastic one.

Mother cats teach kittens how to behave – even how to use a litter tray – so try not to separate them too early or you'll have to teach your kitten what it should have learnt from its mother.

Kittens can start to be litter trained from the age of four weeks.

If your cat keeps weeing in the same spot in the house, try feeding it in this place. It will soon stop using it as a toilet.

If your kitten has a bit of an accident, transfer the puddle or poo to the litter tray. This should attract the cat to it next time it wants to go.

Clean a litter tray at least twice a day – some cats are fastidious and don't like to 'go' if the tray isn't clean. Well, would you go if the chain hadn't been pulled?

If you're busy, stack three clean litter trays on top of each other. You can simply lift off the top tray when it gets dirty and you have a clean one all ready and waiting to be used immediately.

Two cats? Two litter trays.

If your cat doesn't take to the cat litter, try substituting it with soil.

Hooded litter trays are best because cats prefer to pee up a wall rather than into the hole they have just dug.

Get cat hair off your furniture by rubbing the fabric with a scouring pad.

Cats don't like having baths, so if you have to give your cat a bath (because its fur has got contaminated or you are going to be showing it), make sure you have an extra pair of hands to help you. Bathe it in a plastic bowl and use a proper cat shampoo.

Cats have a routine when cleaning themselves: with their paws they clean the face first and then the top of the head, followed by a good lick down of the shoulders and front legs, then the sides and lastly the tail.

Give your cats a glossy coat by dabbing a cotton-wool ball into some diluted vinegar and gently wiping it over their fur.

A great way to groom your cat is by wearing a rubber glove. They enjoy being stroked and you get rid of loose hairs while you are doing it.

To untangle knots in long-haired cats use a crochet hook.

Cut cats' claws with baby nail clippers.

Cats should be bathed twice a year. Put some cotton wool in their ears and hold their front paws while washing them. It's a good idea to get cats used to this while they are still kittens.

Elderly cats find grooming difficult so they need extra help from their owners.

Long-haired cats need to be brushed and have knots and tangles removed each day. Cats with long hair are often more docile than their short-haired cousins.

Get your cat used to being groomed. Always brush it at the same time each day. It's usually best to do this after you have fed it.

Keep eyes and ears clean by wiping carefully with a cotton bud dipped in warm water containing a little diluted baking soda.

If your cat suffers from a lot of hair balls, try rubbing in some hair conditioner. Check that it's not toxic, in case your cat tries to lick it off.

When grooming a cat, put it in a pillowcase or a terry towelling bag with a draw pull, so that you can keep them in one place and you don't get scratched. This is also useful if you have to give them tablets.

Short-haired cats don't need as much looking after as long-haired cats. They can groom themselves and it's easier to spot any problems such as wounds, parasites and bad skin conditions.

A compromise between a long- and a short-haired cat is one with semi-long hair. They have a long top coat and a thinner undercoat, so are easier to look after than the full-blown long-hairs.

Behaviour

If you want a cat, buy two because they will amuse each other.

It can take a month for two cats to get used to each other.

If you have two cats, don't separate them when they get into a fight. They have to learn to live with each other and they need to establish who is top cat.

Cats enjoy playing. Try to give them at least ten to 15 minutes of your time each day.

Cats get bored with their toys easily. Have two or three to hand and keep rotating them every month or so.

Make your own catnip ball. Just cut the ends off a pair of old tights and fill with catnip. Twist the tights and cover the ball several times and then knot the end.

Make mazes out of cardboard boxes to amuse your cats. They love it.

Keep a cat happy for ages – give it a cardboard box with a couple of holes in it. Brown paper bags are fun too.

A cat flap gives your cat freedom to come in and out of the house as it pleases. The best height to fit the cat flap is 6 in/15 cm from the floor.

Get your cat used to its travelling basket by feeding it inside the basket for a while. Your cat will then get used to the sensation of going inside the basket.

Feeding your cat in its travelling basket will make it associate the basket with nice things and not just vets and catteries.

Choose a top-loading cat basket so the cat doesn't feel as if it's entering a long, dark tunnel. Make sure it has open sides for all-round vision.

Read a cat's mood by its tail and ears. An upright tail and pert ears means it likes you. If the tail is wagging or the ears lie flat then watch out!

A yawning cat is a happy cat – even lions and other big cats do it to show each other that they are relaxed. Try yawning at your cat to let it know how much you enjoy its company.

A scared cat will crouch down with its tail held low and its fur fluffed out.

Rubbing their body against an object is a way of marking their territory – and that can include you.

If your cat rolls over on its back and shows you its tummy, it's demonstrating that it's completely at ease with you and trusts you. Don't try to tickle its tummy – cats are very sensitive there and you'll probably get clouted for your efforts.

Don't stare directly at a cat – it's interpreted as a hostile gesture. Scrunch your eyes up and blink slowly and you'll get on fine. Best of all, wear sunglasses. You'll look cool and cats love it.

Cats sleep for around 16 hours a day, so make sure they have somewhere comfortable to sleep.

A cat sleeping with its paws over its nose was believed to indicate that gales were on their way.

It's a myth that cats should be put out at night – most moggies are happy to stay indoors and sleep.

Make sure your cat can sit at a window and see what's going on. Cats love watching the outside world.

Discipline

Cats behaving badly? Have a water pistol to hand. Then, if they do something wrong, they get soaked but don't associate you with the punishment. If only men were so easy to control!

Stop cats from using your lawn as a toilet – sprinkle some pepper on the grass. They hate the smell and won't go near it.

Keep cats off the lawn altogether by placing litre bottles full of water around the area you want to protect. Cats don't like reflections and will steer clear of them.

To stop a cat scratching wooden furniture, use lemon-scented polish.

Alternatively, rub citrus soap on to chairs and sofas. The smell will put the cat off.

If your cat claws your curtains, dab a little peppermint oil on to the fabric to warn it off.

When moving out of a house, put the cat in the bathroom or where no one is likely to go. Put a sign on the door to make sure it isn't opened accidentally – otherwise, your cat will run off to get away from the pandemonium of moving.

When moving to a new house, keep your cat inside for at least a week. When you do let it out for the first time, make sure it goes out on an empty stomach and will therefore return home to be fed.

Prepare your cat for the arrival of a baby by sprinkling baby powder and lotion on your skin so that the smells become familiar.

If you have a new baby, tie a string of noisy rattles across the pram. Not only will the noise alert you if the cat jumps up but it will also scare the cat and put it off trying again.

To discipline your cat, tap it on the nose, say 'no' in a loud voice. Then put the cat straight down and ignore it. Cats crave affection and respect and will hate the cold shoulder.

Prevent cats from climbing over a fence by spraying the wood with surgical spirit.

Angling the top of the fence inwards prevents cats from getting out of the garden so easily.

If your cat continually jumps on to kitchen work surfaces, spray the surface with a little water.

Create an effective scratching post with a carpet tile stuck to a wall 2 ft/60 cm up from the floor. This should prevent your furniture from being reduced to shreds.

Orange and grapefruit peel scattered round the garden will stop cats coming in – they hate the smell of citrus fruits.

To prevent electricity and computer leads from being gnawed to bits, cover them with sturdy rubber tubing such as a hose pipe. Just cut a section length-wise and wrap it round the wires you want to protect.

If your cat continually chews your houseplants, spray them with diluted lemon juice.

You can teach a cat to walk on a lead. Start by getting your cat used to wearing a harness before attaching the lead to it. Practise walking around the house and garden before you try using the lead outdoors.

Don't punish your cat if it brings home a dead bird or mouse. It's only trying to contribute to the family. Punishing it may indicate that you're not satisfied with the offering, so it'll go off and do it again. The best thing you can do is accept it gracefully and dispose of it as soon as possible.

Health & Safety

Always put elasticated collars on your cats – this will let them slip out of trouble. They are always getting caught up in things and a rigid collar can be dangerous.

Having a cat around can be a bit like having a child. They can poke their noses into all sorts of dangerous situations, so be aware of hazards: for example, don't leave small objects lying around which can be swallowed, keep plastic bags out of their reach and don't leave washing-machine doors open.

Administering pills can be a bit of a tussle. Try wrapping the cat in a warm towel, keeping paws and claws out of the way while you slip the medicine down the throat.

If this doesn't work, crush the pill and mix it with some yoghurt. Put the solution into a pet syringe (available from your vet) and squirt it gently into the cat's mouth.

If getting medicine into the cat is proving a real struggle, gently pinch the nostrils. The cat will have to open its mouth to breathe and you can then pop the pill in.

After a cat has swallowed a pill it will usually lick its nose. If this doesn't happen, then be prepared for the pill to reappear!

If you don't intend to breed from your cat, get it neutered. Female cats come into season several times a year, so you'll stop unwanted pregnancies (and antisocial sexual behaviour in males).

Female cats should be neutered when they're four or five months old, while male cats should be done at six months.

Once a male cat is neutered, it becomes less territorial and won't wander as far as a tom.

Toms that have not been neutered are prone to leukaemia.

Cats can never be vegetarians. No matter what your beliefs are, cats need meat to survive.

Make sure your cat's food bowl is always clean – cats are fussy eaters and won't eat from a dirty bowl.

If you have more than one cat, make sure each has its own feeding bowl.

Tinned cat food contains all the right nutrients for a cat's balanced diet. Now and again you can treat them to fresh food: scrambled egg, chicken, meat, pasta, canned tuna or even porridge.

Feed your cat regularly to discourage it from wandering from home and looking elsewhere for its meals.

Cats have a unique sense of taste. They aren't any good at detecting sweetness, but they can detect tiny variations in the taste of water.

Bad breath? Fish may be a feline favourite but it causes smelly breath afterwards.

Too much milk causes diarrhoea – cats were originally desert creatures used only to water so don't give them too much milk.

Cat diarrhoea can be a problem. A bit of cereal crumbled into the food should help clear things up.

Dry food is an excellent diet for cats. Test the quality of the dried food by soaking a piece in water. The superior brands, with a high meat content, will only swell up a little bit.

If your cat refuses to eat, try leaving the dish out with food in it, but make sure it's just out of reach for a while. Cats can't resist thieving and this might be just the challenge it needs to start eating again.

If you have two cats and one of them isn't eating, feed the other one first. Cats hate to be left out.

If your cat has lost its appetite, try heating the food for a few seconds in the microwave. Being natural hunters, cats prefer their food to come at blood temperature.

Most dental problems can be avoided if you get your cat used to having its teeth cleaned regularly.

Cats are regularly sick. It's the best way to get rid of fur balls. Chewing grass helps them to throw up with greater ease. So, for cats who don't go outside, grow a tray of grass indoors.

Cool down your overheated cat by stroking it with a frozen ice-pack wrapped in a towel.

White cats get sunburnt easily. On very hot days, try keeping them in the shade. Their ears are also prone to frostbite.

White cats are prone to deafness.

Cats regularly get into fights with other cats. Keep an eye out for bites and scratches; they can become infected. If this happens, try to bring the abscess to a head by bathing with salt water.

All cats have a third eyelid, which you shouldn't be able to see. If it does become visible, it's usually because your cat is unwell. Take it to the vet immediately.

If a cat is affected by hypothermia, gently bathe the affected area in warm water. Then wrap the cat up in a towel and take it to the vet.

If your cat gets burnt, you must take it to the vet. You can help alleviate the pain by damping the scald with cold water (don't use butter on the area). Hold an ice-pack against the affected area and then put some petroleum jelly on to the wound to keep fur out of it.

Protect your cat's paws when it goes outside by rubbing in some hair conditioner – it stops mud getting stuck between their toes.

To get rid of warts, you could try this old wives' remedy: stroke the afflicted area with the tail of a tortoiseshell cat… but only in May.

You think your cat has got fleas? If you find black grains of dirt in your pet's fur, take a grain and place it on a damp piece of toilet paper. If it turns red, it's flea droppings.

If your cat gets cat flu, leave it in a steamy shower room for a short while to help its breathing.

CATERERS

Fiona Bowyer, Fine Food Ltd; Parties & Co.

Perfect Parties

People usually try too hard when entertaining. Stick to dishes you have made before rather than launching into an ambitious recipe plucked out of a book. And don't try to put together a really exotic menu – if the main course is rich, try some sliced melon for starters. Likewise, if fancy puds are your thing, serve a simple main course of grilled fish or steak and salad.

Don't be a stranger to your guests. The worst mistake people make is to throw a dinner party but spend all evening in the kitchen. Always choose menus that you can prepare in advance.

Provide contrast and variety – go for different flavours and textures. Meat, followed by fish or the other way round. Don't have too many spicy tastes in one meal.

Use music to change the mood when entertaining. Something pacy will get you moving in the kitchen, then slow things down with something relaxing so you can enjoy your meal with everyone else.

For comfortable guests, remember to set your heating thermostat a few degrees lower than usual. All those bodies will create their own heat.

If you're having a party, set up drinks in a different corner to the food so that people aren't climbing on top of each other – it will also encourage guest to 'circulate'.

Don't feel you have to do all the cooking for a dinner party. If your guests ask if they can bring anything, suggest they bring a pudding – fresh cream cakes, Danish pastries and patisserie all go down a treat.

If your tablecloth is stained and you've got guests arriving any minute, don't panic! Scatter some rose petals on to the cloth for an effective and pretty solution.

If you are worried about staining your table, put some cling film across the wood before placing the tablecloth on top. If you are concerned about hot dishes burning the wood, put a blanket underneath the tablecloth.

Candles add atmosphere to a meal. Make sure yours are below eye-level, though, so that your guests can see each other.

Don't Panic

When grilling, keep a spray bottle filled with water handy to douse any flare ups.

To keep the kitchen smelling sweet, put some orange peel in the oven (at 180 °C/350 °F/ Gas Mark 4).

To disguise lingering cooking odours, boil some cloves in a mixture of one cup of water to one tablespoon of vinegar.

To clean up any spills in the oven, sprinkle some salt and cinnamon over the spill. This stops the house from filling with that acrid smoky smell and the spill will be easy to lift off with a spatula.

If disaster strikes and you burn a pan, leave some cold tea to soak in the pan for a few hours. The black burnt-in crust will then come away quite easily.

If your hands are stained from beetroot or red cabbage, rub them with a raw potato.

If you've burnt your hand, make up a paste of baking soda and water and apply to the burnt area. This will take some of the pain away.

If you burn your hands while handling chilli, rub a little vinegar over them.

Has a vegetarian turned up without warning? Take a tin of baked beans, stir in some wine, pour the mixture over a selection of your vegetables, and bake it in the oven for 20 minutes while you recover from the shock with a glass of wine. Result – one tasty vegetable bake.

If an extra guest turns up, most things can be stretched by turning them into casseroles. Salmon steaks can be flaked and covered with a sauce, meat and vegetables can be put into a stewing dish.

If you have run out of breadcrumbs, use some crushed cheese biscuits instead.

If you've overcooked your vegetables, put them in icy cold water for a few minutes then microwave them very briefly before serving.

Sloppy mashed potato? Fold in a stiffly beaten egg white and bake in the oven.

Always throw a can of food away if the can has an outward bulge – the contents will be bad.

Here's a handy tip to rescue brown sugar that has gone hard: put half a cup of boiling water in a microwave. Next to it put your sugar in a microwave-proof container. Put the microwave on high until the sugar has gone soft. Allow three minutes for every pound of sugar.

To make a meal out of lettuce that has started to go brown, sauté it in a little olive oil with some garlic and salt.

If your cooking oil goes black while heating it, add a few drops of vinegar and cover with a saucepan lid. Continue heating like this for about 30 seconds and the oil should have returned to a lighter colour.

Too much garlic in a sauce or stew? Add some parsley to neutralise it.

To absorb the smell of frying fish whilst cooking, add celery to the pan. It tastes good too.

If you run out of eggs while baking a cake, add a teaspoon of vinegar – one teaspoon per egg.

Run out of dishwasher powder? Try baking soda.

Planning Ahead

Prepare your potatoes the night before. To stop them becoming discoloured, leave them in a pan of water along with a small lump of rinsed coal. They will stay looking fresh until the next day.

If you're tight for oven space, all meats can be half cooked the day before, stored in the fridge and then finished off when needed.

If you only need to use the tomatoes from the tin and not the juice, pour the left-over juice into an ice-cube tray for use in gravy at a later date.

If you are marinating ingredients, make sure you do so for long enough. Marinades only work if left for at least 24 hours.

To stop you cutting the end of your fingers when grating cheese, wear thimbles.

To make a more imaginative basting brush, take sprigs of fresh herbs and bind them together to make a brush. The taste of the herbs will transfer to the meat.

To fill a piping bag, stand it in a tall glass. Fold the edges of the bag over the top of the glass and fill.

To clean a cheese-grater after grating the cheese, grate a raw potato. The potato will clear the cheesy gunk from the holes.

Use different sides of the chopping board for different things – one for things with strong odours and one for things that you don't want to be affected by strong odours. Write on the board (with an indelible felt-tip pen) what each side is for.

Fill your testing spoon from your stirring spoon – it's more hygienic.

If you've got no time for sifting, put all the dry ingredients in a bowl and stir briskly with a whisk.

Put a sheet of tin foil between a casserole dish and its lid – this saves having to wash up the grimy lid afterwards.

Warm plates for a dinner party in the drying cycle of your dishwasher.

If you always get in a mess with cling film, try storing it in the fridge. It's easier to use when cold.

Some foods, such as bacon or rhubarb, can be difficult to chop – try using scissors instead of a knife.

To cover a saucepan or wok, use kitchen foil. The 'lid' can be used several times.

The waxed bags inside cereal boxes make excellent linings for cake tins.

Line kitchen scales with cling film before weighing out ingredients, so you don't need to wash them afterwards. The correct amount also goes into the mixture rather than staying in the scales – great for sticky butter!

To check whether the fat in your deep-fat fryer is hot enough, to start cooking drop a popcorn kernel into the fat. When the kernel pops, the fat is hot enough.

Soups

When making soup, put a crustless piece of bread in the blender with the other ingredients to give the soup a lovely texture.

To make soup go further, add wine, cream or stock. This will enhance the taste as well.

To thicken home-made soup, just add some instant mashed potato before serving.

To get rid of congealed fat in a soup or stew, drop in an ice cube. It should attract the excess grease to it, gathering it in one place for you to remove.

If you like adding yoghurt to soups and casseroles but find that it separates, mix the yoghurt with a few spoonfuls of cooling stock beforehand.

Remember, when you're making a purée to decorate soup, make sure it's the same consistency – if it's heavier it will sink to the bottom.

If you've got room in your fridge, save potato-cooking water and use it for soups and sauces. It's more nutritious than plain water and adds flavour and body to your cooking. Potato water will keep in a fridge for three or four days.

Reserve the liquid used to soak dried mushrooms and freeze it. It will be a real boost to soups and sauces in the future.

Jazz up plain tinned soup by stirring in some sherry or port.

Pep up boring bean or vegetable soup with a large spoonful of balsamic vinegar.

A dash of lemon juice added to cream of mushroom soup just before serving will cut through the richness of the soup and bring out the full flavour.

Draw a slice of bread across soups or stews to soak up excess grease.

To remove fat from tinned soup, place the can in the fridge. When it's cold, open the tin and scoop the separated fat off from the top.

Snacks & Sandwiches

When making sandwiches in bulk, pour a cup of boiling milk over a stick of butter in a bowl, allow to cool, beat together until creamy and the resulting mixture will spread very readily.

For a yummy sandwich filling, mix honey and mayonnaise.

To make better cheese on toast, take the cheese out of the fridge 30 minutes before melting it. Cheese melts better and will not separate if you start off with it at room temperature.

Fancy some de luxe cheese on toast? Mix grated cheese with an egg for a scrummy bubbly topping. A pinch of chilli powder will give the mixture a bit of bite or try some chopped spring onion for a delicious extra flavour.

Caviare must be served on cold toast – hot toast will make the eggs separate.

To prevent scrambled eggs sticking to the pan, add two tablespoons of cold water to the pan before you put the eggs in.

Make a super topping for fish pies and vegetable bakes by whizzing some hard cheese and crusts of bread together in a food processor.

To get baked beans out of the can, remove the tin from the shelf and turn the can upside down, open as normal and you'll find all of the beans shoot out – simple but very effective.

To make sure that every single bean comes out, use a can-opener to remove the top. Place a plate over the top and turn over quickly. Then, use the can-opener on the other end, but don't throw away the circle of metal. Instead, push it through as you lift up the can.

Saucy Ideas

If your hollandaise sauce curdles, gently stir in an ice cube.

You can disguise gravy made from instant gravy granules by stirring in one main flavour; for example, some apple juice for pork or a tin of chopped tomatoes for lamb.

To avoid lumpy white sauce, heat the milk first.

For handy ready-made portions of apple sauce, freeze large quantities of stewed apples in an ice-cube tray and defrost as required.

Instead of using plain water as a base for gravies and sauces, save the water from boiling vegetables. It has more flavour, more goodness and it saves water.

To get really rich curry sauces, add a little sugar to the butter or ghee while melting it.

To thicken gravy, add instant mashed potato powder.

Create your own flavoured vinegars, oils and mustards using your favourite herbs and spices – place them into the bottles or jars and seal for at least a week.

Save left-over red wine in a screw-top bottle and keep for sauces and salad dressings.

Left-over chicken, beef bones or vegetables? Don't throw them out. If you've got room in your freezer put the whole lot in a sealed bag and freeze. You'll have all the ingredients to make a stock when required.

Try adding mustard or Marmite to your gravy for a special mixture that packs a punch.

Caramel sauces must not be allowed to boil. But if yours does, don't worry. Just stir in some milk or cream and turn it into toffee sauce.

Overcooked sauces will never improve so don't waste your time. Some melted butter will be a delicious alternative sauce for any dish.

When making stocks or gravy, put a chip basket inside the pan to hold bones, bay leaves and other chunky ingredients. This will make it easier to lift them all out when you have finished.

Veg Out

Peeling garlic can be fiddly. Peel down the stem of the clove and soak in boiling water for a few minutes. The skin will then come straight off.

If you do have to keep your tomatoes in the fridge, take them out a couple of hours before eating, as they become juicier at room temperature.

An egg-slicer is perfect for slicing mushrooms.

Avocado pears make excellent face masks. Just mash them up and smear them on for that perfect complexion.

To tart up new potatoes or chips, try a couple of teaspoons of mint jelly over the top instead of butter or ketchup.

To give cauliflower a bit more flavour, substitute chicken stock for plain water – alternatively just add a stock cube to the water.

If your string beans have been around for a week and are starting to toughen, add some sugar to the water when cooking.

If your red cabbage turns blue or purple during boiling, add a tablespoon of vinegar to the water and the cabbage will turn red again.

To get the best out of slightly old vegetables while boiling, add salt to the boiling water to help retain flavour and colour.

Make raw carrots more tasty. Add a little vinegar to a pot of iced water in the fridge. Stand the carrots in the pot overnight.

Left-over cucumber? Slice, sauté on both sides until brown and serve with cream cheese. Lovely!

To prevent potatoes sprouting before you have a chance to use them, put an apple in the same bag as the spuds.

If you want whiter than white cauliflower, add some milk to the water when cooking.

Carrots are easier to scrape if dunked in boiling water first.

Mushrooms won't shrink when cooked if you soak them in a little boiling water first.

To make the best of left-over veggies, keep them in a plastic container in the fridge. When the container is full, make the contents into a soup or stew.

For firm corn-on-the-cob, add salt to the water while boiling.

If you prefer your corn soft, add sugar.

Celery keeps longer if wrapped in foil.

Don't throw out the dark, outside leaves of cauliflowers. De-stalk them and chop up finely, then add to soups.

If you've been told to reduce your salt intake, try using dill seeds, crushed or ground, as a substitute.

Reduce the cooking smells from cabbage water by adding a few caraway seeds to the pan.

Pop a bay leaf into stored flour to deter weevils.

Remember, basil is one of the few herbs that increases in flavour when cooked, so always add it at the end of cooking unless you want a really strong flavour.

Sage is the ideal herb to use with meat as it aids digestion of fat and its antiseptic qualities help to kill off any bugs in the meat as it cooks.

To cook delicious broad beans, add some chopped parsley to the water.

Presentation is everything. Some fresh herbs sprinkled on top of the most ordinary-looking dish will turn it into something special.

Make sure your parsley stays green – only add it to a sauce once the liquid has boiled.

If a recipe calls for 'finely chopped onions', just grate or blend some of them to save you time.

To make onions brown more quickly when frying, add a pinch of sugar. They'll also taste delicious and be slightly caramelised.

To absorb the smell when frying onions, put a sheet of wet newspaper close to the hob.

Salad Days

If you want raw onions in your salad but are worried that they will taste too strong, soak them in some tepid water first.

To keep lettuce fresh for longer, wrap it in a paper towel, put in a plastic bag and keep in the fridge.

If your lettuce has gone limp, put it in a bowl with a piece of rinsed coal and leave for several minutes.

Soggy tomatoes will firm up if soaked in salty water for ten minutes.

To make mayonnaise more interesting, add a pinch of curry powder or even some brown sauce.

Make your own chutney. Simply empty a packet of dates into a clean jam jar, cover with your favourite flavoured vinegar and leave for at least a week. It's cheap and delicious.

For a fresh-tasting, home-made salad dressing, mix a pinch of paprika and a squeeze of lemon juice into a carton of plain yoghurt.

Rice & Pasta

Rice is one of the most common culinary disasters. Cook yours well in advance if you're having a dinner party. Then, before it's quite done, turn off the heat. Leave the lid on and it will retain its heat whilst also losing some of its stodginess.

To stop rice sticking together, add a few drops of lemon juice to the boiling water.

Bored with rice? Go for great presentation by packing it into small shaped moulds (a small tea cup will do). Spray the moulds with a non-stick cooking spray first.

Remember, rice triples its volume when cooked, so use a big enough pan.

Always fluff cooked rice with a fork – this allows the steam to escape and stops the grains sticking together.

Cooked rice keeps well in the freezer, so make plenty and freeze the extra.

For bright white rice, squeeze some lemon juice into the water while boiling.

Add toasted nuts to rice while boiling to enhance the nuttiness.

Don't add oil to boiling pasta water because the sauce will slip off. A really good sauce should literally coat the pasta.

Never rinse your pasta – the starch helps the sauce stick to the pasta.

Raw spaghetti makes an excellent firelighter.

To check if your pasta is cooked, try flinging a piece against the oven door or the fridge. If it sticks, it's cooked.

Children love coloured pasta – add food colouring to the cooking water.

Pasta bake is cheap and easy and an excellent way to use up left-overs. Simply pile any left-over vegetables in a dish with some cooked pasta, add a tin of tomatoes or some baked beans, and cook.

Main Courses

Before plucking a chicken, soak the bird in boiling water for a minute or two. The feathers will come out more easily.

To stop dishes like lasagne and cottage pie sticking to the baking tin, grease it with butter and line with breadcrumbs.

If sliced ham or tongue has dried out, soak it in a little milk for five minutes to restore its flavour and texture.

Does the meat seem a bit tough? Squirt a little lemon juice into it before carving.

Fruit

Remember to remove the zest of oranges and lemons whenever you squeeze them. Pop the rinds into the freezer or store them in a jar and use them to flavour salads, stews and cakes.

The smoother a lemon skin – the juicier the lemon.

Save money on lemons – buy lots when they're on special offer. Squeeze the juice out and freeze it in ice-cube trays. When a recipe calls for lemon juice, just take out the required number of lemon ice cubes and add to the pot.

To freeze fruit, use the waxed paper from the inside of cereal packets to line the trays.

To make peeling grapefruit easier, pour boiling water over the fruit and leave to stand for five minutes.

Bananas gone brown? Don't fancy eating them? Use them to make some delicious banana bread.

An alternative use for brown bananas is in banana milkshakes, where you don't see that they've gone brown.

Ripen green bananas by leaving a red tomato next to them.

Banana trees (for hanging bananas from) are great because bananas kept in the fruit bowl make the other fruit go off. But what happens when you're down to your last banana? Make sure that the last one has a long stem and then poke the banana tree's hook through the stem.

To chop dried fruit, wet the blade of the knife so the fruit doesn't stick to it.

If rhubarb is too acidic for you, try leaving it to soak in cold black tea for an hour before using.

Alternatively, before cooking, chop the rhubarb into 2 in/5 cm pieces and soak it in a bowl of cold water containing a teaspoon of bicarbonate of soda.

The simplest way to achieve a healthy diet is to eat more fruit and vegetables. You should ideally eat five different portions a day – remember, 'eat five to stay alive!'

Naughty – but Nice

Love double cream, but you're cutting calories? Evaporated skimmed milk makes an excellent substitute when slightly frozen.

Whipping cream calls for cool temperatures – refrigerate your utensils before you start.

Put ice-cream bowls in the fridge for 30 minutes before serving the ice-cream – it won't melt so quickly.

Substitute dessicated coconut for some of the sugar when making the topping for fruit crumble.

For a healthy but tasty pudding, add some low-calorie drinking chocolate powder and some dried fruit (such as sultanas, apricots or raisins) to natural yoghurt. Leave overnight to allow the flavours to mingle.

A sugar-free way to enjoy a rhubarb tart is to add chopped dates instead.

Plain, low-fat yoghurt makes a healthier alternative to sour cream in recipes.

A frozen banana will stop hunger cravings – its natural sweetness will give you energy without adding extra pounds. Peel, wrap in cling film and freeze. It will take ages to eat as well.

Do you love gingerbread, but could do without the fat? Try replacing the fat in the recipe with pumpkin. It's tasty, low in calories and cholesterol, and extremely good for you.

Frozen sheets of filo pastry can be used as a low-fat alternative to shortcrust or puff.

Replace full-fat chocolate with cocoa powder in cakes and desserts for a low-calorie treat.

For a sweet treat at a barbecue, toast marshmallows above the hot coals.

To stop honey or syrup sticking to your spoon, grease it first with a little oil.

Also try dipping the spoon in boiling water before you dip it in the honey.

For really simple frozen yoghurt, put a lollipop stick into a carton of yoghurt, freeze and remove the carton. Try different flavours and low-fat yoghurts for a tasty slimming treat.

Try adding a layer of banana to apple pie.

When making toffee, pour the mixture into greased ice-cube trays for ready-made bite-sized pieces.

If you love peanuts and ice-cream, try mixing them together for a yummy dessert.

Instead of sugar, try golden syrup in your porridge or your favourite jam.

Drinks for Everyone

Pour wine from a height to add air and flavour.

When serving wine at a dinner party, give everyone some mineral water too. They'll quench their thirst with the water and sip the wine more slowly.

To prevent pieces of cork getting into wine glasses, pour the wine through a coffee filter paper.

To add that certain something to drinks, frost the edge of the glass. Just dip the rim in some egg white followed immediately by some castor sugar. For a jazzy look, mix some food colouring into the sugar.

To serve beautiful drinks in no time at all, add pieces of sliced fruit to an ice-cube tray and chill in the freezer beforehand. It's then easy to add the ice cubes without all the fiddly chopping when your guests arrive.

When holding a garden party, fill a child's paddling pool with ice to keep the bottles cold.

If you are using baking recipes that call for liqueurs, rather than buy a whole bottle of one, buy a range of miniatures.

Had a bit too much to drink? A slice of toast with honey before you go to bed will avoid a hangover.

Make iced coffee quickly and easily with a couple of teaspoons of Camp coffee stirred into a pint of cold milk. Add a few ice cubes for a refreshing drink.

If you don't have a cocktail shaker, use a smaller glass inverted inside a pint glass.

Traditionally whisky should be served two parts whisky to one part water – the water brings out the flavour. Use mineral water instead of tap water, which can have too strong a taste and affect the flavour.

Do you like fizzy drinks, but worry about tooth decay? Use a straw – it reduces the contact between your teeth and the drink.

Trying to get used to sugar-free drinks? Put a little sugar around the rim of the glass – just enough to taste on the lips.

If you take a lot of medication, lay off the grapefruit juice. It can reduce the body's ability to absorb some drugs.

Store milk on fridge shelves, not in the door, as this usually isn't cold enough.

You can freeze milk for up to three weeks without doing too much harm to it nutritionally. Skimmed freezes better than whole fat milk. If you're off on holiday leave a carton in the freezer so that you can make a cup of tea when you get back. Thaw in the fridge and beat it if it separates.

If your little ones aren't keen on milk, add it to food in place of water – they'll still get all the goodness.

Cleaning Up

To clean an aluminium pan, boil the peel of an apple in some water. This will make it much easier to clean the pan afterwards.

To clean a grater, rub a hard crust of bread over it.

Keep your knives rust-free – plunge them into an onion and leave them there for half an hour. Wash and then polish lightly with some vegetable oil.

Tomato ketchup has a clever second use – to clean the base of copper-bottomed pans. Pour some over the bottom of the pan and leave for a few minutes. Then rub the ketchup in and wash it off.

To stop the bottom of a pan scratching the inside of the one it is stacked on top of, put the lid of a margarine tub inside the larger pan as a 'cushion'.

CHAUFFEURS

Jane Fowler;
Robert Gordon

To be on time is to be late. Always arrive 15 minutes early.

To get in to the most comfortable position for driving, wriggle your bottom into the seat. This way you give your back maximum support.

To get into a low classic car put your bottom in first, then swing your legs around. It avoids twisting your back and shoulders and you look more elegant.

If you are very small, you can use a child's polystyrene car seat, which should give you a bit of a boost for driving.

Stop yourself from falling asleep on long journeys. Always chew gum because it keeps you awake and alert.

Reduce tension when you're driving. Take a deep breath, draw your shoulders to your ears and then let your shoulders drop down again. Repeat this three or four times.

To ease tension in your back, especially if you've been cooped up for a long time, pull your stomach muscles in as you take a deep breath. Hold the breath for a short while, then release it.

When buying an old car, take a bit of carpet with you to lie on so that you can check underneath. Take a torch with you as well so that you can see into all the nooks and crannies of an engine.

To check whether a handbrake is in good working order, stop the car, apply the handbrake and try to move off in one second. If you can, the handbrake needs to be looked at.

To lubricate stiff windows, put a couple of drops of washing-up liquid into the tops of the window channels.

When cleaning the limousine, use boot polish on the interior rubber trim.

Buff the windows with newspaper and a mixture of water and vinegar.

Car a bit smelly? Freshen it up with a fabric-softener sheet placed beneath a seat.

CHEESE MERCHANTS

Paxton & Whitfield at London, Stratford-upon-Avon and Bath

Whole cheeses keep better than sliced ones, so when you buy a slice of cheese eat it as soon as possible.

Large pieces of cheese keep better than small ones.

Some cheeses like to be kept cold, others prefer a warmer atmosphere. It depends on the cheese and its stage of maturity. No cheese likes temperatures above 68 °F/20 °C or below 39 °F/4 °C. Most are happy between 46 °F/8 °C and 59 °F/15 °C.

Keep your cheese in the salad drawer at the bottom of the fridge where it is slightly warmer, and the confined space keeps up the humidity. Don't keep salad in the same drawer though as salad leaves can pose a hygiene threat to the cheese.

In warmer temperatures a cheese will continue to mature. Reduce the temperature to slow down the maturing process. Hard cheeses are more resilient to temperature extremes. Soft cheeses generally prefer a temperature around 54 °F/12 °C.

Nearly all cheeses like a moist atmosphere, but not too damp – a cool cellar is ideal. If you aren't lucky enough to have one, cover your cheese with a damp cloth, or keep it in a container that stops the moisture escaping, such as a cheese bell or cardboard box.

If the atmosphere is too dry, a cheese will crack. Too damp, and white rind or mould will form.

Waxed paper will keep the cheese in the right condition. It allows the cheese to breathe but not to dry out.

Cling film around cheese tends to allow moisture to build up encouraging mould.

Kitchen foil is ideal for blue cheeses.

Unpasteurised cheeses retain more calcium and vitamins than pasteurised ones, but unpasteurised and soft cheeses should be avoided by pregnant women, the very elderly, the very young and those with a depressed immune system.

Always bring cheese to room temperature an hour or two before serving.

If you only need a small amount of cheese, buy one or two good cheeses rather than a wide choice of different cheeses.

For interest either serve a variety of cheeses: one hard, one soft, a blue cheese and a goat or sheep's cheese, or serve a selection from one geographical area.

Stilton and port is a classic match, but try Wensleydale or Caerphilly with white port, Brie de Meaux with late-bottled vintage port and a hard sheep's cheese like Berkswell with ten-year old tawny port.

CHEFS
Preparation

Caroline Stokes, Beakerkent Park School; Sebastian Gougen, Michelle's; Paul Reed, Chester Grosvenor Hotel; Mohammed Ali Haydor, Kushi Restaurant; Enrico Maglifiore, San Carlo; Glen Chadwick; Monica Shaw

Keep a scrapbook of recipes cut from magazines, papers and packets.

Try to draw up your shopping list in the order that you reach the appropriate aisles in the supermarket. That way, you're less likely to waste time criss-crossing the supermarket.

To remember which cans of food you need to replace when you go shopping, put stickers on the wall behind each line of cans (for example canned tomatoes or baked beans). When you use the last can, it will reveal the sticker and remind you to get another one.

To avoid forgetting regular items, type a list on a computer and save. Then, each week, add one-off items and reprint.

To avoid frozen foods from a supermarket thawing out before you get them home, pick them up last, so you don't carry them around the supermarket while you get your other shopping.

Always use the freshest ingredients for the best results.

When sieving, remove the top and bottom of a large tin and place over the mixing bowl as a rest for the sieve. Both your hands are then left free to pour and press.

To loosen a tight jar lid, wind an elastic band around it to form a great grip.

If you're chopping an onion, place a small piece of bread under your top lip – no more tears!

Store onions and garlic in the foot of some sheer tights to keep them dry and fresh.

To peel garlic easily, peel down the stem of the clove and soak in boiling water for a few minutes. The skin will then come straight off.

You can bring water to the boil much more quickly if you place the lid on the pan and put a large scoop of salt on top of the lid.

To get the most juice out of a lemon, cut it in half and warm both halves in the oven for a few minutes before use.

To get the best out of spices, roast them before use.

To dry herbs instantly, place them in the microwave for a few seconds. This works especially well with parsley.

To remove air from freezer bags, use a bicycle pump.

To prevent wooden kebab skewers charring in the oven, soak them in water for 20 minutes before cooking.

When chopping, put a damp tea towel under your chopping board to give it a firm grip on the table.

When cooking in a microwave, paper coffee filters make excellent lids for bowls and dishes.

Do your tortillas break when you roll them? Put them in a plastic bag and pop them in the microwave for 30 seconds – they'll be beautifully soft.

For the lightest shortcrust pastry, try substituting soda water for tap water.

To cut the perfect slice of pâté or gâteau, first run the knife blade under very hot water.

To cook rice, soak it in cold water for an hour or two first. This saves you time and fuel in the long run.

Fabulous Fish & Meat

To cook delicious fish, wrap in cling film and place in boiling water so that none of the natural flavour escapes.

To prevent fish skin from sticking to the frying pan, rub the fish with salt, leave for 15 minutes, rinse and rub dry. Then cook.

To ensure that meat is tender, always carve across the grain.

To serve really thin slices of cold meat, place the joint in the freezer for half an hour before carving – you'll find it much easier to carve thinly.

As an alternative to honey-roast ham, try emptying a can of Coke into the baking tray for really sweet-tasting meat.

To stop your gammon from curling over when frying, simply snip the edges with a pair of scissors.

Marinating meat in distilled vinegar overnight tenderises it.

If you've overdone the chilli in your curry, squeeze half a lemon over it. Then place the half-lemon into the curry, stir for a few minutes, then remove it. The chilli taste will have disappeared.

To rescue a casserole that has been over-salted, just add fizzy water. Or place a potato in the casserole for ten minutes and then remove.

If there's too much fat on the top of your casserole or sauce, gently float a piece of kitchen paper across the top and it will soak up the excess.

Soups, Sauces & Dressings

To thicken stews and soups, don't use flour – porridge oats are very effective and much tastier too.

To give your soup a beautiful golden colour, add some of an onion's outer skin. Remember to remove it before serving.

To give soups a rich flavour and colour, add a tablespoon of prune juice.

If you have some gravy left over and you don't want to throw it away, pour it into a small margarine tub, freeze it and keep it for stock.

Do your sauces stick to the spoon when serving them? Dip the spoon in cold water or cold milk (if a milk-based sauce) before serving and the sauce will run off it more easily.

To get the best from wine in sauces, put it in a pan and bring to the boil beforehand. Then set light to it with a match. The flame will burn off the alcohol and any sharpness. Add a touch of sugar to sweeten and then add to the sauce.

Put too much salt in your sauce? Dip a sugar-cube into the sauce and swirl it around the surface for a minute or two.

To keep olive oil fresh, buy a large jar of olive oil, but pour the oil into a number of smaller jars. Air affects the quality of the oil, so if you leave it in a large jar, as the amount of oil decreases and the amount of air increases, the quality of the oil will diminish.

If you're making a tomato sauce, but the tomatoes are a little tart, try adding finely diced carrots at the start of cooking. They'll mellow the flavour.

Thicken spicy sauces with unsweetened cocoa powder.

As a substitute for salad cream, mix a pinch of paprika and a squeeze of lemon juice into a carton of plain yoghurt.

To make smooth gravy every time, mix equal quantities of flour and cornflour – say two tablespoons of each – in a jar, add some water, put the lid on and shake well, then add the mixture to your gravy and boil to thicken.

A spoonful of cream added to a sauce made with milk will give the impression that it's made with all cream.

For no fuss marinating, pop the marinade and the meat into a self-seal bag. It takes up less room in the fridge than a bowl or plate and just needs a simple turn from time to time.

Remember that cold water brings out flavour and hot seals flavour in. Always start a stock with cold water.

To get the best from vinaigrette, make it at least an hour before dressing the salad to allow time for the flavours to mix together.

To dress a salad evenly, pour the dressing down the sides of the bowl rather than directly on to the salad.

Also try putting your dressing in a spray bottle to coat salad lightly. This usually saves calories too.

Eggs

If you have trouble peeling hard-boiled eggs, crack the shells and soak them in cold water for a minute – the shells will slip off beautifully.

Eggs will whip more easily if left for ten minutes in cold water before breaking.

For perfect poached eggs without a poacher, add a splash of white wine vinegar to the water, bring to the boil, crack in eggs and reduce to simmer.

You can freeze egg whites, but not egg yolks.

To open quails' eggs, use a small knife. Towards the flat end of the egg, gently push the blade of the knife into the shell. Turn the egg, keeping the knife in place, taking a circle of shell from the top of the egg. Then carefully pour out the egg.

To make delicious, creamy scrambled eggs beat in a tablespoon of mayonnaise for every two eggs.

To test whether an egg is fresh or not, hold it up to a burning candle. If there are black spots visible, the egg is bad.

Here's a cracking tip for hard-boiling eggs. Boil ten or 15 eggs at one time. While boiling, add food colouring to the water. The shells of the cooked eggs will take on the colour of the dye. You can then look in the fridge and tell which eggs are hard-boiled and which are raw.

If you've undercooked a boiled egg, just pop the top back on and wrap the egg in cling film. Place gently back into the pan and finish off the cooking.

Eggs are best used at room temperature. If you're one of the misguided souls that keeps them in the fridge, remember to remove them an hour before you want to use them.

Take care when separating eggs – the whites do not whisk up so well if any trace of yolk gets into them.

Eggs stuck to the carton? Don't pull – they'll break. Just soak the box in water and they'll come away easily.

To boil a cracked egg, wrap it in foil, twisting the two ends into a cracker shape. Then boil as normal. When you take the foil and egg out of the water, plunge it into cold water for a moment to stop the egg cooking inside the foil.

Don't wash eggs. They have a natural protective layer on the outside that helps keep them fresh, but do wash your hands after handling eggs. Think where they come from!

Make lighter omelettes by adding a splash of water to the mix, and don't over-beat.

Egg whites thicken up faster when you add a pinch of salt before beating.

For extra fluffy scrambled eggs or omelettes, pour all the ingredients into a large plastic milk container and give it a good shake.

To separate lots of eggs at the same time, gently break them all into a bowl and with clean, careful hands scoop out the yolks.

Don't waste energy boiling eggs continuously – once the water's come to the boil, turn off the heat and leave the eggs in the pan for about 15 minutes.

To test whether an egg is properly hard-boiled, try spinning it on a hard surface. If it doesn't spin easily, it isn't quite cooked.

Milk & Cheese

Don't worry about keeping milk fresh while you're camping. Just mix muesli with milk powder, store in a sealable box until needed, and add water as required.

Toast parmesan cheese before serving for a better taste.

If a recipe calls for milk, for a change, try yoghurt instead.

If a recipe calls for buttermilk and you haven't got any, use quarter of a cup of milk and three quarters of a cup of yoghurt instead of one cup of buttermilk.

Before boiling milk, dampen the inside of the pan with water. When the milk boils, it won't burn the bottom.

Liver too tough? Tenderise it by soaking it in milk for at least an hour. Drain it and dry it before cooking.

When boiling milk to make custard, add a pinch of salt. It gives a lovely ice-cream flavour.

Keep the rinds of parmesan cheese and add to soups while cooking for extra flavour.

To prevent blocks of cheese going mouldy before you have chance to use them, grate the cheese and freeze in a freezer bag.

If you need softened butter, but have forgotten to take it out of the fridge, try grating it on to a warm dish.

Fabulous Fruit

If your cooked apples taste bland, grate some orange or lemon peel over the top and bake for a further ten minutes.

Add a few drops of almond essence when making the topping for apple crumble. It complements the flavour of the apple perfectly.

Prevent a fruit tart from becoming soggy by sprinkling a little semolina powder on to the base before adding the fruit.

Damson stones can be removed more easily when making jam if you cook them in the microwave first before adding the sugar.

When a recipe calls for the juice of a lemon, save the rind. Grate it finely, dry in a slow oven and add to castor sugar for added taste when baking.

Before grating the rind of a lemon or orange, run the grater under the cold tap.

Lay a piece of greaseproof paper over the blunt side of your grater before you grate the rind of a lemon or orange, carefully holding it in place as you grate on the sharp side. You can just lift it off and shake the zest free.

To ensure apples remain crisp and juicy, store them in perforated plastic bags in the salad crisper of your fridge.

Keep fruit and veg longer by storing them in paper bags rather than plastic.

To check if a bunch of grapes is fresh, shake the bunch gently. If any grapes fall off, they are not fresh.

For a tasty Bolognaise sauce, try adding raisins, sliced apricots and apples to the mince.

Chopped fruit often goes brown. It's a good idea to keep some bottled lemon juice in a spray bottle in the fridge. Whenever you chop fruit just give it a quick squirt of lemon and that should stop it browning.

Test to see if a pineapple is ripe. You should be able to pull a leaf from the top easily.

To tell if a shelled nut is fresh or not, shake it. If it rattles, it's not fresh.

For a nutty addition to dishes, add toasted sesame seeds.

Vivacious Vegetables

Never buy artichokes if they have brown patches.

To keep artichokes fresh for a bit longer, cut off the dry ends and put the stems in a jar of water, adding a teaspoon of sugar to the water.

For a perfectly chopped onion, skin it and put it on the chopping board root-end down. Cut downwards, but don't cut all the way through the onion. Turn the onion round and slice across the cuts.

Here's the best way to skin tomatoes: cut a shallow 'x' in the bottom of the tomato. Put it into rapidly boiling water until the skin starts to split. Immediately pop the tomato into a bowl of ice water and leave until cool. The skin should now peel off like magic.

To stop broccoli smelling while cooking, put a piece of red pepper in the pot with it while boiling.

To stop Brussels sprouts falling apart during boiling, cut an 'x' into the stalk end (the bottom) of the sprout with a sharp knife before cooking.

Do a stir-fry in vegetable broth rather than oil to cut down on the fat.

To remove the smell of onions from your hands after chopping, turn on the cold tap and rub your hands up and down the neck of the tap. This only works with stainless steel taps, so if you don't have them, try rubbing your hands with a stainless steel spoon instead.

To cut mushrooms easily and evenly, use an egg slice.

To stop onions making you cry, burn a candle near by while chopping them.

To prevent an unpleasant odour when boiling cauliflower or cabbage, tear a slice of bread into small chunks and add it to the pot. Rye bread works especially well.

When chopping up chilli peppers, avoid getting hot stuff on your skin by coating your hands with vegetable oil before handling them.

To keep potatoes firm while boiling, add vinegar to the water (one part vinegar to two parts water). Add a little salt too.

Be careful if wearing contact lenses when chopping shallots or chillies – the smells have been known to permeate the lens and harm the eye.

To check the quality of raw beans, put them in water. If they sink, they're good. If they float, throw them away.

Tight for time? Chop a quantity of onions, green peppers and celery at the beginning of the week and refrigerate in individual well-sealed containers. Dip into them as required.

If you have half an avocado left over, do not remove the stone. Store it in the fridge – leaving the stone in will stop the flesh browning so quickly.

A lot of people don't like the taste of olives in brine. Try putting them on to simmer in some fresh water for ten minutes. Drain well.

You can have healthy roast potatoes! Parboil, then place on a baking tray lined with parchment paper. Roast in the top half of the oven.

For little burns or scalds in the kitchen, rub the affected part with the inside of a fresh potato peel.

Prevent peeled potatoes from discolouring by covering with water mixed with a few tablespoons of milk.

Avoid soggy mashed potatoes? Instead of adding milk, sprinkle with milk powder.

For neat potato salad, cut the potatoes up before cooking, put them into a deep-frying basket, lower into a pan of simmering water until cooked.

Soft tomatoes can be made firmer by placing them into a bowl of salted water and ice cubes.

The base of asparagus isn't always as tough as people think – it's just the skin. By peeling the base you'll find more you can eat.

Chop parsley at top speed by putting sprigs into a cup and attacking them with scissors.

Cauliflower a little past its best can be restored to whiteness by adding a dash of milk to the water you boil it in.

Keep cauliflower white by dropping a cube of sugar into the cooking water.

Mushrooms can be fried in water as a low-fat alternative to butter or oil.

Dried beans are full of goodness, but they're also full of 'gas'. To reduce their gassy effect always dispose of the soaking water and cook them in fresh water.

Also, if you are prone to wind, rinse tinned beans such as kidney and flageolet in fresh water before using. This will also reduce your salt intake.

Your Very Good Health!

If you want to lose weight from your hips, avoid spicy foods because they over-stimulate the glands that cause fat storage in your hips and bum.

For a healthy pastry base that you can use in quiches and pizzas, substitute whole-meal breadcrumbs mixed with plain low-fat yoghurt for plain flour.

If you're watching your fat intake, but crave take-away curry, buy it, leave it to cool and place in the fridge. When the ghee or fat solidifies, skim it off – and presto, a low-fat curry that will taste delicious.

Eat vegetable soup as a starter to lose weight. The fibre causes the rest of the meal to pass through your digestive system more quickly.

To reduce the amount you eat, turn out the lights. Dim lights make you want to eat less.

Also to reduce the amount you eat use smaller dishes. Large plates make you want to eat as much as you can fit on to them. It's all psychological.

Worried that you eat too quickly? Use chopsticks.

Eat eggs to clear up a cold – they're high in zinc, which helps cure colds.

To get rid of a filthy cold, eat a strong curry – it will 'sweat' the cold out.

If cholesterol's a problem and you want to cut down on the number of eggs you eat, replace eggs in baking recipes with a tablespoon of soya flour mixed in with a tablespoon of water.

To persuade your kids to eat healthier cereal, mix half a portion of healthy stuff with half a helping of something less wholesome.

A simple way to reduce calories and fat in your favourite pies: don't cover the top with pastry – just leave it off for a healthy open pie that is just as tasty.

Need a simple low-fat dip? Prick an aubergine all over and cook on high power in the microwave for ten minutes.

Spice up corn-on-the-cob with a squeeze of lime and a pinch of chilli powder for the delicious flavour of South America without the usual indulgence of butter.

For mashed potato without the butter, cream or milk, try beating in some of the hot cooking water. To make the spuds really light and fluffy you'll need lots of elbow grease but the exercise will help reduce those calories.

Alternatively, try using low-fat buttermilk or yoghurt.

For spuds that are high on flavour, but low on calories, try drizzling some balsamic vinegar over cooked potatoes.

To make thick broths without adding fat or flour, just remove a portion of your soup, purée and put back in.

There's no need to fry French toast in oil or butter. Just pop it into a hot oven for ten minutes, turning once.

Try using minced turkey instead of beef in mince dishes like chilli or spaghetti Bolognaise. It has less fat and calories and you can always 'beef' up the flavour using a beef stock cube.

To remove excess fat from soup and stock, fill a plastic bag with ice and drag it across the surface. The fat will cling to the ice-cold bag.

Alternatively, pour your stock through a large funnel filled with ice cubes.

Fancy a vitamin-packed light dessert to finish off a meal? Try making fruit granita using freshly squeezed grapefruit or orange juice. Add a splash of your favourite liqueur and pour into a shallow plastic container. Freeze the mixture, occasionally removing it from the freezer to stir gently. You should get a pretty, crystal-like consistency.

Add Flavour

If you frequently use fresh herbs, save the measuring cups from medicine bottles. They can be used for measuring herbs and spices.

Try crumbling a vegetable stock cube into Welsh rarebit for a different taste.

Pep up dried stuffing mix. Use a dissolved vegetable stock cube instead of plain water.

To keep ground herbs fresh, store them in a container that doesn't let in light.

To restore the flavour to spices that have been sitting in your cupboard for months, roast them in the oven on a high heat until you start to smell the aroma.

Odds and ends of fresh root ginger can be preserved in rice wine.

If you do a lot of oriental-inspired cooking, it's worth preparing a mix of garlic and ginger in advance. Pop a whole head of peeled garlic cloves and a peeled ginger root in the food processor and whizz them together, then turn the mixture out on to foil, form it into a log shape, wrap tightly and freeze. Next time you make a stir-fry, just cut off as much as you need.

Tomato paste doesn't keep well once opened. Freeze the remains in an ice-cube tray for handy-sized blocks.

For garlic popcorn, just add a peeled clove to the popping oil.

When a recipe calls for you to fry onions and garlic, always add the garlic last to prevent burning.

If you don't have fresh herbs, mix dried with lemon juice and a chopped onion and allow to stand for about 15 minutes.

When making pizzas or bread at home, create a brick-oven-baked flavour. Buy some terracotta tiles from a DIY store. Place a layer of the tiles on an oven shelf. Preheat the oven and place the pizza or bread directly on to the tiles to cook.

To get rid of the starch that rises to the top of the pan when cooking rice, hold a cold serving spoon on the surface of the water and most of the starch will stick to the bottom of the spoon.

Grills & Barbies

Before lighting your barbecue, brush the grid with a dab of vegetable oil to bring out the taste.

Barbecue charcoal is ready for cooking when 80 per cent is covered with grey ash.

For home-made burgers that are cooked right through, poke a hole in the centre when forming. For burgers that are rare on the inside, slip an ice-cube in the centre.

When grilling meat, put a slice of bread underneath in the grill pan to soak up the fat and meat juices that drip down. It reduces smoking fat and makes the grill pan easier to clean.

When frying sausages, fix them together with skewers to make for easier turning over.

To skin a fish, first dip your fingers in water, then in a bowl of salt so as to get a firm grip on the skin.

To cook sprats the low-fat way, roll in seasoned flour then thread on skewers, place on an oiled baking tray and cook for about 20 minutes.

Run out of breadcrumbs for coating fried fish? Use crushed cornflakes instead.

Pots & Pans

Don't throw away foil trays from take-aways – wash them and keep them to use as mini baking trays.

To clean a coffee pot, put in some ice cubes and some salt and swirl round.

To shine the bottom of copper pans, rub with half a lemon and some salt.

If your pan looks like it's about to boil over, put a whisk in and beat quickly. The bubbles will go down like magic.

When a recipe calls for a coating of oil, it's really hard to make that coating even. So try pouring some oil into a spray bottle. Hold it about a foot from the food and spray.

Rice slightly burnt and stuck to the bottom of the pan? Don't scrape it off – it can be salvaged. Place a layer of onion skins over the rice. Leave for quarter of an hour, throw away the onion skins and serve the rice.

The bigger the pan you cook pasta in the better – the pieces won't stick together.

To remove burnt food from the bottom of pans without hassle, wet a cloth in boiling water and then leave it stretched over the top of the pan for half an hour.

Use glycerine to lubricate egg beaters and other kitchen equipment with moving parts. It has a much better taste than machine oil!

To save energy, use the smallest pans you can – less metal, less energy needed to heat. (And less time to wash up afterwards.)

Save more pennies in the kitchen. If you have electric rings on your cooker, turn them off a minute or so before cooking is complete. The rings will stay hot enough to continue to cook the food.

Clearing Up

To clean the microwave, place half a lemon in a bowl of water and boil in the microwave for a few minutes. The lemony steam will vaporise all those greasy stains and clear nasty smells.

Microwaves cook more efficiently if the inside is clean.

Wrap fish, poultry, veg and hot sandwiches, especially bacon, in white paper towels when you microwave them. The towels absorb the grease and moisture, keeping the oven clean, and absorb excess fat from the food, so you don't eat it.

To get rid of the strong smell from new plastic containers, wash, dry and put in the freezer for at least two days.

To clean a food-stained pan, fill with distilled vinegar and soak for half an hour before washing in soapy water.

To clean burnt saucepans, soak in Coca-Cola for a while.

If there are little bits of cork in your wine, give the bottle a really short, sharp flick over the sink and the cork should come flying out. It's all in the wrist action!

Fill an ice-cube tray with left-over wine to use in cooking at a later date.

To clean your hob, try white vinegar. Not only does it bring up a nice shine, but it will eliminate persistent cooking smells in the kitchen too.

Alternatively, if the pong is really strong, boil some cloves in a mixture of one cup of water to quarter of a cup of vinegar.

To keep your fridge smelling nice, stick some cloves in an orange and place it in the fridge.

Clean a grotty roasting tin (not aluminium or non-stick) with a solution of washing soda and water boiled up in the tin. Rinse and then dry in a cool oven.

Cleaning a greasy grill pan is a horrible job. Avoid it by lining the grill pan with foil beneath the wire tray and simply lifting the foil out – complete with dirt and fat – each time after use.

Don't try to keep your baking tins shining like new – once matt and dark they will actually retain the heat much better.

Also keep a good kitchen knife clean by dipping a cork in scouring powder and running it along the side of the blade. Rinse the knife, dry it and wipe it down with vegetable oil.

To clean a rusty knife, cut a potato in half and dip the cut surface in bicarbonate of soda. Rub the potato hard on both sides of the blade for a gleaming finish.

Boiled eggs will turn metal cutlery black if it is not washed soon after use.

To clean really baked-on food from a cooking pan, put a sheet of fabric conditioner in the pan and fill with water. Leave overnight and the next day the food will just lift off with a sponge.

Clean cast-iron skillets on the outside with a commercial oven cleaner. Let stand for two hours. Then remove any accumulated black stains with vinegar and water.

To clean and deodorise wooden boards, combine half a cup of baking soda with some warm water to make a paste. Rub the paste on to the wood. Rinse well with clear water and pat dry.

To restore the sheen on a wooden board, rub in salad oil or linseed oil using a fine steel-wool pad.

Always dry wooden chopping boards upright to stop them warping.

To remove strong food smells from plastic chopping boards, give them a rub down with a cut grapefruit.

To restore whiteness to a plastic chopping board, rub with half a lemon and wash in warm water.

To remove hard-water lime deposits from your draining board, soak in full strength white vinegar, then scrub.

After washing your baking trays, put them back in the oven while it's still warm to prevent them from going rusty.

When you're cooking from a recipe book, cover the open page with some cling film to stop it getting marked.

Remove fruit or berry stains from your hands by rubbing them with lemon juice.

CHILDREN'S ENTERTAINERS

Sue Harthill;
Elegant Days of
Warwick & London

When and Where

Think about children's parties before conception! Christmas-time is often busy for venues. Summer is best as you can have the party in the garden.

Find out which other children in your child's class have birthdays around the same time – and share.

It's a good idea to hire somewhere to hold your party. Children can get very excited and cause a lot of mess, so this solution saves wear and tear on your home.

If you are having the party at a restaurant, check to see that they don't object to you bringing in an outside entertainer.

If you are having the party outside, get your children to decorate some old bed sheets and use them to sit on and have a picnic.

Entertainment

When choosing an entertainer, get the prospective candidate to give you a step-by-step account of their act.

If your child wants a particular entertainer, book well in advance.

Instead of hiring a clown, get your partner or a friend to dress up as a clown, a pirate, Darth Vader or Father Christmas (whatever is appropriate).

Themed parties always go down well. Pirates, cowboys and Indians, spacemen are just a few popular ideas. Don't be too ambitious though, or you'll find nobody will turn up in costume.

Hire a large screen projector from a camera shop and rent a video from your local video store.

Once children reach about seven, they usually only want a small group of friends, not the whole class. Hurrah!

For an older age group, what about booking tickets to the cinema or pantomime, or taking them out for a pizza. It can often work out cheaper than a venue, entertainer and going home presents.

Preparations

Be imaginative when making invitations – use white paper plates, photographs or folded paper shapes, for example.

Help the children get to know each other – make little name badges. This also helps the entertainer and any other adults there.

Create an element of surprise – fill party bags for each child and give them out as the children arrive. Pop in hats, balloons, chocolate, or anything else that you fancy.

Save your puff! Balloons are easier to blow up if soaked in water first.

Keep a few extra prizes wrapped and hidden away for emergencies. You might have to resort to an extra game of musical bumps.

If you have more than ten children attending, split pass the parcel into two groups.

Make a fun jail – get some plywood and a couple of old sheets. Paint bars on to the sheets and use it as a 'detention centre'.

Party bags are expensive. Why not give all the children *one* present as they leave. A football or decent yo-yo and perhaps a balloon can work out cheaper than a bag of nonsense.

Alternatively, have a lucky dip at the door as children leave. It's fun for the children.

To make a lucky dip, go to a pound shop and buy as many gifts as you want. Ask the children to decorate the lucky dip box while you wrap the presents. If you've got things that are particularly for girls or boys, colour-code the wrapping to avoid tantrums.

A great going home present (if you're organised enough) is a party photo. Take a photo of each child during the early part of the party, then send someone out to get them developed at a one-hour service, pop them in cheap wooden frames and present them to each child as they leave as a personal memento.

Organise your little helpers afterwards. Don't be left to clear up on your own. Put sticky name tags on boxes and get the children to fill up the box with their name on it as quickly as they can.

Have plenty of bin liners available for tipping away the mess.

Games

To avoid children getting upset during the party, it is a good idea to avoid elimination games, such as musical chairs. However, if you do want to play them, make sure that the children who are out can take on a different role (like playing the music or arranging the chairs).

If you don't have enough room to play musical chairs, play musical hats instead. Place the children in a circle so that each child is looking at the back of the next child's head. Give all the children, bar two, a home-made cardboard crown and away you go.

Children can get very competitive at parties and it can all end in tears, so make sure that some of the games are team games. Give everyone the chance to win something.

Children love personalised games so get each of the parents to bring a baby photo of their child. The game is to recognise who the baby is in each photo.

Personalise 'pin the tail on the donkey'. Photocopy and enlarge a photo of the birthday girl or boy for the children to pin a red nose on to.

Home-video your party then play it back to the children just before home-time. They'll love seeing themselves.

Organise all your running-around games before tea. You don't want children to be sick on those pretty party frocks!

Children get tired. Have 45 minutes of games, then 30 minutes for tea, then 30 minutes for quieter games like pass the parcel or sleeping lions.

Food

Save yourself a lot of hassle – make a lot of the party food beforehand and freeze it until you need it.

For a culinary delight, sprinkle multi-coloured jelly babies into your jelly mixture before it sets.

If you are no good at making cakes, buy a bag of ready-made fairy cakes, arrange them on a plate in the shape of the birthday child's initial and place a candle on each cake. It saves mess, too, because each guest can have their own little cake.

Cake in party bags often ends up wasted. Offer the cake as pudding at the party tea.

Put the cake candles into their holders then into the cake. Otherwise you squash the cake as you insert the candles.

For younger children, don't include snacks wrapped individually in foil - they are hard to open and you have enough to do.

Children tend to drink far more than they eat so have plenty of jugs of juice or cartons at the ready.

If you don't have a big enough table for everyone, just put a plastic throw-away cloth on the floor and have a 'picnic' indoors.

To save mess, give each child his or her owned packed tea in a small box (you can save them and use them for parties another time).

CHIROPODISTS

Mrs Nickson; Mrs Hill; Liz Warburton; Society of Chiropodists; Chiropodist Association

You can side-step a number of foot complaints just by wearing properly fitted shoes.

To get the most out of your everyday shoes, wear leather uppers and man-made soles.

If you want to avoid aching feet, lie or sit down with your feet higher than your hips for at least 15 minutes.

Aching feet can be caused by shoes with thin soles or rigid heels, so insert a foam insole to alleviate the problem.

You should wash your feet in water that is at a temperature of 140 °F/40 °C.

Bromidrosis can be a problem – that's smelly feet to you or me! Swab your feet with surgical spirit after washing and drying. Don't use too much talcum powder because this will only plug up your pores.

To avoid 'cheesy' feet, only wear wool or cotton next to your feet. Never wear the same pair of shoes two days in a row.

Try not to wear wellies for any great length of time. Your feet won't benefit from it and they'll smell awful, too.

To cure anhydrosis (dry skin on the soles of your feet), try rubbing petroleum jelly into your feet every night without fail. Keep your feet covered overnight with a towelling sock. The dry skin will soon disappear.

Don't disrupt the circulation in your feet. Never wear tight-fitting socks or stockings.

Wear open-toed sandals instead of slippers.

Barefoot is best – give your feet a rest each day and walk about the house with no shoes on.

To avoid blisters, don't wear new shoes for too long.

Blisters can be a pain on a long walk. To avoid them apply surgical spirit to the feet and then wear two pairs of thin socks. Make sure the outer pair is bigger.

To prevent toes chaffing together during a long walk, put petroleum jelly between them.

To cure small verrucas, cover them with a plaster.

To dissolve big verrucas, get a match with a pink head, wet it in warm water and rub it into the verruca. Then cover with an ordinary waterproof plaster.

Stop your feet from sweating too much – wipe them with surgical spirit every morning.

To get rid of athlete's foot, rub surgical spirit between the toes twice a day. Or get a jar of potash, and dissolve one or two crystals in a tub of warm water. Soak your feet in the tub for about quarter of an hour.

As a last resort, cure fungal infections on your feet by soaking them in a bucket of your own urine.

To heal sprains, follow the ICE method: ice, compression and then elevation.

To prevent hangnails or ragged cuticles, avoid soaking your feet in water, and apply a little olive oil to your cuticles.

To get rid of a recurring in-growing toenail, dab hydrogen peroxide (available from pharmacists) down the side of your nails. This should fizz for a bit and then you can wipe away any dead tissue.

Prevent hard skin on your feet – use a pumice stone regularly.

Shoes should be ½ in/1 cm longer than the longest toe.

The maximum heel height for everyday shoes is ½ in/4 cm.

Always buy shoes with a proper fastener that holds the foot in place. Laces are best.

When trying out new shoes, stand up and walk around to see how they feel. Or stand on tiptoe and ask a friend or the shop assistant to pull the back of the shoe. If it comes off, the shoe doesn't fit properly.

If the seams of new shoes rub, hammer them gently. This will soften them.

CLEANERS

Brass & Metal Cleaning

Joan Burke, Lygon Arms; Wendy Croad, Wendy Ann Cleaners; Helen Bowley, Maid to Order; Susan Wooldridge, Molly Maid

Badly tarnished pieces of brass can be restored by leaving them to soak overnight in tomato ketchup. Scrub them with an old toothbrush and rinse in water.

Paint stripper is also good if the brass has been covered with paint. Scrub with a wire suede brush.

Ease an old stiff lock, not with oil, which will seep, but with the shavings from a graphite pencil brushed into the lock with a soft paint-brush.

New-looking brass can be aged by leaving it in an airtight box for a few hours with an open pot of liquid ammonia (from pharmacists). Don't let the brass touch the ammonia, and beware of fumes when you open the box. Rinse the brass items and gently polish them.

Small brass fittings can be fiddly to clean. Secure them to a scrap of wood with a nail or screw to hold them in place while you polish them.

To protect metal fittings that can't be removed from furniture that you are cleaning or restoring, brush them with a layer of candle or beeswax. Beware the methylated spirit in french polish doesn't melt the wax.

Always wear gloves when cleaning metal. Your fingerprints will mark the metal and be hard to rub off.

Keep pewter clean by rubbing with a cabbage leaf. Finish off by polishing with a soft cloth.

Alternatively, rub pewter with petrol and leave to dry. When it's dry, rub over with hot beer. Leave this to dry as well and then buff with a soft cloth.

Bring up the shine on silver with a piece of rhubarb.

Bring new shine back to tarnished silver cutlery, by adding shredded aluminium foil to enough boiling water to cover the silverware in a baking tray. Leave to boil for ten minutes.

Kitchens

To clean any spills in the oven, sprinkle with automatic dish-washing powder, cover with wet paper towels, let stand for a few hours, then clean with a damp sponge.

Keep salt near the cooker to avoid a grease fire. Following a spill, immediately sprinkle with the salt. When the oven cools, brush off, then wipe with a damp sponge.

Make your own oven cleaner from one tablespoon of bicarbonate of soda mixed with a good cup of hot water. Wipe over the whole oven, including the glass door and shelves, and the stains will gradually disappear.

Soak oven shelves, trays and any other removable parts overnight in a solution of biological washing powder and hot water. Next day you can rinse and wipe the stains away.

Remove the chemical smell of oven cleaners by heating lemon rind in a low oven for about 20 minutes.

To rid white appliances of yellowing, mix together half a cup of bleach, quarter of a cup of baking soda and four cups of warm water. Apply with a sponge and leave for ten minutes. Rinse and dry thoroughly. Sparkling white!

Wipe large items like freezers and washing machines with car wax to make them shine and to remove small scratches.

Use rubbing alcohol instead of expensive commercial waxes on all white goods.

Stop a garage freezer becoming rusty by spraying it with furniture polish.

When defrosting your freezer, keep frozen food cold by wrapping it in several layers of newspaper.

After defrosting your freezer, apply a thin layer of glycerine to the inside with a paper towel. It makes the ice much easier to remove next time.

After cleaning out the fridge, wipe down the inside with a solution of bicarbonate of soda in cold water to make it smell brand new.

For a truly sweet-smelling fridge, pour vanilla extract on to a piece of cotton wool and leave it on one of the shelves inside.

Keep the coils at the back of your fridge clean – unplug and pull out the fridge regularly, and use your vacuum to remove dust and dirt. The fridge will stay efficient and last longer too.

To clean beneath the refrigerator, tie a sock around the end of a stick or broom handle.

Dish-washers will work just as effectively if you use the cheapest brand of dish-washing detergent available, but add a few tablespoons of vinegar to the dish-water. The vinegar will cut the grease, leave your dishes sparkling and save you some money.

To remove the sticky film on dishes and the inside of the dish-washer, put a bowl containing one cup of bleach in the bottom of the washer. Run through the wash cycle, but do not dry. Then fill the bowl with one cup of white vinegar and run through an entire cycle.

To clean your dish-washer, simply run a cup of white vinegar through the entire cycle of the empty dishwasher.

Clean a microwave by placing half a lemon in water and setting it to boil.

Remove traces of plastic melted on to toasters by dabbing with nail polish and peeling off when dry or tacky.

To descale your kettle, pour some malt vinegar and water (50/50) over the element in your kettle and boil the kettle.

Clear a blocked sink by tipping a handful of bicarbonate of soda followed by a cup of vinegar straight down the plug. After a couple of hours, pour down a kettleful of boiling water.

Never put celery or other stringy matter in the waste disposal unit.

Cardboard cylinders from inside loo and kitchen rolls make good 'tinder' for lighting a fire.

Drop fresh parsley into hot oil after use to absorb unwanted flavours from a pan. The oil can be reused without affecting the taste of the next food to be cooked.

Keep swing-bin liners in the bottom of your bin. When you take out a full bag, a new liner will always be at hand.

When you wash the kitchen floor, use your rubbish bin instead of a bucket to hold the water. This way you get a fresh bin without the extra job of washing it.

To get rid of unsightly build-up in the bottom of a vase, add a few drops of automatic dish-washer detergent and fill with hot water. Soak overnight, then rinse.

To remove tea or coffee stains from fine china, rub with a damp cloth dipped in baking soda.

Rubber gloves last far longer if you turn them inside out and stick an adhesive plaster across the tips of the fingers.

Before you throw away old rubber gloves, cut strips from the cuffs to use as extra strong rubber bands.

For a clean, sweet-smelling sponge, just run it through the top rack of your dish-washer.

Dirty dishcloths cause germs. Always dry yours thoroughly before storing away – bacteria love nothing more than a nice, warm, damp 'bed'.

Windows

To remove the black mould that can grow in the corners of windows, use an old toothbrush dipped in a mixture of water and bleach.

Water down your glass cleaner to make it go further. It will work just as effectively.

Wipe one side of the window horizontally and the other vertically. That way you will know which side the smears are on.

Polish on a curtain rail will make curtains run smoothly.

Make invisible repairs in your net curtains by dabbing colourless nail varnish on the torn edges and holding them together until the varnish is dry.

Dull net curtains can be transformed into gleaming white ones by putting a denture-cleaning tablet into water and soaking the curtains.

If they are really filthy, soak Venetian blinds in the bath and, wearing a pair of fabric garden gloves, wipe each slat clean. Then hang the blinds over the bath to dry.

Clean aluminium window-frames with cream silver polish.

To keep the corners of window-panes free of dust and moisture save the ends of white candles and rub on the corners of the wood.

Louvred windows and doors are easy to clean with a 2 in/5 cm wide paint-brush dipped in a mild soap solution. Lightly towel dry.

Or, dab lighter fluid on a cloth and rub gently.

Dusting & Cleaning

To keep feathers clean, sprinkle with talcum powder and then brush off.

Blow the dust off a pleated lampshade with a hair-dryer.

Clean a circular electric fan with an old sock over your hand.

Line the top of a tall bookcase with old newspaper. When you want to remove the dust, just throw away the paper and replace it. This works for the tops of kitchen cabinets as well.

Brush dust off shelves with a new paint-brush.

Make your own polishing pad by cutting up some old tights and putting them in a cotton bag.

To ensure your new duster picks up dirt, soak it in equal parts of vinegar and paraffin. When it's completely saturated, take it out of the mixture and store it in a screw top jar until you need it.

Make sure dirt stays in the dustpan – spray the inside with furniture polish so the dust has something to stick to.

Dustpans and brushes are always overlooked, but they get filthy – wash yours out thoroughly at least once a month. They will be much more effective at picking up dirt and more hygienic too.

Stop dried pampas grass from disintegrating by spraying it with hair-spray.

Take care of your chamois leather. Wash it in warm, soapy water and rinse after use. Allow the leather to dry away from direct heat so that it retains its natural oils.

A room will smell clean and polished when you spray furniture polish behind the radiator. The heat will disperse the smell around the room.

No time to whiten trainers before school? Spray them with window cleaner, then wipe with a damp cloth.

Reach cobwebs by taping a children's toy broom to a bamboo cane.

To blow dust or cobwebs out of corners, use a balloon pump or a bicycle pump.

Embossed wallpapers often look grubby. A clean, soft-bristled toothbrush solves the problem.

Mouldings and cornicing can be awkward to clean thoroughly. Put some detergent into a garden spray bottle to get into all the nooks and crannies. After wiping, spray again with clean water to make sure no detergent is left lingering.

A terry nappy is good for wiping cornicing because the loops get into all the detail.

To clean your television/video remote control unit, first take the batteries out. Then with a paint-brush and some methylated spirits give it a good scrub. Leave for half an hour and it will be as good as new.

Dusting your television? Eliminate static electricity from the screen by wiping with a used sheet of fabric softener. It will help prevent dust re-settling.

To clean between computer keys, use cotton buds.

Clean the ball of a computer mouse with a cotton bud dampened with alcohol.

To clean ink and ribbon fibre from typewriter keys, roll Silly Putty into a ball and very carefully press into the keys.

Make life easier when cleaning: put some detergent on, say, a floor or a sink, then move on to the next job, leaving it to work for a while. By the time you return, the detergent will have really got into the dirt and your task will be half done for you.

Floors

Move furniture with ease. Put foil pie dishes under each leg and the furniture will slide easily over the carpet.

Make your own protective castor cups or mats with the lids of coffee jars. Just slide under the castor to protect the pile of the carpet.

Furniture can leave dents in the carpet. A cube of ice left on the dent will restore the pile of the carpet.

Brush the dust away from the corners and edges of carpets with a hand brush and then vacuum it up.

To refresh the colours of a carpet, sprinkle over a mixture of tea-leaves and salt, and then vacuum.

Alternatively, clean with two parts water to one part malt vinegar.

Vacuuming is hard work at the best of times. Change your vacuum bag before it gets too full – a full bag is less efficient and makes the task twice as difficult.

Keep dust from flying around – empty the contents of your vacuum cleaner on to a damp newspaper.

If your vacuum cleaner's hose gets clogged with dust, you can knock out the clog with a broom handle threaded carefully through the hose.

Prevent your vacuum cleaner picking up metal pins and clips by taping a magnet to the front of the cleaner or the outside of the tube. This should stop anything metal getting into the dust bag and damaging it.

To clean a dirty mat, put it in a bin bag and shake it around. The dust will stay in the bag rather than settling on the rest of the furniture.

To neutralise odours and discourage pests, liberally sprinkle bicarbonate of soda on your carpets and leave for 15 minutes before vacuuming up.

If you've dropped a glass, use a piece of white bread to 'blot' up the tiny slivers of glass.

Dropped an egg on the kitchen floor? Add some salt to the egg, leave it for five minutes and it will clean up more easily.

To clean a wooden floor, scatter damp tea-leaves over it to keep the dust in one place when sweeping.

Dark-coloured floors show up scuffs, dust and scratch marks, whilst black heel marks show up more easily on light-coloured floors. Consider your options or face a lifetime on your knees scrubbing.

Make your old linoleum floor look as good as new. Wipe it down with one part fresh milk mixed with one part turpentine. Rub into the floor and polish with a warm, soft cloth.

Get your quarry tile floor shining – use sour milk to wash it down.

Stop your rugs from creeping away – put heavy-duty double-sided tape on the bottom of the rugs.

For heel marks on hard floors, wipe with kerosene or turpentine, or use a pencil eraser.

Nail polish spills can be left to solidify. When just barely pliable, peel them off.

Be careful when cleaning quarry or ceramic tiles. Although the tiles are very tough, the grout surrounding them is not. Rinse thoroughly to avoid the grout deteriorating.

To clean a varnished floor, try adding instant tea granules to your bucket of water.

When choosing a mop, consider this: cotton mops need breaking in, but will dry a floor faster than other alternatives. Rayon mops require no breaking in and will immediately absorb water, often absorbing seven times the mop's weight. Blended mops can offer the best of both worlds: no breaking in, plus immediate absorbency.

To eliminate the re-depositing of dirt as you mop, frequently flip the mop-head as you work.

Top mop tips. Always use cold water, not hot. Keep your back straight. Do not twist your spine. Bend at the knees, not your back. Use your arm muscles to move the mop in a figure of eight pattern. (It's all good exercise too.)

Wipe your guests' feet for them! Most visitors don't wipe their feet. Their minds are focused on where they're going or they're keeping pace with the people in front of them. Ensure you have a good width of matting at entrances.

In icy weather clean the doorstep with a bucket of water to which you have added a crushed aspirin, 8 fl oz/250 ml of warm water and one tablespoon of methylated spirits. This will keep the step clean and stop ice from forming.

Bathrooms

Glass shower doors will stay cleaner longer if you spray them lightly with furniture polish and then shine.

Glass shower doors quickly look grubby, and limescale can be hard work to get rid of. Try using a squeegee – the sort that motoring shops sell for car windscreens – for a sparkling look in minutes!

Remove mildew from shower curtains by scrubbing with a paste of bicarbonate of soda and water. Then rinse in plenty of clear water.

Prevent mildew on shower curtains by soaking them in salt and water before use.

To wash shower curtains, put them in the washing machine along with warm water and two large bath towels. Add half a cup each of detergent and baking soda. Then wash, adding one cup of white vinegar to the rinse cycle. Do not spin dry or wash the vinegar out. Hang immediately and wrinkles will disappear when completely dry.

To stop the bottom of your shower curtain from becoming discoloured or mouldy, coat it with baby oil.

If your shower-head is clogged, pour about 2 in/5 cm of vinegar into a plastic freezer bag and place the shower-head in the bag. Place a tie wrap or elastic band around the neck of the shower-head to hold the bag in place. Leave to soak overnight. In the morning remove the bag, and the head should be clean and function properly. Repeat if necessary.

To descale a clogged shower or clean up hard water stains on tiles, clean with one part water mixed with one part malt vinegar.

Tiling all the wall space in a bathroom can look stunning, but it can be a pain to keep gleaming – a squeegee will do the trick in no time.

Clean fungus from grouting between tiles with a paste of bicarbonate of soda and water. Leave for about an hour, then remove with a damp cloth.

Before you start to clean tiles, run the shower at its hottest water setting. The steam will help to loosen the dirt and make for easier cleaning.

Lemon oil keeps tiles shinier longer and helps keep water stains from building up.

Car wax makes an ideal cleanser and polish for ceramic tiles. Apply it generously and give it a wipe with a soft duster before it's completely dry. Not only will it clean your tiles a treat, but its natural waterproofing will keep them looking good for longer.

Keep taps and bathroom chrome shiny by rubbing them over with a little glycerine on a dry cloth.

For chrome taps or fixtures, try rubbing them with alcohol for a super shine

Dripping taps can cause a stain on the bath or sink enamel. Try rubbing the mark with a cut lemon to get rid of it.

To clear blockages in sinks or basins, cover the overflow holes with a damp cloth to build up the pressure while you are using a plunger.

If your acrylic bath gets scratched, try rubbing the scratches with silver polish.

Safety first – never use two different commercial cleaners in the loo at the same time – they may combine to produce dangerous gases or even explode.

To clean a really grubby toilet, tie a cloth around a toilet brush and push the water out of the bowl. Then soak the bowl in bleach for several hours before flushing again.

Alternatively, rub with a fine grade sandpaper (wet the sandpaper if the rings are very old).

When bleaching your toilet, don't forget to put some bleach into the toilet-brush holder to ensure the brush stays clean.

For bad bathroom stains on tiles and ceramics, mix a paste of peroxide and cream of tartar. Scrub with a small brush and rinse thoroughly. If stains persist, re-apply the paste and add a drop or two of ammonia. Let stand for two hours and scrub again.

Cure condensation by cleaning the affected area with bleach, then dry out with lots of warmth and ventilation.

After a Fire

Nothing causes more dirt and damage than a fire. If you're unfortunate enough to have needed the fire service to hose down your house, here are a few tips to get things back to normal:

If you must use your mattress temporarily, sun dry the mattress on both sides and cover with plastic sheeting. It is almost impossible to get the smell out of pillows as feathers and foam retain odours.

Let rugs and carpets dry out thoroughly. Clean with a wet/dry vacuum or water extractor carpet-cleaning machine. They will remove the standing water and dirt. Rinse, using vinegar and water in the tank of the carpet-cleaning machine. Dry the rugs as quickly as possible. A fan turned on the rug will speed the drying. Any moisture remaining will quickly rot the rug, causing it to fall apart.

Most dishes can be washed in one tablespoon of bleach to one gallon of lukewarm water for 30 minutes prior to washing. Wash in hot soapy water. Dish-washers are excellent for this purpose – use a rinse and hold cycle.

When water is underneath lino, it can cause odour and rot or warp a wooden floor, which could become a major expense. If this happens, remove the entire sheet of lino. If glued, a heat lamp will soften it so that it can be rolled up without breaking.

Walls may be washed down while still wet. Use a mild soap, and wear rubber gloves. Work from the floor up, a small area at a time. Rinse with clear water. Work quickly when washing wallpaper, so that it does not become soaked. Wash ceilings last. Do not paint until dry.

Dry, heat and ventilate rooms for several days to dry plaster and paper. If mildewed, wipe with a cloth wrung with soap. Re-paste edges or loosened sections of paper as necessary.

Protection

To cut down on static, put a few drops of fabric conditioner in some water and wipe down the front of your television.

Wipe bathroom mirrors with some washing-up liquid on a cloth – this will reduce condensation.

Prevent rusty rings in your bathroom. Paint the bottom of aerosol cans with clear nail-varnish.

Spectacles need regular cleaning, but often go rather smeary. A little eau-de-Cologne or some astringent face toner wiped over the glass will prevent the problem.

To keep clean when you are doing dirty work, wear a dustbin liner. Just throw it away when you've finished.

Put some washing-up liquid in the children's paints – it helps to get the paint out of clothes when they're being washed.

To make non-dribbly paint, mix it with wallpaper paste (but not one that has an anti-fungal agent in it).

After cleaning a cast iron pan, and while it is still warm, wipe with a piece of wax paper to prevent rusting. Or, when clean, rub a small amount of vegetable oil on the inside to keep it seasoned.

Steel wool pads won't get rusty if you throw them in a plastic bag and store in the freezer.

Smells

When light bulbs are cool, dab some of your favourite perfume on. When the light is on and the bulb heats up, the room will fill with the aroma.

To prevent the smell of cigarettes from lingering, put a small bowl of vinegar in the corner of the room. Cover the bowl with cling film and pierce several holes in the top – then you won't get vinegar everywhere if the bowl is knocked over.

Prevent cigarette butts from smouldering. Line your ashtrays with bicarbonate of soda.

Keep your waste disposal unit smelling sweet by grinding citrus rind. Or use the discarded baking soda after it has finished absorbing odours in the refrigerator.

Stains

To remove ink stains from all sorts of materials, spray with hair-spray first and then clean.

To remove a cigarette singe stain from the carpet, pour a little milk on the stain and leave it to soak in. This will dilute the colour and stop it browning. Then rub the stain with a raw potato and wash as normal.

Remove chocolate stains with a mixture of borax powder and glycerine. Stretch the fabric over a bowl, dab the mixture on, leave for a few minutes and then wash off.

To give a stainless steel sink a superb finish, rub it down with a scrunched-up ball of newspaper after cleaning.

To descale tap nozzles, put a plastic bag filled with vinegar over the nozzle. Secure it with an elastic band and leave it for at least half an hour.

Save money – cut your steel wool pads in half so they go twice as far.

Preserve steel wool pads for longer by keeping them in soapy water. This will stop them from rusting.

The secret to removing bloodstains on white fabric is to use cold water and a little detergent. You can dab the stain with hydrogen peroxide, but be careful. Then rub on the secret weapon: unseasoned meat tenderiser. Rinse and wash. Do not use warm water – it will set the stain.

To remove oil marks from paper, cover with talcum powder, leave overnight and then brush off.

To get rid of ink stains from furniture, soak a piece of cotton wool in water and cover the stain with it. The mark will be drawn out and into the cotton wool.

Remove lipstick stains from linen napkins by applying petroleum jelly before washing.

To remove crayon marks from walls, apply a thin coat of rubber cement glue and allow to dry thoroughly, then 'roll' it off. If a colour stain remains, try rubbing it with a little liquid detergent mixed with a few drops of ammonia.

Small, irritating marks on a ceiling can be blotted out with a little white shoe polish.

If a ceiling gets really grubby or smoke stained, it is often quicker to whitewash it than clean it. A pair of swimming goggles is a good idea to protect your eyes.

To whitewash a ceiling, use a new sponge mop rather than perch up a ladder with a roller.

Don't try to clean unpainted bricks – water will make any marks worse.

Sticky label marks can be stubborn to remove from glass. Try using a little peanut butter rubbed in on some soft cotton wool.

For scratched woodwork, you can minimise the damage by dabbing with cotton wool that's been dipped in diluted tea.

COBBLERS

New Shoes

Bill Byrd, Blockley, Chipping Campden; Mark Beabey, Leeds; Guy Metcalf, Totnes;

Buy new shoes at the end of the day when your feet are at their 'largest'. If you buy shoes in the morning, they can become uncomfortable later on in the day.

Always try on both shoes because most people have one foot slightly smaller than the other.

Alan Macdonald,
Cheltenham; Su
Randall; Guild of
Master Craftsmen

New shoes often rub at the heel. Make sure yours are comfy from day one. Place the heel of the shoe over the arm of a wooden chair, cover with some cardboard and bash with a hammer – it's a bit like tenderising meat!

If you've got big feet, stick to dark or neutral colours. White or bright colours will only draw attention to them.

If you've got narrow feet, shoe flaps sometimes slip over each other. To prevent this happening, simply place a bit of felt under the flaps before you lace the shoes up.

Cleaning & Polishing

Save your energy. Polish your shoes in the evening and then buff them up the next morning. This gives a better finish anyway.

To make leather shoes last longer, try using some saddle soap in place of ordinary cleaning products.

To clean gents' shoes without damaging the stitching, wrap a thin soft cloth around a knife and rub off any mud or dirt.

When cleaning sandals, slip one hand in a plastic bag then place that hand inside the sandal and clean with the other hand.

Get rid of salt marks during the winter by mixing one tablespoon of vinegar in one cup of water and then wiping over the marks.

To remove grease stains from leather, rub in washing-up liquid. Leave to dry and then polish off.

Satin wedding shoes often get ruined by water marks. Remove the stains by dipping some cotton wool in a little white spirit and dabbing it over the shoe. If the shoe is brightly dyed satin, test a little area inside first.

Wedding shoes come in such subtle colours that it can be hard to find a matching polish. Try rubbing oil pastels over the shoe; they come in a full spectrum of shades. When you find the perfect match, seal the shoe with a little neutral polish.

To remove bad stains from leather, use wood bleach.

If you've run out of shoe polish, you can use floor wax, furniture polish or window-cleaning spray.

For an alternative brown shoe polish, rub the inside of a banana skin along the leather. Leave to dry and don't buff them up.

Polish black shoes with the inside of the rind of a fresh orange.

To give shoes an instant antique look, buy them one shade lighter than you really want but clean them with a slightly darker polish.

Canvas shoes often look grubby very quickly. Carpet shampoo, applied with a small brush, will make them look as good as new.

Prevent your shoes from scuffing by painting a layer of clear nail-varnish on the heel and toe of your shoes.

Keep your suede shoes looking pristine by removing any marks with an eraser.

Freshen up old suede shoes by giving them a good steam over the kettle.

Nubuck shoes quickly lose their downy roughness. To make them furry again, rub gently with some fine sandpaper.

Clean nubuck shoes and bags with baby wipes.

Bring the shine back to patent leather – try rubbing a little vegetable or baby oil over the shoe and then buff with some kitchen paper towel.

Make patent leather sparkle, with furniture polish.

Patent leather shoes come up a treat if rubbed over with petroleum jelly.

Scuff marks can be covered by gently building up layers of felt-tip pen until you reach the perfect colour match.

Even the grubbiest of trainers look fit for Centre Court if you give them a good clean with a baby wipe.

Keep new trainers looking white for longer – spray them with starch when you get them home from the shops. This makes them easier to clean as well.

To clean the white rubber areas (the 'bumpers') on training shoes, use toothpaste.

To clean white training shoes, rub with bathroom cleaner, buff and then wipe off with a rag.

Alternatively, use cheap face-cleansing milk.

To keep your football boots in good condition, avoid products that have paraffin in them because this will rot the leather.

If you've got marks on your white stilettos, try getting rid of them with nail-varnish remover. If you can't get them off, dab some correcting fluid over the marks.

Remove black marks from white leather shoes by gently rubbing with a damp Brillo pad.

White leather shoes appreciate a wipe down with beaten egg white instead of polish. Use cotton wool to clean them and then polish with a soft cloth.

If you're trying to sew stiff leather, first soak the cotton in melted wax.

Many leather-working tools have round wooden handles. Flatten one edge a little with some sandpaper to stop the tools rolling off tables and work surfaces.

Heels & Laces

Stiletto heels always get scuffed and marked. Try spraying them with some matching car paint as a durable solution.

Clean wooden heels with furniture polish.

If flamenco dancing is your thing, make sure your shoes last the distance. Hammer some carpet tacks into the heel. You'll sound the part too!

To keep high heels stain free when you have to walk on wet grass, wrap clear tape round them.

Scuffs on high heels or shoes can be covered up using magic marker or felt-tip pen.

If your leather laces are a bit wide for the holes, dampen them first and then pull them through a small hole punched in some cardboard before trying to lace them up in the actual shoes.

To stop shoelaces coming undone, wet them before you tie them. The knot will then remain in place. Or you could wax the laces with polish before doing them up.

The plastic tips often come off laces and once frayed they're very difficult to thread through shoe holes. For a permanent solution, pull the plastic tips off and burn the ends to seal them.

Comfort

When you get your sandals out of the wardrobe after a long winter they often feel really stiff and uncomfortable. Pop them in the oven for three or four minutes at a bit below 110 °C/225 °F/Gas Mark ¼ and they will soon soften up.

If your boots are really tight, put your foot into a small plastic bag and it will slip in more easily. Once you've got your boot on, you can tear the bag off your foot.

If the bottoms of your shoes feel sticky, sprinkle a little talcum powder over the sole.

If your soles are slippery, rub a piece of sandpaper across them. Or stick a piece of sandpaper to each one.

Give your shoes a rest. Try not to wear them day after day. They'll last longer and it's healthier for your feet to let the shoes dry out.

Stop your shoes losing their shape at the toes – keep your toenails short.

If your shoes are a bit tight, just poke a hairbrush handle down inside the toes to stretch them a little. Or stuff them with potato skins and leave overnight.

Make your Doc Martens last longer. Put a leather insole inside.

For a cheap pair of boot trees roll up some newspapers and stuff them down your boots. Or you could tie some kitchen towel cardboard tubes together.

Keep boots standing to attention by using empty bottles instead of boot trees.

Make your own shoe horn – use a large metal spoon or an old telephone card.

Wet Shoes

If your shoes get soaked, take them off as soon as you get home and stuff with newspaper. Leave them to dry naturally; don't try to speed the process up by putting them in front of a fire or in bright sunshine. When they are dry, use some saddle soap to condition them and then polish.

To dry wet wellies, use a hair-dryer.

Dyed shoes often mark your feet when they get wet. Prevent this from happening by spraying the inside of the shoe with some Scotchguard.

Never wear new leather shoes in the rain. They need a bit of wear and tear to build up water resistance.

For an effective waterproof coating, give your shoes a final polish with a coat of floor wax.

Smelly Feet

Place orange peel in a pair of smelly summer shoes overnight and they'll be much fresher next day.

Or you could try placing a fabric-softener sheet in them.

Deodorise trainers by filling the feet of pop socks with unused cat litter, tie the ends, place inside and leave overnight.

To keep shoes smelling sweet, fill a fine plant spray with water and some cologne and give the shoes a little shower.

If you have smelly feet, sprinkle some bicarbonate of soda in your shoes and leave overnight to cut down on the pong.

Never wear boots in hot weather – your feet will swell and get sticky. You'll find it really difficult to get your boots off – the more you tug, the hotter your feet get and the tighter the boots become!

COCKTAIL BAR TENDERS

Ed Barnes; Jamie Francis; Jack Harrison

Chill Out

To be properly chilled, a glass should be placed in the fridge at least a couple of hours before serving. If you have forgotten to do this, simply fill the glass with ice, swish it around, and then empty it before pouring.

To frost a glass, put it in the freezer until a white, frosted look appears. Alternatively, bury it in ice cubes until the same thing happens.

Handle glasses by the stem – you don't want to warm the glass after you've chilled it or leave fingerprints.

For drinks that call for a sugar frosting, take the frosted glass and wipe the rim with a slice of lemon and lime. After this, dip in powdered sugar to complete the effect.

Margaritas are prepared in the same way, but the rim is coated with lime and dipped in coarse salt. Don't get the glasses mixed up!

If you're making cocktails at home, don't buy an expensive ice crusher: just wrap the ice in a clean tea towel and smash it up with a meat mallet or even an ordinary hammer.

Never scoop up ice for a cocktail using the glass itself – it may break. If this happens, throw the ice away immediately. You don't want to drink ground glass!

When making highballs, make sure the glass is two-thirds full of ice before adding spirits. For lowballs, fill the glass about half-full of ice before pouring the drink.

Ice makes whisky too cold and reduces its flavour.

Be very careful not to keep the ice in a shaker longer than the time it takes to chill the ingredients. The ice will begin to melt and you will be left with a watered down cocktail.

The best way to keep party punch cool is to freeze some of it in ice-cube trays or a ring mould. Float the frozen punch in the bowl to keep the rest of it chilled, but undiluted.

I Can Drink a Rainbow!

A useful tip when layering: if you don't know the specific gravity of a liqueur, read and compare the proofs on the bottles. A lower proof generally means that there is more sugar and that the liqueur is thicker and heavier.

Remember that the same type of flavoured liqueurs made by a different company can sometimes have a different proof (or specific gravity). Ignoring this may have the effect of spoiling the layered presentation.

When layering drinks, rest a spoon against the inside of the glass and pour the liqueur over the back or rounded side of the spoon. The liqueur should run down the inside of the glass and rest on top of the drink.

If the glass is too narrow to place a spoon in, a maraschino cherry should do the job.

If you mess up the layers, place the drink in the fridge for about an hour and the liqueurs will separate themselves.

Something Fruity

When you slice a lemon for your G&T, rather than letting the rest dry out, slice it up and freeze in water in an ice-cube tray for next time.

In fruit drinks, such as strawberry margaritas, always use fresh fruit, not frozen fruit.

To decorate punch for a special occasion, core and slice apples and cut shapes from the slices using pastry cutters or a sharp knife. Dip shapes in lemon juice and float on the punch.

Lemons and oranges give more juice if soaked first in warm water.

When you refrigerate cut fruit, cover it with a damp napkin. This will help to keep the juices in.

When squeezing a wedge of lime, shield it with your hand to prevent lime juice from squirting your guests in the eye – very painful!

For very special party nibbles, inject cherry tomatoes with vodka and Worcestershire sauce – sprinkle with celery salt and black pepper for a very original take on the traditional bloody Mary.

Store fresh ginger in vodka – it will improve the taste of the vodka and the ginger.

Flavoured vodka is all the rage in pubs and clubs so try making your own – cordials or crushed and puréed fruit can be added. Experiment with lighter and heavier cordials than the vodka itself for a pretty, layered drink.

Treat adult party guests to jelly made with a large dash of vodka. Enjoy experimenting with quantities at home.

Orange slices should be cut about ¼ in/5 mm thick. Slices that are thicker than this are not economical and waste orange; slices thinner than this will be too flimsy.

When cutting fruit, slice in half from tip to tip, then slit the pulp down the middle without slicing through the rind. Turn the fruit pulp-side down and slice at right angles to the slit on the other side. This leaves a slit in the middle of each wedge to hang on the glass.

To cut 'twists', slice the ends of a lemon just to the pulp. Then cut slits length-wise through the rind, but not quite down to the pulp. Continue slicing around the lemon with ¼ in/5 mm gaps. Then you can peel the twists off the lemon.

When using a twist, rub the top of the glass with the rind side as it contains more aromatic oil, then actually twist it and place it in the drink.

You should be able to get about 16 wedges per lime.

Always keep a few chillies marinated in sherry to add a kick to a bloody Mary.

Mix'n'Match

Never use the best quality alcohol for cocktails. The less expensive ones work just as well when they are mixed with juices, carbonated drinks and so on.

When mixing the different ingredients, add the cheaper ones first, so that expensive ingredients don't get wasted in the event of a mistake.

A teaspoon of egg white shaken together with the ingredients will give otherwise clear drinks a smooth misty look and a pleasant thin white head, without spoiling the taste.

When inventing your own cocktails, try to balance the flavours in the drink by combining something sweet (such as fruit liqueur) with something sharp or bitter (such as lemon juice). Most classic cocktails achieve this balance.

Rinse your shot glasses frequently. Spirits can taint each other or cloud your drink.

Remember, a 'dash' is four or five drops.

Try to avoid using plastic cocktail sticks as they tend to give a cocktail a slightly artificial appearance.

When using eggs, a handy way to separate yolk and white is to crack the egg in half on the edge of the glass. Pour the egg yolk from one half of the shell to the other, back and forth, until the white runs down into the glass and only the yolk is left in the shell.

Most shaken drinks that contain single cream can also be made as blended drinks, substituting vanilla ice cream for the single cream – a kind of alcoholic smoothie!

Shake any drinks made with juices, sugar, eggs, or cream, or use an electric blender.

No need to stir a drink that contains a carbonated mixer; it does most of its own mixing naturally by bubbling. If you think it needs a helping hand, give it two stirs – but no more.

Don't use soda in whisky – it ruins the taste.

Whisky evaporates very quickly so keep the cap tightly screwed on.

Open champagne without fuss by clamping the cork with a pair of nutcrackers and gently turning the bottle.

Up in Flames

It is always easier to flame brandy, or other high-alcohol spirits, by warming the glass first. Hold the glass by its stem above the flame or electric coil of your stove until it feels warm.

Do not allow the glass to touch the flame or coil, as this can char or crack the glass.

An impressive trick: light a little sambuca in a glass and then put your hand over the glass to extinguish the flame. When the flame goes out, the decrease in air temperature creates a strong suction on your hand – strong enough that you can shake your hand around without the glass falling off.

It may sound obvious, but keep your head away from the cocktail glass when flaming spirits! Many an eyebrow has been lost this way…

The Aftermath

Keep the fizz in an unfinished bottle of champagne by hanging a silver teaspoon, handle downwards, in the neck and keeping the bottle in the fridge. It should last a couple of days.

If you find cocktails often leave you with a nasty hangover, try drinking cocktails with fresh fruit juice in them. The juice will replace the vitamins your body loses through drinking, and the fructose will help to absorb the alcohol.

Prevent hangovers by eating a spoonful of coleslaw before bed. (Honest!)

The prairie oyster is an ideal hangover cure. Rinse a glass with olive oil. Add tomato ketchup and a whole egg yolk. Season with Worcestershire sauce, vinegar, salt and pepper. Swallow the mixture in one gulp.

When cleaning ashtrays after a long night, try using soda water. The bubbles will help to shift the ash, so you don't have to wipe them.

COMPUTER CONSULTANTS

Harry Sanders; Sue Bresnahan

Travels with a Laptop

Make sure your computer is insured. If it's only insured as part of your house contents, it may not be covered for travel.

Back up all data before you set off.

Carry your disks separately from your machine.

Make sure your system is password protected.

Display your name, address (including postcode) and phone somewhere obvious inside the carry case. Also, postcode your machine using ultraviolet-sensitive ink.

Never allow your computer to go in the luggage hold. If you get a reasonable-sized carrying case, you can use it for your other hand-luggage, such as passports, wallet and so on.

Do not allow your computer or any disks to pass through a security X-ray machine, but be prepared to switch it on for airport security staff, to prove that it really is a computer.

Don't carry floppies through a metal detector. Hand them to security staff and collect them on the other side.

Make sure you have an adapter and appropriate transformer for running your machine at different voltages abroad.

Laptops are very nickable, so try disguising it by popping it in a normal overnight bag, well padded with clothes.

Keep a floppy in the disk drive to prevent dust from getting in.

Security & Safety

When you take delivery of new computers, either at work or at home, don't put stacks of empty computer boxes outside on bin day – it advertises to thieves that there are new machines inside.

Try to avoid leaving computers near windows – for a start it's not good for them to get too much sun, and it makes it too easy for thieves to see what you've got.

Take software out of boxes and keep disks in a different place to manuals. It makes them far less attractive to thieves who can sell boxed sets with instruction manuals at boot fairs.

Think about who has authorised access to your office. Contract cleaners are there out of hours and will not have been subject to the same security checks as your own staff.

Be careful about loading free samples of software. They are often time-limited, can take up an awful lot of memory space and may be hard to remove.

If a floppy disk can't be read, try taking it out of the drive and tapping the edge of the disk sharply on your finger. Replace and try again.

If your hard disk is four years old or more, make sure you back up everything on it frequently. Statistics indicate that it's more than 50 per cent likely to go wrong at this age.

Don't use your mouse with your arm straight and your elbow locked – it can cause damage to your elbow. Move your seat and reposition yourself so you can keep your mouse arm relaxed.

Angle your screen so that there are no troublesome reflections from windows or lights.

Be very careful with magnets around computers. If a magnet comes into contact with your screen, the image can become completely distorted, and magnets can wipe floppy disks and other electronic media.

Cleaning Up

Clean a dirty mouse by taking it apart and wiping over with a cotton bud dipped in vodka or gin. If that doesn't work, drink the gin!

To get in between the keys on your computer use a small paint-brush or cotton bud.

Or use the smallest attachment on your vacuum cleaner to get up fluff, crumbs and debris from in between the keys.

If you spill a drink on to the keyboard, save your files, shut down using the mouse and turn off and unplug the computer. Turn the keyboard upside down over a towel to absorb any drips, and unscrew the two parts of the keyboard, keeping an eye on any loose parts. Soak up any moisture using a tissue and cotton bud in awkward places, then dry off with a hair-dryer on its coolest setting. Spray the interior of the keyboard lightly with WD40 before reassembling it.

Never spray cleaner directly on to a computer screen. Spray it on to a lint-free cloth first, then wipe over the screen with the cloth.

Try polishing off a bad scratch on a CD's playing surface with liquid metal polish. It has tiny abrasive particles. Rub it off with proprietary CD cleaner.

If you're getting rid of computers, bear in mind that they could be of use to other people. These organisations that are grateful for unwanted computers:

• Computers for Charity 01636 819043/ 01288 361177 – Paul Webster (pandpw@globalnet.co.uk)

• Jonathan Young Trust 0115 947 0493 – Armorel Young (young@lineone.net)

• Tech. for Special Children 0115 989 0212 – David Carlisle (jenny@carlisle.freeserve.co.uk)

CYCLISTS & BIKERS

Health & Comfort

Simon Matthews, Freewheel; Sandra Barnett

Get more power out of your legs – make sure your leg is straight when you reach the six o'clock position on the pedals.

Don't have your seat at too much of an angle – it should be flat.

Keep your tyres pumped up properly; squishy tyres make cycling harder work and it's much less efficient.

If you have a mountain bike with thick, chunky tyres that you use mainly on the roads – buy some road tyres!

When cycling long distances, wiggle your hands and fingers to avoid numbness.

If you get caught short when out cycling, use your cycle cape as an emergency portaloo.

If you're out in the wind and the rain without much protective gear, stick some newspaper, cardboard or even straw down your front and secure with a bungee cord round your middle. This should keep you nice and dry.

If it's raining, tuck a plastic bag under your saddle. When you reach your destination, you can use it to cover your seat. At least you'll have a dry bottom on your return journey.

Take some kitchen foil with you to cover the seat in case it rains.

When cycling in the hills you can stuff an old magazine up your shirt to stop the air flow cooling down the sweat on your body.

A cycling tip for men only – take a third sock with you when you go cycling in the winter to keep your crown jewels warm (impresses the girls as well).

If you are out touring, make sure you eat little and often, and drink liquid regularly.

Loading up panniers can be a pain, so take two guy ropes and peg one end to the ground and the other end to the bike. Secure both ropes so that the bike stands upright, keeping the panniers off the muddy, damp ground. You can then pack each pannier more easily.

Safety & Security

Be noticed! Now is the time to wear that loud sweater or silly hat.

Covering your bike with stickers is a great anti-theft device; it makes your bike instantly recognisable and difficult for the thieves to strip down.

If people keep stealing the quick release on your bike when you remove the saddle, hit it with a hammer until the thread jams.

For security, two locks are better than one.

Always lock your bike up at home – even if you keep it in a garage or shed.

Don't put the lock on your bike so that it is easy for you to remove – it makes it too easy for the thief as well.

Don't position the lock near the ground because a thief is less obvious to passers-by in this position.

When you're on a cycling holiday, take some dental floss for a washing line. You can also use it at night to tie between your leg and your bike – you'll soon know if anyone tries to nick your wheels.

To secure the bottom clip of your panniers, put a key-ring through the main bolt.

Cleaning & Repairing

For a cheap bike lever, use a spoon.

To check whether your valve is leaking, get a small jar of water and submerge the tip of the valve in the water. If there are air bubbles, the valve is not working properly and should be changed.

Rather than carrying a puncture kit around with you, carry a spare inner tube. Then, if you get a puncture, you can replace the inner tube and repair the old one at home where it's nice and dry and the light is good.

A bike needs to be lubricated once a month if it is being used regularly. Don't be tempted to substitute vegetable oil for bike oil because it can muck up the chain.

Clean the chain and cog system regularly – it will cost a few pennies but will save a fortune in maintenance and repairs in the long run.

Polish any metal and painted surfaces with household wax to stop rust.

To get rid of rust from bicycle-wheel rims, put some emery paper between the brake blocks. Turn the pedals and lightly apply the brakes.

Keep chrome looking shiny – polish with a little bicarbonate of soda on a damp cloth. Rinse off and dry.

If you get bike oil on your clothes, rub the stain with washing-up liquid and then wash as normal.

Tar and oil stains can be removed with toothpaste.

Keep your visor wipe handy – cut a tennis ball in half and tie it around the handle. It makes a great place to store a damp sponge, which you can use to keep your visor clean.

Protect your paintwork – put some sticky-back plastic on to the tank of your bike. It will stop the zips on your jacket and trousers from making scratches. The bike will be easier to sell if it isn't covered in marks.

DANCE INSTRUCTORS

Lucy Pankhurst; Sarah Cramer; Jane Hodgkin, www.jivestories.com; Don McAlpine

Taking Classes

If you don't seem flexible enough for a particular move, don't give yourself a hard time. It may not be lack of practice. The shape of your bones, and other structural differences, can affect your range of motion.

Muscles do not turn to fat when you stop exercising them. What actually happens is the strength of the muscle reduces and it feels softer. Muscle and fat are completely different tissues.

If you injure a muscle, tendon or joint, treat it by resting, applying an ice pack, compressing (applying a bandage or support) and elevating the affected area – remember this routine using the initials RICE.

No pain no gain is a bit drastic – muscular endurance can be increased with light resistance repetitions, and as a general rule, when you start to feel a burning sensation in your muscles, try five more repetitions.

Most people know that you shouldn't eat immediately before a class, but they don't know that this is because during exercise the blood supply to inactive areas, like the digestive system, is reduced to supply more blood to the muscle. If you have just eaten, blood flow to the digestive system is increased, depriving the muscles of an essential blood supply.

It's often best to do class in close-fitting clothes so your teacher can see whether the right muscle groups are working. With loose clothes, it may look right superficially, but the underlying movement itself may be quite wrong.

Having a cold can affect your balance, as the ear canals may become infected. This means that the feedback of information on position and balance to the nervous system can become distorted.

If you don't like performing under blinding lights because you can't see what you're doing, practise with your eyes closed. This strengthens your understanding and reliance on the receptors in your skin, which are sensitive to pressure, and send messages telling the brain where the body weight is placed.

As much as possible, relax and allow your natural reflexes to work, because when you think too much you can start to build up stress and tension.

If you rehearse or perform in trainers, always wear 100 per cent cotton socks to prevent blisters, fungal infections and other nasties.

Just because you look thin doesn't mean you are healthy. Snack-based, high-fat diets may keep you slim, but only because they produce under-developed muscles, which leave space for a substantial layer of fat on a seemingly slim body.

Treat your body like an athlete's, by eating four to six small meals a day and combining all the right food groups to give you the energy you need.

The simple truth is that most dance disciplines never stop hurting. For example pointe work might hurt when you start learning, but it won't stop hurting when you're a professional. It might hurt less, but in performance or training, a dancer is always striving to be better, so you will keep pushing your body to the limit, though those limits might change.

Especially in modern or contemporary dance, there is a lot of physical contact, with lifting, turning and rolling. This makes personal hygiene especially important. Dance kits should be washed every time you wear them.

It can be hard doing very intimate physical work with someone you barely know, and just as difficult if you do know the person. You have to learn to think of them as a body, and a part of the dance, rather than as a person.

Instead of just copying the instructor, try to understand the link between the mind and the body, as this can improve co-ordination. Use feelings to accompany body movement, for example, imagine the feeling of trying to avoid hundreds of pins on the floor, and move accordingly. Or try visual imagery – drawing a picture in your mind of the space or shape your body needs to move within.

If you have trouble learning a step, walk it through in your mind over and over after the class. Even if you get back to class and you've still got it wrong, you've got a context for putting it right.

Use your kitchen or any space you can to practise. Even if you can't get the steps right on your own, the process of practising and being used to moving still improves your dancing.

Always have a count in your head, relating to the beat of the music. To learn a step, weave into the count a reminder of the step you should be doing on each beat: 'one, two, forward, side'.

Joined-up Dancing

If you are dancing socially and want to ask someone to dance, watch them for a while first to see what they're doing, as you have to be able to match your style to theirs. It might take a couple of dances to understand their style.

If you're a woman following the man's lead in a partner dance, you have to learn to concentrate on what your partner is doing. Watch and feel for the physical signs your partner is giving you, but at the same time, relax, and try not to anticipate what's coming next, or you could end up making a wrong assumption.

It can be daunting at first to lead a partner dance. Break the dance down in your mind, and have a few sequences ready. You can look great by recycling just a few steps in different combinations.

Remember you can always mark time by going back to the basic step – you will always look good if you do it with energy and conviction.

Dancing a lot in high heels can damage your lower back, so wear flats whenever possible to compensate.

If you're going out dancing, you know you will get hot and sweaty, so when you're choosing your outfits, buy two or three tops the same, and nip to the loo to change in the middle of the evening.

If you're not very fit, remember that you don't have to join a dance right at the beginning – you can wait 20 or 30 seconds, then join.

Always think about your stomach muscles. Hold them straight, and you will look alert and poised without looking rigid. Make sure you can still breathe, though.

If a dance includes the woman turning under the man's arm, the woman should keep her head up so she looks confident, rather than ducking under his arm apologetically. If you are a tall woman, raise your arm higher to do this, as it also raises the man's arm.

The popular myth that the man should always be taller or the couple won't be able to dance well is untrue. Don't worry if you're a short man or a tall woman; if you're both dancing well, you will both look good.

Turn your head quickly back to face your partner by turning your head faster than the rest of your body. This also stops you feeling dizzy.

To hold yourself straight while turning, feel your body as a column above the foot you're turning on.

It actually takes very little energy to spin on one foot. If you put too much energy behind it, you can lose your balance. Use your partner's energy when they push you into a turn.

DENTISTS

Clare Baines; British Dental Association

Cleaning

Get the last scrape out of a tube of toothpaste by cutting the tube across the middle with scissors – you can usually get enough for at least another day.

Every time you eat sugary foods, bacteria in plaque react to form acids that will attack the enamel of your teeth for up to an hour afterwards. This means it's better to eat a bag of sweets all in one go than to spread them out over a few hours.

Chewing sugar-free gum after a meal really does help by producing more saliva that helps to neutralise the ph in the mouth.

Eating alkaline foods, such as cheese, after a meal also helps to neutralise the damaging acids and can help prevent decay.

Brush before breakfast rather than after. Eating and drinking weaken enamel and brushing straight afterwards can remove tiny pieces of enamel and cumulatively cause damage to the teeth. Leave at least half an hour between eating or drinking and brushing.

Brushing before bed is particularly important because saliva flow decreases at night.

Don't use too much toothpaste. For age seven and over, a pea-sized amount is quite enough. Below the age of seven, just a little dab is sufficient.

Only floss the teeth you want to keep!

Floss once a day, every day. It's no use telling your dentist that you floss if you don't – we can tell!

If you suffer from bad breath, try brushing your gums and tongue at the same time as your teeth.

Bleeding gums is not a reason to stop flossing – on the contrary, it's a sign that you really need to do it regularly.

Don't take fluoride tablets or give them to children without checking with your dentist first.

Acid in fruit juice and fizzy drinks can erode the enamel on your teeth. To reduce this effect, drink through a straw and don't brush your teeth for about half an hour after having them.

To reduce discomfort from sensitive teeth, try applying some sensitive toothpaste around the base of the tooth and to the gum after brushing, and leave it there.

Emergencies

If a second tooth is knocked out whole, try and re-implant it immediately, making sure you get it the right way round!

If you can't re-implant it, store it in some milk and get to a dentist straight away.

If no milk is available, tuck it inside your cheek, up next to the gum, and get to a dentist straight away.

If you have a broken tooth and can't see a dentist straight away, you can minimise scratching to the tongue and the inside of the mouth by taking a little piece of wax from an Edam (or similar) cheese, rolling it up and placing it on the jagged tooth.

You can temporarily fix a broken-off crown by using sugar-free gum or denture fixative.

Denture wearers are at greater risk of oral thrush. To avoid infection, leave dentures out at night and eat plenty of live yoghurt.

If you have toothache, an anti-inflammatory painkiller, such as ibuprofen will give greater pain relief than paracetamol.

Don't put crushed aspirin around a sore tooth – it can lead to an 'aspirin burn' inside the mouth.

For abscesses, don't place a hot-water bottle against your face, as it's likely to lead to a greater build-up of pus.

If you have an abscess and your face is swollen, hold hot, salty water inside your mouth to encourage the abscess to drain into the mouth. Spit, rinse and repeat.

DIY EXPERTS

Roger Staples; Bob
Coltman; Tony Page

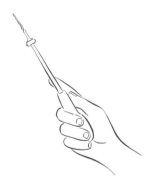

Ease a stiff lock by puffing powdered graphite into it, or by rubbing a key over an ordinary pencil lead.

To get a screw into an awkward position, stick it to the screwdriver with a blob of Blu-Tak.

Remove a rawlplug by putting a screw in about halfway, then using pliers to pull both out together.

Buy small amounts of sand from a pet shop or a builders' merchant. The sand is useful for supporting broken objects so that you can mend them.

To mend a tile, place it on a piece of paper, and apply glue to both broken surfaces. Press these together, and then tape the tile to the work surface to hold the two pieces in place.

When mending glass, like the stem of a wine glass, place the glass upside down and press a piece of putty or plasticine firmly at the point of the break so it can support the glass stem. Glue the two parts together and press the plasticine against the join to support the two parts and leave to dry.

To glue a broken plate, support one part of the plate by standing it in a drawer and closing the drawer against it. This will hold the plate securely while you fix the two parts together.

Rubber bands or tape will also work well to hold two parts of broken china together while they bond.

When finishing off tiling, run a thin piece of dowelling over each grout line – use the blunt end of a pencil or a lolly stick if you don't have dowelling.

When drilling a tile, stick a piece of masking tape or sticky tape over the area where you are going to drill.

If the drill wanders a bit, don't try to put the mistake right by drilling another hole close by. File the hole in the bracket into an oval shape, which will take the screw.

Alternatively, glue the back of the bracket with epoxy resin and fix it to the wall using only one screw.

DOG BREEDERS & TRAINERS

Choosing a Dog

Helen Louise Johnston; Tracy St Clair Pearce; Lynn Bourne; Jude Simmons; Deborah Bragg, canine@behaviour. freewire.net

Having a dog takes commitment – work out how much time you can give a dog, where to exercise it and how to clean up after it. What shape and size of dog will suit your family? Dogs cost money – the bigger the dog, the more money! All dog owners have to pay for visits to the vet, inoculations and food; some will pay for insurance and kennel fees, too.

When choosing the sex of your dog, remember that young un-neutered males can wreak havoc when they go into sexual overdrive. Bitches go on heat twice a year so need to be watched carefully unless you don't mind the inevitable attention of all the neighbouring male dogs and subsequent pregnancies.

Pedigree dogs should be bought from a recognised breeder. Like cars, pedigree dogs come with documents that certify its breeding and confirm its vaccination record.

Cross breeds are cheaper than pedigree dogs and are often less likely to inherit the diseases and ailments that pure pedigree dogs can suffer from.

Show dogs require a lot of attention. They need to be groomed daily and be incredibly well trained.

Working dogs need a lot of exercise and a larger diet than house dogs.

Lap dogs need a lot of exercise because they are usually active breeds, but they won't eat you out of house and home.

Guard dogs give security and protection, but you must be an experienced dog handler and know what the legal requirements are for owning such a dog.

It is illegal to deny a blind person guided by a dog access to any public place. These dogs are usually better behaved than most people.

Labradors, golden retrievers and German shepherds are the most popular breeds for guide dogs. They are generally intelligent, hard workers, large enough to fit a harness and small enough to be controlled.

Hearing dogs are used to alert their owner to a variety of sounds, such as the doorbell, smoke alarms, crying babies and so on.

Puppies

When you bring a puppy home, check that there are no holes or gaps in your fence where it can escape. Pick up all small items that could be swallowed. Have the puppy's bed ready because it will be tired after all the excitement.

Make your puppy feel secure – this will be the first time it has been away from its mother. A quiet spot indoors, with a small pen that it can't escape from at night, is a good idea. Place a cardboard box inside, lined with an old jumper wrapped round a warm hot-water bottle. Put a good wad of newspaper nearby so it won't soil its bedding.

To keep a lonely puppy happy, especially at night, leave a ticking clock nearby. It will be like the beating of its mother's heart so it'll feel more secure.

Decide where the puppy's toilet is going to be in advance of its arrival. Take the puppy there as often as possible. Look for signs that it wants to go (whining, circling, snuffling) and praise it to the skies when it does it in the right place! Don't punish the puppy or rub its nose in it if it makes a mistake – it won't understand.

Healthy puppies are happy to be picked up and should feel firm and heavy.

Watch a puppy interact with the rest of its litter; this should give you a good idea as to its temperament.

When choosing a puppy, check its ears – they should be pink inside with no crusty or waxy discharge (this indicates the presence of mites).

Also look at its eyes; they should be clear and bright, free from any discharge. If the puppy keeps pawing at its eyes, this could mean it has some sort of inflammation or irritation.

A puppy's teeth and gums should be pink (or black and pink) and not smelly.

Check your puppy's skin for oiliness or flakiness. There shouldn't be any sores or lumps. If you run your hand against the lie of the coat, you can check for any parasites.

A puppy's bottom should be clean and dry with no signs of discharge or diarrhoea. If the puppy keeps dragging its bottom along the floor, it could mean it's got blocked anal glands.

Get your puppy used to being picked up and carried. Don't pounce on it, but reassure it first before holding it firmly but comfortably. Put one hand under the puppy's chest and the other under its rump.

Tag your dog as soon as you get it home. More and more vets have the facility to place a microchip under the dog's skin.

Get your puppy used to wearing a collar. Put its first collar on for short periods each day. If you can't be around to keep an eye on your puppy, remove the collar.

When fitting a dog with a collar, you should be able to slip two fingers under the collar.

Puppies need to eat three or four times a day. Once they are six months old, you can reduce that to two feeds a day. When they are between six and nine months old, they can go on to adult dog food.

A crate makes a safe and secure home for a puppy especially if you keep it in a busy area of the home. It's somewhere for the dog to retreat to. Puppies are less likely to make a mess in their sleeping area, so it helps when it comes to house-training.

Never leave a dog in a crate for more than two or three hours a day.

A crate is for security, not for punishment. It's somewhere for your dog to want to go, not be afraid of.

Put the dog bed in a busy part of your home, such as the kitchen.

Cleanliness

Incontinent dogs can make your house smell awful. Put some bicarbonate of soda in their drinking water to reduce the smell of their urine.

If your dog wees on the carpet by accident, don't apply disinfectant: it reacts badly with ammonia and could leave a mark. Instead, try using a soda siphon, and keep blotting the stain until dry. Sprinkle on some baking soda and leave for about quarter of an hour. Vacuum afterwards.

Don't use products that contain ammonia to clean up a dog's mess because it can remind a dog of the smell of its own urine. If a dog can smell its own odour, it will return to that spot and use it again.

Don't buy expensive pooper scoopers – plastic bags over your hand work just as well.

If your dog is in the habit of eating its own poo, try to break this bad habit by sprinkling its latest offering with a hot, peppery sauce.

When your dog has rolled in something unpleasant, wash it with tomato ketchup instead of shampoo. It gets rid of the strongest smells.

Prevent your dog from walking clumps of mud into the house – keep its paws trimmed.

If your dog always jumps out of the tub at bath time, leave its collar and lead on. Hook the lead over the taps. It will know it can't escape and bath time will be less of a struggle for both of you.

Stop your dog from scratching the bath – put a non-slip mat down. The dog can keep its grip and your bath is protected at the same time.

To protect your clothes when bathing your dog wear a bin liner with three holes cut out for your arms and head.

Put dog shampoo in a squeezy bottle and dilute with 50 per cent water. Just squirt it out and the thinner mixture will spread evenly through its coat, avoiding great clumps of bubbles that can be difficult to rinse out.

Use baby shampoo if you don't have any dog shampoo.

To get rid of fleas, start shampooing from both ends of your dog at the same time. The fleas get trapped in the middle and have nowhere to run to!

Discourage fleas with a dash of cider vinegar in the final rinse at bath time.

Add a couple of drops of tea tree oil to some water and sponge your dog's coat. This will get rid of fleas.

The best time to trim a dog's nails is after its bath when they are softer than normal. Don't cut into the pink area of the nail because this is living tissue. If you're not sure where to cut, ask your vet to show you.

Some dogs have the kind of faces that trap dirt and debris – the more wrinkly they are, the more they need keeping clean. Use damp cotton-wool balls to clean out the folds of skin.

Plug your dog's ears with cotton wool when you give it a bath.

Avoid getting shampoo in your dog's eyes and mouth.

After its bath, dry your dog's head first. This is the first thing it will shake so it saves you from getting soaked.

To dry your dog quickly, use a chamois leather. This also makes silky haired dogs lovely and shiny.

You can use a hair-dryer to dry a wet dog, but only if it has healthy skin. Heat tends to aggravate sensitive skin.

If your dog won't stand still while you groom it, put something tasty on the door of your fridge or oven and let your dog lick it off while you get on with the grooming.

Use a non-slip mat to stand your dog on while you groom it.

Grooming is a great opportunity to check your dog for any parasites, sores, bumps and bruises.

Long-coated dogs need their hair brushing daily, and need regular trims.

Some long-haired dogs with silky coats don't have a downy undercoat so need to be groomed carefully so that their skin isn't scratched.

Long-haired dogs should be groomed for at least 15 minutes in order to keep their coats in good condition and looking tidy. Pay attention to particular areas such as under their legs (where hair can get matted), between the toes and on the hind legs.

Dogs with a wiry coat have to be 'hand stripped' every month: pull the dead hair out with your fingers, always going in the direction of the hair's growth.

Curly coats must be clipped every two months to keep them under control.

Smooth-coated dogs are the easiest to look after and only require a weekly brushing.

A chamois leather will bring out the shine on a smooth-coated dog.

Over 75 per cent of dogs require dental attention so keep your dog's teeth clean. Bad breath is often the first sign of a problem.

It's tricky to clean a dog's teeth. Make it easy by wrapping a fabric plaster around one finger and dabbing on some bicarbonate of soda. Use your finger as a toothbrush.

Discipline

Tone of voice is important – dogs will learn to associate your tone of voice with their behaviour. It will soon learn that your stern tone after it has done something wrong isn't much fun. Be clear about the signals you're giving.

To assert your authority, never let a dog go through the door before you. It must know who's boss.

Reinforce a dog's respect for you by ensuring that it is never higher up than you are. Sofas and beds should always be out of bounds.

Do not comfort your dog in a thunderstorm or when fireworks are going off as it will perceive you as being frightened which will in turn make it frightened.

A dog should obey you because you are in charge not because it's frightened of you. Punishment is acceptable as long as it doesn't terrify or hurt the dog.

If you have two or more dogs and one is clearly the boss, do not try to re-arrange the pack order. Instead, enhance its superior status by feeding and greeting it first.

Dogs cannot experience guilt as we understand it. Therefore, it is utterly pointless telling a dog off for trashing the house in your absence since it cannot associate the devastation with its own actions. It looks 'guilty' (slinks under the table) because it has learned to associate its owner with an angry mood when he or she walks in the door.

Catch your dog in the act and then punish it. It's no good punishing it a few minutes afterwards because it won't realise what it's being punished for and will just become confused.

Never hit a dog across the nose – instead, grab it on both sides of the head and growl at it. Mother dogs growl at their offspring and it works a treat.

Don't call a dog over to you to be punished because it will start to associate your call with punishment. Always go over to a dog to admonish it if it has done something wrong.

Never use a lead to punish a dog.

Don't force a puppy's training – ten minutes at a time is about all they can take. Always make it fun for them.

Never train a well-fed puppy – a full tummy means a sleepy mind and the puppy won't be able to concentrate on learning.

When training a puppy or new dog, use a long training lead for outdoors and a long, light house-line for indoors.

It's best to conduct training sessions in quiet places, away from people if that's possible. You don't want your dog to be distracted while it's learning.

Try to finish your training sessions on a positive note. Always encourage your dog.

After your dog has had a training session, follow up the hard work with a bit of play.

Enforce your training commands with praise, physical reassurance and an immediate reward.

Teach your dog to sit to command with a small titbit. Hold slightly below the line of vision and command 'Sit'. Dogs sit down automatically to get a better sight of the titbit.

Gradually reduce the reward treats as training progresses, so that your dog reacts to your voice and body language rather than bribes.

Don't bother with a training session if you or your dog is tired – it will just be a waste of time.

The first thing a dog learns is usually the command 'sit' or 'come'. Start training on the lead. Practice makes perfect.

When using a choke or check chain, keep your dog on your left side.

If your dog is a bit bold or too fearful, fit it with a head halter. Then if it pulls, its own momentum pulls the head down and the jaws shut. This is an alternative to a check chain.

A check or choke chain is ideal for bouncy dogs or ones with a rather short attention span. Make sure you don't put the collar on backwards because this can cause discomfort when it tightens. In the right position, the chain only tightens when tension is applied.

If your dog has to wear a muzzle, make sure that it can open its jaws and pant while the muzzle is on.

Fights usually happen between dogs of the same size, sex and age. When your dog meets another, keep the lead fairly loose (a taut lead encourages aggression) and offer praise when it just sniffs the other dog.

If your dog gets too excited when you get its lead, put the lead back where you keep it and sit down. After a couple of times, it won't get so excited.

A dog that constantly pulls on its lead is a nuisance. Try filling a tin with pebbles to rattle next to its ear every time it pulls.

A bored dog can often indulge in destructive behaviour so it's a good idea to channel its frustration into something such as playing tug of war. Make sure you always win though, you are the dominant one in this partnership, so don't start to play until you've taught it to drop an object on your command.

Keep your dog occupied for hours – make a hole in a rubber dog toy and fill it with dog treats.

Make your own chewy toy – take a hollow bone, sterilise it and then fill it with cheese spread. Show it to your dog and leave it to make a start; it'll have a busy, happy time trying to reach the food.

Train your dog to run to heel so you both get a bit of exercise.

If your puppy has the habit of running off, try hiding. Then call it to you. It won't be able to find you when it returns – it will be worried and stay closer next time!

Dogs that go roaming do so because the experience is rewarding – they can go through people's dustbins, chase cats and so on. Telling the dog off when it returns will do no good and may actually make it more reluctant to return. Better still, ensure that the dog does not have the opportunity to take itself for a walk.

If your dog creeps up on to the sofa when it shouldn't, put a couple of whoopee cushions on the seat. The unexpected noise will deter it from doing it again.

If your dog steals food from kitchen surfaces, make a booby trap by tying a chicken carcass to a string of tin cans or similar noisy objects. When the dog steals the carcass, the shock of the noise that follows will soon teach it restraint.

Incessant barking can be hard to deal with. Squirt water in your dog's face whenever it barks and it will soon stop.

To stop a small dog from yapping, hold it up at arm's length.

If your dog barks incessantly at people walking past the house, do not yell at it to shut up – it will think you are joining in and bark louder! Instead, say 'sshhh' in a very soft voice or leave the room.

If your dog keeps digging holes in your lawn or flowerbeds, fill a sock with pebbles. As your dog starts to dig, throw the sock out of an upstairs window so that it lands near the dog – not on it! It won't know where it came from but will associate the unwelcome shock with digging and soon give it up.

Some dogs dig up newly planted shrubs because they have been planted with bone-meal or chicken manure in the planting hole. Try using a seaweed-based plant food instead.

If your dog starts to chew the furniture, paint on anti-nail-biting fluid or oil of cloves. Better still, if you can catch it in the act, throw a cushion or something that makes a loud noise to startle it.

Stop your dog from chewing furniture by rubbing vapour rub on to the chewed places. The smell lasts for weeks and dogs hate it.

Don't allow your dog to play with old shoes or clothes because they'll assume it's acceptable to chew any shoe or item of clothing.

If your dog likes rummaging around rubbish bins, sprinkle the area with pepper to deter it.

Make sure you keep the lids on bins to deter your dog from having a poke around.

If your dog won't let go of the television remote control (or any other object), get up, ring the doorbell and the dog should drop whatever it has in its mouth and run to the door. Grab the remote (or whatever) before it comes back.

Owners inadvertently encourage their dogs to jump up by telling them to get down. The words are irrelevant: all the dog sees is a response to its enthusiasm. So don't say a word, shrug the dog off and refuse to greet it until it has four paws firmly on the floor.

Keep food treats by the door. Visitors can then feed your dog if it's good and doesn't jump up at them when they enter the house.

Don't give in to begging. It can often become a habit with dogs, especially if they are bored. If you pander to their whims, you'll just reinforce the bad habit and get a fat dog.

Train your dog to eat always from its bowl, which should be kept well away from where you and the family eat.

If your dog doesn't like travelling in the car, sit with it on the back seat, leave the engine running while you do so and just read the paper for a while. The dog will soon learn to relax.

For dogs that suffer from travel sickness, try children's travel sickness tablets. Half a tablet for puppies and a whole one for fully adult dogs.

Alternatively, try sitting your dog on newspaper during journeys.

Also sit the dog in a stationary car with the windows slightly open. Then travel a few yards so the dog gets used to the movement. Do this regularly over a fortnight, gradually increasing the speed and distance travelled until your dog is accustomed to the motion of the car.

If you don't have a car grille or special safety belt for dogs, tie its lead to the seat-belt anchor so that your dog can't move around too much while you're driving.

If you are about to bring a new baby home, let the dog smell something of the baby's, like a blanket or vest, before the arrival.

Introduce your dog to the baby and not the other way round. You are introducing a new member to the 'pack'. Hold the baby on your lap and let your dog have a good smell.

When the baby is home, try to keep the dog's routine the same, so you go for walks at the same time, it gets fed as normal and so on.

When introducing a child to your dog, make sure they stroke the dog on its side, not its front (dogs can interpret that as an aggressive gesture). Dogs and children should always be introduced to each other in the presence of an adult.

Explain to children that they must never rush up to a dog, shout at it or pat it on its head.

Sniffing the ground is a sign that a dog wants to relieve itself. If you're in the throes of house-training, you will have a very short time to get the dog or puppy on to the newspaper that you should always have at hand.

Keep some of the soiled newspaper around to show your dog or puppy, so it can smell where it's been and this will encourage it to use the same spot again.

Don't punish a dog for making a mess in the house – it will only make it more nervous and prone to more accidents.

Train a puppy to relieve itself outdoors as soon as possible. Use the garden first where you can easily remove any mess before moving out to a suitable public place where you can poop-scoop away the evidence.

Walking a dog helps to stimulate it to relieve itself. Always keep your dog on its lead until it has done its business; then let it off its lead to play. It will soon come to realise that it has to poo before playing.

While your dog is relieving itself, say 'hurry up'. As soon as it's finished, praise it. Your dog will soon start to relieve itself on your 'hurry up'.

When a new litter arrives, place a piece of cloth in the bed with their mother. As the puppies leave for new homes, cut the cloth into strips and send one away with each puppy as a comforter.

Health

If your dog keeps licking a wound, try rubbing vapour rub near the sore (not on it).

Fleas hate garlic so drop a garlic capsule into your dog's feed to rid it of troublesome guests.

To get your dog to swallow a pill, cover the tablet with butter. Your dog will love the taste and the pill will slip down easily. Or try hiding the pill in some cheese or meat.

For dogs with a sweet tooth, cover a pill with melted chocolate.

When giving a pill to a dog, you should go to the dog rather than call it to you.

If your dog has an upset tummy, feed it some bio-yoghurt mixed with a little honey to settle it.

When your dog is teething and about to lose a tooth, give it an ice cube to chew. The tooth will fall out and the cold will ease any pain.

To feed a sick dog, treat it as you would a puppy. Give it three or four small meals a day.

A good meal for a recuperating dog or very young puppy is a bowl of lightly scrambled eggs.

If your sick dog refuses to eat solid food, try it with some gravy broth in a saucer.

If your dog hasn't eaten for 24 hours, take it to the vet.

Spaying doesn't make a bitch fat – eating too much food is the only thing that will make her overweight.

If your dog needs to go on a diet, try to give it around 60 per cent of its normal calorie intake.

Overweight dogs benefit from increased daily exercise.

Dogs cannot live on meat alone – make sure you vary their diet, mixing meat with cereals, vegetables, pasta and rice.

Dogs can eat their 'greens' as well as humans: cabbage, potatoes and carrots are all part of a well-balanced diet.

Want to go vegetarian? It can be done, but talk to your vet about getting the right balance at mealtimes.

Chicken is easy to digest and much lower in calories than other doggy meals.

Dried foods have four times as many calories as canned food, so always serve in small quantities. These foods shouldn't be confused with dog biscuits, which are mainly cereal.

For a high-fat content, try serving heart (it has double the calories of kidneys).

Dogs' food should contain protein for growth, fatty acids for a healthy coat and carbohydrates for bulk and bowel movements.

Don't be tempted to substitute dog food with cat food – it's too high in protein for a dog.

Pasta is a good carbohydrate source, but might need to be flavoured before you serve it up.

Serve dog food at room temperature.

If your dog hasn't eaten its canned or wet food after 15 minutes, remove the food and give it a new serving at the next mealtime.

A low-protein diet can help an incontinent dog. Offer cooked chicken, fish and vegetables.

Gnawing on bones is an ideal way to exercise jaw muscles and massage gums. Beef shin or knuckle bones are the best option because they are less likely to splinter.

Dog chews have fewer calories than bones and are often a more convenient (and pleasant) alternative.

Always keep the water bowl clean and refill it each day.

The best kind of feeding bowl is made from stainless steel with a bottom rimmed with rubber to stop it from sliding all over the floor. Ceramic bowls can get chipped and harbour bacteria.

Don't treat your dog like a dustbin. Giving it food it's not used to can lead to stomach upsets. Stick to pet treats instead.

Small dogs have small stomachs so feed them small amounts twice a day.

Pregnant dogs need to eat up to 50 per cent more food.

Old dogs should be fed little and often.

If your dog suffers from incontinence, try fitting it with some disposable toddler training pants (with a hole cut for its tail).

Alternatively, you could try giving cold boiled water.

When travelling, don't feed your dog just before a journey; you don't want to see the meal reappear.

During a long journey, stop every two to three hours to give your dog the chance to stretch its legs, relieve itself and have a drink.

A hot car – in summer or winter – can be a death-trap. Never leave your dog unattended in warm weather or with the heater on.

Excessive panting and drooling can be a sign that your dog is overheated. If this happens, move your dog at once to a cooler spot. Get rid of any excess saliva to help it breathe. Sponge its face with cool water before giving it a drink. If things look really bad, wrap it in a cool, wet towel.

For sea dogs (or any dogs that are going by water) it's worth investing in a dog's life jacket. Dogs can swim, but may drown if they get exhausted.

DRESS AGENCY OWNERS

Roberta Gibbs, Bertie Golightly, 48 Beauchamp Place (near Harrods), London

Don't put clothes away as soon as you've taken them off. Leave them out overnight, hanging over a chair or on the back of a door, then put them away the next day.

Linen has to be steam ironed. There's no getting away from it, and there's no such thing as easy-care linen either!

Remove belts before you hang up your dresses – they pull them all out of shape.

Silk is tough – they used to make parachutes out of it. Hand wash it and it will last you for years.

Get shoes fixed before they need it. They'll last much longer.

Empty everything from your handbag every night. This makes sure you only take with you what you really need (credit cards, lipstick and tampons), and that you sort out paperwork that otherwise accumulates in the depths.

Winter-weight leather handbags will come out of storage looking like new if you apply a leather feed at the end of the season. When you want to use them again, just polish them up.

Remove really fancy buttons and metal trims before you consign your clothes to the dry cleaner.

Cover buttons with tin foil before you send garments for dry cleaning – it'll protect them from damage.

An old double duvet cover is perfect for protecting a wedding dress.

Never use metal hangers from the dry cleaner. Use them to make topiary forms – it's all they're good for – and buy some wooden ones for your clothes.

Always store hats in boxes or on hat stands.

Keep jackets and long-sleeved dresses looking like new by stuffing the sleeves with scrumpled-up tissue paper.

Never put woollens away dirty. Moths always attack stains first.

Pack cleaned woollens away with cedar balls to discourage moths, but replace them every year.

DRESSERS

Duncan Newman; Claire Hartley; Jimmy Flockhart; Joe Hobbs; Nujma Yousaf

Washing

For the best wash results, mix small and large items of clothing together so that they can move more freely during the wash.

Minimise the amount of detergent you use – always place it in a detergent ball so that it gets right into the wash and isn't wasted in the system.

Left-over detergent in fabric will attract dirt. Use slightly less than the manufacturer's recommended amount and if you think there's some left in the clothes after rinsing, give them an extra rinse.

To prevent soap scum, add a tablespoon of white vinegar to the rinsing water.

For really clean clothes, make sure your washing machine is clean. Fill the washer with warm water and pour in 1 gallon/4.5 litres of distilled vinegar. Run through an entire cycle. The vinegar cleans the hoses and cleans away soap scum.

If your machine overflows from too many suds, adding some fabric softener will get rid of the suds.

To eliminate lint, add one cup of white vinegar to the final rinse cycle.

Too many suds when hand washing? Sprinkle talcum powder on them and they will subside.

Stop tights and stockings from getting in a tangle during washing. Place them in an old pillow case or cushion cover. This works for delicate items as well.

Make a 'delicates' bag out of old net curtains for use in the washing machine.

To stop ladders in tights, starch the tights lightly before you wash them.

To make tights and stockings last longer, wet them thoroughly, wring out the excess water and then freeze them in a plastic bag. When you want to wear them, thaw them out and dry thoroughly.

If you're pushed for time and don't have a chance to mend tears and sew loose buttons, put garments in a pillow case so they don't tear further in the wash.

Don't ruin your best clothes in the wash. Zips, buttons, hooks and eyes, and poppers may cause damage to other items, so do them up first.

Put your woollies in a pillow case when you spin dry them to prevent them losing their shape.

Rinse washable wool garments in lukewarm water and add a few tablespoons of glycerine to keep them soft. It also helps to prevent itching.

If your jumper cuffs go baggy after washing, try dipping them in cold water then drying them with a very hot hair-dryer – they should shrink back to shape.

Wash teddy bears with carpet shampoo and then just fluff them up afterwards.

When washing silk, a couple of lumps of sugar added to the final rinse will give the silk more body and make life all the sweeter.

Wash silk garments after every wear, otherwise perspiration stains may be impossible to remove and will actually weaken the fabric.

If you're unsure whether a coloured garment will run, pop a white hanky in with the load to pick up any dye. If the hanky stays white, you're safe to wash these clothes with your whites.

Alternatively, to check whether an item is colour fast when dry, iron a corner of it between two white cloths. If any dye runs, you'll know it needs to be washed separately.

When soaking an item of clothing to remove a stain, always immerse the whole garment even if the stain itself is only small. This avoids a patchy result.

Keep tough stains away from hot water or steam. Lots of foods contain albumen, a protein that is fixed by heat. So tackle the stain first, before putting in a hot wash, for instance.

To remove rust stains, cover with salt. Rinse, then put some lemon juice over the stain. Leave for an hour and then wash.

One way to get bloodstains out of clothes, is to get the person whose blood it is to suck it off. Their own saliva should dissolve the blood. Tell that to Dracula!

To remove grass stains, place a clean cloth under the fabric and dab another cloth in methylated spirits. Clean the stain with a small circular movement, working from the centre outwards.

Use wet wipes to clean patent leather or bring a shine to your PVC trousers!

To clean white training shoes, rub with bathroom cleaner, buff and then wipe off with a rag.

Milk-stained clothes should be rinsed in cool water. Then washed in cold water using liquid detergent.

Remove fresh coffee stains by applying a mixture of egg yolk and glycerine to the area. Wash out with warm water.

Really grimy work clothes? Empty a can of Coca-Cola all over the clothes, add detergent and run through your regular wash cycle.

Dirty rings on shirt collars can be removed with oily hair shampoo – the principle is the same.

To remove sweat stains, spray with vinegar before washing.

As an extra measure on ground-in sweat, you can also add a couple of crushed aspirin tablets to the washing water.

White cotton socks gone a bit grey? Add a slice of lemon to the water and boil them for five minutes to restore whiteness.

To remove rain spots from suede, rub lightly with an emery board.

To remove grease spots from suede, dip a cloth in vinegar and blot out the stain. Brush with a suede brush to restore the nap.

As soon as dirt appears on your treasured sheepskin coat or suede jacket, get it cleaned. Ground in dirt will never come out.

Ballpoint pen on your best suede jacket or bag? Very carefully, try gently rubbing an emery board or fine sandpaper on the offending mark.

Drying

Turn white T-shirts and shirts inside out and, if possible, dry in the shade so that direct sunlight doesn't turn them yellow.

To ensure that the pleats stay in a pleated skirt while it's drying on a washing line, hang by the waistband and clip clothes pegs to the bottom of the pleats. (Dry all skirts by the waistband.)

Save space on the washing line, peg your socks and tights to a hanger and hang it on the line.

When drying socks on a line – peg them by the heels – this keeps the stretch in the right direction.

Instead of using bleach, leave newly washed clothes out in the sun to dry – the sun acts as a natural bleach.

Wash your clothes pegs once in a while – put them inside a pillow case in the machine to make sure the pegs don't leave dirty marks on clean washing.

Ironing

Start your ironing with items that need a cool iron. Gradually work through the ironing, finishing with items that need a hotter setting.

If your pile of ironing has become bone dry, pop it back into the tumble dryer with a wet towel for a minute. This will get the items slightly damp again and they will be easier to iron. If you don't have a tumble dryer, wrap them in a wet towel instead.

To remove fabric shine, dampen a cloth and wring out the excess water. Put this cloth on top of the shiny fabric and steam press. Do this several times, pressing the area until it is almost dry.

To iron velvet, fold a thick towel in two and place it over the reverse side of the velvet. The iron should only ever touch the towel and not the velvet itself.

To put a good, lasting crease in trousers, apply a thin line of paper glue along the inside of the crease and then iron it.

When ironing the collar of a shirt, go from one tip to the middle and then repeat. Never iron straight across the collar because this pushes the fibre across to one end and makes the collar uneven.

Iron on the reverse side of clothes to help them to retain their colour for longer.

Protect delicate buttons when ironing – place a metal spoon over them.

Avoid ironing altogether – silk and velvet will lose their creases if hung in a steamy bathroom.

Clean the bottom of your iron with wet wipes.

For a rusty iron, tie a piece of beeswax inside a rag and rub the iron when hot. Then rub with another rag sprinkled with salt.

Storing

A great way to keep trousers looking good is to do as sailors do, roll them up when you're not wearing them.

If you hang trousers on a wire coat hanger, put sheets of newspaper over the hanger first to avoid creasing.

Avoid creases – don't fold trousers over a hanger, peg them to the hanger by the ends of the legs.

If clothes keep falling off their hangers, put a rubber band around each end of the hanger.

Keep jackets in good shape by stuffing the arms with tissue paper or newspaper.

Roll up silk scarves inside loo-roll or kitchen-roll cardboard tubes.

Linen should be rolled up rather than folded to avoid excessive creasing.

Skirts will keep their pleats if you pack them lengthways in a pair of old tights.

If you're worried about damp in your cupboards, tie a handful of sticks of chalk together and hang them inside. They will absorb any moisture.

Moths don't like bay leaves, allspice berries or cedar chip so put some in your wardrobe.

Make your own pomander by sticking whole cloves into an orange. Then place a teaspoon of ground cinnamon and a teaspoon of orris root in a plastic bag along with the studded orange. Shake until the orange is coated all over. Store it in tissue paper for at least two weeks before hanging in your wardrobe.

Mending

Scuffs on high heels or shoes can be covered up using magic marker or felt-tip pen.

Clear nail-varnish stops ladders in tights from running.

If buttons have a habit of popping off, dab a bit of clear nail-varnish over the button thread to strengthen the fibres.

To mend a dropped hem in an emergency, use a stapler.

A fishing tackle box makes a good sewing box.

Use wax on ordinary thread to stop it sticking.

When threading a needle, don't use the end you have just cut from the reel because it will twirl and knot. Use the other end.

If your needle keeps sticking, rub some talcum powder over it.

Emergency mending kits should always include double-sided tape and safety pins.

Before you cut a button off a jacket, slip a comb underneath to protect the jacket.

If a button is to take a lot of weight, stitch another smaller one on the inside of the jacket to anchor the main button.

White line down your jeans? Mix some permanent blue ink with water until you've got the right shade. Paint down the line with a small brush and leave the jeans to dry.

To stop your jeans fading, soak them in a mixture of four tablespoons of vinegar and 8 pints/4.5 litres of water for about 30 minutes.

To dye satin or fabric shoes, use ordinary hand dye but add methylated spirits to the mixture.

Give leather shoes a radical new colour – paint them with acrylic paint.

Don't throw out unwanted shoulder pads from that 1980s power suit – they make great shoe stuffers, polishing pads and pin cushions.

Wearing

To prevent the fluff from your angora jumper getting all over the inside of a jacket, put the jumper in the freezer before wearing it.

Alternatively, give your mohair and angora woollies the occasional squirt of hair-spray to stop them from moulting.

Get rid of static electricity by running a wire coat hanger over the offending garment.

To get a jacket to hang straight, put pennies (or spare foreign coins) into the bottom of the hem.

To look after a jacket when driving, turn it inside out and place on the back seat of your car so that it doesn't get covered in fluff and muck.

If your shirt collar is too tight, move the button over. It won't be seen behind your tie.

To get rid of the shine from black trousers, brush them with black coffee and then press with a damp cloth.

When buying socks, wrap them round your clenched fist. If the heel just meets the toe, they will fit you perfectly.

If shoes are too tight, put damp newspaper in them or spray the outsides with water and leave to stretch.

To stretch canvas shoes, dampen them and then wear them. They will dry to fit your feet.

For extra emergency heat insulation, cut out a polystyrene shape to fit in the bottom of your shoes or boots.

Stop bras from rubbing by soaking them regularly in hair conditioner.

You can treat wigs with fabric conditioner. This also works on your own hair.

Stop blouses and shirts from escaping from the waistband of skirts and trousers. Sew the elastic from the top of some old stay-up stockings into the waistband.

Stop the end of a ribbon from fraying – put a drop of clear nail-varnish on the end.

Wash your make-up brushes and sponges regularly in washing-up liquid.

Get extra life from your roll-on deodorant – store it upside down and it will last much longer.

DRESSMAKERS

Equipment

Paula Carpenter;
Julia Dee;
Julie Weiner

Make things easy for yourself – put all your bits and bobs on a trolley so you can wheel it round with you and have everything to hand.

Keep different sized scissors in order – hang them from a row of hooks.

Fabric tape-measures often stretch. This can leave you with inaccurate measurements. For accuracy, buy a fibreglass or coated one.

Don't make your thread too long. The longer the thread, the more it gets weakened as it's drawn through the fabric. Shorter threads are less work – your arm doesn't have to move as much!

Put synthetic thread in the fridge for a couple of hours before you use it. This will stop it clinging to the fabric.

Always cut thread at an angle.

To keep loose embroidery threads tidy, cut strips off a cereal box, punch holes along one edge and put the threads through the holes. Use bulldog clips to hold the strips together.

Pins can damage delicate fabric. Use sticky tape instead.

To avoid messy or ragged edges scissors must always be razor-sharp.

Use an old tailor's trick and rub your needle along the side of your nose. It picks up just enough grease to 'oil' its passage through the fabric.

Keep your sewing machine needle sharp – stitch it through some fine sandpaper for a few inches.

Always keep a spool of clear thread for emergency repairs when you can't match any of your threads with a fabric.

If you're finding it hard to push the needle through a fabric, rub some soap over the cloth on the wrong side.

Making Clothes

When choosing a pattern, it's more important to get the right measurement for the bust than for the hips. The hip measurements are normally much easier to adjust.

When drawing patterns, especially tricky curves, be bold and draw quickly. You'll achieve a much smoother line than if you go at it more cautiously.

To achieve the best possible fit, start making adjustments at the neckline and shoulders, as these will affect the whole hang and style of a garment.

When trying a garment on, make it easier by putting it on inside out. Adjust it, tack it up and then try it on again the right way round.

A waistline will be much more flattering if it dips slightly at the back.

To make a small bust look fuller, use long darts round the chest area.

To prevent bra straps from showing fix Velcro strips to your bra and on the inside of the dress strap.

Fabrics like tartan and complicated checks will fray badly. Cut them with pinking shears to reduce the problem.

To choose a practical fabric, try squashing it in your hand to see how easily it will crease.

Don't ruin beautiful chintz. Always iron the reverse side to protect the special glaze.

Protect your fabrics (such as velvet or silk) by wrapping them around a tube rather than folding them. This will prevent creases.

When mending a small tear in very fine fabric, tape on some stiff paper behind the tear to stop the fabric from slipping.

Silk slips and slides, making pattern cutting a problem. Try putting an old cotton sheet underneath the silk to give it a firmer grip.

To make fur cuffs and collars neater, use a lightweight material for the inner layer.

To recycle your old dresses, cut off the skirt below the hip line, sew a hem, and wear it as a blouse.

If you have clothes you won't be wearing for a while, hang them up inside out.

Dressing-up Clothes

Get your children involved in helping to make dressing up clothes. It'll double the fun.

Don't throw out old sheets, curtains, worn-out clothes or off-cuts until you have explored all the possibilities for recycling them.

Even if the material you have doesn't look very promising, bear in mind that dye can transform a fabric beyond recognition.

Look out at jumble sales and in charity shops for suitable garments and fabrics.

Keep a selection of interesting buttons, particularly large or metallic ones.

For an instant Peter Pan or Robin Hood hat, cut a large padded envelope across from corner to corner. The piece with two closed edges can be painted green and, once you've attached a feather, you'll be off to Never-land.

An old tail jacket makes a great ring-master's outfit.

Shirring elastic sewn on the outside of a black T-shirt gives a cobweb effect for Halloween.

Make a creepy zombie hand by gluing rice crispies or cornflakes to a rubber glove. Paint the whole lot green – yuk!

For cowboys and Indians, sew lampshade fringing down the sides of a pair of jeans, and break up a couple of feather dusters to make an Indian head-dress or just sew them on to a simple T-shirt dress.

Old velvet curtains, still gathered, make terrific cloaks for princes and princesses. Attach some Velcro for a quick escape – cloaks are always getting stepped on, so you don't want anything that could hurt round the neck.

Finally, don't worry about making dressing-up clothes look perfect – once the imagination is in gear, the simplest outfits will delight your children.

DRY CLEANERS & LAUNDERERS

Fountain Cleaners;
Jenny Miles

Difficult stain? Don't try to remove it yourself. Take it to a dry cleaner as soon as possible, they will have the appropriate chemicals for particular stains.

If you have to cut the cleaning instructions label out of a garment, make a note of them to take with you when you have it dry cleaned.

Add half a cup of baking soda to the washing machine along with your usual amount of liquid laundry detergent for more effective cleaning. You'll have whiter socks and clothes, and brighter colours. (It doesn't boost powdered detergents, however.)

Flush out acid spills on clothing (acid drain openers, toilet bowl cleaners, battery acid, film developer, vomit and urine) with cool water immediately, then neutralise by sprinkling baking soda on them. If acid has dried on clothing, neutralise it with baking soda before putting it in the wash, otherwise the water will reactivate the acid, which will continue to damage the garment.

Crayons left in a child's pocket can colour a whole wash. Re-wash the clothes in the hottest water allowable for the fabrics and add a generous amount of baking soda (half to a whole tub). Repeat if necessary.

Add baking soda to the washing machine (or bowl for hand washing) to remove stains from linens and clothing. In addition, the baking soda softens the water, so you can use less detergent.

Run out of fabric softener? Add half a cup of baking soda to the softener dispenser instead.

If some horror has left chewing gun in a pocket, clean out the inside of the drum (on the drier or washing machine) with a soft abrasive sponge and use a paste of baking soda to scrub the inside clean.

Before leaving a jacket for dry cleaning, go through all the pockets and check the lining for any valuables and for biros, which can cause havoc if they go through a dry cleaning machine.

ENVIRONMENTALISTS

Chris Crean; Friends of
the Earth; Wastewatch

Never ignore a skip! When you pass one in the street, always have a look for old pieces of wood and a host of other useful things. One man's rubbish is another's salvation!

To help developing countries, don't throw your old spectacles away. Take them to your nearest Oxfam shop.

Save the rainforest! Avoid buying hardwoods like mahogany.

In the Kitchen

Avoid excess packaging. Buy in bulk – it's much cheaper, too.

Save space in your dustbin. When a plastic milk bottle is empty, pour in the left-over boiling water from the kettle. Swill it round the plastic bottle several times and then pour it away. The plastic will have become pliable and can be rolled up like a sausage.

Recycle milk cartons for planting seedlings. Cut them in half and use the bottom half as a planter.

Better still, make friends with your local milkman. He recycles the bottles for you.

Put plastic shopping bags in your car, not under the kitchen sink. Then you can reuse them on shopping trips.

If you have your own canvas shopping bag or basket, you won't need so many plastic carrier bags.

When disinfecting your sink, don't bother with strong chemical solutions. Just use ordinary household salt.

Don't put kitchen fat down the sink – let it solidify in a container, such as a yoghurt pot, and then put it in the bin.

Make your kitchen utensils last longer. Always buy items made for the professional catering trade. They are more durable than domestic ranges and often have less of a mark-up.

There's no need to buy kitchen paper towels. Drain food on brown paper bags instead.

Put lids on your pots when cooking – it will save time and energy.

Line up the bottoms of your pans with the rings on the hob so that you don't lose too much heat.

When cooking vegetables, steam fast-cooking vegetables over slow-cooking ones. It saves energy, preserves the goodness in the food and makes a wonderful meal.

To stop ants going into your kitchen cupboards, you don't have to buy pesticides. Just sprinkle around some dried tansy.

Avoid using toxic oven cleaners. Sprinkle the oven with water and bicarbonate of soda then start scrubbing. This also works well on baths.

Forget specialist oven cleaners. For an inexpensive alternative that will remove even hard, baked-on grease put your oven on warm for about two minutes, then turn it off. Place a small dish of full-strength ammonia on the top shelf and a large pan of boiling water on the bottom shelf and leave overnight. In the morning, open and air for a while before washing down with soapy water.

Check that you're not wasting electricity – make sure that your fridge and freezer door seals are still effective. Place a piece of paper in between the seal and the door. If it falls out or slides down easily, you are losing energy, the food isn't being stored safely and you need new door seals.

Fill your freezer compartment so that it doesn't waste energy trying to keep a large space cold. You can always fill it with loaves of bread or even newspaper.

To conserve energy, avoid placing your freezer next to a cooker or a window that gets direct sunlight.

A cheap and natural alternative to bleach is to put freshly washed clothes outside in direct sunlight.

For home-made furniture polish, mix up one part lemon juice to two parts olive oil.

Save money! Put your washing machine on after midnight and before 7 am so that you're using off-peak electricity.

Minimise the amount of detergent you use. Always place it in a detergent ball so that it gets right into the wash and isn't wasted in the system.

Don't throw away empty washing-powder boxes. Use them to keep magazines or files in. Just cut a large corner away and cover the box with left-over wallpaper or wrapping paper.

Tumble drying can use a lot of electricity. Put a dry towel in with the wet clothes to absorb the excess moisture.

Roll clothes in a towel before putting them into the dryer. This will soak up excess moisture.

If you've mislaid your dustpan, wet the edge of a newspaper, brush the dirt over the edge and roll up the paper.

Preserve steel-wool pads for longer by keeping them in soapy water. This will stop them from rusting.

If your steel-wool pads are rusting, wrap them in kitchen foil after use.

Save those soap slivers. Mix them in the blender with some water and make your own liquid soap.

Or collect them in an old nylon stocking and hang near an outside tap use after gardening.

Don't buy soap. Use natural oatmeal – it works just as well.

To soften your lips, use a little almond oil.

Make your own ceramic tile cleaner by mixing quarter of a cup of baking soda, half a cup of white vinegar, one cup of ammonia and 1 gallon/4.5 litres of warm water in a bucket. Stir and apply with a sponge or brush. This mixture will not keep between cleaning, so you'll need to make a fresh batch each time, and always wear rubber gloves as the solution is quite harsh.

Get rid of tobacco fumes – leave a bowl of cider vinegar in the room overnight.

Avoid shiny fruit. It's probably been coated in pesticides.

There's no need to use a sticky plaster when you cut yourself. Press the inside of a clear onion skin on to the cut. Leave it there for as long as you can. Onion is a natural antiseptic.

Save Energy & Water

Keep the electricity bill down by using energy-efficient light bulbs. They use 80 per cent less energy than normal bulbs.

To insulate your house hang heavy drapes from the ceiling to the floor. It's much cheaper than double-glazing.

Keep warmth in – don't hang long curtains over radiators because you'll lose the heat behind them. Make sure your curtains hang just above the radiators.

Close curtains at north-facing windows during the day in winter so that they don't let any heat out.

Fix cracks in windows – seal with some tape.

Make your own draught excluders – roll up a towel and fix with rubber bands at either end.

Save money during the winter – put a pan of water near a radiator to humidify the room. A warm and humid atmosphere feels warmer so you will be less inclined to turn the thermostat up.

Clean your radiators as well as the furniture. Dust can insulate a radiator, keeping down the amount of heat that it gives off.

To save water, clean your teeth using a mug rather than having the water running constantly. Also replace one bath with a shower each week.

To save water in the cistern, place a 3 ½ pint/2 litre plastic bottle filled with water in the cistern; position it away from the handle.

Keep your toilet bowl looking clean – put 5 fl oz/150 ml white wine vinegar in the bowl, leave for about five minutes and then flush.

In the Garden

To absorb chemicals from the air, plant azaleas (to counteract formaldehyde), English ivy (for benzene) and peace lily (for trichloroethylene). Such chemicals are found in paints and varnishes.

Get a water butt – rain water is soft and much better for your plants. It will save water as well.

Don't waste time and energy watering lawns – they can be left for longer than you think.

Speed up the composting process – put some fresh horse manure inside and you'll soon be rewarded with wonderful organic compost.

To construct your own composter, put some holes in the side and base of an old dustbin and stand on some bricks for drainage.

Make sure you put some carbon in your compost – cereal packets, egg boxes and so on will give the compost some bulk.

Create a cheap mulch for the garden by shredding any left-over bits of wood.

Using peat is not environmentally friendly so investigate the alternatives.

To make your hot-water bottle last longer, put a couple of drops of glycerine inside the first time you use it.

In the Car

Keep your engine properly tuned – it will save petrol in the long run.

Braking sharply and accelerating uses up more fuel – so don't!

Don't sit for ages letting the car warm up – an engine will warm up quickly when the car is moving and it uses up less fuel doing so.

If you're stuck in a bad traffic jam, turn off your engine.

Take any unnecessary items out of the car – the heavier the car, the more fuel you use.

Don't just throw your old car oil away. Take it to your local garage so it can be reused.

To save on petrol consumption, slow down! Going at 70 mph/110 kph uses 30 per cent more energy than driving at 50 mph/ 80 kph. Better still…

Leave the car at home and go to work on a bike.

EQUESTRIANS

Horse Care

Eric Mackechnie, Mark Phillips Equestrian Centre; Lucy Henderson; PC Mark Wood, Mounted Horse Division; Delia Cunningham; Shona Kinnear & Sharon Burt, Warwick Equestrian Centre

When buying a pony, ask to ride it away from the stables or house, rather than just back again. If it swishes its tail or is stubborn you know it's likely to be trouble.

When buying a horse, ask the owner to ride it first and then get a friend to ride it for you. You can thus see what its action and temperament are like before you have a go yourself.

Always ask to see a horse being ridden in traffic before you buy. A traffic-shy horse can be a liability if you enjoy hacking out. Don't try to ride a strange horse yourself in traffic.

Encourage children to look up when jumping. Stand the other side of the jump and ask them to shout out how many fingers you're holding up.

Persuade children to keep their hands up while riding – ask them to hold a cup of water and see how much they spill.

Teach children to relax and breathe while they're riding – encourage them to sing a song when doing rising trotting.

Horses are sensitive souls so don't shout at them. Tone of voice is important. Speak calmly and with authority.

And they have sensitive spots... well, ticklish ones anyway. Be careful around the stomach, flanks and inside thighs.

Always warn a horse if you are going to walk behind it. Horses don't like surprises. Run your hand along its back and quarters as you move behind it so it knows where you are all the time. You're harder to kick if you're close.

Keep an eye on the ears. They are a good barometer of mood. Pricked forward, they mean that a horse is alert. Ears back could mean the horse has heard something behind him or that it's unhappy about something. Ears flattened back is a sure sign of anger.

Signs of distress (due to fear or pain) are showing the whites of the eyes, snorting a lot, sweating and rapid, shallow breathing.

Horses are creatures of habit; they love routine, so make sure you feed, clean and exercise them regularly.

A 'cob' horse is known for its dependability and strength.

When tacking up, talk to your horse. Approach it so it can see you and keep talking to give reassurance.

When you are about to mount, make sure the horse is standing still and squarely. You don't want to catch it or yourself off balance.

As you mount your horse, try to avoid digging your toes into its side. This will only make it move away from you and it will be harder to mount properly.

Mounting a horse can be tricky if you've had a hip replacement or are arthritic. Always use a mounting block. Climb on with short stirrups and lengthen them once you're seated.

When turning your horse, make sure you haven't gone so far into a corner that its hind quarters can't follow properly.

Keep your shoulders parallel with your horse's shoulders.

When trotting, your hands should remain still and you should absorb the rise and fall motion through the ankles, knees and hips. Lean slightly forward and stay relaxed.

If you are going out in the country for a ride for the first time, plan your route carefully in advance. Let someone know that you are going out, what your route is and what time you plan to return.

When riding out in the countryside, if in doubt, walk. Keep an eye open for potential hazards such as boggy ground, low branches or slippery surfaces.

As you ride uphill, lean forward and let your horse stretch its neck out. This allows your horse to use its hind quarters and legs more effectively.

Always walk through water unless it is very shallow. Galloping at full tilt through water may look great on the movies, but you want to be sure that the footing is safe and secure for both you and your horse.

Don't frighten a horse by throwing the whole rug over it, fold the rug in half, place it over the horse and then gently unfold it.

If loudspeakers or low-flying planes distract a horse, just put a little cotton wool in both its ears, being careful not to push it too far down.

To calm a young foal, scratch its neck.

If a horse is difficult to catch, always approach it from a 45° angle; it's much less threatening than head on.

Try not to throttle a horse. When fitting the bridle, put your hand beneath the throatleash to check that there is enough room to allow it to breathe.

Strengthen a horse's shoulder muscles by holding a carrot to one side of its head, let it take a bite and then move the carrot to the other side. Make sure you exercise each side equally.

You can use a carrot to strengthen a horse's legs. Place the carrot between its front and back legs and it will reach down to eat it. Again, always make sure you repeat this exercise equally on each side of the horse.

If a foal won't suckle, try tickling its bottom; it stimulates the sucking reflex.

Never dice carrots – always chop lengthwise otherwise you run the risk of your horse choking.

Feed little and often. Horses have small stomachs, digest food slowly and can't take a huge meal in one go.

Don't feed a horse if it's hot and tired.

When feeding a horse titbits, keep your hand flat. You don't want your fingers to become part of the snack.

To make bran mash put 2–3 lb/900–1350 g of bran in a bucket and pour boiling water over it. Stir, adding some salt and a handful of oats to taste. Place a sack over the bucket and let the mixture steep until it is cool. You can add chopped carrots and apples as extra treats.

If you must change a horse's diet, do it gradually. They don't like sudden changes and it could lead to colic.

For fussy feeders, add molasses to their feed.

After exercising during the winter, give a horse warm water to drink, rather than straight from the tap. Cold water can cause colic.

Never feed or water a horse straight before or after heavy work – this can cause colic.

If a horse is allergic to dust or spores, use shredded paper as bedding rather than sawdust, straw, shavings or peat.

Try looking a gift horse in the mouth. You can tell the age of a horse by looking at its teeth. The more angular they are, the older the horse is.

A piggy eye, where too much white is showing, is often thought to indicate a mean nature.

Grooming

When washing greys, use a blue-rinse shampoo for that whiter than white tail.

When plaiting your horse's tail before travelling, cut one leg off some tights and stretch it over the plait to stop it falling out.

To keep a horse's tail shiny and tangle-free, put a little baby oil in some water and spray on to the tail. Run your fingers through to the tips.

For a shiny, tangle-free tail, try washing it with some fabric conditioner.

If a tail is in a tangle, comb some hair conditioner through it to get rid of the knots.

When a foal is first born, push the mane neatly to one side while it is still damp and it will stay like that.

Plaiting a mane can be difficult, but a little hair gel rubbed through before you start will make all the difference.

For showing, set the mane to one side of your horse's neck with a little egg white.

When pulling a mane, a little oil of cloves rubbed into the hair will prevent it from hurting your horse.

To get a horse's mane to lie over, comb it the way you want it to lie and then dampen it down every day.

To make a horse's features stand out, rub a little Vaseline round its muzzle and eyes.

If a horse or pony lives out during the winter, don't groom it. The mud that they get themselves covered in acts as a second coat and insulates them against the cold. They may look scruffy, but they'll be warm too.

If you need to get a horse looking clean in a hurry, damp a cloth (an old dishcloth will do) and wipe it over its coat to produce a clean-looking shine.

Keep two sponges handy for cleaning a horse: one for the eyes, nose and mouth area and the other for the dock area. It's a good idea to have them in different colours so you won't confuse the two.

To give a shine to a horse's hooves, rub in some hair conditioner.

Pick your horse's feet out at least twice a day and after exercise. Horses should be shod every four to six weeks.

To take the sweat off a horse, try winding some bale twine around your hand; it makes a great scraper and you'll be able to get into all the curves of a horse's body.

If a horse gets really greasy, it can be difficult to clean. Dip a towel in some methylated spirits and hot water, and wipe over the coat; this will draw out the grease.

Clothes & Equipment

Don't make your saddle too slippery when polishing it; clean the straps and underneath but never the top part where you actually sit.

Saddle racks can quickly mark saddles, so glue a couple of pieces of foam on to the racks to protect expensive tack.

Make saddle soap go further – melt it down in some milk before using.

Don't saddle soap the seat of your saddle (try saying that quickly after a few drinks!) or you'll end up with a black bottom.

To stop your saddle drying out, try putting some hair conditioner on it. Rub it in as you would polish.

Don't wear one stirrup out faster than the other. Although you always mount from the right, you can cut down wear on stirrups by swapping them around every couple of weeks.

To check that the stirrups are at the right length, adjust the leathers so that when your fingertips rest on the stirrup bar, the base of the stirrup reaches your armpit.

To check the length of the stirrup leathers once you are on the horse, ensure that the base of the stirrup reaches your ankles when you let your leg dangle.

Always run up both stirrup irons after dismounting. This avoids them hitting the horse when it moves and it's easier for you to carry the saddle this way.

Put oil on your tack to make is soft and supple – especially when new.

If you have to leave a horse when you've tacked up, loop the reins under the stirrups so that they don't get in the way.

Soak a new pair of boots in manure overnight. It will draw out any excess grease and they'll stay easier to clean.

Get a great shine on your boots without too much elbow grease. Polish them with washing-up liquid and leave overnight.

Shine boots with furniture polish. For extra sparkle, try a final rub down with some nylon tights.

For a really rich shine on boots, the penultimate layer of polish on black boots should be brown.

To harden up new boots, add a few drops of methylated spirits to the water when first cleaning.

Tight-fitting boots can be hard to pull on. Wear a pair of pop socks over the top of your jodhpurs and the boots should slip on more easily.

To keep boots in pristine condition, don't go to the expense of buying inner woods. Old nut bags scrunched up inside a soft pillow case and stuffed inside the boots will work just as well.

Keep your grip when riding – don't polish the insteps of your boots.

Avoid unnecessary discomfort when riding – don't wear skimpy underwear that can rub. Really big pants may not be glamorous but they will be far more comfortable and won't show under tight-fitting jodhpurs either.

For extra grip, wear jodhpurs with a suede bottom or chaps.

When learning to ride, wear fitted clothing so your teacher can correct your position.

Buff up your velvet hat by leaving it in the bathroom when you take a hot, steamy shower.

Keep your hoof pick clean – just ask your vet for an old syringe holder to keep it in.

To muck out, you don't really need an expensive shovel and broom. The side of your foot and an old washing basket is just as good.

To stop your horse becoming cast (stuck against the wall), always bed it down with big bales of straw.

Soak hay overnight in a wheelie bin. Just pierce a hole or two in the bottom to let the water drain out. Once soaked, the hay will be much easier to move around.

To open a bale of hay or straw, use another piece of twine to cut it open. Slip the piece of twine under where you want to cut and then saw it backwards and forwards. The twine holding the hay together will always come apart first.

Always tie hay nets up high so your horse doesn't get tangled in them.

Donkeys

Donkeys have a strong sense of self-preservation; if they think something is dangerous, they won't do it… so don't make them.

Like horses, donkeys are sociable creatures – it's best to keep them with another donkey or horse.

Donkeys were originally desert creatures so they don't handle the cold as well as some other animals. Make sure they have adequate shelter.

A dirty donkey is a happy donkey. They use dust and grit like shampoo to keep their coats in good condition.

Donkeys can live to a ripe old age, sometimes over 40 years – they are a long-term commitment.

ESTATE AGENTS

Selling

Steve Daly; David
Snell; Avril Majors

Check whether an estate agent is the right one for you. Look at their adverts in the local paper. Are they clearly laid out? Do they feature good photographs and do they sell properties in a similar bracket to your own?

To judge the sort of efficiency you're likely to get from your selling agent, register with them first as a would-be buyer and see what sort of service you get.

To check your agent is doing everything necessary to sell your property, ask a friend to register as a buyer looking for a similar type of property to your own and see how well your home is being marketed.

To calculate the approximate value of your property, find the average asking price of four properties in your area, then deduct five per cent from this figure to give you the average difference between the asking price and actual selling price.

Avoid a low valuation – never admit to wanting a quick sale.

To sell an empty house, arrange for someone to clear away mail regularly and open the windows from time to time.

Present your property at its best – make sure any photos the agent takes are in colour and not black and white.

Find out what sort of impression your house makes on a potential buyer. Ask a friend to come round, show them the house and then ask them to be brutally honest. Don't be offended at what they say… you did ask for honesty!

Make your house more appealing to potential buyers. Take down any net curtains and let as much light as possible flood into the rooms.

Keep your windows clean – it makes a huge difference.

Be tidy. Keep kitchens and bathrooms tidy, clear up hallways and stairs and make sure the garden looks neat.

Deal with any potential problems such as sticking doors or dripping taps.

Make potential buyers feel welcome. Turn off the television, offer them a drink and be friendly.

Don't be too friendly! Traditional clichés like brewing coffee can make people nervous. What are you trying to hide?

Don't use strong room fragrances – people will think you're covering up a damp smell – or worse!

Many people don't like pets. Make sure yours are well out of the way.

Don't have too many people in the house. It can be off-putting for potential buyers.

Look efficient. Have an information pack with guarantees, plans and local information ready to show prospective buyers. Have an idea how much your last electricity, gas and water bills were.

Speed things up. Chase your agent regularly and find out how things are progressing.

When choosing a solicitor, don't go to the one suggested by the agents. Personal recommendations are much better.

If you are in a hurry to sell, appoint a solicitor when you first put your house on the market and not at completion. When the time for completion comes, your solicitor will have had plenty of time to find all the deeds and relevant information.

Keep track of all dealings with your solicitor – just in case things do go wrong.

Unusual properties can be hard to price but often do well at auctions.

Buying

If you've targeted an area you want to move to, walk or drive round the streets every day on the lookout for new 'For Sale' or 'To Let' signs. They often go up before the property is advertised in a paper or the details have been printed, and you can get an offer in ahead of the competition.

Avoid the mad rush and over-competitive markets. Try looking for a home over Christmas or during the summer holidays, which are traditionally quiet times for buying and selling houses. You'll get more of the estate agent's attention, too.

Don't get carried away at an auction. Ask a friend to bid on your behalf with clear instructions not to go over your affordable price.

Try to assess what a house will look like all year round. For example, once the trees don't have leaves on them will the house be overlooked?

Check that nearby roots haven't caused any damage by looking for bulges in the main wall.

Underground streams or a damp environment can cause structural problems. See if there are any willow trees nearby because they are often a good indicator for these conditions.

Check whether a house gets good television reception. Do neighbouring houses have over-sized aerials?

To see how good the water pressure is in a house, turn on the highest tap in the building. Water should still come pouring out at a good rate.

To check for woodworm, look round the base of a toilet. The grubs are attracted to the protein found in urine-soaked floorboards.

To discover whether a house has wet rot, slide a penknife into the wood at right angles to the grain. If the blade slips in, then there's rot about.

Dry rot shows itself by cube-shaped cracks in timbers.

If you buy a house with plans to extend it, check what building regulations are relevant before exchange of contract to avoid disappointment.

To find a redundant church to buy up and convert, contact the local diocese to see if there are any available properties that haven't come on to the market yet.

For security reasons, always change the locks in a house as soon as you move in.

To calculate the insurance for a thatched cottage, allow four times as much premium as normal insurance to cover the potential fire hazard.

To get the most from your survey, let your surveyor know of any plans you may have so that he can check out the suitability of the house and plot.

EVENTS ORGANISERS

Elegant Days of Warwick and London

Arranging nuptials? Fix the date as soon as possible. Then book the church and/or wedding venue and reception venue. Once these details are confirmed you can relax for a while.

Once you have made any confirmation over the phone, put it in writing. This will protect you from any misunderstandings later.

Any reputable marquee company should comply with relevant BS standards and be able to produce a MUTA safety certificate.

Don't take short cuts with heating arrangements: use ducted hot-air heaters with thermostatic controls. Space heaters should not even be considered.

Winter or summer, make sure there is a back-up generator at the ready. Who wants warm white wine and no lighting?

If you are intending that your guests park in a field, imagine what the ground will look like once 50 cars have driven over it. Keep the grass short and use boards at the gate entrance to avoid a mud bath. No one wants to have to push a car while wearing a long dress and stiletto heels!

Allow 6 ft²/0.5 m² per person for a cocktail reception without furniture. Allow 12 ft²/1.1 m² per person for a seated served dinner and 15 ft²/1.4 m² per person for a seated buffet. To work out space, pace out a square yard (one big stride on four directions to form a square). Be strict and don't fudge it. You want a party, not a bun-fight.

Golden rule of any event: always have a wet weather strategy.

Don't be bullied by contractors. If you want limbo dancers, a chocolate wedding cake or fireworks at dawn – why not? It's your party.

If you are nervous about organising a big event, you can save money in the long run by employing an events organiser to shoulder the responsibility.

Any wine merchant worth their Sauvignon should be happy to offer you a couple of sample bottles to try out at home. It's worth his while if you are likely to order several cases as a result.

Arrange sale or return: most wine merchants should be happy to arrange this so you aren't left with cases after an abstemious party.

Don't forget drivers and non-drinkers: if you have drawn the short straw and are left with the car keys, there is nothing more dull than being plied with warm orange juice all evening. Consider offering interesting alternatives like sparkling apple juice or elderflower champagne.

EXPLORERS
Made for Walking

Simon Tarver & Rebecca Drury, Raleigh International; Hilary Bradt; Paul Cammack; Major Anrezej Frank; Peter Hill, Highlander Mountaineering

Keep blisters at bay – wear thin liner socks under thick outer socks.

Buying boots should take place during the afternoon when you've been walking around for a while. Your feet can be up to half a size smaller in the morning.

For the perfect fit, take along the socks you would normally wear for walking when you go to buy a pair of boots.

The best way to dry socks is to stuff them under your armpits.

For sea-level traversing (or coasteering), wear sturdy, supportive shoes to deal with all kinds of terrain, from seaweed to sand dunes, rocks to boulders. Modern climbing shoes are tight, lightweight and close-fitting and aren't really suitable for this activity.

Dressed for the Occasion

Don't wear gaiters over the top of your outer trousers because water will dribble down into your boots. It's better to wear them under your outer trousers.

Secure your gaiters to plastic boots with a strong glue to stop snow or mud getting inside.

Waterproof over-trousers often fall down – spare your blushes and wear braces to keep them up.

Wear layers of clothes. Cotton T-shirts get wet and clammy from sweat. Wearing a thermal T-shirt not only keeps you warm but also draws sweat off the body and out through the clothes.

Make sure your clothes can 'breathe' – this goes for inner and outer layers. The more layers you have, the more you can draw the sweat away from your body. Putting another layer on once you've worked up a sweat may warm you up for a minute or so but it will cool you down in the long run.

For coasteering, you need to be amphibious and you should dress accordingly. Wear modern, tight-fitting synthetics such as lycra or polyester. They'll keep you warm in the water by trapping a layer of water underneath, but they will also dry out very quickly.

Wear a hat – 70 per cent of your body heat is lost through the head.

Mittens are warmer than gloves because fingers preserve heat next to each other. Mittens also allow you to wiggle your fingers around to generate more heat.

If you don't have any gloves, use socks.

When putting on a jacket on a windy day, face away from the wind to put your arm in the first sleeve. Then turn and let the wind wrap the jacket round the rest of your body.

Packed & Prepared

Give your knees a bit of help – use two trekking poles, setting them so that there is a slight bend in your arms as you walk. This can take up to 200 tons of pressure off your knees in a single day!

Improve your grip when climbing – take a bag full of chalk to dust on your hands and sprinkle in hand-holds.

Always carry non-stretch strapping tape (¾ in/2 cm wide and easy to tear). It's useful for plastering over cuts, acting as a bandage support for any weak joints and wrapping around the back of hands and fingers to make them more effective for jamming into rocks.

Sticking plaster is a versatile piece of equipment – for example, it is excellent for binding up tent poles.

Panty liners make wonderful first-aid dressings because they are sterile on one side and waterproof on the other. The padding won't allow blood to soak through and they are just the right size.

To light fires in wet weather, be prepared in advance. Dip a tampon in methylated spirits and wrap in a plastic bag until needed.

Belly-button fluff makes great kindling for fires.

Stop your meths-fuelled stove from smelling or sooting and clogging; put a few drops of water into the methylated spirits.

Line your rucksack with a bin liner to make it waterproof in case it falls into a river.

Keep precious items waterproof – use a condom. They are ideal for keeping matches dry or protecting specimens such as insects or plants.

Condoms make great water carriers – they expand, and are strong and sealable.

Make your own buoyancy aids – when crossing rivers, blow up condoms and put them in your rucksack and clothing to stop that sinking feeling.

Always carry an ID card on you no matter how remote the area. If you are found by a rescue party they will know who you are!

Protect your maps – cover them with sticky-back plastic.

Use a down-filled sleeping bag rather than a synthetic one. It will be much more expensive but it is lighter to carry and much warmer.

Always use a tent with a sewn-in ground sheet. Use a mosquito net in hot climates and always hang your pack above ground.

Techniques for Safety & Survival

Warm up before a climb by hanging from rocks. This will help to prevent any injury and stop you becoming stiff and inflexible in dangerous situations.

Always try to turn a fall into a jump to give you a chance of choosing where you land.

If you fall off rocks into deep water, fill your lungs with air before you hit the water. Streamline your body shape to get you through the surface of the water with the least impact. Then immediately spread your limbs and start to swim up in order to slow your descent.

To traverse a zawn (a crevice cut in a cliff), make a giant lasso, hook over a jutting rock on the opposite side and secure the other end to your side. You should now have two lengths of rope stretched across the crevice. Lie on the rope, hang one leg down as ballast and crook the other one over the rope. Keeping the rope in the bend of your ankle, shuffle across. This is called the Tyrolean traverse.

Always carry your pickaxe in the arrest position (facing up and out) so you can dig it into a slope quickly if you fall.

When climbing, 'jam' rather than grip – insert a hand, foot, knee or arm into a crack and expand it to hold you up. This puts less strain on fingers.

Stop snow sticking to your crampons – snow can quickly form large lumps making it difficult to walk. Fix a plastic bag over the crampons, leaving them free to grip.

Keep an eye out for thin ice – it is grey rather than white. Avoid thin ice whenever possible, but as ice cracks are constantly opening and closing, you have to take risks at times.

If you've lost your sunglasses and you find yourself on a glacier or elsewhere where there is a strong glare, use a long piece of cardboard with a slit in it to see through. Wrap it round your head – like wrap-around sunglasses!

Use the sun to navigate – make sure you know in advance where it should be in the sky at what time of day.

Use pace counting when visibility is poor – count in advance how many of your paces make up 110 yd/100 m. Then, when you have walked that number of paces put a little pebble in one pocket to mark each 110 yd/100 m.

If you get hopelessly lost in the jungle (or forest), follow a river and it will lead you out. Sometimes turning back takes more courage than going on.

Don't be confrontational – always preserve the self-esteem of border guards, soldiers and potentially hostile strangers. Don't be either aggressive or too submissive.

Don't just read books by travel writers before leaving home. Read accounts by anthropologists and naturalists. Know the culture of the people so that you don't end up causing offence (for example, in some parts of Africa a firm handshake and direct eye contact is offensive).

To avoid hypothermia in the snow, dig a bivouac as an emergency shelter. Wind is the greatest cooling factor, even in summer, and the bivouac will protect you from the wind chill.

If you've got frostbite, ease the pain by gently dabbing on some warmed olive oil.

The easy way to put up a tent on a windy day, is to lay it out on the ground with the tip folded and into the wind. Hammer in pegs or snow stakes upwind. Lift the top of the tent up and the wind will take the fabric and erect the tent for you.

To sleep on a mountain where there are no ledges, attach your hammock to the rock face and abseil into it.

Food & Water

Avoid dehydration – if you are tired and have a headache, you're probably not getting enough water. You should drink about 3 ½ pints/2 litres a day.

Drink fluids in snowy regions – the climate is as dry as the Sahara because cold air carries less moisture. When breathing out, your breath is full of water vapour, but in a snowy climate, you don't breathe any in. Also, you are using up a lot of energy and sweating a lot so you need to replenish your water levels.

Carry a pipe to suck snow through when you are in snowy regions.

When shipwrecked or stranded on pack ice you can break off ice from the highest point because the brine will already have drained out making it drinkable.

Purify water – put a couple of drops of iodine in it.

Save water – wash steel or enamel plates in sand. They come up a treat. Just wipe over with a damp cloth when you've finished.

Keep water cool – dig a hole and put your water bottle in it or float it in water.

Make instant hot-water bottles – fill your large, metal drinking bottles with boiled water at night. Pop the bottles straight into your sleeping bag to warm it up. The water cools overnight and will be ready to drink.

Carry dehydrated powdered food – 96 per cent of food is made up of water so lighten your pack and save energy.

Culinary tip – stir in a lump of lard to thicken low-fat yoghurt.

Never take plain chocolate to cold regions – it freezes so hard you'll probably break your teeth on it. Rather, take milk chocolate because this won't freeze as hard.

To stop chocolate from melting – put it in some water and keep it in the shade.

If you run out of food in Arctic regions, eat the dog food first and then the dogs. (Dogs are now banned from the Antarctic in case they infect the seals – so don't run out of food there.)

When you run out of food in the jungle, don't eat any old insect you come across. Insects protect themselves against predators with warning colours. If they're brightly coloured (such as red or yellow), then you should avoid them because they will probably be poisonous.

In the jungle, rainwater collects in air plants called bromeliads. They grow low down on trees and are an easily accessible source of water and food. (Insects often live, or drown, in them.)

Observe the social etiquette of the bathroom... even in the wilds – either dig a hole or cover it up with a stone.

Never use a leaf to wipe your bottom because any insects and larva living on the leaf may decide that your bottom makes a more attractive habitat.

Animals

Always look before you touch – danger comes from small creatures as well as large. For example, scorpions seek out dark places during the day so check out your rucksack before plunging your hand inside.

Worried about inquisitive polar bears? Make your own early warning system. Place ski poles around your campsite and thread a string between them. Hang anything that rattles or makes a noise on the string.

To frighten off polar bears shout as loud as you can and wave your arms about. Look as big and aggressive as possible!

If you get stung by an insect, put some bleach on the afflicted area – the ammonia will help lessen the pain. If you don't have any bleach, just pee on the stung spot.

Llamas are intelligent and easy to train.

Become the best friend of weavers and knitters – give them llama hair to spin or knit into warm, luxurious garments.

If a llama spits at you, take notice. He's telling you to push off.

Generally, llamas are gentle and easy to get along with. They are extremely sociable and therefore shouldn't be kept on their own.

Llamas are multi-functional: they can carry heavy loads (up to 100 lb/45 kg) and travel between 12.4 to 18.6 miles/20 to 30 km a day. Some exclusive golf courses use them as caddies. They can be trained to pull a cart and they make great guard dogs (they're very territorial and protective).

Owing to their efficient digestive system, llamas can polish off hay, grass, weeds, shrubs and trees.

If you want to keep a monkey as a pet, be warned – they can't be toilet-trained.

Never keep a monkey on its own – it needs companions of its own kind.

Capuchin monkeys like strong smells. They have been known to rub food such as onions or orange peel over their bodies.

A cage can never be strong enough for a monkey – don't ever underestimate their power to escape.

Some monkeys scent mark their cage so don't sterilise it when you clean it. Always clean the nest-box and the cage at different times so a familiar smell remains.

Gorillas are great bluffers – all that rushing about and chest-beating is usually just to try to scare away intruders, while the rest of the gorilla band slope off quietly into the forest.

Gorillas and chimps love termites and ants, but hate getting bitten, so they slap the ground to stun the insects before eating them.

If you come across a beached whale or dolphin, make sure its blow-hole is clear so it can breathe. Try to keep it upright (don't drag it by its tail). The skin should be kept cool and wet; you can use damp cloths and seaweed to cover it, if necessary. Call the fire brigade for assistance.

If you are bitten by a venomous snake, forget what you saw in the old Western movies. Don't try to suck the poison out with your mouth or try to cut into the bite. Let the bite bleed freely for 15–30 seconds. Cleanse and disinfect the area quickly with iodine. Apply hard, direct pressure over the bite and tape an adhesive bandage in place (tightly, as if it were a sprain). Then get to a hospital as quickly as possible.

If you come across a snake in the field and don't know what it is, don't approach it, try to examine it or take a photo (unless you've got a zoom lens).

To scare off grizzly bears, have bells round your ankles or walking sticks.

Grizzlies have a great sense of smell so don't walk along eating, and don't leave half-eaten food around your camp. Seal any left-overs away in plastic bags and take them with you.

FARMERS

Simon Bowyer; Mark Verity; Richard Smith

Wildlife

Hang bars of soap around your crops to keep deer away.

If you are worried about hedgehogs getting trapped in cattle grids, put a brick or little ramp on the inside so that they have an escape route.

Fences provide the ideal site for bird boxes or standing posts for birds of prey. Just put in the occasional tall pole and fix a bird box or perch to the pole.

To attract wildlife on to your land, plant mountain ash or alder. They are fast-growing trees and produce lots of fruit for the birds.

Give the birds a treat – place small piles of wood and branches around your land. These 'islands' will soon fill up with insects, providing a welcome source of food for the birds.

Ensure that your hedges are stocked with fruits for birds and mammals – trim the hedges in the winter.

Minimise the threat to wildlife when getting rid of rats. Put bait down intensively for one week and then remove it.

To avoid disturbing birds that may be nesting around your pond, try mowing towards the end of August.

Owls can be fatally attracted to water troughs so float a piece of wood on the surface – this will allow the bird to get itself out of danger.

Farm Animals

To keep your cattle troughs clear, put goldfish in them.

For the optimum shelter for your animals, keep hedges at a minimum of 6½ ft/2 m high.

Keep your ducks happy while they are moulting. They can't fly at this time so check on them regularly during the summer.

If you are worried that a fox might eat your duck eggs, don't go looking for the nest. Your scent will lead the fox straight to the clutch of eggs.

Never trust a bull even if you know him really well. Bulls respond to dominant behaviour; twist the nose ring slightly to let him know who is boss.

To keep a cow from fidgeting, hold her tail near the base and lift it up. This will keep her still.

Raising your own chickens means you have your own supply of fresh eggs and meat. Gardeners like them because they keep pests and weeds down and are a good source of nitrogen-rich manure.

Choose the right breed for your purpose. Some chickens are better layers while others are better for eating. Some, like Rhode Island Reds, serve both purposes.

If you want your hens to lay eggs, provide them with nesting boxes. These should feel enclosed and secure. A laying hen will produce an egg every one or two days.

Try to keep your poultry yard in two halves. The chickens can be kept in one half while the grass grows in the other half. Once there is enough grass there, the chickens can be moved across.

Like other birds, chickens need grit to help with digestion.

If a goose tries to attack you, call its bluff and advance towards it rather than retreat. It will usually turn tail and run, unless it's protecting a nest.

Always stand behind the head of a billy goat to avoid being thumped.

Pigs are intelligent animals. They respond well to being talked to quietly.

Only pick up a piglet if the sow is restrained. Piglets tend to make an almighty row when handled and this could alarm the mother.

Sheep have a blind spot so if you want to catch one, approach it from behind.

Some sheep have a habit of falling over on to their backs and being unable to right themselves. If this happens, you must get them on their feet as soon as possible. They can develop acute indigestion in this position and may even die.

Sheep hate being on their own. They're happiest in a group and are then much easier to handle.

Sheep are great ones for panicking. If they are going to make a run for it, they tend to aim uphill or towards the light.

If you are shepherding sheep, make sure they can see an opening in front of them. They hate entering dark places, walking into their own shadows or going into water.

To examine a sheep, get it into a 'docile' position. This involves sitting it on its back legs. One way to do this is to lift its front end, then walk the sheep backwards until it sits down.

If an animal is suffering badly from bloat (when one of its stomachs blows up with gas), you may need to resort to emergency remedies. Try peanut oil (1 pint/600 ml in warm water for cattle), liquid paraffin (2 floz/50 ml for a goat), washing soda crystals (for cattle, ¼ lb/100 g dissolved in hot water then diluted to about a pint with cold). These remedies should be administered as a drench by somebody who knows what they're doing.

On the Farm

To stay warm in winter wear lots of light layers, making sure you've got wool next to your skin.

To reuse an old jacket, cut the sleeves off and wear it under your boiler suit for extra warmth.

Don't throw old string away. Use it again. It's ideal for tying up kidney beans or trees laden with apples.

To make fencing last longer, soak the wood in creosote first. When it changes colour, take it out and put it in the ground. Then paint it with creosote as normal.

Make sure newly planted trees have a good start in life by providing shelter for them as they grow and by keeping them clear of weeds.

FASHION DESIGNERS

Keeping Clean

Serafina Grafton-Beaves, Kensington & Chelsea College, London; Julia Dee, Designer Alterations, London; Karen Spurgin, London; Raj Mairs, Exclusively Mairs, Birmingham; Janine Watson

Remove a water stain from silk by placing a dry cloth underneath and dabbing the spot with a damp cloth.

Cut down on creases when washing your sari – fold it up and place it in a pillow case before putting it in to the wash.

To get an old black grease stain off fabric, rub gently with margarine and then wash as normal.

Get rid of black spots on white shoes and handbags with nail-varnish remover.

Dirty marks on white material can be covered up with white chalk.

Remove pencil marks from embroidery material by rubbing the fabric with kneaded white bread.

Clean a felt hat by wrapping sticky tape round your hand and gently dabbing the fluff away.

Alternatively, brush a felt hat vigorously with a nail brush and then steam over a kettle to bring the pile back up.

Remove stubborn stains from a felt hat by brushing with sandpaper. If that fails, colour in the mark with an appropriately coloured felt-tip pen.

Remove the shine from velvet, wool or viscose by spraying the affected area with water and then leaving to dry. Give the material a good brush when it's completely dry.

Get rid of fluff and cat hairs by wrapping sticky tape around your hand and rubbing up and down the item of clothing.

Ironing

Iron your sleeves by hanging the jacket on the door and placing the sleeve board vertically up the sleeve.

To iron a shoulder pad, wrap your hand in a towel and place under the shoulder.

Remove creases from silk after a long journey with a hair-dryer. If you're on the road, you can use a hot-air hand dryer in a service station.

When ironing delicate fabrics, place tissue paper over the top.

Sewing

To get a good hem on chiffon or silk, fold an inch of the material over and sew as close as possible to the edge. Cut the excess, fold over again and then sew.

Make a thimble from an old elbow patch.

To thread a needle easily, hold a piece of white paper behind the eye of the needle.

Never put pins in your mouth if you wear lipstick because it will stain the material. Instead, use a small pin cushion attached to your wrist by a band.

Stop your embroidery thread ending up like a rat's nest – simply tie it into a braid and the threads will come away easily.

Creating 'The Look'

To give you good luck on your wedding day, whoever sews your dress should place a lock of their hair in the hem.

To look slimmer, tuck the flaps of your pockets into your jacket thus creating a smoother line.

Wear a V-neck for a slimmer-looking neckline.

To make your bust look larger, dust a little bit of blusher on your cleavage.

To draw attention away from a large bust, wear a very simple, plain white shirt.

To draw attention away from your hips, wear a scarf around your neck.

To give an old jacket a new lease of life, simply sew on a velvet collar.

To really jazz up an old jacket, put it on a hanger in the garage and throw a large tin of fabric paint all over it.

Stop the hem of your silk skirt or sari from flying away – sew a 2p piece into the hem.

To stop the pleats in your sari from coming undone, use two safety pins to hold them in place.

To make a hat smaller, line it with draft excluder.

When you try on a straight skirt, have a practice at sitting in a chair (especially a low one) and getting up out of it to make sure it's decent in any situation.

If a skirt keeps swivelling round when you wear it, tuck the hanging loops into the waistband of your tights.

Keeping Clothes

Protect your wedding dress – sew two cotton sheets together as a protective cover.

Clothes keep their shape longer if you do up all the buttons when you hang them in the wardrobe.

Make zips run more efficiently by running a lead pencil along the metal teeth.

If you want to reuse your bindi, just place a little bit of blu tack on the back.

Prevent your shoes from scuffing by painting a layer of clear nail-varnish on to the heel and toe of your shoes.

To stop a new pair of shoes rubbing on your heel, rub some candle wax along the edge to soften the leather.

FINANCIAL ADVISORS

Michael Bates, Granville Bates Independent Financial Advisors (tel: 01789 450443, granvillebates@msn.com); David Graham.

If you have money to invest, make every single penny of it work for you by minimising charges and avoiding up-front costs. An IFA (independent financial advisor) who knows the market place should be able to advise you where to go to achieve this.

Do put all your eggs in one basket – lots of baskets mean lots of standing charges. Make sure your basket has integral pockets that allow you to change money from pocket to pocket without charge.

Fixed terms on any investment are a bad idea. It is hard to predict markets far into the future and you will want to get your money out when it is advantageous to do so.

Don't invest in anything that depends on a certain market result being obtained at a certain date – this is a pure gamble.

Study the degree of risk attached to an investment, then weigh up the risk against the potential gain.

Aim for a tax advantageous investment for long-term savings. For example a pension plan will attract a minimum uplift of 20 per cent (by way of tax relief) on the investment at the stroke of a pen (before it starts performing). Work out how many years it would take to earn that in a deposit account.

To achieve a balanced investment, do not expose your money directly to any one market whether it is deposit, equity, property or whatever. The money should be 'mixed'. A professional manager will invariably achieve the best results (it's his job to have in-depth knowledge of the markets). An IFA specialising in investments should know which mixed funds would best suit your requirements.

IFAs are bound by law to give 'best advice' and take all circumstances into account. Product providers cannot give advice, only information – so if you deal direct – *caveat emptor*.

Before investing any money, have between three and six month's salary in the bank, which will cover you for emergencies like redundancy, illness or a rainy day.

Save effectively, by putting ten per cent of your salary straight into a savings account. Studies show people don't miss this amount, but that we are apathetic about saving. When once we put away ten per cent, the figure these days is nearer three per cent.

When taking out cash, work out what you need for the week and only go to the cash machine once in the week. Give yourself a daily budget.

Avoid temptation by only taking one cheque and one credit card out with you.

Lower your repayments by cutting up your credit card with the highest rate of interest, then transfering all your debts to the card with the lowest rate – and pay that off.

Leave your credit cards behind at the weekends when you go out shopping. Just take cash.

Think before you spend on impulse. Wait for 48 hours, and think about whether you really need those new shoes.

FISH BREEDERS

Mary Bailey; Nick Fletcher; Richard Mills, Slough; Ben Helm, Brooksby College, Warwick; John Mulvana, Aquatica, Wakefield

First Fish

If you've never kept fish before, start with freshwater species rather than the more demanding marine fishes. Tropical freshwater fish can be just as colourful and attractive to look at as their marine counterparts.

Tropical marine fish are more expensive than freshwater ones so it's worth getting a bit of experience with other (cheaper) fish before you move into this area.

Some fish need more expert care and handling than others: for example, the moray eel, sea horses and the venomous tailbar lionfish are really only for the more experienced fish keeper.

Make sure your fish will get along together. Some fish can't stand the company of their own species but will happily share a tank with others. This might be a bit 'obvious' but don't put carnivorous fish into an aquarium with small fish… you might start to notice numbers dwindling. Carnivorous fish should be kept on their own or with fish of a similar size to themselves.

A mix of species is a good idea because different fish tend to have different habits, live in different parts of the aquarium and move around during different parts of the day. For example, catfish feed at the bottom of a tank, while tetras move happily around all areas.

Koi and goldfish can live for over 20 years, while killifish only last for a year. A good rule of thumb is: the larger the fish, the longer it will live.

When choosing fish, check what size they will grow to. You could end up with a very large fish in a very small aquarium. Piranhas can grow up to 12 in/30 cm long while some angelfishes can reach 16 in/40 cm.

You don't need to buy a net for catching fish – a plastic bag will do just as well.

When transporting koi in a car, make sure the fish is in a container that doesn't allow it to turn round. Then place the container so that the fish is lying across the car and not back to front. This stops the fish from banging its nose every time you brake.

When transporting very small fish, twist the corners of the plastic bag and secure with an elastic band. This stops the fish from getting crushed in the corners.

When bringing new fish home, put their plastic bags or containers inside brown paper bags. This stops them from getting too stressed on the journey.

Imported fish can suffer from jet lag, so it's not always a good idea to take them straight home from the shop. A good breeder will allow you to reserve fish.

Health

A healthy fish should have a good strong colour with no blurring, and it should be eating.

A healthy fish always has an erect dorsal fin.

An unhealthy fish can swim with its fins held flat against its body. Avoid fish covered in spots, lumps, wounds or split fins. Don't buy a fish if the tank also contains dead fish.

If your male fish refuses to mate, make him jealous. Introduce a bit of competition by making a false fish out of paper. Wriggle it about in the tank for a while. It should make your male get his act together.

To encourage egg laying, cut nylon wool into strips. Tie one end to the bottom of the tank then secure the other end to a piece of cork so that it floats. Your fish will lay their eggs along the small pieces of wool.

A great way to catch flies for your fish is to attach a piece of fine net to the side of your car in the summer.

To feed your fish using a timer, drill three holes into a clock face at the times you want the fish to be fed. Remove the minute hand and place some food over the holes. Suspend the clock face over the tank. When it's dinner time, the big hand will knock the food into the tank.

Fishy food treats are pieces of cucumber, lettuce or orange.

Don't overfeed your fish. They should have finished eating within two minutes. Anything left over just mucks up the water.

A good way to hatch brine shrimps is to place them in a milk bottle.

Feeding fish with fresh fish is nutritionally very good for them. Always feed freshwater fish to salt-water fish and vice versa.

To stop big fish eating small eggs, put some net curtain or glass marbles into the tank. The eggs will drop between the holes and cracks to safety.

To feed fry fish (and stop the bigger fish from getting more than their share), use a gravy baster to squirt the fry food in the right direction.

Feed fish little and often. Like all animals, fish thrive on a balanced diet.

Nominate one member of the family as the fish feeder or have set feeding times so you don't run the risk of the whole family dropping meals into the water and overfeeding the fish.

Grow your own whiteworms. Buy a few to start off with from a fish dealer. Put the worms in a box of earth and cover with a slice of wet bread. This should give you a continuous supply of worms for your fish.

Aquariums & Tanks

Cold freshwater systems don't need as many bits of technology as the tropical systems but they are more difficult to maintain. Cold-water fish consume more oxygen than tropical fish; therefore you will need a larger tank with aquatic plants to oxygenate the water.

A tropical freshwater aquarium should be kept at a temperature of around 77 °F/25 °C.

Rainwater is ideal for aquariums, but not if it comes from a dirty roof or metal containers.

Think carefully where you are going to place your aquarium. Try not to put it in a window; the sun can cause too much algae to grow and the water to overheat. You need to be near an electrical point to run the filter, air pumps and heaters.

You will need a heater if you intend to keep tropical fish. Allow ten watts of power per 9 pints/5 litres of water for a tank in a normally heated room. If you have a large tank (over 36 in/90 cm), install two heaters.

Filling your tank with plants and rocks makes it look more attractive but don't go overboard. Your aim is to try to copy the natural habitat of the fish as well as make it look good.

Plants are a good way of absorbing carbon dioxide and producing oxygen; they also remove nitrate from the water, and some plants are part of a fish's diet.

Plants are also an ideal way of hiding the technical bits and pieces which you need to run your aquarium.

When planting up your aquarium, put the taller plants at the back, but don't place them too densely together. The odd gap here and there will give an illusion of distance and space.

You can't keep live plants in a marine aquarium, but you can use synthetic plants and corals to liven things up.

Purify the water in a tank by putting watercress in the filter chamber. Buy it ready-prepared from a supermarket or grocer. If you introduce it from the wild, you run the risk of introducing diseases into the water.

Don't overcrowd your aquarium. You should keep three fish for every 2 gallons/9 litres of water. If you've got more fish than that, you should get an air pump.

Don't tip your new fish into their aquarium straight away. You have to let the temperature of the water in the bag equalise with the aquarium water. The easiest solution is to float the bag in the tank for a couple of hours before letting the fish into the water.

If you are planning to introduce new fish to an established tank, keep them in quarantine for a couple of weeks. Keep expensive fish in quarantine for longer (at least a couple of months).

When you set up a new aquarium, let it 'settle' for at least a week before you start introducing fish. The first fish to go in should just be a couple of goldfish. If something's wrong with the tank and the fish die, you won't have wasted lots of money on expensive fish.

When setting up a new tank, use the filter from an old tank to establish beneficial bacteria into the new water immediately.

If you have to take your fish out of the water, place it on a baby-changing mat. The raised edges will stop it sliding off. Also, cover the fish with a soft, damp cloth.

If you want to dispose of a terminally ill fish, don't flush it down the loo. Fish can survive for some time in the warm water of the sewers. The humane way is to put water in a jam jar, put the fish in the jar and place in the freezer.

Rocks in tanks shouldn't contain calcium – test them by dabbing them with a bit of vinegar. If they fizz, don't put them in the tank.

For fish that like caves, use terracotta plant pots in tanks. They make great breeding grounds.

A good alternative plant fertiliser for tanks is rabbit or guinea pig droppings. They won't harm the fish and they do a lot for the plants.

If your fish like alkaline conditions, sprinkle a bit of baking powder into the water.

For fish that like more acidic water, put a tea-bag in the tank. This will also encourage plants to grow.

To stop fish getting cold during a power cut, put a plastic bottle filled with hot water inside their tank. Replace it as necessary.

When cleaning out your fish tank, don't throw away the water. Put it on your garden instead. It's full of nitrates that will do your plants good.

To clean a tank, remove one-third of the water every fortnight, replacing it with clean water.

Bring out the exotic colours of your fish by exchanging the gravel in your tank with coal.

Get fish used to shows – place their tank in a busy part of the house.

To make male fish display themselves effectively for competitions, place them in adjacent tanks so they can show off to each other.

Ponds

If you're planning to build a fish-pond, don't make it too involved. Awkward shapes can cause water to stagnate in odd nooks and crannies.

Don't situate your pond underneath trees because you'll have your hands full keeping the surface clear of fallen leaves.

To remove blanket weed from the side of a pond, use a windscreen ice scraper.

During a frost, make sure you leave an air hole for your fish to breathe. Float a rubber ball on the surface overnight. During the day, you can take the ball away and, if possible, draw off some of the water so that oxygen can reach the surface. Never break the ice with a hammer – it's like a bomb going off at close quarters and the shock waves can kill the fish.

If you've forgotten to leave an air hole, heat a pan of water and hold it on top of the ice so that it melts, leaving a perfect hole.

FISHMONGERS

Fresh is Best

Ralph Easton,
Blackburn Fishmarket;
Peter Preece,
Queensgate Market

To ensure that you get the best range and quality of fish, choose a fishmonger that supplies local restaurants.

The most important thing when buying fish is to ensure that it's really fresh.

Fresh fish should have a firm texture. Push your fingers into the flesh; if your indentation stays there, the fish is not really fresh.

To tell if a fish is fresh, check the brightness of the scales and the pinkness of the gills. The eyes must be clear, bright and not sunken.

The tail of a truly fresh fish will be stiff.

Fresh sea fish should be bright and not noticeably dry.

Fresh trout should be slightly slimy to the touch.

When buying white fish fillets, look for neat, trim fillets and a white, translucent appearance.

Smoked fish should have a fresh smoky aroma and a glossy appearance.

Frozen fish should be frozen hard with no signs of partial thawing and the packaging should be undamaged.

Don't buy plaice that has roe in it because it will be absolutely tasteless.

To tell if a salmon is wild or farmed, hold the tail between your thumb and forefinger. Farmed fish have far fewer scales and are more slippery. If it slips through your fingers, the fish is farmed.

Fresh fish should be used as soon as possible. However, it can be stored in the fridge overnight.

Keep fish cool. Remove from the packaging and rinse in cold water. Pat dry, cover and store near the bottom of the fridge.

Store fresh fish and smoked fish separately so that the flavours don't get mixed up.

Store cooked, ready-to-eat fish (such as smoked mackerel, prawns and crab) separately from raw fish.

Before freezing your fish, rinse it in water to create a protective glaze around the fish when it's frozen.

Soak fish such as shark, ray and skate in salt water for 20 minutes before cooking to remove the smell of ammonia.

Choose mussels with undamaged shells. To make sure that all the mussels open when cooking, stir them regularly in the saucepan. The sheer number of them may prevent some mussels from opening.

Crab and lobster should feel heavier than you would expect. This means that they will be meaty and juicy.

Gutting & Filleting

When preparing fish, always use a sharp knife.

Before filleting and skinning fish, dip your fingers in salt. You'll get a much better grip.

Cut the fish from the bottom to the neck and then chop off the head. The innards will pull out easily.

Use a spoon to scrape out the guts, especially of larger fish.

When filleting a plaice, start with the white side first. The head is on this side; it's quite knobbly so it's easier to grip.

In trout and salmon, there is a line along the spine of the fish (a black kidney shape in a trout and a red blood patch in a salmon) which doesn't taste very nice. You can remove it easily by running your fingernail along the spine.

The head-end third of cod contains all the large, noticeable bones. Run your thumb along the top of the fish. Where the bumps stop marks the end of these bones (the tail-end of cod only has small bones). If you cut a V-shape in the back of the fish up to where the bumps end, you will have a fairly boneless piece of fish.

When preparing monkfish, cut the head off and pull the skin off from the tail. Then remove the membrane that covers the flesh of the fish before cooking, otherwise the fish will have a chewy texture.

Remove fiddly bones from salmon fillets with tweezers.

To remove the bones from raw fish, use a vegetable peeler. Run the peeler along the flesh, catching bones in the centre slit. Twist the peeler and pull the bones out.

To clear fish guts and scales from your chopping board, use a window squeegee.

Clean fish on newspaper. This keeps your board clean and means you can wrap the waste up and put it straight into the bin.

Mustard removes fishy smells from wooden boards.

Clean wooden chopping boards with half a lemon dipped in salt. This also prevents the surface from staining.

To remove strong food smells from plastic chopping boards, give them a rub down with a cut lemon.

Stop wooden chopping boards from warping by drying them upright and not flat.

To remove a fishy smell, rinse your hands in lemon juice.

Always pick a hake up by its eyes so you don't cut your hands.

Fishy Dishes

Crab should be placed alive in cold water over a low heat. If you place it in hot water, its membrane will let water in and parts of it will fall off. Always heat it up slowly to make sure your presentation is perfect.

When crab has been cooked, get the shell off and remove the 'dead man's fingers'; these are the gills and taste nasty. There are five on either side of the inner body.

Don't crush crab and lobster claws – use the handle of a teaspoon to get the meat out instead.

A clean and easy way to coat fish in batter or breadcrumbs is to place the fish in a freezer bag with the batter or crumbs and shake gently until it is covered.

Before shallow-frying fish, first dip it into well-seasoned flour. This will create a protective layer, which helps to form a good crust and keep the fish moist.

Always mix the pre-mixed batter from supermarkets with chilled water (46 °F/8 °C). If the water is too warm, the batter will ferment. Whisk the batter so it's light and fluffy, then drop the batter-covered fish into hot fat (375 °F/190 °C). If your fat isn't hot enough, the fish will absorb the fat and the batter won't be crispy. Hot fat instantly seals the batter.

To make an unusual and delicious batter, replace the milk in the batter-mix with the same quantity of beer. Allow to stand in the fridge for half an hour before using. This gives the starch grains in the flour time to absorb liquid and swell, producing a lighter mixture.

To make batter stick properly to fish or whatever else you're battering, add half a teaspoon of sugar to the mix.

When keeping fried fish warm don't stack it or cover it up because this will make it soggy.

To stop fish from falling apart after it's been fried, dip it in boiling water before you fry it.

To test whether fish is cooked, look for flesh that is opaque and feels firm to the touch. You should be able to insert a knife easily and peel the skin away.

Fish can be cooked straight from the freezer – just add a couple of extra minutes to the cooking time.

Pieces of bacon laid over skinned white fish fillets will keep them moist while cooking.

Cook fish in foil parcels to give delicious, moist morsels of fish.

You don't need an expensive steamer for fish, just put a colander over a pan of boiling water and cover the colander with a large lid.

If grilling a whole fish (mackerel, for example), slash the skin three or four times on the diagonal on both sides. This prevents the skin from breaking open when cooked.

Skinning a fish is fiddly. Flash grill the fish first under a very hot grill and the crispy, scorched skin will lift off effortlessly.

If you need only a couple of drops of lemon juice for fish, simply pierce the lemon with a cocktail stick and it will then stay fresh for use later.

Fish cooks quickly and the golden rule is never to overcook it.

To make haddock less salty, poach it in milk.

To cook delicious juicy fish, wrap it in cling film and place in boiling water so that none of the natural flavour escapes.

To prevent fish skin from sticking to the frying pan rub the skin with salt, leave for 15 minutes, rinse and rub dry. Then cook.

For a tasty, crunchy coating for fish or potato croquettes, first dip in egg and then roll in crushed crisps – just choose your favourite flavour.

It's easy to cook trout in the microwave – try brushing each side with some balsamic vinegar for a lovely flavour.

To slice tuna thinly, pop it in the freezer for an hour beforehand.

To stop fish going soggy during cooking, sprinkle it with salt and leave for half an hour before cooking.

To store lobster, soak some sheets of newspaper in cold water. Roll up the lobster in the newspaper and put in the fridge. The lobster will keep fresh for a couple of days longer.

To reduce the unpleasant fishy smell when poaching fish, add some celery leaves to the pot.

Prevent that lingering fish smell on plates and in pots and pans, by putting a tablespoon of vinegar in the washing-up water.

To clean a pan after cooking and to remove the fishy smell, leave some cold tea in the pan for ten minutes before you wash it.

To make opening sardine tins easy, don't even try to use the troublesome key. Just turn the tin upside down and use a tin opener.

FITNESS INSTRUCTORS

Anne-Marie Millard

Exercise

Start off moderately – you don't have to go at things like a bull at a gate.

Listen to your body – if it hurts then don't do it. Gone are the days of Jane Fonda's 'going for the burn'.

Warm up and cool down every time.

Always do your least favourite exercise first so you can get it over with and enjoy the rest of your workout.

Exercise can become addictive so be careful that you don't overdo things.

Get a partner – exercising with someone is more interesting. You'll be more likely to turn up at the gym or exercise class if you have to meet your partner there.

Don't weigh yourself when training. You'll get despondent because muscle weighs more than fat and you'll think you're getting fatter! Measure yourself instead and you'll realise the good you're achieving as your body changes shape.

Smile from time to time while you're exercising. It stops you getting cramps in your cheeks!

If you are running out of steam, it is psychologically easier to count backwards when exercising. So… 5, 4, 3, 2, 1!

To keep your muscles warm when exercising, rub some fat over your body before you begin.

To firm up your bum, walk up the stairs backwards.

To improve the front of your thighs and your bum muscles, walk up the stairs two at a time.

To strengthen your thighs, sit against a wall without a chair and build up the time you can hold this position. Always remember to stretch out before and after the exercise.

Increase your leg strength by exercising with a small child. Let them sit on the bottom of your legs, ankles together, and raise your legs up and down. They'll enjoy the ride and you'll feel the benefit.

Make your own body liniment for strains and sprains. Mix two drops of lavender oil with two tablespoons of grapeseed oil.

Keep yourself motivated when out walking or running – aim for visual reference points. Also alternate between fast and slow.

If you get stressed before a competition, try juggling. The sheer concentration will stop you feeling anxious.

Food & Drink

For real energy, eat a banana before exercising.

A wonderful home-made isotonic drink is to mix ½ pint/300 ml each of filtered water and orange juice. Add two pinches of salt and two pinches of glucose to the mixture.

For a great energy shake, blend old bananas, honey, brown sugar, two or three ice cubes and one small pot of plain yoghurt together – sweeten to taste.

Don't get despondent on a diet. Think of all the positive points rather than the negative ones – like that size 12 you're going to get into, rather than all the cream cakes you're not eating.

Boredom can kill a diet stone dead so experiment with low-fat recipes. Low-fat foods don't have to be boring.

If you are too nervous to eat before a big event, one healthy helping of rice pudding will give you enough energy for the whole day.

Losing weight is all about good diet and healthy exercise.

Equipment

You don't need to buy expensive dumb-bells for basic work – use large plastic bottles of water.

You can make your own cheap weights by using baked-bean cans.

If you don't have an exercise bike, sit on an ordinary cycle propped against a wall and cycle backwards.

To make your legs work harder when swimming, tie some sponges to your calves. Because they absorb so much water, you'll really feel the difference.

For a cheap pair of training shorts, cut the legs off some old tights or leggings.

To keep trainers smelling sweet, splash them with a shot of Dettox.

FLIGHT CREW

Philip Lelliott; Jenny Bates; Angus Milligan

The first rule of air travel: as soon as you set off, set your watch to local time at your destination. That way you start thinking of your day around the time it is there. When you arrive, even if it is bedtime on your body clock, do everything you can to stay awake until it's the right time to go to bed.

If your legs are long, make sure you secure a seat by an emergency exit where there is a bit more leg room.

Don't drink too much alcohol, no matter how much the stewardesses ply you with it. You won't be able to see straight when you arrive, and you may be hiring a car.

Try to arrange your flights to and from your destination through the same carrier so you can make the most of air miles.

The secret to getting yourself upgraded to first class: ask if the flight is full, and if the check-in steward says it is getting that way, ask if they are looking for people to up-grade. In order to be SFU (Suitable for Upgrade) you need to be looking fairly smart. As airlines always overbook, there's a good chance of getting lucky.

When in Europe check in 45 minutes before take off, then get to the gate five minutes before they close the doors (ten minutes before take off). There will be no need to stand in queues and there will be a better chance of being upgraded.

In the USA, check in and get on the plane as soon as possible. Americans take more hand luggage and the overhead lockers get full very quickly.

If at all possible, only ever take carry-on luggage. If you have a connecting flight to catch, it will save you time if you don't have to wait for luggage to come out of the hold. It also reduces the chances of your luggage ending up in Timbuktu.

If you don't want to be bothered by kids on a flight, don't sit near the bulkhead.

And if it all becomes too much, get your own plane!

FLORISTS

Vases & Containers

Paula Pryke; Linda Trompetto, Society of Floristry; Hilary West; Jinnie McCabe; Sandy Martin, Branching Out, Glasgow; John Carter

Store oasis in a bucket of water – it should never be allowed to dry out.

Oasis should stand higher than the edge of the vase so you can have flowers and foliage hanging down rather than all standing to attention.

Stop oasis from floating around in a vase or bowl – secure it to the bottom with double-sided tape or blu tack.

To reuse oasis, just turn it over and start again.

If you don't have any oasis put sticky tape across the top of the vase in a criss-cross pattern to form a grid to hold the flowers upright.

Use pebbles from the garden (make sure they are clean first) instead of oasis in the bottom of the vase.

Marbles hold flowers in place. If used in a glass vase, they look attractive too.

To make flower arranging easy, put a wire scouring pad in the bottom of the vase and push the flower stems into the wire. The pad will last longer than oasis and, unlike oasis, can be used again even after it dries out.

Use polystyrene for drainage instead of stones.

If your vase has a small crack in it, seal the leak with a piece of soft candle wax.

If your vase is too big for the number of flowers you have, put a smaller tumbler inside the vase, fill it with water and put the flowers in that. The flowers will stand upright in the vase and won't look overwhelmed and droopy.

Clean vases regularly with bleach – not washing-up liquid – to kill the bacteria residue. Flowers are dirty things!

Vases with green stains at the bottom can be cleaned with biological washing powder and water. Leave to soak, then add a few drops of ammonia to the final rinsing water for a great shine.

Stubborn stains inside a glass vase will shift if you fill with warm water and a little silver sand. Shake well, then rinse.

To clean a smelly vase, half fill it with water and add a tablespoon of mustard. Shake the mixture and then leave for an hour.

Cut flowers in the late evening and they'll last longer.

Add a shot of vodka to the water in your vases – it will keep your flowers fresh for longer.

Alternatively, add a splash of lemonade to the water.

Fresh Flowers & Foliage

Never buy roses or spray carnations in tight bud but make sure the petals are unfurling. Very tight buds may never open.

Use lukewarm water when arranging flowers; it has less oxygen in it and so you don't get so many air bubbles up the stems of flowers.

When arranging flowers, strip off all leaves below the water line to prevent them rotting.

When buying foliage with flowers, avoid dowdy, yellow leaves. Foliage dies before flowers so make sure it's healthy and vibrant.

Smash hard woody stems but cut soft stems before placing them in your arrangement.

Don't place flowers in direct sunlight, near central heating or on top of the television. Make sure they are in a well-ventilated part of the room.

If your flower arrangement is going to be in a warm room, keep the blooms looking lovely by popping some ice cubes into the water each morning.

Don't put flowers next to fruit because the fruit produces ethylene gas, which increases the maturity rate of flowers, so they die more quickly. Equally, remove dying flowers from a bunch or arrangement because they produce the same gas.

Don't mix daffodils with other blooms – they release a poison that kills off other flowers.

Cut wide-stemmed flowers under water and then, keeping your finger over the cut end to stop air from getting into the stem, transfer to the vase.

Cut poppies will loose sap quickly and therefore won't last long unless you carefully singe the ends in a candle flame to create a seal.

Rubber plants leak sap when cut so use cigarette ash to stem the sap.

Gardenias leak white sap that can cause a rash if it comes into contact with your skin. Seal the cut stem over a naked flame.

Remove the stamens from lilies to prevent the pollen from staining clothes and furnishing fabrics. Wipe up any pollen that falls on to polished wood surfaces because, if left, it will eat into the wood.

If the pollen from flowers has fallen on to your carpet or furnishing fabrics, lift it off gently with sticky tape so that you don't rub it in and leave an indelible stain.

If the stem of a lily splits, wrap it in sticky tape.

Sharpen scissors by cutting tin foil.

Revive droopy tulips and roses – wrap them tightly in wet newspaper and put them in a deep bucket of water overnight.

Alternatively, revive droopy flowers with a soluble aspirin in their vase – it's a great pick-me-up.

Perk up woody-stemmed flowers (such as roses) by putting the stems in boiling water for ten seconds, and then immediately plunging them into deep, cold water. This will move the air lock that has formed in the stem up to the flower.

To keep your posy of roses fresh, punch holes in a raw potato and insert each stem into a hole separately. Your flowers will stay fresh and pretty for a considerable time.

Scented flowers don't last as long as non-scented varieties because they use up extra energy creating the smell.

To keep fresh tulips closed, paint them with unbeaten egg white.

Use all the same flowers and stick to one colour to create a glamorous arrangement at half the price.

Always use flowers that are in season: daffodils for spring and roses for summer.

When arranging flowers with soft stems, make a hole for the stem in the oasis using a knitting needle.

For flowers in an opaque vase, broken stems can by disguised by sliding them inside a plastic straw, and inserting that into the oasis.

Dried Flowers

Preserve dried flowers by spraying with hair-spray. It acts like an adhesive and prevents them from falling apart.

Revitalise dried roses by holding them over a kettle of boiling water.

Make your own dried flowers – use the microwave. A rose, for example, will take three minutes on medium power.

If you don't have a microwave, hang the flowers upside down in the airing cupboard for a couple of days.

To crystallise flowers, mix one part sugar to one part water, simmer until the sugar has dissolved. Then put the flowers in the syrup and simmer gently for a short while. Remove and leave to dry.

Pot Plants

Repot a plant without making a mess. Simply place the old pot inside the new larger pot and fill the gap with soil. Then remove the smaller pot, take the plant out of the old pot and place into the hole in the new pot.

To repot cacti, use old carpet scraps to hold the plant so you don't damage your hands.

Alternatively, fold a length of brown paper into a wide band, wrap it round the cactus and hold both ends in one hand. Pull the pot away with the other hand.

Don't waste your money on expensive leaf shine – give your potted plants a good wipe down with milk.

House plants are used to being warm so when you are taking them home, keep them in the plastic sleeves the shops put them in. If it's really quite cold, add an extra layer of insulation by putting the plants in a cardboard box.

House plants grow towards the source of light so turn them regularly to encourage even growth.

Many house plants benefit from a humid atmosphere. Grouping them together is one way to increase humidity.

To clean a large plant with small leaves, put it in the bath and spray it with tepid water using the shower attachment.

Keep plants with hairy leaves clean by brushing away dust using a small, soft paint-brush.

Golden barrel cactus likes a dry atmosphere. Don't water it during its rest period in the winter.

Spotted dumb cane likes shady conditions, but keep it away from children because its sap is poisonous.

Herringbone plant is another one that likes shady conditions. Don't leave it in too bright a light because the bright colours of its leaves will fade.

Create a tower of flowers. Stack pots one on top of the other to create a dramatic display.

To water plants while you are away, stick one end of a pipe cleaner into a bowl of water and place the other end into the plant pot. The plant will then suck up the water when required.

Alternatively, fill your bath with about 1 in/2.5 cm of water and place a thick bath towel on top. Stand your plants on the towel so that they can take up water when they require it.

To give plants a really good watering take them into the shower with you. A verse of 'Everything's coming up roses' goes down well too.

Devon violets drink water through their leaves so always dunk them right under water.

To revive a bone-dry plant, plunge it in a bucket of water and then drain. Don't pour water over it: this will just wash out the soil.

Always keep one set of tools for house plants and another for the garden so you don't run the risk of introducing damaging diseases or pests.

Garden Flowers

Protect roses from frost by piling the soil up into a mound round the stems. Remove the soil once the weather improves.

When deadheading long-stemmed plants, cut back to the next growth point or set of leaves.

As rhododendron flowers fade, remove them, but be careful not to damage the plant as you do so.

Deadhead soft-stemmed plants by hand. You get better access to the flower heads and it's easier than using secateurs.

Lily bulbs can rot in damp weather, so put a layer of gravel in the planting hole to encourage the water to drain away.

Alternatively, plant lily bulbs on their side so that water doesn't gather round the crown of the bulb and cause it to rot.

Put marigold flowers in your bath to soften the water.

Love-in-a-mist (*Nigella damascena*) produces spice-scented seeds, which can be used in cooking.

Heartsease can be added to salads, sundaes and drinks.

Use rose petals in cream, ice-cream, cordials and salads.

Try adding the flowers of pinks to salads or vinegar, or even use them to decorate cakes.

Nasturtiums have a strong, peppery flavour, which works well in salads and sandwiches.

FOOTBALLERS

Boot, Shirts & Gloves

Andrew Collins;
Erroll Hibbert

When you have brought your new football boots home, soak them in water, then stuff with newspaper. Allow them to dry naturally. When they are fully dry, rub them with petroleum jelly.

To get your new boots to fit perfectly, sit in the bath with them on – as practised by the professionals!

After the game fill your boots with scrunched-up newspaper to keep them dry and in shape.

To stop studs rusting into the soles of football boots, unscrew them and rub Vaseline on to the screw before screwing back in.

Don't knock mud off the soles of football boots, by banging them against a wall – you'll damage both the wall and the studs. Instead, leave the mud to dry and peel it off.

Many football boots – despite appearances – aren't actually made of leather, but are synthetic. Avoid the hassle of polishing – synthetic boots can be cleaned with soapy water.

Contrary to popular belief, use shoe polish on leather football boots rather than dubbin. Dubbin stops the leather breathing.

Leave boots to dry naturally – drying them under a radiator or in an airing cupboard will dry out the oils in the leather and it will crack.

The best thing for cleaning white stripes on football boots is a bit of kitchen cleaner cream. Second best is toothpaste.

And the best way to touch up trendy coloured boots is with a crayon of the right colour.

Never tumble dry football shirts with names and numbers on the back – the transfers will melt.

Hang football shirts on your wall between washing and wearing – they make great posters.

When folding up football shirts after washing, avoid folding along the line of the sponsor's name on the front of the shirt – the print will crack.

If your team has two kits, wear them alternately to get the life back into them between matches.

To air sweaty, smelly goalkeepers' gloves, turn them inside out and attach them to the handle-bars of a bike with rubber bands. Then ride round on the bike.

Training

For your own home-made isotonic drink, mix together 3 teaspoons of glucose powder, a teaspoon of salt and 1 litre of water.

A fun way to get your team warmed up is to put your players in a confined area with their shirts tucked into their shorts. One player starts out trying to pull the back of the shirts out of the shorts. Once you've 'lost your shirt', you grab others' shirts.

To practise heading, use balloons. This is particularly useful in building confidence when heading the ball at the same time as another player. Throw the balloon between two people; they have to go for the balloon carefully and slowly.

To build confidence in dribbling, place several kit bags on top of each other and dribble around them. Don't use anything small, like a cone or disc on the ground, until later.

Keep in touch with the rest of the team – improve your communication with your team members. Give everyone a number from one to ten. Then, in a confined area, pass the ball from one to two to three and so on. Each person has to shout out his or her number to get the ball.

Improve your thinking and sharpen your reactions – get someone to shout out the points of the compass. React as quickly as you can by diving in the correct direction: left for west, for example.

Speed up reaction time by throwing the ball at a player and shouting 'Head it' – except they must catch it. Likewise, when you shout 'Catch it', they have to head it.

To bend the ball in flight, hit the ball on the outside and point your foot in the direction you want the ball to go. Follow through with the kick.

When throwing the ball in, stand sideways and turn like a javelin player, dragging your foot on the ground as you turn (don't let your foot come away from the floor).

To improve your goal-keeping skills, make sure you keep your arms up as you dive to save the ball. People normally dive with their arms down, bringing them up as they move towards the ball – by which time it can often be too late.

The proper stance for a goalie comes straight from a gunslinger's book. Stand with your hands spread out by the side of your body – as if you are about to go for your gun, cowboy!

When in goal, never cross your feet: side-step along the goal line.

Every time goalies catch or hold the ball, they should spread their fingers, making sure that their thumbs are touching (so that there is a W-shape at the back of the ball).

To get children to control the ball, set out a 6 ft/1.8 m square. Keep throwing the ball into and through the square; the child has to stop and control it and, in doing so, they will learn how to trap, stop and control the ball naturally.

When playing with small children, don't use small goals because they'll never score! Use a large adult goal: the scoring opportunities increase and they remain interested.

After any exercise, stretch your muscles out, keeping each one tense for 30 seconds, to keep them free from aches and pains.

If you have sprained yourself, stick a bag of frozen peas on the affected area.

FURNITURE REPAIRERS

Andrew Barnet;
Angela Ring

Stripping & Polishing

Stand smaller pieces of furniture on an old sheet on an old table. It will stop you from straining your back as you work.

Old toothbrushes are ideal for removing bits of paint from awkward crevices.

When trying to strip a piece of furniture caked in many layers of paint, brush on a layer of gel or paint stripper thickly and cover with a piece of old newspaper. With a plant sprayer filled with soapy water, keep the paper and stripper wet. Leave it for an hour or so (keeping it wet), then lift the paper and scrape gently at a test area to see if the stripper has worked. Hey presto, when you lift the paper the paint should come off with it.

Keep water handy in case you splash any stripper on your skin.

Don't throw away old paint-brushes – they are great for applying paint stripper. Leave the brushes in the stripper for an hour or so before you start to remove residual paint from the brush.

Restore the finish of French polish by flicking on a little baby oil and rubbing in into the surface. Then rub it over gently with a little methylated spirits.

If you have any suspicions that a piece of furniture might be valuable, leave it well alone. Removing the patina (sheen produced by age) can dramatically lower the value of an antique piece.

Wax and oil test – rub a concealed area of finish with a little meths on a cloth and if it leaves a smear on the cloth it has been waxed. If it turns slippery it has been oiled.

Make your own wax polish by melting 18 oz/500 g of beeswax by placing it in a metal container sat in a saucepan over a heat source. When the wax has melted take it off the heat and remove the metal container. Slowly add ½ pint/300 ml of white spirit to the hot wax, stirring all the time. It makes an ideal first treatment on bare wood.

Test a waxed area by drawing your finger across it. If you can see a mark, keep on buffing!

Bare wood will absorb first coats of wax better if you warm the surface of the wood with a hair-dryer immediately after you have applied the wax, then rub the surface with a terry towel.

Save time by treating wood first with a shellac or cellulose sanding sealer, then apply wax polish.

Boiled linseed oil dries quicker than the raw product. Thin initial coats with white spirit to speed absorption.

Drop oily cloths in water before throwing them away. They will be highly inflammable otherwise.

Repairing

If a veneer has bubbled, iron it through a sheet of kitchen foil. Use the tip of the iron and keep it moving. Try to press it down but if the veneer doesn't stick, wipe over it with a dry cloth and press it down with a weight for an hour or so.

If that fails, cut along one edge of the bubble with a sharp blade, then insert a little PVA glue under the veneer, holding it up gently with an artist's palette knife. Press the veneer down lightly and wipe away any glue that oozes out with a damp cloth. Seal with masking tape and press the bubble down with a weight until the glue has dried.

If a veneer has been stuck down with traditional scotch glue, you may be able to reseal it with a cool iron. Hold the iron about 2 in/5 cm from your hand. It should feel warm but not uncomfortably hot.

Chair with a wobbly leg? Rather than take a chair apart, try drilling a small hole into the loose joint where it cannot be easily seen and injecting glue into the hole. Plug the hole with putty until the glue has dried.

Strong gluing relies on some absorption of glue into the wood. Melt old glue with meths or scrape it off with a chisel, without removing any good wood at the same time.

When mending the stretchers between two legs on an old chair, make a tourniquet to hold the legs tight whilst the glue sets. Loop rope around the legs (protecting the wood with pieces of cardboard) and twist a stick or screwdriver to tighten the rope.

No wax? Fill small holes – like woodworm homes – by melting a child's crayon in a spoon over a candle. Mix the colours to match the wood and trickle the warmed wax into the holes, smoothing it out with a knife dipped in hot water. Use a plastic scraper to remove any excess wax.

Car-body filler is a good alternative for filling damaged wood, even MDF. Small screws driven into the damaged area will help the filler to bond and stop it cracking.

Sawdust mixed with PVA glue into a paste also makes a good filler.

Glass fibre resin from car accessory shops is also good for reinforcing woodworm-damaged furniture or for reinforcing damaged cupboard-hinge areas.

Don't waste money on lots of different coloured fillers. Buy one tin of light filler and stain it with wood dust each time you use it.

Ingrained grime in wood can be washed away with a home-made mixture of equal quantities of vinegar, white spirit and water. Add a squirt of washing-up liquid and apply with a water sprayer. Wipe it off before it hardens.

Use car-rubbing compound and metal polish to remove white rings on furniture – rub gently though as they are both abrasives.

Salt and lemon juice rubbed in to an ink stain on furniture will work well on bare wood. On polished or finished surfaces, leave them well alone.

Clear nail varnish will cover scratches and chips in varnish. Leave it to dry and rub down gently with a fine sandpaper.

Use a child's felt-tipped pen to camouflage scratches in wood. Artists' oil paints will also do the trick. Thicken it up with wax and apply with a paint-brush.

GAMEKEEPERS

Leslie Ferguson, Representative of BASC; Country Landowners Association; Game Conservancy

Give your dog a good rub down after a wet day's shooting. Use discarded newspapers instead of towels.

Get the most out of your trap or snare. Bury it in the ground for several weeks to remove all traces of manufactured smells.

Stop foxes from eating your pheasants. Place mirrors or plastic bags round the pen and it should help to deter them.

Encourage pheasant chicks to peck at their food by mixing the corn with chocolate 'hundreds and thousands'.

Make wheat more palatable to young pheasants. Soak it in water first.

For an indestructible beater's flag, use old plastic fertiliser sacks. As well as being completely waterproof, they have the added advantage of 'cracking' when used for driving partridges and grouse.

Prevent your shot game from turning green and deteriorating within a matter of hours. Never leave it in a heap. The body heat must be allowed to disperse as quickly as possible.

GARDENERS
Seeds & Young Plants

Ken Hollingsworth; Andy Flitney; Mary Griffin; Michael Walker; David Parker; Guy Dagul

When storing seeds, make sure moisture doesn't ruin them. Keep them in an airtight tin. As an added precaution, wrap some milk powder in tissue, seal with a rubber band and leave it in the tin.

Sow seeds evenly. Punch holes in the top of a jam jar or coffee jar and use this to shake out the seeds.

The smaller the seed, the shallower it should be sown.

Mix small seeds with sand for easy planting.

Plant seedlings in bits of old guttering – they are easy to slide off the end for repotting.

To collect seeds, put the ripe seed head in a paper bag and shake.

Seeds in pods should not be stored in airtight containers. They need a flow of air round them. When the pods are dry, you can remove the seeds and put them in a paper bag.

Small seeds can stick to your hands when you're sowing. Keep your hands cool by running cold water over your wrists and then drying your hands thoroughly before you start.

Dry seeds by putting them on a piece of kitchen paper and leaving them to dry thoroughly. If seeds are still damp, they may start to rot or germinate.

The best place to store seeds is in the fridge.

Always label your seeds; some will keep for ages, while others only last a year.

Use cardboard egg-boxes filled with compost to sow seeds, then cut up the sections and plant them out straight into the ground. Water well and the cardboard will soon break down.

Use your linen cupboard to propagate seeds that don't need much light. Cover seed trays with cling film and check daily. As soon as the first seedlings appear, remove the trays.

Conserve moisture – cover seedling pots with cling film; this keeps out draughts and ensures that the temperature remains constant. Take the cling film off from time to time to prevent too much moisture building up.

If you use a propagator for seedlings, make sure you wipe the inside surface regularly to remove any condensation. Too much condensation cuts down the amount of light reaching the seedlings.

If the light levels are low where your seeds are growing, stand the pots of seedlings on kitchen foil so that they benefit from the reflected light.

To separate very small seedlings, use an old fork to lift them and divide them carefully.

Settle small seeds into the compost by wetting them with a plant mister.

To test if the soil is warm enough for sowing, gardeners of old would remove their trousers and sit on it. If you don't want to bare all, test the ground with your elbow as you would a baby's bath water.

To avoid disturbing the roots of plants roll newspaper strips into tubes. Fill with compost and moisten before sowing seeds into each one. Plant out the tubes and the roots will go down through the newspaper.

Seeds with hard coats can be soaked in water overnight. This will give them a head start when they are planted.

Always dry seeds before storing them: use paper towels or newspaper.

To avoid damping off in seed boxes, always use seedling compost and never garden soil. Don't reuse compost either.

Collect seeds from flowers – it's a lot cheaper than buying them in packets.

Cut up old magazines to make seed packets.

Empty film canisters make excellent containers for storing seeds.

Cover seed trays with cling film to prevent the compost from drying out while the seeds germinate.

Seed vegetables in the clean plastic containers from ready-cooked meals.

Instead of using pots or boxes to grow your seedlings, plant them in soil blocks. The advantage is that you can plant them straight out as soon as the roots emerge. Take a short length of plastic piping, 2–3 in/5–7.5 cm in diameter. Find a glass bottle that fits inside snugly. Stand the tube on a flat surface and fill with compost mixture. Pound down with the bottle several times. Lift off with a twisting motion. You are left with a solid soil block.

Cover a piece of cardboard with silver foil and place it behind a seedling. The foil reflects light from the window on to the plants, helping them to grow.

Transporting young plants can be difficult. Try using cereal boxes. Cut the box in half lengthwise. Punch a few holes in the bottom and then slip over the top of the seedling tray.

Protect a small plant from the sun by covering it with a large empty flowerpot before the temperature starts to rise.

Nobody likes getting into a cold bed and seeds are no different. Warm the soil before you plant by putting a dustbin liner over the soil and holding it in place with stones.

Avoid sowing in cold, damp conditions – you don't want the seeds to rot before they've had a chance to start growing. Delay sowing until conditions improve.

For an alternative seed starter, use tea-bags.

Thin delicate seedlings with a pair of tweezers. This doesn't disturb the roots of the remaining seedlings.

To support small plants, remove the inner part of a ballpoint pen and use the transparent outer skin as a support.

Make a mini-greenhouse – cut the top off a plastic drinks bottle and place it over your seedlings.

Sow lawn seeds using a plant pot with holes in the bottom as a shaker.

Once you've sown grass seed, gently rake over some soil to protect it from birds. This will help to give it a good start.

Make sure you have a ready supply of plants for next year – pot cuttings from perennials in late summer.

When taking cuttings, put them in a plastic bag until you're ready to plant them up.

To stimulate a cutting and encourage root formation, cut a sliver of bark from one side of the cutting's base.

Cover yourself before moving a plant – take some cuttings just in case the move doesn't work.

Swap cuttings with other gardeners.

To kick-start woody cuttings, slit the end of the stem and put a grain of wheat into the cut. As the wheat germinates, it encourages the root of the cutting to form.

Try growing a cutting from a shrub by bending a low branch over and pegging it into the ground. Within a few weeks, you can often find you've got a new plant growing apace.

Watering

When planting a shrub in dry soil, put a pot of gravel around the roots. When you water it, the water should go straight through to the roots.

In hot weather, line a pot with damp paper before potting up a plant. This conserves moisture.

To make a self-watering plant pot, cut a plastic bottle in half, remove the lid and pull a piece of fabric partly through the spout end. Then place the plant in the top, on the fabric. Fill the bottom half of the bottle with water and place the spout end, complete with 'wick' and plant, on top. The fabric will soak up the water from below.

Alternatively, fill an old jam jar or container with water, cut a hole in the lid and thread through one end of a long strip from an old pair of tights so that it reaches the bottom of the jar. Put the other end of the strip through the hole in the bottom of the plant pot. Stand the pot on top of the container.

Many pots have inadequate drainage holes, so don't overwater – you can always add more but you can't take it away.

For moisture-loving plants such as ferns, you can line the inside of a terracotta pot with polythene to prevent water loss.

A self-watering plant pot using a plastic bottle

A self-watering plant pot using a jam jar

Stop twigs, leaves and other bits and pieces from getting into your water butt by securely fixing a pair of old tights to the end of the downpipe. Clear out regularly, especially after heavy rainfall.

A water butt should be kept clear of algae. Scrub it out with a stiff, long-handled brush and soapy water.

Stop your wooden water butt from splitting during a freeze – place a piece of wood in the barrel.

Make sure you can get a watering can under the tap of a water butt. Raise the butt off the ground using some old bricks if necessary.

Tap water is fine for most plants. However, if you live in an area with a high lime content, boil the water first, particularly if you have a lot of lime-hating plants (like azaleas).

Don't use water that has been put through a water filter because the chemicals in the filter can damage your plants.

For drainage in window boxes, use small pine cones. They are a great lightweight drainage material.

Poke four holes into the bottom of a plastic milk bottle and half bury it in the soil. Plant cucumber seeds around the outside. When you need to water or fertilise the cucumber plants, fill up the bottle. The moisture will go straight to the roots without wetting the foliage.

Watering is required every five to seven days during a period of drought in summer. There's no need to water every day or two just because the plants droop or are not growing.

Don't waste time and energy watering lawns. They can be left for longer.

When you do water a dry lawn, spike it with a fork to ensure the water runs down to the roots rather than evaporates on the surface.

A sign of over-watering is if moss starts to grow on top of the potting compost.

If you have over-watered a potted plant, take it out of its pot and re-pot it using fresh potting mixture. Mix in some sand to help with drainage.

To rescue a parched potted plant, break up the potting mixture slightly with a fork (being careful not to damage the roots). Put the pot in a bowl of water until bubbles stop rising to the surface. Spray the leaves with a plant spray. Drain and leave in a cool place.

Pots that need lots of watering – sink in a bucket of water before you go away, then leave so the pot is wet as well as the compost. It should last the weekend.

Be careful when watering plants in a greenhouse or on a window-sill. A drop of water on a leaf can act like a magnifying glass and cause damage to the plant. Try to water in the early morning or avoid getting water on the leaves.

Never pour water directly into the tuber of a florist's cyclamen; just immerse the pot in water for 15 minutes.

Keep moisture in a hanging basket by placing an old saucer in the base of the basket when planting up.

Don't blast dry compost out of hanging baskets when you water them in the summer. Place half a dozen ice cubes in a perforated food bag and place overnight in the hanging basket. By the morning, the plants will have been watered.

To make sure the soil in hanging baskets is properly watered, punch holes in empty yoghurt cartons and bury in the middle of the hanging baskets. The soil gets watered and doesn't run off the top.

If the compost in a hanging basket has dried out so much that water just runs off it, add a few drops of washing-up liquid to the water. The water will then be able to penetrate the surface.

Alternatively, take down the hanging basket and put it in a bowl of water until the compost becomes moist.

To avoid lifting heavy watering cans up to hanging baskets, use a one-litre plastic bottle – it contains just about the right amount of water for the task.

Save water. Put pots under hanging baskets to catch any over-spill of water.

To check if you've had the sprinkler on long enough put an empty jam jar by the sprinkler. When there's an inch of water in the bottom, it's time to move the sprinkler.

Buying Plants

The best time to buy plants is in the spring because you can get a good idea of their health by checking their foliage.

When buying a plant, there's nothing wrong with taking the plant out of its pot and checking its root system.

Try not to buy plants that have moss, algae or weeds growing in their compost. This could mean that the plant has been in its pot too long.

When buying shrubs, look for young, small plants. They will grow more rapidly and establish themselves more successfully than larger shrubs… and they'll probably be cheaper too.

If you come across a shrub for sale that's been pruned in an odd fashion, don't touch it. It probably means that the plant was damaged in some way.

Don't buy new heather plants; just place a heap of cuttings compost in the centre of your old heather plant and moisten. New heather roots will start to form in about six months' time.

Planting & Maintaining

When you have divided your perennials, you may be left with spare sections of plants; use them in containers as well as other parts of the garden.

Always check the roots of a plant. If they are all knotted up and congested, soak the root-ball in water for a few hours, tease the roots out and then plant it.

Before moving a plant, water the ground thoroughly for several days.

When moving a plant, tie up any loose stems or branches. This makes it easier to carry and reduces the risk of bits and pieces snapping off.

After moving a plant, cut back the foliage to reduce stress from moisture loss.

If there is a delay before replanting, wrap the roots in a plastic bag to retain moisture.

After transplanting an evergreen shrub, spray the foliage every day for two weeks.

Don't stick too rigidly to a planting timetable. Try sowing spring-sown annuals in the autumn. If it works, you can often get a much longer flowering period out of them.

Use annual climbers to cover a bare trellis while the slower-growing plants get a chance to establish themselves.

Protect a young clematis by planting it several inches deeper than it was in its container and surround the base with a cylinder of cardboard or plastic to prevent slugs from nibbling at it. Put some grease round the top of the cylinder to stop slugs and snails from climbing over it.

You can give a new lease of life to a hawthorn hedge by bending some of the pliable stems down into the soil. Secure them using metal hooks. In time, they will take root and start to fill out the bottom of the hedge.

When growing azaleas and rhododendrons, plant some foxgloves next to them. They help to keep the other plants healthy.

When planting against a brick wall, remember that the wall will take moisture from the soil so choose your plants accordingly (*Euonymus* and *Alchemilla mollis* are good choices).

Removing flowers and large leaves from a perennial when planting helps give it a good start in life and prevents moisture loss.

Don't do too much digging and moving of plants in winter – you'll only run the risk of damaging their roots and your back. Wait until spring.

You can store a plant for a while before planting it. Evergreen shrubs and conifers should stay in a sheltered spot to protect them from extreme temperatures.

Bare-root plants can be left in an unheated shed or garage for a few days before planting. Cover the roots loosely with an old sack or polythene bag so they don't dry out.

If you are planning to store a plant for a while, don't feed it. You want it to rest, not get all stimulated.

Protect tender perennials from frost by lining a hanging basket with straw and placing it over the top of the plants.

Don't replace a sick or dying plant with something similar. If you put the new shrub in the same spot, it may pick up the same disease.

Pinch out the tips of ivy to encourage bushiness.

Tweak out the first shoot from perennials like foxgloves and though they will flower a bit later, you will get a larger clump of flowers.

Brush your hedge before you cut it. Sounds mad, but a wet hedge is hard to cut, so sweep along it with a household broom to knock the water off.

Box is often used to edge lawns and paths. After trimming, it can smell a bit 'catty'. One remedy is to leave hard limestones in some water for three to four hours and then water the box with this water.

Cordylines in pots – put in shelter, wrap with raffia and sacking to protect leaves from wind damage.

Tender plants can be protected from cold snaps in winter by putting an old frost-proof pot over the top. Remember to remove it after the frost has passed – you don't want to encourage mildew.

For a large pot planted with a standard, such as box or bay, surrounded by lower-growing plants, keep the standard inside a plastic pot rather than in the pot soil, and replant around it regularly without disturbing its roots. It also keeps the growth in check and ensures that it doesn't outgrow its pot.

When sweeping up the leaves in autumn, first check which way the wind is blowing and then sweep with the wind.

If you have a piece of lawn that isn't doing too well, why not turn it into a wildflower area? Wildflowers love poor soils.

When storing bulbs, make sure they are kept dry. Put them on dry sand or newspaper so that they're not touching each other.

To check if a bulb is healthy give it a squeeze. It should be firm to the touch.

Planting bulbs in baskets means you can easily lift them when they start to fade and leave them out of sight while the foliage dies down.

Plant bulbs under deciduous shrubs. They will flower and fill the bare patch of earth. When the shrub's in leaf, it will hide the dying plants.

A container for bulbs should have lots of holes for drainage. A pond basket is a good alternative.

Ponds

New water plants often contain tiny duckweed plants which, once in situ, can multiply at an alarming rate. Rinse new pond plants under the tap before planting.

Always line the baskets of pond plants to keep soil round the roots. A bit of old sacking is fine.

Adding floating plants to a pond not only makes it look attractive but will also help to prevent the water getting too warm and give shelter to the pond's inhabitants.

Use an old colander to remove algae from ponds.

A good way to prevent algae from growing in your pond is to stuff the leg of a pair of old tights with barley straw. Tie the open end securely, attach a weight to one end and then submerge in the pond.

Keep pond surfaces clear of fallen leaves. If left, they can cause a build-up of toxic gases, which can kill fish and wildlife.

Use an old net curtain to cover your pond in winter. This will catch falling leaves for you. Shake it out regularly and then replace.

Blanket weed is best removed from your pond using a stick. Wind it round and round as if it were candyfloss.

To remove duckweed from a pond, draw a plank vertically across the surface and then remove the weed using an old colander or sieve.

Always bury duckweed in a hole, or put it in the dustbin or on the compost heap. It's a tough little plant and can spread easily.

Weeds

Use an old potato peeler to dig up weeds from your lawn.

To slaughter stubborn weeds, blast them with a mixture of gin and detergent.

To make your own funnel to administer weed-killer more easily, cut off the top of a plastic drinks bottle. You can then just throw it away after you've used it.

When using weedkiller, be careful not to get any on your boots or gardening shoes. You don't want to tramp it all over the garden.

Keep weeds down by planting up the gaps and cracks between paving stones with seeds of hardy annuals.

Alternatively, ensure that the grouting between paving stones is done properly in the first place.

Try not to walk on frost-covered grass because you can damage the blades which make it vulnerable to disease.

Garden Pests

Protect your vegetable patch with an 'instant snake'. Take an old piece of garden hose, about the length of a snake and wind it on the ground around your plants. Cats and birds will stay away at the sight of a 'snake'.

Orange and grapefruit peel scattered around the garden will stop cats coming in – they hate the smell of citrus fruits.

Keep cats off your garden with a judicious sprinkling of pepper.

Leave your rose prunings on the ground; rabbits and cats don't like a prickly surface.

Sink empty bottles up to their necks in the garden. Moles don't like the sound of the wind across the empty tops.

Stick a child's windmill in the ground near a mole's run; it causes vibrations to run down the stem and into the run which disturbs the mole.

Deter moles by lining the bottom of their run with gorse. Moles hate having their noses pricked.

Marauding deer won't trouble you if you tie a few children's silvery helium balloons round the perimeter of your garden.

If your dog keeps digging up newly planted shrubs, he might be after the bonemeal from the fertiliser. Try using pelleted chicken manure instead.

Protect the bark of young trees from rabbits by wrapping a 'skirt' of chicken wire round the tree. Check that it doesn't restrict the tree as it grows.

To keep rabbits out of your garden remember:

R	Rosemary		
A	Azaleas	B	Bay
B	Bluebells	A	Asters
B	Box	N	Nasturtiums
I	Iris		
T	Tulips		

Don't be too tidy – leave some areas for helpful garden animals to hide in.

When the birds have flown, take down their nest and either throw it away or burn it. Nests are great places for insects to live.

Keep pests out of the shed and house – spray insect repellent across the edge of the door and along the window-sill.

Remove woodlice temporarily from a terrace by spraying the ground with a high-pressure water spray.

Mix up your own insect spray from a mixture of water and a little washing-up liquid.

To get rid of pests from plants, spray with garlic tea. To make the tea, infuse garlic cloves in hot water and leave to stand for half an hour before using.

Clear flying insects and their eggs from your greenhouse – use a vacuum cleaner.

Rhubarb leaves help to deter pests.

Protect your carrots by sprinkling coffee granules around them.

Keep greenfly down – put on some rubber gloves and go and squash them.

A 5 in/13 cm square of carpet underlay placed around your cabbages protects them from the root fly maggot.

Grow carnivorous plants in the greenhouse – it's one way to keep pests at bay!

Garden pests can be controlled using Jeyes fluid. Pop some in your spray bottle and use on blackfly and greenfly.

If you are plagued by blackfly, just sprinkle some soil from the base of the plant over the pests.

To catch codling moths, wrap a piece of old sacking round the trunk of an apple tree in the summer. The moths crawl into the sacking and you can then take it down and burn it.

A bruised garlic clove left at the entrance of a wasp's nest will clear it.

Protect carrot plants from carrot flies by surrounding them with a fence, 2 ft/60 cm high, made of polythene or old bin liners. Carrot flies aren't high flyers and so won't be able to clear the fence.

Exposed colonies of mealy bugs can be treated by touching them with a cotton-wool bud dipped in methylated spirits. Repeat when necessary.

To control clubroot, insert a small stick of rhubarb into the planting hole.

To avoid phlox eelworm, take root cuttings – this pest doesn't enter by the roots.

To keeps wasps off ripening fruit, spoon a layer of jam into the bottom of a jar, cover this with water and put a hole in the lid – hang the jar near the fruit to catch the wasps.

The red spider mite loves hot, dry conditions so make sure you wet the floor of your greenhouse several times a day. This increases the humidity and lowers the overall temperature.

Get rid of wireworms, which can attack root vegetables, by making traps. Cut potatoes into pieces and put them on a wooden skewer. Bury the chunks in the ground, leaving enough of the skewer above ground to act as a marker.

To prevent aphids from attacking your apple trees, grow nasturtiums up the trunk.

Aphids can wreck plants in hanging baskets. Spray the baskets with soapy water to kill off the aphids.

Flea beetles can cause a lot of damage. To get rid of them smear a piece of bright yellow card (flea beetles love yellow) with grease and leave by the threatened plants.

Insects hate the smell of lemongrass, melissa, eucalyptus, tea tree and citronella. Use them (in the form of essential oils) when eating outside in the summer.

Pots of basil will keep whitefly at bay in the greenhouse.

Not all creepy crawlies are pests. Many insects will help you wage war against pests so encourage them. Ladybirds, spiders, lacewings, hoverflies, centipedes, ground beetles, many birds and wasps are all friends of the gardener.

Slug pubs are a great bait. Cut slug-sized holes in the lid of a cottage cheese tub, fill it with beer and sink it into the ground. Slugs will be attracted to the beer, and drown in it.

Place half-empty beer cans on their sides in the garden as slug traps (the snails won't be able to get through the ring-pull hole).

Half a grapefruit left upside down, with the cut surface on the ground, makes a great slug trap.

Stop slugs and snails in their tracks. Smear petroleum jelly on the rim of a flowerpot to stop your plants getting attacked.

When planting up a pot, place rocks in the bottom for drainage, then follow with a layer of grit – to deter slugs from entering.

Deter slugs by scattering crushed eggshells around your tender plants. Slugs hate to crawl over such a rough surface.

Ash, hawthorn twigs and holly leaves will all deter slugs.

Don't place pots close to a wall – it gives slugs a good route up.

Wave goodbye to slugs by smearing lettuce or cabbage leaves with lard and leaving them dotted around the garden. When they are covered with slugs, pick them up and throw them away.

Slugs don't like strands of horse hair rope laid across the soil surface.

Encourage frogs and toads into the garden; they love slugs. Victorian gardeners used to keep a couple of toads in the greenhouse to keep down the slug population.

Protect delicate seedlings from slugs by surrounding them with the cardboard centres of loo rolls or milk cartons with the top and bottom cut off.

Use Jeyes fluid in your watering can to combat slugs and snails.

Compost & Fertiliser

Peaches and cherries in pots can be fed throughout the summer by making a mix of manure, water and soil, and rolling to make a 'snake' that can be fitted inside the rim of the pot, on top of the soil.

Banana skins are rich in potash, beneficial for flowering plants, so don't throw them away; place them round the bottom of your roses for a great fertiliser.

Fertilise your azaleas and camellias by placing used tea-bags around their roots.

Give azaleas the odd drink of 2 pints/1.2 litres of water mixed with two tablespoons of white vinegar.

Urine is a great fertiliser if you dilute it ten to one.

When you clean your coffee-maker, sprinkle a thin layer of coffee grounds on to the soil surfaces of your potted plants. As the coffee grounds are high in nitrogen and other nutrients, they will decompose into a slightly acid-forming nutrient source.

Pigeon poo, and rabbit and goat droppings all make good compost activators.

If you're friendly with a brewery, try getting some of their spent hops to use as a soil conditioner. Use them as mulch or compost.

Gardeners living near the sea have a ready source of rich fertiliser. Seaweed can be used straight away or put into the compost heap.

Collect sheep droppings in a hessian sack, then suspend the sack in a barrel of water. Use the water as liquid fertiliser.

To improve the texture of the soil, add a handful of chopped bracken when planting. Bracken is slightly acidic, so don't use with lime-loving plants.

Leaf mould, cocoa fibre and organic matter will all improve the soil's moisture retention, drainage and texture.

Make your own leaf mould. Collect the leaves and put them in a large bin bag. Make some holes in the side of the bag and fold the top over. Weigh down with a brick and leave for six to twelve months.

Apply humus mulch at the right time – when the soil is warm and moist. May is ideal.

Keep grass cuttings. Throw them on to the compost heap (or into a black bag) and cover with a piece of carpet until they've mulched down.

To preserve nutrients in grass, only cut the top third of the grass and leave the other two-thirds; that way, the grass keeps its nutrients and doesn't die.

An inexpensive alternative to mulch is to lay wet newspaper on to wet soil around a shrub. Cover with soil to disguise it.

Use hedge trimmings in compost, but don't put them into a compost heap if you know that the hedge is diseased.

Lay an old sheet before you start to trim your hedge. When you finish, you can simply gather them up and take them to your compost heap in one go.

After trimming your garden hedge, leave the cuttings on the ground. When you mow the lawn, the twigs and leaves can be collected with the grass cuttings.

Don't feed a plant if it's been suffering from lack of water. It won't be able to absorb the fertiliser properly.

To protect tender plants in winter, use chicken wire held in place by wooden stakes. Cover it with a piece of old carpet.

Natural fibre knitted items such as jumpers and cardigans can be cut up and added to your compost. Don't use your mum's cashmere sweater though.

Old carpet can be used in compost as well as being an effective lid on your compost heap. Chop it up into small squares.

Alternatively, old feather pillows make a good compost ingredient.

Always layer your compost. Try not to add too much of any ingredient at one time and try to alternate a moist ingredient (like grass clippings) with something drier.

Accelerate your compost by mixing green manure into it.

Alternatively, put some fresh horse manure in your compost and you'll soon be rewarded with wonderful organic compost.

If the weather gets hot, give your compost a drink of water. This encourages the ingredients to break down.

When it's cold, make sure your compost wraps up nice and warm. If it gets too cold, it won't rot down.

To construct your own composter, put some holes in the side and base of an old dustbin, and stand it on some bricks for drainage.

Make sure you put some carbon in your compost such as cereal packets, egg boxes and so on which will give the compost some bulk.

To encourage geranium growth, keep all your eggshells in a bucket of water. After a few weeks remove the eggshells and water your geraniums with this liquid.

Put crushed eggshells in the bottom of a planting hole for extra calcium. Eggshells are alkaline, so don't use for plants that like acid soil.

Make your own liquid fertiliser from nettles. Put freshly picked nettles into a large bucket. Cover with water (around 18 pints/10 litres of water to 2lb/1 kg of nettles) and seal with cling film. Leave for a few weeks, stirring now and again. When the nettles have rotted down, strain the mixture into a bucket. Dilute the liquid with water about ten times before using.

Alternatively, soak nettles together with thistles for a few months and use that as a fertiliser.

If you can't be bothered to dig in organic matter, spread it over the soil in the autumn and leave the winter weather to break it down for you.

Improve the texture of your soil by digging in coarse sand and gravel. Avoid using builder's sand because it can contain harmful contaminants.

If you want to improve the alkalinity of your soil, use mushroom compost.

If you plant a wildflower area, don't fertilise the ground. Always wait until the flowers have set seed before cutting.

Fruit

Don't plant potatoes too near your apple trees – they just don't get on together.

Peeing on your apple trees (especially if old men are doing the watering) is said to encourage fruiting.

To grow an apple tree from a pip, half fill a plastic food container with damp compost and put several pips in it. Put the lid on, place somewhere warm (like an airing cupboard) and leave for several weeks.

Alternatively, drop all your apple cores in a chosen spot in the garden. Cover them with compost occasionally and eventually one will start to grow.

Plum trees thrive on a mixture of urine, left-over wine and some water.

Beating a tree is a sure-fire way to encourage fruit growth.

To protect peach trees from leaf curl, grow garlic at the base of the trunk.

Put saucers of water under gooseberry bushes to keep the atmosphere moist.

Gooseberries grow well from hardwood cuttings.

Melon seeds should be kept in a warm place for six to eight hours before sowing.

To get rid of freckles, follow this old recipe. Take 1 pint/600 ml of white wine vinegar and put it into a glass with six oak apples and a few elder leaves. Set it in the sun and wash your face with the mixture.

Vegetables

When sowing vegetable seeds, put two seeds in each hole to allow for poor germination. Thin if more than one seed starts to grow.

To kick-start parsnip, early carrots, onions and parsley, sow the seeds on damp kitchen paper. Leave somewhere warm until they germinate. When the roots emerge, wash the seeds in a sieve and then mix into wallpaper paste. Prepare a small trench in your vegetable plot. Fill a plastic bag with the wallpaper mix and cut the corner off. Go along the trench, squeezing out the paste and seeds as if you were icing a cake.

You can save space by sowing two different crops in a single row. Mix a slow-growing crop such as parsnips or carrots with something faster such as lettuces and radishes.

In addition, you can save space by growing trailing varieties of marrow and squash up an arch or pergola.

Use newspapers to line a bean trench before filling up with compost and soil. This helps retain moisture, especially if there's a dry spell, while the rotting paper will feed the roots.

Pigeon or poultry dung in your asparagus beds will help the vegetables grow to a larger than average size.

Keep onions away from runner beans.

Peas and beans will increase the nitrogen levels in the soil, so include them in your planting scheme.

Remember to cut peas and beans down to ground level once they have finished cropping. Leave the roots to add nourishment to the soil.

Peas and beans don't like garlic (maybe they're closet vampires), so never plant them next to each other.

When growing leeks, give them some stout to drink to stimulate their growth.

Encourage leeks to grow by applying soot to the soil.

A pair of old tights slipped over a marrow will protect it from the birds.

Make a trench alongside your rows of vegetables. Water into the trench so that the moisture gets down to the roots.

To water long rows of vegetables, lay plastic guttering between the rows. Make small holes along its length. Pour water into the guttering.

Always water vegetables in the evening.

Don't grow large areas of vegetables. It's like hanging up a neon sign to pests saying, 'Come and eat me.' Grow small areas, interspersed with other plants and vegetables.

The simplest way of storing carrots, beetroot and swedes is to leave them in the ground. Lay some straw down for frost protection in the colder months.

When you've harvested your cabbages, leave the stumps to grow again. Cut them at an angle so that the rain and snow won't settle and start to rot what's left.

Cabbage can stink when it's being cooked. A bay leaf added to the boiling water will stop the smell without affecting the taste of the vegetables.

Carrots are easier to scrape if dunked in boiling water first.

To cook delicious broad beans, add some chopped parsley to the water.

If your hands smell of onions, soak them in some milk.

There's no need to use a sticking plaster when you cut yourself. Press the inside of a clear onion skin onto the cut. Leave it there for as long as you can. Onion is a natural antiseptic.

Store onions and garlic in the foot of some sheer tights to keep them dry and fresh.

Tools & Furniture

To remove rust from garden tools, mix two tablespoons of salt with one tablespoon of lemon juice. Apply this mixture to the rust and rub hard.

To store garden tools over winter, grease lightly with cooking oil.

To prevent your tools from rusting, store them in buckets of sand and oil mixed together.

Prevent rust by using left-over engine oil. Leave the bottle to drain into a jar, then brush the oil on to your garden tools or furniture to keep them in good condition. Wipe off before using.

Always push – never pull – your wheelbarrow; you have more control this way.

Keep the tyres of your wheelbarrow free of mud. If you allow mud to build up, it could conceal sharp stones that may cause a puncture.

Put a couple of drops of food colouring into your rain gauge to make it easier to read.

Turn your electric drill into a bulb planter with extra large drill bits. Use a 2¼ in/5.5 cm wide bit for small bulbs, try a 2½ in/6 cm for medium bulbs, and a 3 in/7.5 cm wide bit for larger bulbs.

To make the handle of your spade or fork more comfortable to hold, put a small section of pipe-insulating foam over the handle. Hold it in place with some insulating tape.

Make your own dibber. Use a broken fork handle or a couple of bits of wood screwed together in the shape of a T.

If you have an external tap, make sure it doesn't drip. The water can encourage algae growth, which can cause unattractive green marks and dangerous slippery patches.

If your soil is heavy, stand on a board when digging it to avoid compacting it further.

If you have clay soil, use a fork, not a spade. A spade can seal the edges and make it hard for water to drain through.

Use a staple gun to fix climbing plants to a fence.

The best support for clematis is nylon wire wrapped round sheds, posts and tree trunks.

Tie up delicate climbers with old tights cut into strips.

To support your herbaceous plants, pull a wire coat-hanger into a square and hook on to supporting canes.

To fill a watering can with a narrow opening, insert a large plastic funnel first.

Cane caps, essential to protect your eyes from damage, can be made from recycled miniature jam pots from hotel breakfasts.

To prevent a hose from being dragged across flowerbeds drive small stakes of wood into the corners and edges of beds so the hose runs round these rather than damaging plants.

Pour some baking soda into your garden hose, replace the nozzle and turn the water on. The spray will wash the grime off the garden furniture and garage doors.

Sitting on the ground or stone can be wet and cold. Make your own insulated cushion from a sheet of kitchen foil sandwiched between two pieces of foam.

Make your own garden kneeling pads from off-cuts of garden underlay, a child's plastic sledge or an old hot water bottle stuffed with bits of material.

Alternatively, sew old shoulder pads inside your gardening trousers.

Protect your arms when pruning old brambles or holly. Cut the top and bottom off a couple of old, plastic sweet jars and use as arm protectors.

Always protect your hands – wear gloves.

Some people are allergic to the scales on bulbs so wear gloves when handling hyacinth, iris, narcissus, bluebell and tulip bulbs.

Put soap under your fingernails before gardening. They'll be much easier to clean afterwards.

Keep odds and ends of soap in an empty supermarket orange bag, twist and tie the top and hang it up by the sink – ideal for washing and scrubbing soily hands in one go!

Get hands clean after a hard day's gardening with soap, water and sugar.

Don't wash your hands in very hot water because it strips the skin of its natural oils. Warm water and a gentle soap are just as effective. Always apply hand cream after you've got your hands wet.

If your hands become stained or discoloured, rub the skin with half a lemon. Rinse off and dry your hands carefully, then massage in some hand cream, because lemon has a drying effect on the skin.

Clean grubby nails with minty toothpaste (this is especially effective for smokers).

For heavy-duty hand cream, mix virgin olive oil and petroleum jelly together. Rub the mixture into your hands and then put them in freezer bags. Sit and have a cuppa or read the paper while your hands absorb this perfect conditioner.

If you've been on your feet all day, give them a treat. A cup of baking soda or Epsom salts dissolved in a bowl of warm water makes a wonderful foot-bath.

Try not to wear wellies for any great length of time. Your feet won't benefit from it and they'll smell awful as well.

An old American recipe for waterproofing gardener's boots: 1 pint/600 ml boiled linseed oil, ½lb/225 g mutton suet, 6 oz/175 g clean beeswax, 4 oz/100 g resin. Melt them down and mix together. While the mixture is still warm, brush on to new boots or shoes that are dry and clean.

It's more hygienic if the layer next to your skin is cotton.

Hang an old curtain over the shed door to keep out draughts.

Bubble wrap is an effective way to insulate your greenhouse. Use clips to attach the wrap to an aluminium frame, or pin it to a wooden frame. Cover the ventilators separately so they can be opened.

To keep an eye on your greenhouse in winter, place a small dish of water inside and you'll know when the temperature reaches freezing.

To make a cheap cold frame, get a wooden apple box and cover with a rigid piece of plastic held in place with twine or a strong elastic band. To shade the contents, use a piece of greenhouse shade netting or an old onion bag.

Age a new statue or pot by rubbing over with natural yoghurt. Within a few weeks algae and bacteria will have begun to 'age' it.

Shift stains from plastic garden furniture with a paste made from bicarbonate of soda and water. Leave the paste on the stain for about two minutes and then wipe off.

To preserve aluminium garden furniture over winter, lightly wipe down with cooking oil. Remember to wipe it off when you want to use the furniture again.

Scrub a wooden deck with a mixture of two cups of bicarbonate of soda and 1 gallon/4.5 litres of water, for a weathered look. The solution may affect stains and finishes so test a small area first.

Treat oil stains (baby oil, sun tan oil) on wooden decks by sprinkling bicarbonate of soda liberally on the affected area. Let it set for an hour or so before sweeping it up. The soda may turn yellow as it absorbs. Or wet the stain with a bit of paint thinner and immediately sprinkle soda on to the area to prevent the thinner from soaking into the wood.

Wipe down garden furniture with a solution of bicarbonate of soda and water before putting it away for the winter. Sprinkle soda directly on to canvas chairs, hammocks and the like. Shake off the excess and store.

Check your insurance policy if you have window boxes or hanging baskets. Are you covered if they fall and damage someone or something?

Clean above-ground swimming pool liners easily with a damp rag and a bicarbonate of soda paste. The soda even helps to keep the pool ph balanced.

Flowers & House Plants

Cut, hollow-stemmed flowers last longer if you turn them upside down and fill the stem with water.

Bring the shine back to dusty house plants by wiping the leaves with a mixture of milk and water.

To keep cacti dust-free, brush gently every week with a pastry brush.

If you've bought decorative plant pots with no drainage holes line the base with a lot of gravel.

To stop soil from leaking out of a pot, line the base with a coffee filter paper.

GOLFERS

Dennis Sheehy; Martin Tyson, Dainton Park Golf Club; Jamie Waugh, Dartmouth Golf Club; Simon Lloyd, Bigbury Golf Club; Owen Mckenna, Elsenham Golf Club, Stansted; Joan Walsh & Pam Dick, Finham Golf Club

Clothing

Your gloves should be kept in mint condition at all times. Golf gloves are made from first-class leather and cost a lot of money so keep them in a small plastic bag when not in use.

Retain the shape of your gloves – store them with a golf ball inside.

Keep a grip in wet weather – try wearing rubber gloves! The other players will soon stop laughing once they see that you are beating them.

Jewellery can get in the way while you're playing. Put a loop on your golf bag to thread your jewellery on so you don't lose it.

Use balls of various different colours for practising chipping. This helps you to keep track of which ball is which… remember, you should be keeping your head down all the time!

Pick up your metal markers using a magnet stuck to the end of a club. Put the markers at the top of your bag so you know where they are when you need one.

Clubs & Tees

To clean the grooves in your clubs, use an old toothbrush.

Smart wooden clubs can soon look shoddy when the paint becomes chipped. Instead of buying expensive paints, try applying two layers of permanent marker pen – first black, then red – which together make a lovely deep brown. Seal with a varnish and your clubs will look the part for ages.

A left-handed club is a useful addition to your golf bag. Use it when you're up against an object and can't use your right-handed clubs. If you're left-handed, read this trade secret back to front!

Keep your grips clean. Dirt commonly gets trapped in the ridges of the grips and, if they get wet, they can become slippery and hard to hold. Clean with soapy water and a nail-brush and dry thoroughly with a towel.

Metal-headed woods allow more latitude for error, and tend to give straighter and longer results.

It's never too early to start – ask a pro to cut down a club for toddlers to practise swinging with.

If you want to mark your ball when you are out on the course, scratch some of the paint off the ball with a wooden tee-peg.

Make your own tee that will stand up in the windiest weather – snip off a 2-in/5-cm length of hosepipe.

If you wear your glove on your left hand, put your tees in your right-hand pocket. They will be easier to get out.

When the ground is frozen, use a plastic bottle top as a tee.

To keep your score use a knitting counter. This is especially useful for beginners.

Technique

Low expectations can help. After a break from play, when you're not expecting to do well, you can often achieve amazing results. The trick is not to try too hard. Just let the shots happen and you'll be agreeably surprised.

Work hard at visualising the perfect shot every time you take a swing. Really live it in your mind, and you'll get your subconscious on your side.

Strengthen your hands by squeezing a squash ball into the palm of your hand using your fingers. Repeat with both hands several times a day.

Don't worry if you can't achieve a full back swing. Much better to optimise the swing you can manage than to force yourself and possibly lose control.

To help you keep your back straight when adopting the stance, imagine you're sitting on a shooting stick. Another way is to hold a club across your shoulders with a hand at each end. Lean forwards a little from the hip, then bend your knees, making sure your knees don't collapse inwards in a 'knock-kneed' stance.

A good practice technique is achieved by fixing your belt round your upper arms just above the elbow. Get a friend to do it up so it fits snugly when you address the ball, then take your swing. It forces you to keep your arms closer to your body and makes for a more consistent swing.

Professionals never play with their arms too close to their body. Practise swinging wearing a couple of blow-up arm bands and you'll soon look like a pro – at least you will once you've taken the arm bands off!

Keep your head down. It's disastrous to look up when putting, even after you've hit the ball. Try perfecting your putting on a carpet. Put a coin under the ball and, even after you've made your stroke, keep staring at the coin.

To time your swing to perfection, just say 'Alexander Cadogan' – Alexander for the back swing and hit the ball on 'dog'.

Check your alignment. Look at the target – if you can see your left shoulder, you are facing the wrong direction and will have to compensate if you want the ball to reach your target. When correctly aligned, your left shoulder should be just, and only just, out of sight.

Improve the pressure of your golf swing by driving a heavy piece of wood along the floor. The resistance will build muscle.

Perfect your swing – stand in front of patio doors. Put masking tape in a V-shape on the window; it should have a 45° angle in the point of the V. The position of your arms at the beginning and end of your swing should be parallel to the V-shape.

Practise chipping at home – invert a tee on the carpet and try to chip it up.

To get your putt straight, practise putting along the skirting board at home.

It's important not to let your legs collapse when hitting a golf ball – try practising with a beach ball between your knees. You mustn't let it go when you hit the ball.

To stop yourself bending your arm at the elbow during shots, take a 2-litre Coca-Cola bottle and cut the top and bottom off. Slice down the side of the remaining middle section and place it over your elbow. This will prevent you from bending your arm.

Don't bend your wrists when putting. Pop a comb or ruler under your wrist-watch and you won't be able to.

Teach yourself to stand up straight and still. Place your golf bag on the side you have a tendency to sway towards. Then if you do sway that way, you will knock the bag over.

Keep your balance when driving off – stand on concrete while wearing spiked golfing shoes. This will force you to keep upright and well-balanced.

To make sure you stand on the balls of your feet and don't move around, practise standing on two bricks.

Bunker shots aren't really difficult! It's all psychological. Here's a cracking idea to overcome those bunker fears: just imagine the ball is a fried egg and you're trying to scoop it out without breaking the yolk.

Save your lawn from ugly divots – practise on a door mat.

Always replace divots – one day you might land in one you failed to replace on your last round.

GRAPHIC DESIGNERS

Gary Beard;
David Mason

To look after your computer, keep it out of direct sunlight.

For security reasons, keep your computer, printer and scanner away from the window. You don't want people to see all the equipment you've got.

When travelling, always protect your work. Make sure you carry it in a waterproof container.

To ensure that you are always relaxed when working, arrange your desk and chair so that you have easy access to everything you need.

To remove glue from a piece of artwork, you don't need to buy expensive art-shop equipment. Lighter fuel does just as well.

To remember where and what colour your ink pens are, stain MDF boxes the appropriate colour and fill with your pens.

GREENGROCERS

Fruit

Robin Blair, J J Blair;
Connie Lucas

To find out if a Cox's apple is ready to eat, shake it. If the pips rattle, it's perfect.

When buying Golden Delicious apples, choose the ones with more brown spots on the skin. The more spots, the more flavour.

To peel apples in half the time, blanch them first in boiling water.

Make great teethers for babies using dried apple rings.

Stop cut apples from going brown – sprinkle with lemon juice.

Don't lose all the filling when cooking baked apples – before you put them in the oven, plug the top of the hole with a little piece of marzipan.

To stop fruit in a bowl going mouldy, place a piece of kitchen roll in the bottom. It absorbs all the moisture.

Bounce your cranberries to find out if they are fresh or not. If they bounce, they are!

To trim gooseberries, use baby nail clippers.

When choosing lemons and oranges, always go for the fruit that feels too heavy for its size.

If you need to keep lemons fresh for a long time, store them covered in cold water.

Old, wrinkly lemons can be restored to their former glory by boiling them in water for a few minutes, then leaving to cool.

If your lemons are overripe, squeeze the juice into hot water and use this to clean your windows.

Before you grate citrus fruit, rinse the grater in cold water. After use, the peel will come away from the grater much more easily.

Citrus peel makes a barbecue smell great and helps to get it going.

Oranges look much prettier in fruit salad if you can remove the white pith. To make it easy, soak the fruit in boiling water before you peel off the skin and the pith should come away too.

For fruit salad with a difference, use lemonade instead of fruit juices. For a celebration, try champagne instead.

Dry orange peel in the oven to make useful fire-lighters.

If you suffer from constipation, a couple of drops of linseed oil in orange juice will help to get things moving.

To chop dried fruit, wet the blade of the knife so the fruit doesn't stick to it.

To stop bananas from turning black in a fruit salad, cover the unpeeled fruit with cold water for ten to 15 minutes before peeling.

Rhubarb is a great blood purifier.

Don't always buy with your eyes – the more crinkly the skin on a honeydew melon, the sweeter it will be inside.

To ripen tomatoes quickly, place them in a brown paper bag along with one ripe tomato.

Don't store tomatoes in the fridge because they will blister.

Vegetables

Make your lettuce last longer by cutting out the core and sprinkling sugar into the cavity.

Tear lettuce instead of cutting it to avoid the leaves turning brown.

It doesn't have to end in tears – store an onion in the fridge for several hours before using and you won't cry when you peel it.

The more wrinkled a red pepper is, the sweeter and riper the taste.

Store mushrooms in a paper bag to stop them sweating.

Freeze parsley on its stem in a clear plastic bag. When you need it, remove it from the freezer and rub it between your fingers – the parsley is automatically chopped.

To keep watercress fresh for longer, immerse the leaves – but not the roots – in a jug of water.

Freshen up bad breath instantly by chewing two or three sprigs of watercress and a couple of grapes.

To get rid of garlic breath, chew some parsley.

To keep drinking water fresh, put a watercress leaf into a jug before filling with water and leave it there.

Keep flies away – place fresh mint on the kitchen window-sill.

When buying cabbage, check its bottom. If it's too white, don't buy it – it's a sign that the leaves and root have been trimmed off.

Always buy broccoli with tight heads – this way they won't drop off when you cook them.

Look out for really purple turnips – the more purple the turnip, the better it will taste.

Aubergines can be either male or female – both taste equally good.

Add herbs to your barbecue for extra sweet aromas.

Prevent car sickness – chew some crystallised ginger.

If you smoke but want to kick the habit, try chewing on liquorice root.

Ease painful indigestion – drop cardamom pods into your coffee.

HAIRDRESSERS & BARBERS
Washing & Conditioning

Errol Douglas; Paula Jerem, Mad P; Daniel Field, Organic & Mineral Hairdresser; Dominic Flynn, Capelli; Ian Matthews, Geo F Trumper

Don't pile long hair on top of your head when washing. It will cause it to tangle. Instead wash hair hanging straight down.

Hair is more fragile when wet, so be careful when brushing after washing. Using a wide-toothed comb helps to minimise the damage.

Make your own egg shampoo by mixing two eggs and half an eggshell of olive oil. Massage into your scalp and rinse thoroughly.

Body shampoo is just as good as hair shampoo – and half the price.

Heal and prevent split ends by rubbing corn oil into your hair, making sure the ends are covered. Leave on for several minutes, then rinse your hair.

Reduce split ends by using a pure bristle brush.

Give your hair a really deep condition by massaging in lots of mayonnaise and then leaving it on for ten minutes before rinsing off.

If your hair is brittle, mix two eggs with a dash of warm oil and massage in. Leave for about ten minutes and then rinse out.

Most conditioners work better if left on for a 20-minute soak.

To make your own conditioner, mash up an avocado and smear over your hair and scalp. Leave for at least ten to 15 minutes and then wash off.

For extra shine, add a spoonful of honey or vinegar to your conditioner.

To give your hair a treat, warm a couple of tablespoons of olive or almond oil in a cup (more if your hair is very long). Rub into your hair and then wrap your head in cling film. Cover with a warm towel and leave for at least half an hour, but much longer if you can manage it – try not to answer the door! Shampoo and rinse.

If you run out of hair conditioner, fabric conditioner will do just as well.

Olive oil makes a fabulous conditioner. Rub some through your hair, then wrap in a warm towel. Put your feet up and relax for ten minutes, then shampoo out.

If you suffer from dandruff, beat together one egg and a teaspoon of parsley. Massage into your hair and leave for five minutes, then rinse out thoroughly.

Another good cure for dandruff is to put about ten or 12 stinging nettle heads into a bowl. Pour boiling water over them and leave to cool. Strain so that any bits are removed. The left-over liquid can be used as a final rinse after shampooing.

To ease itching caused by dandruff or a dry scalp, soak some dried thyme and sage in warm water, and use it as a final rinse.

Don't buy expensive dandruff shampoos – just add some olive oil to your conditioner.

To stop dandruff proliferating, soak your comb in vinegar.

Cutting, Styling & Colouring

To cut children's hair without tears or mistakes, trim the ends while they're asleep.

If cutting children's hair when they're awake, try putting them in front of a fish tank – it should hold their attention.

Alternatively, draw a blank face on a piece of paper. As you cut your child's hair, get them to stick the cut pieces around the face on the paper.

If you don't usually have time to blow dry your hair at home, don't let your hairdresser do it after a cut either. Let it dry on its own to test whether you're happy with the basic cut.

If your funds are limited, spend all you have on one really good cut rather than all the fancy (and overpriced) products on the market.

If your hair is thinning, have a shorter, blunter cut to give the illusion of thickness.

Even if you only wear specs occasionally, take them with you when you get a haircut to check that your style suits them.

Try and sit very straight when you're having your hair cut. Even crossing your legs can make your shoulders tilt and may result in an uneven cut.

If you have long, lank hair, try drying it with your head upside down to get more lift and body.

Add body to your long tresses by scooping your hair up into a high ponytail for an hour or so before you go out. When you let it down it will be full of bounce.

To straighten out your curls, spread your hair between some brown paper and get a friend to smooth it down using a cool iron.

Make your own styling wax – use petroleum jelly.

For an alternative setting lotion, use pale ale.

Detangle knotty hair – just comb some lemonade through it.

To give your hair a firm hold, use sugared water.

For the ultimate beehive, nothing works better than egg white.

Fancy hairstyles can be held in place with a little discreet sticky tape.

After a dye job, you can remove stains from your skin by rubbing them with cotton wool dipped in milk.

Dyed blonde hair often turns slightly green after swimming. Retrieve your bombshell glory by rubbing in some tomato ketchup and then rinsing your hair.

When colouring with henna, you could add some coffee, tea or red wine to enhance and deepen the colour.

If you are getting the odd grey hair, don't bother to dye your whole head, just cover up the offending hairs with a mascara wand.

Use an old tie to hold hair ornaments and scrunchies.

Make your own hair curlers – use old toilet roll tubes for big curls.

Clean a hairbrush by using a nailbrush.

Shaving

No shaving foam? Use peanut butter or olive oil.

Take your shower or bath before you shave to soften up the bristles. If you don't have time for full ablutions, try pressing a warm flannel against your stubble instead.

Don't put shaving foam all over your brush because you'll end up with far too much. Instead, separate the bristles, put a little foam inside and then close the bristles round the foam. This way, you'll get the amount you need gently released as you apply the foam.

If you have a rather broad face, shave a concave line upwards under the chin to make your face look thinner.

To sharpen razor blades press the blade flat against the inside of a glass and move it firmly backwards and forwards. The glass will sharpen the metal edges so you'll always have a perfect blade.

For a silky-smooth, kissable chin, first shave down with the grain, then a second time against the grain.

After shaving, rinse thoroughly in cold water to close up your pores.

HEALTH VISITORS, DOCTORS & NURSES

Caroline Donley; Dr
Kate Crockers; Glynis
Fletcher

Nappies & Later

If a child – or an adult, come to that – has a urine infection and is reluctant to wee because of the pain, let them sit in a warm bath and wee in that – far less painful.

During toilet training, a little boy's aim can be rather inaccurate. Try placing a ping-pong ball or an (unflushable) cork in the loo and get him to aim at it when weeing. This not only reduces the wayward stream but will encourage him to stand still and concentrate for longer than a nano-second. Hopefully, this will result in a properly emptied bladder and reduce the damp patch on the carpet as well as in pants and trousers.

When you reach the 'nappy off, pants on, lots of reminders' stage, there's no point asking the child 'Do you want a wee', because at this stage the child only gets a few seconds' warning from the bladder, so the chances are they'll always truthfully answer no. Instead say (firmly but positively), 'It's time to try' or 'Let's go to the loo before we have our lunch/go out in the car/watch Sesame Street'.

Try building regular loo times into the day so that the child learns the routine and the question doesn't come as a surprise, particularly when they're busy doing something else.

Night-time wetting can be reduced by not giving fizzy drinks or drinks containing caffeine, such as Coca-Cola, coffee or tea, as these are diuretic.

If you decide to try 'lifting' your child for a wee when you go to bed, try to make sure they are awake enough to walk to the loo themselves. If you carry them to the loo and have to support them as they wee in their sleep, the sensation is more or less the same as weeing in their bed. They need to be making a conscious action or they won't learn to get up by themselves.

Constipation or not? Filling the nappy is usually accompanied by straining and going red in the face. Babies may also go several days without a soiled nappy. Knowing if it's constipation all comes down to consistency, I'm afraid. Think toothpaste. If the stool is firmer than toothpaste, the baby is heading towards being constipated, so offer more fluids. Once it reaches 'rabbit droppings' stage, it is definitely constipated and probably quite uncomfortable.

Feeding & Cleaning Teeth

For a baby that clamps its mouth firmly shut as the spoon approaches, give it a spoon of its own to mess around with. Rather than trying to feed face to face and from on high, try a sitting position at the side of the baby, and approach from an angle.

Play 'hide the veggies' with reluctant eaters to ensure adequate vitamin intake without the tears (yours as well as theirs).

Courgette, broccoli, leek, peas and carrot can be cooked and puréed into a tomato-based sauce for pasta, with the colour of carrot and tomato disguising the dreaded green.

Home-made carrot soup (with or without coriander) can disguise other veg and pulses, cooked and puréed. Orange seems to be more acceptable to children than other colours. Making it quite thick and letting them use their hands to dip chunks of bread is an obligatory factor in the success of the project, I'm afraid.

If your toddler is put out by you breastfeeding a new baby, and starts acting up, try getting a small, quiet, age-appropriate toy, game or book and keeping in a special bag with the child's name on it. When you feed, present the bag to your child, and let him or her play with it until the end of the feed. Then, they must put it back in the bag until next time. This only works if you keep the bag exclusively for feed times.

If your child is feeling a bit queasy, do yourself a favour and don't give them black-currant to drink – a pool of dark purple puke is somehow very depressing, and stains clothes terribly.

Fed up of battling over tooth cleaning? Stand behind the child and let them look at themselves in the mirror while brushing their own teeth. Once they've had a go themselves, you can hold the brush with them and finish off the areas they missed. This is less threatening than a face-to-face confrontation with you brandishing the toothbrush in their face, and helps them learn the correct strokes.

To encourage more thorough brushing, make up a little tooth-brushing song! Three verses of 'Brush the peggies' to the tune of 'Oh my darling Clementine' should be plenty.

Medicine & Inoculations

Never run out of Calpol.

When giving eye-drops to a child, get them to lie down with their eyes closed and place the drops on the inside corner of the closed eye, then ask them to play 'peep-bo'. Enough of the eye-drops will get in to be effective, and it's far better than trying to hold a wriggling child still.

If you are unfortunate enough to have to give eye-ointment to a child, hold the tube across the bridge of the nose with the nozzle just above the eye. That way, if the child moves suddenly at least you won't poke them in the eye with the nozzle.

Homoeopathic teething granules work like a dream for some kids, but even if you're not convinced of their efficacy, the process of shaking the little packet, tearing the corner and tipping the contents into a teething baby's mouth can distract them from the misery of new teeth.

Chicken pox can be miserable. To distract your child from the itchiness, stand them on an old towel and let them apply calamine lotion themselves using a child's paint-brush. They can join the dots and have fun creating pictures – butterflies, ladybirds, even 101 dalmations if it's a bad case!

To give medicine to an uncooperative child, remember that smell is a key factor. Get your child to hold its nose before taking it.

To give a baby medicine, using a syringe or dropper, insert it into the side of the mouth and gently trickle the medicine while holding the baby in the crook of your arm. If you squirt it straight into the middle of the mouth, it can go over the baby's tongue and is likely to evoke a gag response, resulting in it being spat right out again.

Burns go on damaging the layers of skin long after the source of heat has been removed, but holding the affected part under cold running water is almost impossible with a distressed child, and applying ice directly to the skin can cause skin damage too. Cool the skin straight away with running cold water, then wrap the area in cling film and secure an ice source, such as a pack of frozen peas or an ice-cube bag, on to the burn area using another layer of cling film. Then seek medical advice.

A cut or swollen lip can be frightening to a child. After washing the area, give them an ice lolly to suck on so as to calm them down and reduce the swelling and bleeding so that a further assessment can be made.

To remove an eyelash or speck of dirt from a baby's or child's eye, soak a cotton-wool ball in previously boiled and cooled water, and gently squeeze the cotton wool to allow the water to wash over the eye and flush the object away.

Sore, red noses during colds can be soothed with the camomile-based cream used for sore nipples during breastfeeding. So hold on to it for later.

When taking a child for an injection, ask them to count 1–2–3–4–5 out loud with you when they feel the scratch (of the needle). It will be over by the time they get to 3, and helps to distract them from the process.

At inoculation time, sit your child astride your lap, facing you. This means they can't see the needle coming, although you can, and makes it difficult for them to pull away.

For the primary course of immunisations for babies, which involves two or three injections and polio drops by mouth, have the polio drops checked and ready so you can place them carefully in the baby's open mouth when it cries.

Equipment & Advice

When you have a baby, it's worth always having a kettle of boiled cooled water around. After making tea, just refill the kettle and boil it again straight away. You can use it for so many things, from rinsing dummies to wiping hands (and other places).

Keep losing baby socks? In colder weather put both girls and boys in baby tights. Under trousers, who is to know his cosy secret?

Graduating to a cot? Place the Moses basket or carry cot inside the cot for a few days so your baby can get used to the new surroundings, sounds and smells.

When buying combination prams/pushchairs, bear in mind that the pushchair part will be used for far longer than the pram, so make sure it will suit your needs.

Baby baths have a limited period of use as babies rapidly grow out of them, but they make great sledges in winter and brilliant pretend play boats in summer when the children are older.

Repeated unwanted behaviour can drive you mad, but remember to state that it is the behaviour that is unacceptable, not the child. The child then gets a clear message about what he or she has to change. Say, 'Biting is naughty' rather than 'You naughty boy/girl' or 'Kicking hurts me,' rather than 'You little monster thug'.

Most children go through a stage of non-fluency (stammering) as part of normal speech development. It's because the speed of their thoughts exceeds their fluency. Don't draw attention to it and don't ask them to repeat it properly. In most cases it will go on its own.

HERBALISTS

Christopher Robbins;
Jenny Steel

For Pleasure

For a bath-time treat, make your own herbal infusion. Put dried herbs in a muslin bag (you can use fresh herbs but these are not as concentrated as dried ones), tie it to the hot-water tap so that the water flows over and through the bag. When the bath is ready, put the bag in the water and leave it to float around while you bathe.

For a reviving bath, use herbs such as mint, thyme, nettles (to boost circulation) and pine (which is refreshing).

For a relaxing bath, use lavender, marjoram (a great natural tranquilliser), sage (an antidote for stress) and lemon balm (which relieves tension).

Put marigold flowers into your bath water to soften the water.

For a soothing hand lotion, soak marigold petals in almond oil for a couple of weeks.

To make your own herb tea, put one small handful of the fresh herb or one heaped teaspoon of the dried herb in a cup of boiling water. Leave to stand for about five to ten minutes. Strain and then drink the tea while it's still hot.

For a restful night, drink some camomile tea before bed. It's a good idea to make a hop pillow too – sew dried hops into a muslin bag.

A natural way of darkening one's hair is to get a large handful of sage leaves, cover with a teaspoon of borax and ½ pint/300 ml of boiling water. Leave until cold, then apply carefully to your hair with a brush.

If you run out of starch and you've got bluebells in your garden, you can use the juice from the white part of the stems as a substitute.

For a natural dye, use elderberry leaves for green, the flowers for yellow and the berries for purple.

For Pain

Soothe a nasty sore throat – try gargling with tea made from sage leaves (you can buy them from most supermarkets).

To fight the onslaught of a cold, use rose-hip berries. Crush the berries and then pour on boiling water. It makes delicious tea.

To make your own poultice it's best to use powdered herbs. Mix them up into a paste with hot water. Put the mixture on to some muslin or a sterile dressing and place on the affected area.

To reduce travel sickness or morning sickness, try camomile, fennel or ginger tea.

To get rid of warts, rub them with the milky sap from the stalk of a dandelion.

Combat acne with some comfrey or marigold ointment. Dabbing on lemon juice and garlic also helps to dry up spots.

Feeling bruised and battered? A comfrey or arnica poultice will help keep bruises down (don't apply arnica to broken skin).

For indigestion, make up some camomile or marigold tea. If your indigestion is of a 'windy' nature, try fennel or peppermint tea. Meadowsweet tea will bring quick relief.

If you are suffering from toothache, try sucking on a clove next to the bad tooth (or put a drop of clove oil on to the tooth). Take sage tea as a mouthwash if your gums are bleeding; if they become infected, suck a clove of garlic. Sage tea is also good dabbed on to mouth ulcers.

Colds and flu don't like peppermint and elderflower tea. If you have a headache as well, add some limeflowers.

When you have a really bad cough, eat loads of garlic. Elderflower and thyme tea will also help ease the cough and make breathing easier.

If you're bunged up with a bad cold, try inhaling the steam from thyme and peppermint tea. Put your head over a bowl of the tea, cover your head with a towel and breathe deeply.

If you're really blocked solid, try sniffing some salt water or beetroot juice up your nose through a straw. It sounds disgusting, but it can move the blockage and bring relief.

Bunged up at the other end? Try dandelion root tea to get things moving again. Increase your intake of fibre as well.

An alternative antiseptic cream can be made from thyme leaves, scraped off the stem and then crushed on a board. Apply this paste to the affected area.

For sore breasts, make up a camomile poultice. Put two tablespoons of camomile flowers into a mug of boiling water and leave it to stand for about ten minutes. Soak a flannel in the tea, then hold it gently on the affected area. Leave until the flannel has cooled.

If your nipples are sore from breastfeeding, you can put on marigold ointment, but you should wipe it off carefully before feeding your baby.

If you suffer from hay fever, try drinking a mixture of equal parts of elderflower and nettle tea.

When your chilblains get really bad, squeeze fresh root ginger or lemon juice over the unbroken skin. Eating a lot of garlic will help to improve your circulation.

To get rid of nasty splinters, mash up some bread and mix with water to make a gooey paste. Apply to the splinter, which should then be drawn out by the paste.

After a bee sting, crush some marigold petals on the affected area.

To soothe a bite or sting, rub some fresh sage leaves on it.

To speed up the repair of broken bones, take comfrey.

Dock leaves really do work to soothe nettle stings, but so do other members of the Rumex family: spinach and sorrel, for instance. Really crush them up well before rubbing on the sting – it's the sap that does the trick.

Make your own toothpaste, take some juniper twigs and leaves that are full of sap. Dry them in the airing cupboard. Place them on a large metal tray and set fire to them. The resulting ash can be used to clean your teeth.

To cure dandruff, put ten to 12 stinging nettle heads into a bowl, pour boiling water over them and leave to cool. Strain, and use the left-over liquid as a final rinse after shampooing.

If you get a bit too much sun, dab some sage tea on to your skin.

Feverfew can help to reduce migraine attacks. Pop a few young leaves into a sandwich on a regular basis. Feverfew should not be taken by pregnant women.

In the Garden

When planting herbs in a container, plant frost-tender herbs in their own pot so you can easily replace them if they succumb to the bad weather.

To cut lavender for drying, trim the stalks as the buds open or cut back after flowers have faded. Lightly prune the whole bush at the same time.

Rosemary needs regular trimming.

Mint can run amok if not kept under control. Plant it in its own container.

Camomile lawns are wonderful and give off a fabulous scent when crushed under foot. They need weeding by hand and like an open, sunny space.

Thyme lawns are a good idea if you want to cover an uneven, sunny area.

Plant camomile next to sickly plants to perk them up.

In the Kitchen

Use the flowers of chives and pansies in salads to give colour.

Presentation is everything. Some fresh herbs sprinkled on top of the most ordinary looking dish will turn it into something special.

Make sure your parsley stays green – only add it to a sauce once the liquid has boiled.

To clean up any spills in the oven, sprinkle some salt and cinnamon over the spill. This stops the house from filling with that acrid, smoky smell and the spill will be easy to lift off with a spatula.

HOME SAFETY OFFICERS

Helen Richardson, Child Accident Prevention Trust; Cindy Allen; Linda Milne; James Black; Jo Downie; Philip Davies

Going Away

Make sure your house looks secure. During an evening when the family is in, go outside and see how the house looks (which curtains are open, which lights are on and so on). This is how the house should look when you are out for the evening. Just leaving the hall light on isn't enough.

Take the back-door keys with you when you go out. A burglar may be able to break a small window to get in but will need to be able to open a door to get your stuff out. It is less risky for the burglar to use the back door than the front.

When going on holiday, make sure that curtains aren't caught behind a chair or hanging in an unusual way. People will notice that this hasn't changed for a while. Make sure they are straight or get a neighbour to rearrange them every few days.

Taking children on holiday? Dress them in a similar fashion for the journey so that if one gets lost, you can give an accurate idea of what they look like by showing what their sibling is wearing.

Plant hedges and build walls in such a way that the entrance to your house can always be seen from the road.

Staying In

Save yourself from a scalding. Turn your thermostat down to 130 °F/54 °C so that water never comes out of the tap boiling hot (and it saves you money, too).

Sharp knives can be dangerous. Never leave them in the bottom of a washing-up bowl. Always wash and dry them straight away and put them back where they belong.

Lots of accidents happen on or near stairs. Make sure this is one area that you have clearly lit and keep the stairs clear of objects.

To prevent people falling downstairs, replace 60-watt light bulbs in hallways with 100-watt bulbs.

Throw away novelty slippers. They cause people to slip and fall all the time. And they look really stupid.

Don't store newspapers for recycling under the stairs. If they catch fire you won't be able to use the stairs to get out of the house.

Don't store bottles by the kitchen door. People can trip over them and cut themselves. You can put them under the stairs: they're not flammable.

If a frying pan catches fire, turn off the heat immediately and cover with a lid or damp towel. Don't move the pan or throw water on it. Leave it covered for at least half an hour to allow any flames to die away.

If your television or computer catches fire, pull the plug out or turn off the main fuse box, then cover with a blanket or rug. Don't throw water over it because there could be a danger from the residual electricity.

Child Safety

Use a wipe-clean board or blackboard at child-eye level near the phone for emergency numbers and numbers where you can be contacted if needed.

Stop children from getting into cupboards and drawers. Elastic bands make ideal safety catches. Just stretch them across adjacent doorknobs and the doors can only open a short distance.

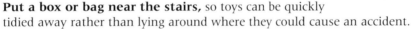

Children have a habit of running into glass patio doors, thinking that they're open when they're not. Avoid a nasty accident by putting a few stickers on any glass door.

Before storing carrier bags, tie them in a knot. It will then be much more difficult for a child to put one over his head without thinking.

Put a box or bag near the stairs, so toys can be quickly tidied away rather than lying around where they could cause an accident.

To stop little fingers getting trapped in slamming doors, glue a small cork to the door-frame so that the doors cannot actually slam shut.

Alternatively, make a sausage out of old tights and bend it round the edge of door, attaching the ends to the door handles.

To test the safety of folding toys, insert a pencil in any nooks or crannies where little fingers could go and see if you can snap the pencil. If you can, then don't let your child play with the toy.

Make windows safe for children. Instead of child bars, fix garden trellis across the bottom of the window.

Keep an eye on children but stop them from getting under your feet. Fix a garden gate, which you can lock, across your kitchen doorway. You can still see them but they won't get in your way.

If your house opens on to a busy road, a sensible precaution with toddlers about is to fix a baby gate across your porch or front doorway.

HOTELIERS

Food & Drink

Judy & David Green, Teviotdale Lodge Country Hotel; Steven Morris, Grafton Manor Hotel; Alison Purchon

To serve white wine immediately without having to put it in an ice cooler, just store it at a temperature of 50–55 °F/10–12.8 °C.

If you haven't got a corkscrew, put a long screw into the top of the cork and pull it out with a piece of string.

When grilling lots of sausages, thread them on to skewers so that it's easier to keep turning them.

Your bacon will be really crispy if you trim the rind with pinking shears before cooking it.

If you get a little bit of yolk in the white when you are separating eggs, take a bit of tightly rolled kitchen towel that you have heated up in some boiling water and hold it near the yolk. The heat will draw the yolk towards the towel.

Scramble eggs in a heatproof glass bowl placed in a pan of boiling water. This way, you don't have to scrub lots of eggy saucepans afterwards.

For really fluffy omelettes, add a squirt of soda water to the egg mixture before cooking.

To stop oil from spitting in a frying pan, add a pinch of salt when melting the butter.

Brazil nuts are easier to crack when frozen in the freezer.

To keep salad really fresh, put a saucer upside down in the bottom of the bowl to collect any spare moisture.

Make consommé look more appetising – drop a lump of sugar into the soup before serving.

If your hands are stained, rub with a piece of raw potato. This works on kitchen work-tops too.

To keep cheese fresh for longer, wrap it in a cloth that you have dampened with white wine vinegar.

A sugar cube in the cheese box will keep cheese fresh for longer.

Keep teapots smelling fresh – put a sugar lump or dry tea-bag inside until you want to use it.

Rooms & Service

When booking a room at the last minute, you may be able to negotiate down the published tariff.

Negotiate up to 50 per cent off for a Sunday night stay (accommodation only) in London and regional hotels, though not resort hotels in high season.

If you want tea or coffee in your four- or five-star hotel room, try requesting a free hospitality tray, rather than ordering from room service. (Check it is free though!)

Ask for an ironing board and iron, rather than pay for a pressing service.

When you're not sure if a hotel is good enough, ask to see a selection of the rooms before booking in.

Going to the theatre? Ask to have your starter and main course before you go, and your pudding and coffee when you return.

Avoid cleaning shoes with free in-room shoe cleaners. They often lay down an impenetrable layer of silicone. Better to put shoes outside your room at night for a traditional clean.

When booking into a four- or five-star hotel, ask if you can be upgraded to a suite, for a small supplement. If the hotel has unsold suites, they should be prepared to offer them to guests for less than the normal rate.

When you need to stay beyond official check-out time, ask reception nicely the night before. Often they will allow you a free late check-out, but on busy days this may not be possible or a charge may be added to your bill.

To avoid embarrassment, always check the dress code for hotel restaurants.

Not guaranteed your booking with a credit card? The hotel has the legal right to cancel your booking after 6pm. Equally if you have guaranteed your reservation with a credit card, you will be charged even if you do not arrive.

If the hotel bed is too soft, contact the housekeeper. Most good hotels can supply you with a bed-board during your stay.

HOUSEKEEPERS

Maureen Cummins;
Liz Foley; Jill Wright;
Janet Reaney

Bathrooms

To clean glass shower doors, try using left-over white wine.

Get rid of soap scum from shower doors by rubbing with a used fabric-conditioner strip.

Shower curtains (plastic or polyester) with mildew spots should be soaked in a solution of one part domestic bleach to four parts water. Then rinse thoroughly or machine-wash if possible.

Grimy shower curtains should be wiped with distilled vinegar then rinsed with water.

To deep clean shower surrounds use a sponge mop dipped in a solution of half a cup of vinegar, one cup of ammonia, a quarter cup of baking soda in 1 gallon/4.5 litres of warm water. After cleaning, rinse with warm water.

For clogged shower heads, unscrew and place in a bowl of vinegar for 20 minutes – remove the rubber washer – but don't lose it! Brush out any sediment with an old toothbrush before reassembling.

Bathroom tile grout a bit grotty? Simply camouflage with some liquid paper.

Clean soap splashes from tiles with a solution of one part white vinegar to four parts water. Rinse and wipe down.

If hard water has caused splashes on tiles or glass that are hard to remove, rub malt vinegar over the surface. Leave for ten minutes before rinsing off.

Always wipe the bath down after use. Some essential oils can mark plastic baths if they are left on the surface.

Avoid hard-to-remove tide marks on the bath – don't use concentrated bath oils.

Dripping taps can cause a stain on the bath or sink enamel. Remove such stains by rubbing with a cut lemon.

Mould spots on bath sealant should be tackled with domestic bleach and a toothbrush. Rinse thoroughly.

To clean a bath, use an old net curtain. It's mildly abrasive and gets the marks off brilliantly.

For a yellowing bath, rub with a solution of salt and turpentine. Rinse well.

To clean delicate bathroom surfaces, sheer tights make an excellent, non-abrasive scouring pad.

Make your own spray cleaner by filling a spray bottle with three tablespoons of ammonia, one tablespoon of vinegar and some cool water.

When descaling tap nozzles, put a plastic bag filled with vinegar over the nozzle. Secure it with an elastic band and leave it for at least half an hour.

Shift hard water deposits from around the base of taps with an old toothbrush dipped in vinegar. Rinse well afterwards.

Chrome taps come up a treat if you rub them with some plain flour, then wash off.

To remove toilet rings, flush first to wet sides and apply a paste of borax and lemon juice. Let sit for two hours, then scrub.

To clean a toilet bowl, pour a can of Coca-Cola around the rim. Leave it for one hour and then brush and flush.

Alternatively, drop several denture-cleaning tablets into the toilet bowl.

To remove dark stains from well water in a toilet or sink sprinkle some citrus drink powder and swirl around. Let stand for a few minutes, then rinse.

Prevent the bottom of a bathroom pull cord getting discoloured – place the casing from a clear ball-point pen over the 'pulling' end.

To prevent mildew from forming in your bathroom, fill a small, flat box with cat litter and place in the bottom of the bath. This is especially important if you're going to be away for a long time – but remember to keep the door shut if you've got cats!

Reduce steam in the bathroom by running cold water into the bath before turning the hot water on. The less steam you get, the fewer mould spots there will be.

Kitchens

If your sponge has become slimy, soak it in one tablespoon of vinegar to 1 pint/600 ml of water for an hour, then wash thoroughly.

If your steel wool scourers are rusting, wrap them in kitchen foil after use.

Rubber spatula ready for the bin? Trim off the tattered edges and keep trimming until there's nothing left.

Spray vegetable oil on a grater before use for a fast clean-up.

Graters are impossible to clean without losing a bit of your own finger. An old toothbrush does the trick and is ideal for sieves as well.

Use baking soda to remove coffee and tea stains from plastic cups and dishes.

Remove tannin stains from your teapot – put a tablespoon of bicarbonate of soda into the teapot, add boiling water and leave to soak overnight. Rinse out and wash thoroughly.

To shift tea and coffee stains from china cups, mix equal amounts of salt and vinegar, put in the cups and leave to soak, then rinse thoroughly.

Get rid of limescale from your kettle – just put a cup of vinegar in the kettle and boil it up. Rinse out thoroughly afterwards.

To get rid of odours from plastic containers, fill with crumpled black-and-white newspaper. Cover tightly and leave overnight. Next day the smell is gone.

To get rid of the strong plastic smell from new containers, wash, dry and put in the freezer for at least two days.

To remove unpleasant odours in your waste-disposal unit, grind orange rinds or a half lemon.

If your waste disposal still has bad breath, try feeding it a handful of ice cubes, a splash of vinegar, a lemon and a pinch of allspice.

When disinfecting your sink, don't bother with strong chemical solutions. Just use ordinary household salt.

Baking soda is excellent for cleaning stainless steel sinks.

To give a stainless steel sink a superb finish, rub it down with a scrunched up ball of newspaper after cleaning.

To remove water spots from a stainless steel sink, use a cloth dampened with rubbing alcohol or white vinegar.

Rub stainless sinks with lighter fluid if rust marks appear. After the rust disappears, wipe with your regular kitchen cleaner.

For a sparkling white sink, bleach is best. But it is expensive to fill a sink with bleach. Instead, line it first with kitchen paper then soak the paper in bleach. Leave for an hour or so before throwing the paper away.

Never use bleach in coloured porcelain sinks because it will fade the colour. Instead, clean with mild liquid detergents, vinegar or baking soda.

To rid your sink of soap suds after washing up, wipe around the sink with a bar of soap with the tap running.

Messy ovens needn't take hours to clean. A sheet of aluminium foil on the bottom will catch all the drips and spills. Replace as necessary.

When you empty a pedal or swing bin, place a few folded liners at the bottom before you fit the new one, so there's always one ready for next time.

Keep a tub of talc by the kitchen sink and sprinkle a little into your rubber gloves before you put them on, to make them easier to slip on and off.

To shift limescale from a steam iron, fill the water tank with cider vinegar, turn the iron to 'steam' and run it over a soft cloth for several minutes. You'll need to rinse out the inside of your iron thoroughly afterwards.

Starch can get stuck to the plate of an iron – to remove it, run the iron over a piece of kitchen foil.

Remove rust and stains from plastic worktops with lemon juice (neat or mixed with water).

Wooden work surfaces can be cleaned using a nylon scouring pad dipped in hot water. Rub in the direction of the grain.

Floors, Carpets & Rugs

A good hallway mat should be four lazy steps in length or about 15 ft/4.5 m. By the time the average visitor has taken those steps, most of the grit and dirt is off their shoes and on the mat where you can collect it regularly.

The average small doormat is fairly useless for trapping dirt. Fit the entrance to your hall with coconut matting, instead of carpet, to capture dust and mud. Edge it with some simple brass tread and it will look stylish too.

Fold a few sheets of newspaper and place underneath the doormat to catch the dirt. Remember to change it frequently.

Remove dirt, sand, small rock particles and debris from your entrance way so it can't be tracked into the home. A simple solution that will save you time in the long run.

Brooms can be cleaned with a mild detergent and warm water.

The bristles on your new broom will last much longer if you dip the broom head in salted water before you use it. (This will only work on real bristles though.)

Storing your broom on its head will damage the bristles. Bang a couple of cotton reels into a cupboard door or wall to hang the head on, with the handle hanging down, to preserve the life of your broom.

Check your broom handle is the right length for you. Held upright, it should reach the bridge of your nose.

Always use a mop for one job only – mark the handles or have different colour mops for different purposes.

For really mucky floors, a squeegee is perfect for scraping up the mud and grime before you give it a wash.

When you are applying polish, wrap an old towel around a broom head to buff up afterwards. The towel will ensure there isn't too much excess polish left on the wood and also bring up a wonderful shine.

Or bring up a shine by rubbing the floor with a bundle of old nylon tights.

Wooden floors needn't be hard to maintain. The trick is not to use too much polish – it just traps more dirt. So only use polish every few months.

Scratched floors look messy, but the scratches are often caused by old mops. Change the sponge on your mop before it gets too worn down and make sure your floor stays looking as good as new.

To clean a wooden floor, scatter damp tea-leaves over it to keep the dust in one place when sweeping.

To clean a varnished floor, try adding instant tea granules to your bucket of water.

Linoleum and vinyl are often used in children's rooms in place of carpets. If little fingers mark it with wax crayons, there's no need for tears. A little bit of silver polish will remove the damage.

Remove grease marks from vinyl by holding an ice cube on the stain before washing it with some soapy water.

Remove shoe marks from linoleum by scrubbing gently with fine steel wool dipped in white spirit or turpentine.

Always vacuum your carpet as you would mow your lawn, in neat rows, back and forth so that you don't miss a spot. Each section needs two or three passes at least.

Sooty footprints: sprinkle with salt, let stand for 30 minutes, then vacuum. On light-coloured carpets try an art gum eraser.

When shampooing carpet, put small plastic bags or glass jars around furniture legs to prevent rust stains from forming.

Freshen carpets by sprinkling liberally with salt, oatmeal or cornflour. Leave for a couple of hours and then vacuum.

Revive the colour in a faded carpet using a mix of one part vinegar to two parts boiling water. Soak a cloth in this solution, rub into the carpet and watch the colours come back.

Catch a carpet stain within the first few days. The longer a stain chemically reacts with the carpet the harder it will be to remove it.

Fountain-pen ink should be blotted up with absorbent paper and sponged with cold water until the stain lifts. Use carpet shampoo to finish off.

For bloodstains on the carpet, sponge with cold water and blot firmly with a towel as often as you need. Finish off with carpet shampoo.

Pet puddles needn't be a problem. To get rid of stains from a carpet, mix equal parts of white vinegar and cool water, blot up the stain, rinse and allow to dry.

To clean up muddy paws or footprints, resist the temptation to remove them straight away. Leave the mud to dry completely before vacuuming it up. Sponge off any marks that are left with carpet shampoo.

To remove curry stains from carpets, use a little lemon juice with water.

To remove a cigarette stain from the carpet, pour a small amount of milk on the stain and leave it to soak in. This will dilute the colour and stop it browning. Then rub the stain with a raw potato and wash as normal.

Beer stains can be removed from carpets with soda water.

Raise dents in carpets made by heavy furniture by rubbing the dent with the edge of a coin.

Alternatively, remove dents in carpet pile by covering with a damp cloth and then quickly placing a hot iron on top. The steam lifts the pile.

Lambskin rugs can be brushed with lots of dry, powdered magnesia. Leave for a day, shake well and brush thoroughly.

To vacuum the fringes on rugs, slip an old stocking over the end of the hose attachment.

To retrieve a contact lens from the floor, cover the end of the vacuum hose with a stocking, as above, and vacuum the area. The stocking will stop the lens disappearing into the bowels of the cleaner.

Keep dust from flying around – empty the contents of your vacuum on to a damp newspaper.

Prevent rugs getting worn and bald too quickly. Turn them regularly so that they get even wear.

To clean scorch marks on rugs or carpets, use the edge of a coin to loosen the burn fibres and then sweep them up. Really bad scorch marks are impossible to get rid of but you can minimise the effect of light marks by trimming with a pair of scissors.

Walls

When washing walls, start off at the bottom and work upwards so that any dirty trickles are absorbed by the already wet surface. Skirting boards are usually the dirtiest part of the room so leave cleaning them until last.

To clean wallpaper, use stale but still slightly moist bread. This gets the marks off without the need for soap and water.

Tobacco stains on walls can be removed by lightly scrubbing them with a soft brush dipped in a weak solution of washing-up liquid.

Dirty marks around light switches can be removed using a soft india rubber.

To protect the wall while you clean light switches, make a cardboard template.

Furniture

For scratched woodwork, you can minimise the damage by dabbing with cotton wool that has been dipped in diluted tea.

Scratches on dark woods can be disguised by rubbing with the cut edge of a Brazil nut. For light woods, use a wax crayon or shoe polish.

Water marks on wooden surfaces (left by a glass or made by spirits) can be removed by rubbing dampened cigarette or cigar ash into the mark with a soft cloth (you can make it into a paste using a little vegetable oil). Make sure you rub with the grain of the wood. Wipe with a damp cloth, then a dry cloth, and re-polish. Buff with a soft duster.

Alternatively, try mayonnaise on a soft cloth or toothpaste applied to the water mark on a damp cloth.

White rings on waxed surfaces can be removed using a paste made from salt and olive oil. Leave the stain covered with the paste overnight and then wipe off. The surface can then be re-waxed.

Remove greasy marks from wood veneers by sprinkling the surface with talcum powder. Cover with a couple of sheets of tissue paper and, using the tip of a warm iron, gently press on to the surface to draw out the grease.

Scratches on wood can be concealed by rubbing in a little cod liver oil.

To get rid of rings or minor scratches on wood cover with petroleum jelly and leave for 24 hours. Rub it into the wood, wipe off the excess and then polish as normal.

Polish wood with metal polish instead of the normal woody kind and it should come up a treat.

You can raise dents in wood by placing a damp cloth over the dent and holding a warm iron (don't get it too hot) over the cloth for a few minutes. The moisture from the cloth swells the grain. Allow the wood to dry before polishing.

Repair a dent in wood by filling with a few drops of clear nail-varnish.

To get rid of dog or cat hair on furniture, use a damp rubber glove.

Collect cat or dog hairs from furniture with a fabric-conditioner sheet.

Saggy cane seats can be re-tightened by wetting the top and bottom of the seat with hot, soapy water. Leave the chair to dry in the open air. As the cane dries, it shrinks and tightens. Unfortunately, this method doesn't work on saggy bottoms!

If you've lost a castor off the bottom of a chair, place a cotton bobbin there instead. If it shows too much, colour it first with dark felt-tip pen.

If your furniture drawers keep sticking, try rubbing vegetable soap on the runners.

Fires & Fireplaces

When cleaning away ashes from a fireplace, sprinkle damp tea-leaves over them to keep the dust down.

Remove soot from bricks around a fireplace by scrubbing with neat malt vinegar. Rinse well and then blot the surface with a sponge.

Prevent cigarette butts from smouldering. Line your ashtrays with bicarbonate of soda.

To clean a room quickly of cigarette smoke odour, soak a towel in equal parts of hot water and vinegar, wring it out completely and wave it like a flag over your head several times around the room (you'll feel very silly but your room will smell wonderful).

Windows

Wash windows on a dull day. Too much sun can dry a window too quickly and leave the glass all streaky.

Never clean windows on a very cold or frosty day – the glass will be brittle and liable to break.

When you've cleaned your windows, for a really fine shine, after the windows are dry, rub a clean blackboard eraser over them.

Here's a pithy tip: for sparkling glass, if your lemons are over-ripe, squeeze them into hot water and use them to clean your windows.

Windows can be made to sparkle using a little vinegar and water mixed together (methylated spirits works just as well). Work the mixture around the glass with a piece of chamois leather or newspaper.

Alternatively, to make windows and mirrors sparkle, rub them with scrunched-up paper coffee filters.

Windows can be buffed using crumpled newspaper – the printer's ink gives added sparkle.

Stop windows steaming up by putting glycerine or a little washing-up liquid in some water and wiping over the glass.

Ugly insect or fly spots on windows can be removed with cold tea.

To keep frost off windows, add antifreeze to your cleaning water. Rub the inside of windows with a sponge dipped in the solution. Polish with newspapers or paper towels.

To clean venetian blinds, wear thick cotton gloves and wipe along the slats with your fingers. Reverse the slats and repeat to clean the other side.

Dull net curtains can be transformed back to gleaming white by putting a denture-cleaning tablet into water and soaking the curtains in the solution.

Glass, China & Metal

To pack glassware for a move, wrap wet newspaper around the glass and let it dry. It will act like a cast around the glass.

Scratches in glassware will disappear if polished with toothpaste.

To remove a stubborn stain from the bottom of a glass vase just fill it with water and put in one denture-cleaning tablet. Leave for 20 minutes and then rinse out.

When cleaning a chandelier, you should always wear cotton gloves. This stops you from leaving greasy finger-marks on the crystal. If you have to dry a chandelier in situ, use a hair-dryer.

To clean small glass and china ornaments, put them in a sink and spray with liquid window cleaner. Dry them on a towel.

Clean porcelain or china figures by placing them on a cloth in a plastic bowl. Put a solution of warm water and washing-up liquid in a spray bottle. Wash and then rinse the figure. Empty the water as it accumulates. Leave to dry on a towel.

To clean delicate porcelain or china figurines, hold the base and work from top to bottom. Brush off the dirt with a long-haired, soft make-up brush dipped in a warm solution of washing-up liquid (or soap flakes if the finish is matt). Rinse in the same way and leave to dry on a paper towel.

Store valuable china without it chipping. Place a paper coffee filter between each plate or bowl.

Avoid catastrophes when dusting by sticking precious ornaments down with blu tack.

Valuable embossed or gilded china should be cleaned with a small eyebrow brush kept specifically for the purpose.

Bone china should not be a museum piece. Take it out and clean it every year.

Tarnish can be removed from silver cutlery by placing the knives, forks and spoons in a saucepan with some scrunched-up kitchen foil and water and boiling for about ten minutes.

Alternatively, put a strip of kitchen foil in a plastic bowl and place the silver cutlery on top. Cover with hot water and add a handful of washing soda. Leave for thirty minutes and the rinse the cutlery thoroughly afterwards.

Get rid of those stubborn black spots from silver salt cellars – immerse in a solution of one tablespoon of salt to 1 pint/ 600 ml of hot water for five minutes. Remove and wash the salt cellar.

To clean engraved silver napkin rings or intricate handles on silver cutlery, rub in a little minty toothpaste with a soft cloth then wipe off.

To shine badly tarnished brass, use a mixture of salt and vinegar and rub the tarnish off with a soft cloth.

Tarnished copper benefits from a rub down with lemon juice (neat or mixed with water). For very dirty areas, dip half a lemon in salt and rub it over the offending part.

Bronze is improved by regularly cleaning the surface with dark brown shoe polish and buffing vigorously with a soft cloth.

To clean pewter, mix wood ash with some water into a paste. Rub this over the pewter and then polish off.

Stain Removal & Other Cleaning

Leave your wastebaskets smelling sweet – put a fabric conditioner sheet in the bottom.

Keep moths away! Place conkers or bay leaves in your wardrobes and drawers.

To leave the air fresh in wardrobes and cupboards, use a fabric conditioner sheet in among the clothes.

Make your clothes smell nice by placing empty perfume bottles in your wardrobes and drawers.

Absorb smells in any closed closet – use charcoal bricks placed in a small muslin sack – ideal for families with teenage boys!

Stop the smell of dirty clothes from becoming too overpowering – an empty perfume bottle at the bottom of a laundry bag keeps things sweet.

Remove unwanted blobs of chewing gum by placing a bag of ice cubes over the gum to freeze it. Tap the frozen gum with a hammer to break it up and then pick off as much as you can. Any remaining bits can be removed using a cloth dipped in methylated spirits.

To get rid of sticky-label adhesive, wipe the surface with methylated spirits.

Alternatively, sprinkle talcum powder on to the adhesive and rub with your finger to remove.

Children's stickers can be removed from wood by 'painting' the sticker with white vinegar, letting it soak in and then scraping off.

Ball-point-ink stains need to be removed quickly – dab them with a cotton-wool bud dipped in methylated spirits.

To remove children's crayon marks from walls, brush with toothpaste using an old toothbrush. Wipe the excess off afterwards – for minty, clean walls!

For crayon stains, rub lightly with a dry, soap-filled steel wool pad.

Or use a damp cloth sprinkled with baking soda.

To remove biro from a shirt, rub gently with washing-up liquid, then lift off the biro mark with a knife.

Alternatively, soak the stain in milk, then wash as normal.

If you want to get biro marks off a photograph, rub the mark with some silver-polish wadding. Then rub the same spot with some cotton wool and the mark vanishes.

Has Blu-Tak marked your walls? Dab a little toothpaste on to the stain and leave to harden. When you wash off the toothpaste, the Blu-Tak will come off with it.

Remove light stains from marble using lemon juice or white wine vinegar. Don't leave the juice or vinegar on the marble for longer than two minutes. Rinse off and repeat if necessary. Marble stains easily so get to work as quickly as possible.

For stubborn stains on marble, use a solution of one part hydrogen peroxide (which you can get from a chemist) to two parts water. Put a teaspoon of this solution on to the stain and then add a few drops of ammonia. When the solution stops bubbling, rinse with lots of cold water. Great fun for budding Dr Frankensteins.

Ivory should never be washed because it can discolour. Clean ivory only when absolutely necessary by using a cotton-wool bud dampened in methylated spirits.

Laminated playing cards can be effectively cleaned by rubbing with some white bread.

Don't use chemical cleaners on stains caused by drinks with chemicals in them (such as orange squash or Coca-Cola) because the chemicals in the cleaner may react with the chemicals in the drink.

Light stains can be rubbed with a cut lemon.

For dark stains or rust, rub with a paste of borax and lemon juice.

For glue stains, saturate the spot with a vinegar-soaked cloth.

Protect an unused piano from damp by covering the working parts and keyboard with sheets of brown paper.

To clean ivory piano keys, squeeze a little fluoride toothpaste on to a damp cloth. Rub the keys quite hard and buff with a soft dry cloth.

Alternatively, you can try the Victorian way and clean the keys with milk.

To clean perspex and get rid of scratches, rub with toothpaste and then buff up with a cloth.

When the artificial coal in an electric fire becomes faded and grey, soak a cloth in blackcurrant jelly and rub over the coals. Leave to dry and they'll come up really glossy.

When using a hot-water bottle for the first time, tip in a few drops of glycerine before you add the water, to prolong the life of the rubber.

To clean in the tiniest nooks and crannies, use a camera lens-cleaning brush, the sort with an air-sac attached.

For difficult areas such as stair railings, chairs and so on, use old socks as mitts to clean. (Just make sure they're clean before you start.)

Dust louvred doors by wrapping a cloth around a ruler. Spray the cloth with polish and run the flat end across each slat.

To remove sticky-back shelf paper, use your hair-dryer to 'warm' the adhesive. Use the lowest setting first, holding the dryer over a small area. When it is warmed enough, it should just lift away from the shelf. Continue warming and lifting small sections until the job is done.

When cleaning light bulbs, rub a little vanilla essence around the bulb with a soft cloth. When the light is switched back on, a lovely smell will be gently released.

Cleaning behind radiators is tricky and often gets overlooked altogether. A sock placed over a broom handle will reach the parts other cleaners cannot.

Tapestry work can be sprinkled with powdered magnesia. Work in well with finger-tips covered with a clean cloth. Leave for several hours at least, then brush out gently.

To clean the inside of a clock, soak a small piece of cotton wool in kerosene or paraffin and place in the base of the clock. Leave for a few days. This will draw down all the dust and leave the clock clean.

Some fluffy toys can't be washed. When teddy needs a clean, shake him in a plastic bag with some bicarbonate of soda, then brush him well afterwards (and there'll be no tearful nights waiting for him to dry either).

Fountain pens are fiddly things to clean – they're best soaked in some neat vinegar for ten minutes or so, then left to dry on some blotting paper.

If a bulb breaks while you are removing it, press an old cork on to the broken glass and twist.

Damp dusters pick up dust more effectively.

Pin a plastic bag to your clothes as you work your way around the house. You can empty bins as you go, without constantly running up and down the stairs.

Blow dust off dried or artificial flowers using a hair-dryer (on its lowest setting).

To clean silk flowers, put them into a large paper bag with a generous scoop of salt. Shake vigorously until all the dust is removed from the flowers.

To remove difficult, dried-on stains, sew a button on to the corner of the cloth you use for wiping down surfaces. Use the edge of the button to scrape off any stubborn crusty stains you come across.

Changing duvet covers needn't end up as a wrestling match. Put one corner of the duvet into its cover and hold it in position with a clothes peg. Repeat with the other corner and shake the duvet down into the cover.

Light a Candle

Candle wax can be removed from a surface by warming a knife over a candle flame. Use the heated knife to lift the wax gently from the surface. If the candle wax has left a stain, dab it with a cotton-wool bud dipped in methylated spirits.

You can get rid of candle wax by covering it with brown paper and running a warm iron (switched off) over it. Change the position of the paper as the wax is absorbed. This works well with other grease stains, too.

To shift wax from metal candlesticks, carefully pour boiling water over the candlestick – this will melt the wax.

Alternatively, to remove wax from a candlestick, use a hair-dryer on a low setting to blow hot air over the surface until the wax has melted.

Keep night-light candles burning for ages. Put a pinch of salt in each one.

To stop candles dripping, sharpen the ends like a pencil. This stops the wax from collecting in a pool and then suddenly spilling over.

Candles burn more evenly and won't drip if you pop them in a freezer before use.

Strong cooking smells will be minimised by lighting a candle in the kitchen while you're cooking – useful in the loo, too!

For scented candles, wrap them in tissue paper on to which a few drops of scented oil have been dripped. Wrap in a plastic bag and leave for a couple of weeks for the scent to impregnate the wax. As they burn down, they release the smell into the room. Ideal for candle-lit dinners!

Recycle candles by melting down all the left-over stubs in a heat-proof bowl in a warm oven. Take a yoghurt pot and make a small hole in the bottom, thread some

string through the hole, and tie to a pencil balanced horizontally on the rim of the pot. Pour in the melted wax and leave to set. Remove the yoghurt pot for a perfectly formed candle.

Creaking door hinges and stiff zips can be miraculously transformed by rubbing a candle along the offending hinge or zip.

Sash windows will run more smoothly if you rub a candle on all the sliding surfaces.

Doors can be unstuck by rubbing the sticky edge with a candle.

Outside

When hanging out washing, make sure the wind is at your back, or you'll get wrapped in wet cloth.

In icy weather, clean the doorstep with a bucket of water to which you have added a crushed aspirin, 8 fl oz/250 ml of warm water and one tablespoon of methylated spirits. This will keep the step clean and stop ice from forming.

Unclog grease from your drains: pour a cup of salt water and a cup of fizzy soda into the drain followed by a pan of boiling water. The grease will usually dissolve immediately and open the drain.

Take a water hose and spray the outside of your house. This will remove the dust and cobwebs. On textured walls attach a car-washing brush to the hose to remove dirt.

For outside windows, dip a long-handled mop in your cleaning solution, wash, then hose off. Throw a clean towel over the mop to dry.

IMAGE CONSULTANTS

Mary Spillane,
www.imageworksuk.com;
Colour Me Beautiful,
www.cmb.co.uk;
Fashion Department,
Women & Home Magazine

Research illustrates that visual image matters. The impact that we make on each other depends 55 per cent on how we look and behave, 38 per cent on how we speak and only 7 per cent on what we say.

Storing Clothes

Take a good look through your wardrobe and weed out anything you haven't worn in over a year. Unless you love it to pieces, throw it out to make room for something you will wear.

Hang your belts and handbags up on hooks inside the cupboard door. It makes them easier to spot than when they're inside a drawer.

Dry-cleaning bags don't protect clothes – they attract dust, can cause whites to go yellow and prevent fibres from breathing.

Never use the wire hangers given away by dry cleaners. They push your garments out of shape.

Use padded hangers for knits, jerseys and silks.

Shaped wooden hangers take up a lot of space in the wardrobe so reserve them for jackets and coats.

Organise your clothes by category – shirts together, trousers together and so on. Within each category, organise by colour and adopt the same scheme for all categories.

Don't stuff drawers – things will get crushed, lost and maybe even emptied out over the floor when you pull out a single item.

Women

Make sure your clothes and accessories are in proportion to your build. Large-framed, tall women should go for looser-fitting clothes, medium to bold prints, medium to large accessories and longer lengths, whereas small and petite women should choose neat-fitting clothes in fine to medium-weight fabrics, patterns only on the top half (if at all), and average to small accessories.

On people with soft, rounded features, black can look jarring, so choose darker versions of warm tones, such as browns and khaki greens.

Overly baggy clothes can look shapeless – aim to flatter curves rather than disguise them completely.

Worried about your hips? Look out for shirts and jackets that sit just below the hips as they are very slimming. Avoid boxy jackets – they draw attention to wide hips.

For instantly longer legs, choose skirts and trousers with a small slit up the side which give the illusion of length and slenderness.

Skirts should always end at a flattering (slim) point of your leg.

Front pleats are a nightmare – flat-fronted trousers and skirts avoid extra bulk.

If you're petite, avoid wearing more that two colours or two garments at the same time as this will make you look cluttered and smaller than you are.

Columns of colour give the illusion of extra height; wearing a darker colour on your bottom half is more slimming.

If you are of angular build, choose fabrics that drape softly over waist and hips. Stiff fabrics and block shapes can look harsh. It's also worth exploring colours such as rust or cinnamon, which suggest approachability, rather than black.

If you are a classic English pear shape and find skirts hard to buy, go for an A-line style, which falls around or just below the knee and which has some pleating or fluting towards the hem.

Buy suits in February and September in 'transitional' weight fabrics. They'll be useful pretty much all year round, especially for office wear, in environments that are heated or air-conditioned to suit.

Buy for today's weight, not your goal weight. If it doesn't flatter now, you won't get the use out of it.

Don't buy a skirt or trousers that you wouldn't be prepared to wear without a jacket.

If you wear a trouser suit, you'll have to be better groomed to look as professional as a woman in a skirt suit.

Jackets with raglan sleeves look modern and deconstructed, but are death for women with sloping or narrow shoulders.

What you wear underneath affects the whole look. Ensure that you are measured and wearing underwear that fits.

A fashionable handbag and pair of shoes will update a classic look with minimum investment.

Coats and jackets get seen first, so make sure yours is the very best you can afford. Buy a classic expensive one in a sale where you will get the best value.

Avoid shopping for a specific item under pressure. Allow plenty of time and take an objective friend along with you who is willing to be honest about items that you try on.

Fashion – note the latest styles and include some in your wardrobe but make sure they are not the major part of your wardrobe budget.

When looking for a really glamorous evening dress, it's a good idea to be fitted for a fabulous bra which will give you the shape you love, then buy the dress to show off your shape. (Needless to say, always try on the dress wearing your super bra.)

A very French tip – buy one or two things of really good quality and keep the rest very simple. A good pair of shoes and a decent haircut (regularly maintained) are the true secrets of style.

Once you have discovered a clothing style that suits you, stick to it. You can update your look with the latest shoes and bags each season.

When buying a new expensive handbag, always fill it to see how it looks (some bags look ugly when packed) and try it on in front of a mirror to check that its proportions suit yours.

Working Mothers

Avoid florals – they look mumsy.

Wear full make-up, not just lipstick and powder.

Wear earrings to work for a business-like look but nothing dangly.

Never carry shopping bags to a meeting. Buy a smart leather 'shopper' that can carry papers as well as a pint of milk without giving the game away.

Take trouble over shoes and hosiery. Make sure they match and are in good condition.

Wear perfume, not eau de baby wipe.

Make sure you arrive at meeting ten minutes early to give you time to 'change gear' from mum to colleague.

Check your handbag and remove pea-shooters, stickers, dummies and anything else you might pull out when hunting for a pen.

Men

Avoid double-breasted suits if you're short or stout, and avoid them like the plague if you're both! They add bulk to the abdomen, which is the last thing you want.

Single-breasted suits are preferable on stocky men, and look fine on anyone except bean-poles.

A three-buttoned suit makes you look taller than two-buttoned, and has a more modern look.

Sit down when trying on a suit. If the collar gapes, it needs adjusting. Hand-sewn collars always sit better.

Sleeve and trouser lengths must be perfect. If not, even the most expensive suit will look tatty. Be prepared to pay extra to have them adjusted, if necessary. Turn-ups are a no-no.

If you wear a handkerchief tucked into your jacket pocket, don't match it exactly to your tie or buy it in a set – you'll look as if your mum's dressed you! Make sure the colour of your handkerchief is co-ordinated with your tie (which should also be chosen to go well with your suit and shirt). Never, ever blow your nose on it.

The width of your tie should echo the width of your lapels.

Keep a full-Windsor for spread collars and double-breasted suits – half-Windsor looks better in most other situations.

Designer silk ties don't hold a knot as well as ordinary silk or other fabrics.

If your suit pattern is bold, make sure your tie is plain or has a vanishingly minimal pattern.

The life of a tie is about five years. Don't try and keep them beyond that life span – they'll never look impressive.

Always give suits at least 24 hours off between wearings. Leave them out of the wardrobe with everything removed from the pockets for a good airing before you put them away.

If you wear a suit regularly, treat yourself to a trouser press – it's a sure sign of joining the grown-ups.

Grooming

Invest in a good haircut with a sympathetic and creative stylist. 'Dress the part' when visiting the stylist as this is how he or she will interpret your image. Return every five to six weeks to keep the cut trim.

Wash your hair daily or every other day.

If you have a busy lifestyle and little time to 'style' your hair every morning, choose a tousled and less structured hairstyle.

Use one of the many light waxes and gels available for quick and easy styling.

If you have longer hair, a low ponytail is simple and can also look smart.

Develop a basic skin-care regime. Cleanse and moisturise daily.

Expose your face to a bowl of steaming water once a week. This will open pores and cleanse grime build-up.

Keep eyebrows well-shaped and tidy. Remember that they frame the eyes, and must therefore do your eyes justice.

A weekly manicure is essential. This is easy to do yourself once you have had a professional manicure and watched how it's done.

Keep hand cream with you and apply each time you wash your hands.

Teeth should be professionally checked and cleaned twice yearly to avoid gum problems that may lead to bad breath.

Brush your teeth at least twice daily. If possible, brush them after lunch as well to ensure fresh breath.

Make-up

Applying make-up should take no more than ten minutes, and should give a natural look that will last all day.

Always apply your make-up while facing daylight.

Apply foundation with a foam sponge, a little at a time evenly in downward strokes all over your face and lips but not your eyelids.

Press in translucent powder with a cotton-wool pad, this will 'set' the foundation so that it will last all day.

Apply blusher using upward strokes to lift the face. For the best effect, blend two shades: lighter on the cheekbone and slightly darker underneath.

A dab of eye base cream to cover your lids and orbital bone lightly before applying eye colour will help to keep your make-up fresh all day without creasing. It will also mean that you use less eye-shadow.

Several thin coats of mascara are better than one heavy one for thick and glossy eyelashes.

Define your eyebrows softly with an eyebrow pencil in a colour slightly darker than your hair colouring.

Use a lip pencil in a natural shade to outline as well as fill in the lips. It will provide a good, lasting base for lipstick.

Blot with a tissue once applied, then reapply lightly.

Colour

Colour analysis is a careful assessment of your natural colouring, which determines what colours for clothes and make-up are most complimentary. It enables you to develop a wardrobe that co-ordinates since the colours within each palette work together. Wearing naturally flattering colours will make you look healthier and feel more confident. Importantly also, it eliminates the unnecessary expense of investing in clothes and make-up that you do not feel comfortable with and therefore do not wear.

Whether you want people to listen to you or talk to you, different colours are appropriate:

Red is upbeat and assertive, a good colour to wear if you want to catch someone's eye. It can also give you an energy boost and project authority. It's not a good colour to wear if you want someone to open up to you.

Pink is gentle and accessible. It expresses femininity so needs to be worn with care. In the office, a totally pink outfit will let others think you are a walk-over, however a pink shirt or scarf can soften an austere look.

Blue is trustworthy and orderly. A colour to wear when you want others to think you are a safe bet – good for the bank manager. If you want others to think of you as more creative, blue is not the right choice.

Green is self-reliant and dependable. Wear green when you are over-stressed or tired as it produces restorative results. After days of wearing more flamboyant colours, wearing green will help you feel more relaxed and balanced. It can also be seen as stubborn and unpredictable, so is not good for interviews.

Brown is earthy and gregarious and a great alternative to black or navy in business as people find brown less threatening. Wear it when you want others to talk to you.

Purple is sensitive and intuitive. If you want to project confidence and individuality, purple is your colour. It is great for evening wear as an alternative to black.

Yellow is cheerful and uninhibited. It is a good colour to wear when working with children and can make you feel better on a dreary day.

INSECT OWNERS

Most insects are easier to handle if they're cool. Pop them in the fridge for a few minutes to slow down their metabolism.

If you have a wounded arthropod (that includes spiders, millipedes, centipedes, crustaceans and insects) with a damaged outer body casing, you can stick them back together with glue.

Spiders

Tarantulas make great pets, but they're not ideal to 'play' with. Enjoy the look of them rather than expecting them to play 'fetch'.

When buying a tarantula, avoid one that is huddled up in the corner with its legs tucked under it. If it doesn't react quickly (or at all) to touch, don't buy it. It's probably dying.

A male tarantula will have little hooks on the undersides of its front legs.

Mature males live from a couple of months to two or three years, depending on the species. Adult females can live for decades; again, it depends on the species.

Different species of tarantula need different living conditions. Arboreals live in trees and make their homes in holes in the bark. Burrowers live in holes. You will need to reflect this when you put them in their cage.

Some tarantulas require very little attention and are therefore easy to keep. Generally, the ground-dwelling tarantulas from arid climates are the easiest. Arboreals and spiders from wet regions need a lot more care. A good choice for the beginner is the Chilean Rose tarantula.

A home for a tarantula can be a 5 gallon/22.5 litre aquarium, a large plastic jar, plastic shoebox or custom-made cage. The top should be covered with screen, mesh or cheesecloth so that there is enough ventilation and secured tightly so there are no escapes.

Tarantulas are the Victor Meldrews of the creepy-crawly world: they don't really enjoy company and are best kept in solitary confinement.

Ground-dwelling tarantulas can easily be killed by a fall, even a short one. So don't let them climb too high.

Tarantulas love crickets. Larger spiders will also eat baby mice and bits of meat.

When a tarantula is about to moult, it will stop feeding, so remove food from the cage. For a small spider, this can be a few days before it moults; for adults, it can be up to several months before they moult.

Spiders that are upside down with their legs in the air are almost certainly moulting. Just leave them to get on with it.

Don't feed a spider that has just moulted. Leave it for a week until the new exoskeleton has hardened (usually when the fangs turn from white to black).

Tarantulas are venomous – that doesn't mean that they are lethal, but bites from some species can be extremely painful and cause unpleasant symptoms. Some people can be allergic to the venom. If you are bitten and experience difficulty breathing, see a doctor.

Stick Insects

Always handle gently – the limbs of a stick insect are easily snapped in two.

Overcrowding can lead to cannibalism so give them enough space.

Make sure there is enough ventilation for your insects – damp conditions can harm eggs as well as adult insects.

Size is important when it comes to housing your stick insect – some species require more space than others. As a general rule, the height of the tank must be at least twice the insect's length.

You can use newspaper to line the floor of your insect's home. Some species, like the Giant Spiny, also like to rest on the floor, so they will need a layer of peat to sit on or cork bark to hide under.

Sphagnum moss in the corner of the tank sprayed regularly can keep the atmosphere humid.

A good temporary home can be made from an empty sweet jar. Make sure you put some air holes in the lid.

Some stick insects need extra heat in order to thrive. You can use a screened light bulb with a low wattage. A tungsten light bulb gives a very concentrated heat but make sure your insects don't dehydrate.

Stick insects are masters of camouflage – some use shape and colour to blend into the background. Others will rock back and forward like leaves or twigs in a breeze.

Food isn't a problem especially if you have access to bramble leaves throughout the year. Avoid leaves with brown edges or other insects' eggs planted on the underside. Leave the leaves on the stem.

To keep food supplies fresh, make a cut in the base of the stem and then set it in a heavy, narrow-necked water container (some stick insects are quite large and could knock over a container). Plug the top of the container with some cotton wool or tissue paper.

Try to vary the diet now and again. The Javanese and Green stick insects are quite partial to rhododendron leaves. Some species will also take privet leaves as well as rose leaves, oak and pyracantha.

Stick insects tend to prefer large leaves to smaller ones.

If you want to experiment with your insect's diet, do so after their moult when new food is more likely to be accepted.

Moults occur several times before the insect reaches adulthood. The higher the temperature, the greater the tendency for the insect to moult. Before a moult your pet will become less active, even losing its appetite for a day or two.

Once a moult is complete, the insect will stay still for several hours while its 'new' skin hardens. Don't handle it during this stage.

Help your stick insect to exercise – put some dried twigs in its cage.

A rose by any other name – some stick insects give off a chemical secretion that smells like rather pleasant perfume.

Don't let your stick insects escape into the wild in case they manage to establish themselves. There are at least two species of New Zealand stick insects living wild in parts of south-western England.

If you want to encourage your stick insects to mate, take them on a car journey. Apparently this can arouse their romantic inclinations, especially with the Giant Spiny stick insect.

Mantids are distant relatives of stick insects, but don't be tempted to keep them together. For many mantids a stick insect is a tasty snack.

INTERIOR DESIGNERS

Special Effects

Jenny Hooper, J H D; Claire Shread, Inardec Art Decor; Karen Mae Birch

Brighten up a dark room. Yellow will make it feel sunny, pink will create a dramatic, warm effect and orange will give it a warm and welcoming feel.

If a room feels claustrophobic, remove any picture rails and paper the walls with vertical stripes.

If a room feels too tall, make a feature of a picture rail or create the same effect with a paper border. Or try painting the ceiling to match the floor.

If a room feels very large, break up the expanse with scattered rugs or pretty screens.

For north-facing rooms, you need to create a feeling of warmth. Try shades of terracotta or sunny, warm yellow.

Natural materials such as wood or brick give a warm feeling.

Test out colour combinations on the back of an old cereal packet.

Get free advice. Many paint and wallpaper companies offer free advice about colour schemes.

Decorative paint effects needn't be hard to achieve. Try scrunching up a plastic bag, dipping it lightly in paint and dabbing it on to a wall for a stunning, dappled effect.

Create an interesting paint effect by dipping a toothbrush in paint and flicking the paint on to a wall.

Transform a wall by cutting a simple design into a potato, dipping it in paint and stamping it on to the wall in a regular pattern.

Want to know where to put a dado rail? Remember that they were originally there to protect the wall from chairs so they should generally be fixed at the height of the back of a chair.

Cover a wall cheaply by stapling large pieces of fabric to it.

Save money on expensive wallpapers – use old sheet music, maps, newspaper cuttings or comics.

When choosing wallpaper, look at it from a distance. You never really stand up close to the wall in your own room.

Paint your radiators to match your walls – it looks better than just leaving them plain white.

Paint shelves and storage units the same colour as skirting boards and picture rails to tie them in to the room and make them an integral part of the overall theme.

After painting the walls, mix up the left-over paint with some clear varnish and use it on the woodwork for a cohesive effect.

You can create an illusion of loads of floor space by painting the skirting boards the same colour as the floor.

If your woodwork is less than perfect, use eggshell paint rather than gloss; its semi-matt finish will hide imperfections.

To brighten up a dark hallway, paint the wall or door at the far end a sunny, bright colour. This has the effect of shortening the long corridor. A wall of mirror also lightens and brightens the space.

When hanging a picture, mark your holes on to masking tape rather than the wall so you don't leave marks on the wall.

Never get a tall person to hang your pictures – you'll always be craning your neck to see them.

When shopping for curtains, take a cushion off your sofa to help you match the exact shade you want.

To change the colour of an old light fitting, spray it with car paint (ordinary paint can be flammable).

Jazz up old light cords by threading them with beads.

Tablecloths can look elegant if trimmed with braid or tassels. However, it can be expensive to trim all the way round a piece of fabric. Instead, decorate the edges of a much smaller top cloth.

Fire surrounds can be expensive. For an effective but cheaper alternative, fix some wall brackets and a shelf over the fireplace.

Give old chairs a new look by painting them with fabric paint.

Transform ordinary-looking boxes or storage cases by covering them in black-and-white photocopies of interesting images. Finish off with a layer of varnish for extra protection.

Make a feature of storage – hang baskets and bags from the kitchen ceiling.

To age pictures, stain with a used tea-bag.

To block out an unattractive view, use stained or etched glass in the window.

The more fabric you use for curtains, the more effective they will look.

Make cheap and cheerful curtains by hanging colourful sheets from a broom handle.

Alternatively, make your own mini greenhouse using double-glazing. Put glass shelves with plants on them between two sheets of double-glazing glass. The plants will thrive in this atmosphere.

Keep an eye out for second-hand sheets. If they are in good condition, you can dye them and use them as curtains, throws, tablecloths or cushion covers.

For inexpensive curtains, clip key-rings to the top of a blanket and thread on to a curtain rail.

For the ultimate snappy shower curtain, use a sheet of bubble wrap.

Make a splash! Decorate the side of your bath with images cut out of wrapping paper or postcards, which you can laminate with sticky-back plastic. Alternatively, get a printer to do it for you – it's very inexpensive.

Refitting a bathroom can be an expensive business. To save money, stick with a basic theme and colour. Try picking up different fittings from end-of-range models.

Old kitchen doors can be transformed by putting new fittings (handles, beading) on them.

If your kitchen is very small, simply re-hang the door so that it swings outwards.

Bring more light into your home – replace the upper panels in your doors with glass.

Light the object and not yourself. To see where you could do with more lighting use a table lamp on an extension lead to experiment with light in different sections of your rooms.

Create the illusion of extra space by hanging a really large mirror on one wall (try to fill the wall space if possible).

Transform a cheap plastic garden container into a sophisticated jardinière with a few coats of emulsion.

Take photos of features or buildings that you like and want to duplicate at home.

Spend most money on the things that you use or touch the most – a chair rather than a poster, for example.

Keep it simple. People often put too much into a room.

Space Saving

When you need more space, look at wasted areas in your house. Space under the stairs is ideal for storing wine (racks can be assembled to fill the awkward shape). Space above a picture rail or around a door is ideal for bookshelves.

Disused fireplaces are ideal for filling with shelves, and their depth makes them ideal for storing larger items.

Areas above your head can be used in the kitchen for hanging pots, pans and utensils.

The blank side of a kitchen cupboard door could accommodate narrow shelves for herbs and spices, jars and even cookery books.

When space is short in a kitchen, buy chairs that stack on to each other.

Stack tins and jars on top of each other in cupboards with cheap space-saver shelves.

Put a run of cupboards above a double bed for hiding away extra blankets, pillows and linen, or out-of-season clothes.

Choose mops, brushes and dustpans with loops so they can be hung on the wall when not in use.

Make the most of ceiling space for airing and drying clothes.

Replace the kick-board under kitchen units with a hinged drawer for storing roasting tins and baking trays.

Fix hooks to the top of a window recess and use them to hang mugs in the kitchen.

Ask your local sweet shop if they have any old sweet jars. These are ideal for storing pasta, coloured pulses and preserves.

Use oil-based paint (gloss, eggshell or enamel), to paint large jars for storing flour and sugar.

Cork tiles, glued to a piece of chipboard or plywood, make perfect notice boards. Use pins with coloured ends or drawing pins to secure invitations and billets doux.

Make shelving look prettier by edging it with wallpaper or thick cartridge paper cut into an interesting shape and decorated with a simple motif.

Use a cardboard template and a jigsaw to cut around thin MDF for edging shelves in a bedroom or playroom.

In the bathroom, use empty wall space for stacking towels and flannels on shelves made from painted MDF.

Strong wire mesh from DIY stores or garden centres makes modern, high tech shelving in a bathroom for storing towels and linen.

An office trolley – very cheap from office suppliers and furniture stores – works well in the bathroom for storing toiletries and towels.

Panel your bath with a home-made wooden panel and turn one section of it into a drop-down flap or removable panel. It will provide extra space for toiletries and cleaning products.

In tight spaces, for example galley kitchens, replace doors with hinged, fold-back doors or even curtains.

Cover old shoe-boxes with wrapping paper or cut-offs of wallpaper, and stack them to store a sewing kit and odds and ends.

Shoe-boxes covered in off-cuts of fabric can be used to store CDs.

Fix small hooks into the inside of a wardrobe door and use them to hang ties, belts and necklaces.

Tights can be stored in a string shopping bag hung on the inside of a wardrobe door.

Multi-hanging hangers allow you to hang three or four times as much clothing in the same space.

Paint old fruit boxes and use them for storing socks and shoes, belts and shoe-cleaning equipment at the bottom of a wardrobe.

Use trunks and boxes as bed-side tables – they can then double up as storage space.

Window seats create more seating space when it is in short supply. Hinged lids allow them to become extra storage space.

Windows

When an expensive patterned fabric takes your fancy, use ungathered headings on your curtains and you won't need so many widths of fabric – try tabs, ties or hooks.

When you collect ordered fabric, check for imperfections (you will not be able to take it back once it is cut) and make sure it is all off one roll. Colours can vary enormously roll to roll.

Always allow for shrinkage when estimating how much fabric you need to buy.

Avoid using precious fabric for lining curtains – it is the part of the curtain most likely to fade.

Put the track or rail up on the window before you start making curtains, so you can get the measurements just right.

When measuring fabric, measure twice and cut once!

When cutting out, make sure you have a square edge by laying the fabric along a rectangular table, with the selvedge edge running exactly down the long side. Run tailor's chalk along the fabric where it bends over the edge of the table. Cut along the chalk line.

Keep an iron and ironing board close at hand when making curtains, so you can press out seams and fabric as you go along.

Measure both sides of a window as floors can be uneven, especially in old houses.

Curtains with drawstrings get handled less so stay clean longer.

Try to use washable fabric when making curtains that hang near doorways. They will get dirty.

When hanging curtains near a doorway on a hard floor, hem them so they hang just above the floor.

A pelmet should be one-fifth of the total length of the curtain.

For a flounced valance or pelmet, use a brightly coloured silk sari.

To calculate the amount of fabric you need for a flounced valance, hang a piece of cord or string over the pole and down each side of the window to the length required.

A plywood pelmet, painted in a colour to co-ordinate with the curtains, will be cheaper then buying and making a fabric pelmet.

Where there is no room for a pelmet, stencil or paint freehand a design around the edge of the window.

If sewing a trim is difficult, glue it on with fabric glue.

No good with a needle? Felt or blankets make good curtains, are good insulators against the cold and come in bright jewel colours. Hang them using clip-on curtain hooks.

Save time and money on tie-backs by using thick rope from ship's chandlers.

When making a bed valance to co-ordinate with curtain fabric, attach the valance to an old sheet.

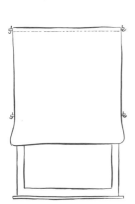

Cheat's blinds: cut two lengths of bamboo (available from garden centres) slightly wider then the window. Cut a length of stiff cloth or raffia, painting the edges with clear glue to stop them fraying. Stitch a narrow casing hem top and bottom and push the bamboo through each casing. Hook the ends of the bamboo over cup hooks screwed into the window architrave.

Thread coloured beads on to strong nylon thread tied around a dowel for an effective beaded curtain.

Flooring

Before choosing a floor, make a list of the activities that will take place in the room: eating, access to outside, cooking, sleeping, playing with toys, bathing, sitting on the floor?

If you want to carpet a kitchen, use carpet tiles that can be replaced individually if they become stained.

Buy a few more carpet tiles than you need.

Bathroom flooring has heavy use and damp conditions, so make a good investment initially, or buy a floor that is cheap enough to replace often.

If you suffer from allergies, sealed wooden flooring works well in a bedroom.

Always ask for the largest sample of flooring to take home and try.

If a carpet seller gives you an all-in price, check you are happy with the quality of underlay he is including in the price.

Make sure you have got measurements right – especially for tiles you are laying yourself. The shop may not take back the tiles if you miscalculate and extra tiles bought later may come from a different production run and vary in colour.

Pale shades will make a room look bigger, dark colours will be warmer and cosier.

In a small house or flat, use the same carpet or flooring colour throughout to give the appearance of space.

If using the same colour throughout, ask your carpet supplier if they do the same carpet in different weights for use in a hall, bedroom and bathroom.

Tiles laid in broad lines or diagonally will make a narrow room look broader, and a border on tiles or in a carpet can help to draw in the walls on a wide room.

Patterned carpeting can also reduce the dimensions of a large room.

Make sure the carpet layer is willing to take away the old carpet or you may be lumbered with its disposal.

Check that colour and pattern are consistent in a tile batch or carpet before it is laid.

Cork is a cheap option for a bathroom floor, but make sure it is flooring quality and seal it with polyurethane.

Where flooring puts up with heavy traffic, use industrial flooring (like textured rubber). Look in shops and offices to see what they use.

Natural flooring, like sisal or coir, should be laid out for 48 hours before it is installed so it can acclimatise to the atmosphere.

Don't use natural matting near an open fire or in the kitchen. It is a fire risk.

If you are laying flooring round a basin or toilet, make a template out of paper first and use that as a guide when cutting the tiles or flooring.

Slight scratches in vinyl flooring can be covered up by rubbing in a matching colour of shoe polish with cotton wool. Remove the excess with a cotton-wool bud previously dampened with a little white spirit. Polish with a soft, clean cloth.

Wooden floors can be painted with marine paint. This is strong and hard wearing, but it takes a long time to dry.

Sounds obvious – but always paint a floor working towards the door. You wouldn't be the first to get stuck on the wrong side of a painted floor!

Always secure mats and rugs to a wooden or vinyl floor with sticky-backed tape or matting available from carpet shops. They can be lethal otherwise.

Add an extra length of carpet at the top and bottom of a flight of stairs so the carpet can be shifted periodically to avoid wear.

Make sure the edge of each stair tread is smooth so it doesn't snag the carpet.

Buy a sample of the carpet you are laying, or use an off-cut to lay near a front door. It will stop wear and the carpet becoming ingrained with dirt.

Don't try to save money by re-using underlay. It will have lost its resilience, so the new carpet won't lie evenly and will wear out more quickly.

Compare prices with underlay. Some expensive underlays may just be marked up so that a particular carpet can be offered at a keener price.

If your carpet is continuing into different rooms, or throughout the house, use the same underlay (most suitable for heavy use). It is likely to be the one most suitable for the stairs.

Newspaper put under underlay will stop dust rising up through gappy floorboards.

Check that there is enough space to get a wide carpet upstairs – it may have to make its entrance though a window otherwise!

If a new carpet is thicker than the one you are replacing, make sure you can open doors and wardrobes. Most carpet layers won't plane off doors for you.

Children's Rooms

If you are preparing a room for a baby, give yourself lots of time – you won't want to be spending hours poring over fabric samples in shops or up ladders when your baby is imminent.

Ensure that plug sockets are fixed to the wall securely and use plastic covers on ones that are not in use.

Keep flexes and wires well out of reach of small children.

Low level panes of glass should be safety glass standard and windows should have safety latches on, which can be detached in an emergency.

Double-glazing should be easily removable in an emergency. Free-standing wardrobes should be fixed to the wall.

Secure any pictures close to a child's cot or bed with mirror plates.

Avoid hanging mobiles above a cot, bed or changing mat, but keep them where the child can see them.

Furniture should have rounded edges and not be splintered.

A thermostatic heater will keep the temperature of a baby's room at a steady 64 °F/18 °C.

Blackout blinds are ideal for keeping in warmth and blocking out early morning light.

Put soft toys in the freezer once a month for at least six hours to kill dust mites, which can cause allergies. Once you take it out of the freezer, vacuum the toy to remove the mite faeces.

To plan a child's room, get down on the floor and view things from a child's perspective.

Brighten up a child's room by making fun borders. Get long strips of paper and let the children walk up and down them with painted feet.

It is easier to re-paint a room than re-paper it. Also children can't resist tearing off any unglued wallpaper they can lay their hands on. Select a brand of paint that is recommended as wipe-clean.

Striped fabrics are fresh looking and won't look too babyish as your child grows.

Pictures to decorate the walls need not be expensive. Use old birthday or greetings cards with bold colourful pictures framed in off-the-shelf frames.

Make your own mobile by hanging interesting items – coloured shapes of animals, stars and moons, card covered in silver paper, pictures cut from greetings cards – secured with string from pieces of dowel.

Painting a mural isn't as hard as it sounds. Choose a simple drawing from a children's book, and draw a grid over the picture using tracing paper. With a soft pencil mark out a larger grid on to the wall, with the same number of squares, and transfer the design to the wall square by square. The number of grid squares will depend on how complicated your chosen design is.

Yes, your children can scribble on walls! Just paint a section with matt black paint and have a tub of chalks to hand.

If your children's bedroom will double up as a playroom, leave one area of it uncarpeted with wipe clean vinyl tiles for messy play.

Choose furniture and finished surfaces that can be wiped clean.

If storage is a problem in a toddler's room, double up the rails in their wardrobe. Their clothes aren't long enough to need the extra hanging space.

Paint or decorate a plastic bin for a child's room. You can use it as a toy 'box'.

Don't put pegs at an adult height in a child's room. This won't encourage kids to clear their own mess up. Put pegs where they can reach them.

For hanging small dresses, fix a rail under a shelf or use chunky wooden pegs.

Use an umbrella stand for storing tennis rackets and cricket bats.

If two children are sharing a room, partition off their own space with a curtain or open bookshelf.

A row of plain wooden pegs running along the wall is useful for hanging sports kit, or soft toys in string bags, and makes use of wasted space on the walls.

If there is space, put a single bed in your baby's room even when he or she is still in a cot. It is useful to crawl into if your child is ill and you want to stay nearby. It can double up as a sofa during the day.

Cot beds are a good investment because a child will get many years' wear out of it.

However when you come to buy a full-sized bed, get one with a divan base (the extra drawer space will be useful) – children cannot resist bouncing on beds and beds on legs with castors will not cope with the athletics.

A weekend bed, with a pull-out mattress underneath, will be ideal for sleep-overs and weekend guests.

Custom-made changing stations are expensive and unnecessary. Use a sturdy chest of drawers for your baby's changing mat – but make sure it is at waist height so you don't strain your back. Alternatively use the floor.

Instead of a desk for a growing child, rest hardboard on two small matching chests of drawers.

Jazz up an old table as a desk, by painting it with coloured stripes. Mark out the stripes with masking tape, prime and undercoat it and use eggshell as the top colours. Cover the piece with two coats of acrylic clear varnish.

You can make curtain poles and finials more interesting by cutting out a shape (perhaps a car or teddy) painting it and fixing it with a screw to the end of the curtain pole.

Make your own play kitchen or workbench with plywood or MDF, painted with spray paints recommended for children's furniture. Then paint on a hob, and stick on knobs as controls for the 'oven'. Chunky hooks can be screwed in for hanging plastic play utensils.

Give a teenager more space in his room by erecting a hammock for him to lie in when listening to music.

If space is tight, fix a triangle of MDF across the corner of a room as a desk with smaller triangles above for shelving.

INTERVIEWERS

Charlie Blackwood;
Mike Coigley

Never, ever be late! Allow for traffic jams and train cancellations. Even if you are far too early, better to take a walk round the block, than rush in out of breath.

If you are taking a briefcase, pack in a clean top or shirt, and tie. You are almost bound to spill coffee down yourself on the way to the interview.

Interviewers often make up their minds in the first four minutes of an interview. As a prospective employee, you need to make an impression immediately. Maintain eye contact, smile and be congenial and positive.

Find out as much about the company as possible, and the position they are offering. Information is power and the more information you have the more powerful you can be in the interview.

Dress according to the image you want to project. Be smart, unfussy and understated.

Don't wear anything that is too tight (you'll be uncomfortable and it will put pounds on you).

Keep perfume to the minimum (they want to remember you, not your smell).

Refuse coffee. If you are nervous, a cup and saucer is one more thing to worry about.

Prepare yourself for tricky questions. The interviewer may throw in something you were not anticipating. Would you be ready to outline your five biggest accomplishments in your present job, give your views on minority groups, describe your personality, know what your subordinates think of you?

An intelligent person thinks through an answer. Take a moment to plan what you are going to say – try not to be glib.

A bit of sparkle goes a long way. Show your sense of humour (that doesn't mean cracking an hysterical joke).

Don't slag off your previous employer. It is not an attractive trait.

Don't invent skills you do not have or embellish your educational achievements.

Don't be afraid to ask how you have done and when the company expect to make a decision. Make it clear you are interested in the job.

INVENTORS & PATENT AGENTS

Richard Brown,
Inventor, Sybre
Innovations

Most inventions come about by solving a problem. Try to think about what really annoys you and then work out what you could do to overcome it.

Has someone else beaten you to it? Scour shops, catalogues, talk to 'shopaholic' friends and of course use the internet.

If you think that a search of published patents is required, use the internet as a first stop. Many on-line patent offices have some on-line searching facilities, though they may be limited. It may be worth filing a patent application with the Patent Office and pay the official fee for the search. This is cheaper than paying for commercial searchers.

Free advice is available from government agencies, the Patent Office, the Chartered Institute of Patent Agents and even the European Commission. Make use of them before parting with money.

Have your list of whom to contact with your invention ready so you can start 'knocking on doors' the minute the patent has been filed.

Keep Mum! Don't disclose your idea until the patent application has been filed. Insist that interested companies sign a confidentiality agreement. Some will object, but most will be impressed that you are taking the protection of your rights seriously.

Use professional advice when filing an application. Tempting as it is to do it yourself as a financial short cut, there are mind-boggling rules to be complied with before a patent can be granted.

The odds are against you ever making money on your idea. So only spend money where absolutely necessary. You are very unlikely to become a millionaire from your brilliant idea, but you never know…

IRONING SERVICES

Trinny Mycroft;
Angela Simms; Henry
Brookes

To iron silk ties, slip a piece of card inside the tie so that no creases come through.

Keep creases in your trousers for longer. Put soap on the inside of the crease when pressing your trouser leg.

Don't press the hems of skirts and trousers if there's a possibility you might need to let them down. Just press up to a few millimetres of the hem and stop there.

Get used to ironing sitting down. If you prefer to stand, try taking off your shoes and standing on a cushion to prevent your legs getting tired.

A small damp sponge is handy when ironing – rub it lightly over a dry crease then iron it away.

After ironing, fold matching sheets and duvet covers and place inside matching pillow cases. This way sets will be much easier to find.

When ironing bed linen, spray it with water infused with lavender oil. The smell will help you sleep.

Make your own version of scented ironing spray with a few drops of lavender oil added to distilled water. Place in a dark glass bottle with a spray top and shake well before you use it.

When ironing, put a drop of essential oil into your steam iron water to make clothes smell nice.

Freshly ironed clothes crease very readily, so hang them up for a few hours before packing or wearing.

Keep corduroy, embroidery, appliqué or damask from flattening, by ironing the fabric on the reverse side.

Woollens should be ironed dry, but place a damp cloth (a white hankie or tea towel will do) over the wool and press down with the iron – don't rub as you would on cotton. Keep the iron cool.

Pleated skirts and dresses? Position a couple of the pleats on the ironing board and pin them at the base of each pleat to the board. Press using a damp pressing cloth (see above). Remove the pins and move to the next pair of pleats, repeating the process.

Use an old blanket as an ironing board cover.

A dab of clear nail varnish on buttons, will fuse the threads together and they won't fall off.

Use melted ice as sterilised water in your steam iron.

Wait until your steam iron reaches the right temperature before using it. Too cool, and it may drip on your clothes, leaving water stains.

Dirty iron? Put a piece of brown paper on the ironing board, sprinkle it with salt and slide the iron around in the salt until the bottom is clean.

Remove starch from the bottom of an iron by wrapping a piece of white candle in a scrap of clean cloth and running it over a warm iron. Do not do this if the iron has a non-stick finish.

Empty the water from a steam iron while it is still hot. The heat will evaporate any remaining moisture (and mineral deposits which can clog up the iron) from the reservoir.

If your iron is spitting brown water on to your clothes, the vents are clogged. Unplug the iron and use the end of an unbent paperclip to clean residue out of the vents. Then fill the iron with equal parts water and vinegar. Put it on the rack over a grill pan, plug it in and set the iron to steam. After the iron has stopped steaming, set the temperature to max and leave it for half an hour. (Don't leave it unattended.) Before using the iron again, run it over a damp cloth to wipe off any sediment.

Store a steam iron upright – residual moisture can discolour the plate.

If your iron sticks to your clothes, wrap a bar of soap in a hanky and rub it over the hot face of the iron – it will be as smooth as new.

JEWELLERS

Louise Callow;
Anthony Boyd

Safe & Sound

For security when going on holiday, use eggcups as jewellery cases and store them in the fridge.

When washing up, attach your precious rings to a safety pin and pin them to your clothing.

If you need to wash your hands in a public loo, don't put your rings down – it's too easy to forget them. Instead, pop them in your mouth, but do not swallow!

Make sure you don't lose your valuables – hang a few hooks inside your bathroom cabinet. Not only will your jewellery be safely away from plug holes but also away from the damaging steam.

To prevent your gold rings from getting misshapen, dented or scratched, cover your car steering-wheel with some soft foam or fabric (apparently gripping the wheel too tight is the most common cause of damage).

If you've lost a lot of weight, get your wedding ring altered.

If your family heirloom is too large for your finger, use the ring as a scarf clasp or as a pendant.

If a ring becomes stuck on your finger, use window cleaner rather than soap to unstick it.

Cleaning

For a good, general jewellery cleaner, try a weak solution of washing-up liquid in warm water with a drop of household ammonia.

Don't be conned into buying expensive gold cleaners: most are just variations on common household bleach.

Useful cleaning tools are old toothbrushes and mascara wands.

Some stones shouldn't be put in cleaning solution: jade, coral and lapis lazuli only need a gentle polish. Opals and turquoise are fragile so polish carefully with a cloth.

Clean amber in some warm milk, dry, and polish with a soft silk cloth.

Jet can be cleaned with soft breadcrumbs.

You can wash jade from time to time in soapy warm water. Jade should be handled as much as possible.

Emeralds are naturally fragile – always get them cleaned professionally.

Never put your emeralds in hot water: the gems will absorb the liquid and crack.

If your emeralds dry out, pour a little almond oil on the stones, wrap them in a towel and leave them on the radiator overnight.

Opals are very porous so avoid washing them altogether. Instead buff them up with a soft chamois leather.

Clean set stones by scrubbing gently with a toothbrush and warm soapy water. Pay careful attention to the back of the setting where dirt can build up unnoticed.

For gold plate or soft stones such as amber, opals or emeralds, a gentle scrub with a toothbrush dipped in washing-up liquid in some water is quite enough.

For tougher stones and gold settings, you can mix your own cleaner with one part ammonia, one part washing-up liquid and three parts water. Allow jewellery to soak for a few minutes, then scrub gently with a toothbrush.

If your diamonds have lost their sparkle, drop them into a glass of water, add one denture-cleaning tablet and leave them to soak for a couple of minutes.

Gold chains need careful handling. Soapy water is the best thing to clean them with but try rubbing the gold gently in a chamois leather afterwards to make them really sparkle.

For really sparkling gold, soak it for several minutes in gin.

Bring up a nine-carat shine with a soft-bristled toothbrush.

The best thing to buff up gold jewellery is a spectacle-cleaning cloth.

To maintain a gleam, remove all gold before bathing. The soapy water simply builds up a film and your precious jewellery will soon look dull.

To store your gold and silver without damage, line your jewellery box with an empty egg tray, so you can keep each piece of jewellery in a separate compartment.

To stop jewellery becoming tarnished, place a piece of chalk in your trinket box.

Clean silver jewellery by coating with a little toothpaste (not gel or stripey), then leave for an hour or so and rub off with a dry cloth.

To create a lovely antique effect, paint egg yolk on to silver bracelets and necklaces.

To stop silver jewellery from tarnishing, wrap in black tissue.

Cameos should never be immersed in water. Use a brush dipped in the cleaner and brush the surface gently. Rinse in the same way with clean water. Blot off excess water and rub with a chamois leather.

Pearls

To test whether pearls are real or not, simply place them between your teeth. Real pearls have a gritty surface; fake pearls are smooth.

Real pearls should be worn regularly so that they can absorb the moisture from your body that will keep them looking lustrous. They should be the first thing to go on in the morning and the last thing to come off at night.

Don't wear your pearls in the shower – the silk thread will become damaged and rot.

If your string of pearls breaks, pick up all the pearls and put them on a round tea tray. You can then use the curve to sort the pearls out so that they are in the right order for restringing.

Wash real pearls in very salty water. Let them to dry and then polish with a piece of velvet.

Shine pearls with a dab of olive oil and wipe dry with a chamois.

Clean artificial pearls with a chamois leather. Just rub it carefully over the beads.

Ear, Ear

Fishing flies make great earrings.

Store earrings by poking them through a piece of fabric.

Aluminium wire that has been wound around a small paint-brush or pencil makes effective earrings.

Lost the butterfly from the back of your earring? Use a piece of pencil rubber as a temporary measure.

Arms & Necks

Make a great bracelet from the inside of a vacuum-cleaner belt.

Can't find your cufflinks? Buff up a couple of nuts and bolts and use them instead.

To untangle your chains, simply use a drop of almond oil, some needles and a lot of patience.

Alternatively, dust lightly with talcum powder.

Make a necklace from electrical wire.

To store necklaces, hang them on tiny nails or a key-ring holder in your wardrobe.

If you are getting a rash from a piece of jewellery but can't bear to get rid of it, try cleaning it first, then apply a coat of clear nail-varnish to all the parts that touch your skin.

To stop stones falling out of your costume jewellery, paint them with clear nail-varnish.

KNITTERS

Rachel Myers

When unpicking wool, wrap it round a hot-water bottle filled with hot water, to help the wool to straighten again.

Put mohair or angora in the fridge for a few hours before you start knitting, to help keep the fluff under control.

When knitting with dark-coloured wool, cover your lap with a white cloth – you'll be able to see what you're doing without straining your eyes.

If your knitting needles stick, just run them through your hair to oil them lightly.

Keep track of where you are on your knitting pattern. Use a hair grip as a guide. Slide it down the pattern as you work your way through.

Check if you've got enough wool to finish a row – the wool has to be three times the width of the piece you're knitting.

For travelling with cable knitting, get some babies' nappy pins and secure the various bits of the pattern on separate pins, rather than risking them on a double-ended needle.

When knitting children's jumpers, do both arms at the same time to save having to work out all the shaping twice, and to make sure both are the same length! Grown-up's jumpers are too big to fit two sleeves on one needle.

LANDSCAPE GARDENERS
Design in Practice

Jane Williams-Thomas, Pershore; Glyn Jones, Cambridge; Gordon MacVity, Coventry; Richard Thomas, Bath; Peter Philips, Bristol; Stephen Welch, Doncaster; Karen Cole, Cambridge

Feeling generous? Donate a plant to the neighbours to create a visual link between small gardens.

If you've inherited an overgrown, neglected garden and don't know where to start, begin by clearing away the rubbish and cutting the lawn. Things will start to look better immediately.

If you're taking over an established garden, leave things for at least a year to see what the garden looks like in different seasons.

Draw a plan out on paper first. Take photographs of your garden from lots of different viewpoints (winter is usually a good time for this). With a felt-tip pen, you can then sketch in the features that you are thinking of adding.

To help your planting plan, take note of which part of the garden the sun reaches and for how long.

Allow for growth. Plants are like children. . . they grow up, so leave them enough room. Check with the nursery if you're not sure.

Never look at your garden at midday because flowers will rarely look their best. As the angle of light changes, the flowers will come into their own.

Tall plants give focus. Plants such as cardoons, angelica or globe artichokes provide a wonderful background. Artichokes are notorious for smothering smaller neighbours, so give them at least a square metre each to expand.

Not sure about plants, but can't resist them? Pot them up in tubs, if you really must have them. Don't rush to put plants into the ground if you're not sure what your final plan will be.

Green glass wine bottles make good edging for your beds.

Plant a quick-growing climber next to your newly erected trellis or screen. Make sure you choose a plant that won't outgrow the trellis.

Clumps of bamboo make an effective screen and can hide unsightly objects such as compost heaps, dustbins and so on.

Get rid of boring stretches of grass. Alter the shape by adding curves or making an island bed.

Alternatively, create a focal point by planting a specimen tree.

Island beds break up big expanses of grass, but make sure the proportions are in keeping with the size of the lawn.

A trellis arch can divide a garden in two. Plant two evergreen shrubs either side to mark the boundary.

A curved lawn gives the garden a more casual look while straight edges are suitable for a formal look.

To make curves in the edge of the lawn, drive a small stake into the ground and attach some string to it. Attach a funnel filled with sand to the other end, pull the string taut and use it to make an even curve.

An ornamental divider breaks up a long lawn.

Old baler twine makes a bright and cheap way to mark out your garden.

Hide hanging basket chains by growing trailing plants up them.

If you've got a pile of unwanted rubble, don't bother to move it. Plant a climber next to it to disguise it, such as a rose or clematis. If the rubble includes concrete, don't use lime-hating plants.

If screening something in your garden is difficult, you could make a feature of it or highlight it in some way, rather than trying to hide it.

If you've got a post or an old tree stump that you don't like but can't get rid of, grow a climber up it.

Pergolas are a useful way of adding shelter and giving an element of privacy if your garden is overlooked.

If your garden is overlooked, add a section of trellis to the top of your fence and plant some evergreen climbers.

Optical Illusions

To make a border look longer, plant brightly coloured flowers and plants in the foreground. Put pale colours at the back of the garden.

Grey plants will make a border seem longer.

Hot, fiery-coloured flowers shorten the distance.

Glossy foliage perks up dull, dark corners.

Grow copper maples, dark red roses and pink camellias in the west of your garden to catch the rays of the setting sun.

If your garden slopes away from the house, put progressively taller shrubs down the slope – an effective way of seeing more garden.

Divide a long, narrow garden into a series of 'rooms' using screens, hedges and trellis.

In a short garden surrounded by a hedge, cut the top of the hedge slightly lower towards the back of the garden to give the illusion that the end of the garden is further away than it actually is.

Alternatively, lay a path that tapers to a point away from the house. Plant trees and shrubs along it that get gradually shorter as you move away from the house.

Planting two pots in a similar way, but one larger than the other will give the feeling of space. Put the larger one in the foreground and the smaller one to the rear.

Secret nooks and crannies add a sense of mystery to a garden.

Direct night-lights away from your garden and towards nearby trees for a magical green backdrop.

Use mirrors to enlarge a small garden.

Water Features

If you want to create a bog garden, think big. A larger bog garden won't dry out as quickly as a smaller one.

When creating a water feature, make sure any container you use is frost proof.

If you are building a pond, make sure animals can get in and out easily – incorporate shallow, sloping sides and rocks for them to use.

Don't situate your pond beneath trees because you'll have your hands full keeping the surface clear of falling leaves.

Weigh a new pond plant down with several large stones. This will keep the roots beneath the water and the plant in position.

Deep-water plants, such as waterlilies, can be planted up in old washing-up bowls. Use a heavy soil and cover with gravel to keep in place. Put the bowl in a shallow part of the pond to start with and then move it into deeper water in a couple of weeks.

Paths & Patios

When sinking slabs into the lawn, make sure they are deep enough that the lawn-mower runs over them easily.

Stepping stones make an ideal alternative pathway across a lawn.

When laying paths through the garden, you should ensure that they are wide enough for one person to walk along with ease.

When building an archway, make sure it's wide enough for two people to walk through and tall enough to take into account the kind of plants you're going to grow up it.

Make a quick and easy arch for a lightweight plant. Get a length of old hosepipe and stop up the ends. Push both ends into the ground and you have an instant arch.

If your garden is full of curves, make sure your paths follow the curves rather than cut right through them.

A path should lead somewhere, even if it's just to a shed, greenhouse, different part of the garden, a seat or a statue. Paths that don't go anywhere look odd.

If you have a dark path running through your garden, lighten it up by planting the borders with evergreens that have brightly variegated leaves.

Combine different materials for a more interesting effect: slabs, bricks, paving stones, gravel and cobble stones can all be mixed and matched.

To achieve an even pointing finish, use a piece of old garden hose. Push it against the mortar to get the desired result.

To break up a long flight of steps, place terracotta pots along the edge.

Alternatively, soften the line of steps by growing plants along the treads. Make sure you use plants that aren't going to take over too much.

You can make a flight of steps look more formal by placing two matching containers at either side of the bottom or top step. Plants such as rose trees, bay trees, box plants or spiralling wire with ivy growing up it are ideal.

If you want a patio, you will need a space at least 8 ft/2.4 m by 8 ft/2.4 m to accommodate a standard garden table and four chairs.

Make your own paving slabs from concrete. Create the shape you want using two semi-rigid pieces of metal or plastic held together by string. Put this on a wooden base and pour your concrete mix in, making sure there are no gaps for it to seep out. Leave it for 48 hours and then untie the mould. Protect from frost until completely dry.

When making your own paving slabs, add concrete dye to make different colours.

When laying out slabs for a patio, dab the cement out in the shape of a number five on a dice. It's more economical and a lot easier to handle because there's less of it.

If you can't find a replacement for a cracked slab, move the offending piece to a less noticeable area and swap it with a better one.

Make sure your wheelbarrow is facing the direction you want to go before you fill it up. It will be a lot easier to manoeuvre.

Plant compact annuals between patio slabs to soften the look of your patio.

In a patio, don't use plants that have a vigorous root system because they may start to displace the slabs in the future.

Remove broken slabs or whole sections of your patio and plant directly into the soil. Make sure that you prepare the soil carefully; it won't have had many nutrients and will probably be severely compacted.

If your patio is too small, you can extend it by simply laying some gravel and surrounding it with brick.

If your patio doesn't get enough sun, consider pruning, even moving, a tree or painting the surrounding walls white.

Use yoghurt or liquid manure to age your patio. Just paint it on and leave for a while.

To age new bricks, brush them with milk.

Trees

Check the growing habits of a tree before planting it. Some roots can undermine large structural foundations (especially if you have a clay-based soil).

To avoid tree roots damaging drains, find out the ultimate height of the tree you want. Then plant it at least one and a half times this distance from your buildings and drains.

If your garden is dominated by trees, use plants that like woodland conditions.

For a natural woodland look, go for plants that are self-seeding, have small flowers and simple foliage.

Don't forget to water plants under trees. The leaves and branches act like an umbrella and keep most of the rain off them.

The further away from a tree you go, the more light the plants on the ground will receive, so plant accordingly.

When planting under trees, be careful not to damage the tree roots.

Make sure newly planted trees have a good start in life by providing shelter for them as they grow and by keeping them clear of weeds.

When planting a tree in a lawn, leave a circle of bare earth three to four times the diameter of the root-ball. You can feed a tree more easily this way and it prevents direct competition from the grass.

When planting a tree, cut off a bit of old hose and place one end next to the roots. When you fill in the hole, leave the other end poking out of the soil. Then you can water the roots directly.

To encourage young trees to grow, spank them!

If you want something screening from spring to autumn, plant a deciduous tree.

Bulbs that flower in the spring are a nice feature to plant under a tree. Don't worry about them not getting enough sun because the tree doesn't cast much shade at this time.

If you want to put a bench or seat round a tree, make sure you leave enough room for the trunk to expand.

Snow can damage trees. Protect conifers and similar densely branched trees by tying together with wire or rope.

Problems Solved

When putting up a shed or greenhouse, choose your site carefully. You don't want to create a wind tunnel and damage your plants.

Where wind is a problem, a hedge is better than a wall. Hedges disrupt the wind, creating calm, whereas wind simply rushes over and around walls.

If you have a sloping garden, make sure you use plants that don't need much looking after. They can be difficult to get to.

It can often be damper at the bottom of a slope so make sure you plant moisture-loving plants there.

Got a garden with a slope like the side of Everest? Cut terraces into the slope and build retaining walls to keep the soil in place.

To keep soil in place on a slope, use netting pegged into the ground.

Noise is a nuisance in built-up areas. A solid hedge will block quite a lot of noise. Even a fairly big tree will reduce road noise.

Well-planted pergolas will reduce overhead aircraft noise.

Alternatively, rustling trees, water and birds will detract from other more unpleasant noises.

Perk up a dull brick wall by painting it, growing fruit trees or climbers against it, adding a mirror or be really creative and paint a mural.

Containers & Raised Beds

Use old car tyres to make simple, cheap plant holders for your patio.

If you've just had a new bathroom put in and find yourself with an old bath you don't need, put it in the garden. It's ideal for large plants that need a big growing space.

Little plastic crates available from supermarkets and DIY stores make an ideal alternative to special pond baskets.

Old watering cans, chamber pots, vegetable crates, metal drums and so on make ideal plant containers. Always make sure there are enough drainage holes in the bottom.

Keep container-grown plants warm over winter – line the pot with sheets of bubble wrap before planting up.

You don't have to put plants in containers. If they are interesting shapes, they can be a focal point in their own right.

Group several plants together in a container, especially ones with interesting foliage or when they're in full flower. Choose plants that need similar growing conditions.

Containers don't have to sit on patios or walls. They are useful when it comes to filling in gaps in your borders as well.

When planting up a terracotta or stone container, water both it and the plants before planting to stop the compost from drying out.

If your container is quite tall, make sure you stabilise it by putting large stones or rubble in the bottom before planting up.

When planting up a tall container, save compost by planting up a smaller pot which will fit into the top of the container.

Don't put a plant that will grow a lot into a barrel or urn-shaped container. You will only be able to remove it by smashing the pot.

When planting up hanging baskets, wrap plants in pieces of polythene shaped into a cone. This will protect the root-ball when you pull it through the basket. Once the plant is in position, remove the polythene.

Alternative linings for hanging baskets are newspaper, knitwear or blanket weed.

Make your own hanging basket – use an old colander or large sieve with some chains attached.

Alternatively, large catering containers may not look attractive but plant them up with trailing plants to hide the sides and you have a handy pot.

For a different hanging basket, transform unwanted lampshades by turning them upside down and planting them up.

In winter, put an old plate on top of your hanging basket and use it as a bird table. At this height, it should also be cat-proof.

When grouping container-grown plants together, choose pots that are of a similar shape or size. If you don't have the same sort of containers, make sure that you put similar plants in them in order to link the group together.

If you're planting up a bottomless container (like an old chimney pot), put a piece of old net curtain across the bottom to keep pests out.

To stop thieves walking off with your planters and tubs put several stones in the bottom of each tub before filling and planting. They will be then too heavy to lift.

Create a herb garden using old bricks laid out in the shape of the spokes of a wheel.

Raised beds are a good way of adding interest to a patio. If you are using bricks, make sure they are frost proof and that they blend into their surroundings.

Alternatively, use concrete blocks to make a raised bed. If you want to grow lime-hating plants, line the sides of the bed with heavy-duty polythene.

Always put drainage holes in the bottom of raised beds.

Fences, Hedges & Boundaries

Stain your fences a variety of colours for a stunning effect.

A cheap way to preserve your fence is to paint it with engine oil from your car.

Don't creosote a fence if you want to grow climbers up it because it takes time for the fumes to die away.

Fences need to be checked regularly and patched up. If a post rots at its base, sink a new one beside it and bolt the two together.

If your fence leans, large wooden struts wedged against the posts at angles will bring it back upright. Once plants grow, the struts will be hidden.

You can make a cheap fence from old floorboards.

If you have to replace or treat a section of fence, do so in the autumn or winter so that you don't damage plants.

A dense trellis is more beneficial to plants than fencing because it creates an air flow through the garden.

If you are putting up a wooden trellis, make sure the base is at least 2–3 in/5–7.5 cm above the soil to avoid damp and wood rot.

When fixing a trellis to a wall, always set it slightly away from the wall so that air can circulate around the plants. Use small wooden blocks or old cotton reels to make a space between the trellis and the wall.

A wooden frame will support a trellis more effectively than a plastic one – it will look better and last longer. Use pressure-treated timber for your support.

Use galvanised nails and screws when fitting a trellis to prevent rust from forming.

Drill a pilot hole into wood so that it will accept a screw. A pilot hole is a hole smaller than the actual screw size.

Don't be a square when it comes to choosing the shape of your trellis. They come in all sorts of shapes and sizes nowadays so you don't have to go for the more traditional look.

For a dramatic effect paint your trellis with coloured wood preservative. You can choose something that either complements your colour scheme or strongly contrasts with it.

To ensure that you get a level edge when trimming a hedge, tie a piece of string to two points along the top.

When pruning a hedge for the first time, only cut one side right back to encourage new growth. In the second year, trim the new growth lightly and cut back the other side hard.

Avoid clipping or trimming your hedge during the nesting season. Wait for at least two weeks until the birds have flown the nest. The hedge can wait that little bit longer and you're doing your bit for wildlife.

Always clip hedges so that the upper surface slopes. This will stop snow from collecting on top and damaging the shape of the hedge.

Hedges need to be fed and watered regularly because they are constantly being clipped and trimmed so they tend to use up a lot of energy replacing the lost growth.

If your hedge is situated next to a road, make sure you screen it with polythene. This will prevent the roots from taking up de-icing salt during the winter.

Fill old pairs of tights with compost to make 'bricks' that can be used to build a retaining wall.

When building a wall, always spray the bricks with water to keep the mortar wet.

Don't put plants too near a wall – a climber should be about 12 in/30 cm from the wall while shrubs can be up to 3 ft/90 cm away.

Make your own screen using chicken wire. You can shape it into columns or stretch it across a space.

Alternatively, use willow or hazel as a screen.

Grow a variety of climbers up a wall. If they have different flowering times, you will always have something attractive to look at.

Weeding & Pests

Don't throw away the salted boiling water that you've cooked your potatoes in. Use it as a weed-killer on paths and drives.

To deter weeds, sprinkle sand on garden paths.

Wear an old woolly glove over a rubber glove. Dip your hand into weed-killer and then stroke the weeds you want to destroy.

Use old carpets as mulch to kill weeds.

Use Epsom salts to kill weeds.

Slugs hate seaweed so use it on your beds. It makes a great fertiliser as well.

To stop mice and birds eating your peas, soak the packet of peas in paraffin and leave for 24 hours. Cut off the end of the packet, drain the peas and then plant when needed.

For a cheap and effective bird scarer, cut flaps in a plastic bottle, put it over the top of a cane and secure with a nail. The wind will spin the bottle around, which will scare the birds away.

Scare the birds by sticking feathers in the ground amongst the vegetables. Being territorial creatures, they'll keep off another bird's patch.

Cut nettles down to the ground the moment they appear. Under constant persecution, they will eventually give up.

Cover garden beds with pine bark to prevent weeds.

Leaving soil uncovered will only encourage weeds. Use some form of ground cover, either a mulch or ground-cover plants.

When tackling bindweed, grow it up a cane before applying weed-killer. This way you won't damage other garden plants.

Remember this rhyme:
Thistles cut in May return next day,
Thistles cut in June come up soon,
But cut them in July and they're sure to die.

When weeding, attach your rings to a safety pin and pin them to your clothing so you don't lose them.

Use an old kitchen knife to dig up dandelions and daisies from a lawn. Keep the blade vertical and cut in a circle round the weed. Pull out with the root intact.

If you're using a weed-killer, protect your plants with a sheet of cardboard or bin liner while you are spraying.

To make your own funnel to administer weed-killer more easily, cut off the top of a plastic bottle. You can then throw it away after you've used it.

Some weeds will absorb chemicals more easily if you crush their foliage before applying the weed-killer. So stamp your feet.

To get rid of green slime from your patio, scrub with a stiff brush and soapy water.

Weeds like water – so remove them regularly and make sure your plants get the moisture instead.

In hot weather, leave uprooted weeds on the soil surface. They'll act as a layer of mulch and help retain moisture in the soil.

Stop your neighbour's weeds from creeping into your garden. Dig a trench 12 in/30 cm deep alongside the fence. Line on one side with dustbin bags, then replace the soil.

When the birds have flown, take down their nest and either throw it away or burn it. Nests are great places for insects to live in.

Make your own insect spray by soaking 3 oz/75 g of chopped onion or garlic in two teaspoons of liquid paraffin for 24 hours. Strain the liquid. Mix with a solution of $\frac{1}{4}$ oz/10 g soft soap in 1 pint/600 ml of warm water. Shake well. Dilute two tablespoons to 1 pint/600 ml of water and fill your spray bottle. Go get 'em!

To control aphids, soak nettle and wormwood leaves in a bucket of water for a week and then spray.

To control flea beetle, soak elder leaves in a bucket of water for a week and spray.

To control caterpillar damage to cabbages, soak tomato leaves in a bucket of water for a week and spray.

Deter rose pests by planting marigolds round the base of a rose bush.

Alternatively, growing alliums and catmint next to your roses will help combat aphids.

To protect your dahlias from earwigs dip a piece of cotton wool in machine oil and tie it round the stem of the plant (about 1ft/30 cm from the ground). Tie some round any canes as well to stop them climbing up to reach the flowers.

To stop earwigs nibbling your fruit and veg, place an empty matchbox, half open, at the top of the plant canes.

If earwigs are causing a problem on your fruit trees, tie some cloths round the branches. Once a week take the cloths off the branches and shake them out – well away from your garden.

Marigolds attract hoverflies, which control pests as well as repel whitefly. Grow some in your hanging baskets, grow bags and vegetable plots.

Marigolds, nasturtiums and flax will help protect potatoes from pests.

Alternatively, growing peas next to your potatoes is thought to deter pests.

Plant caper spurge near a mole run. Some people consider it a weed, but moles hate the smell.

Moles also don't get along with cats.

Try putting sweet chewing-gum into mole holes. Some say the moles eat the gum and it clogs their digestive system.

Daisy-like flowering plants are very attractive to insects that will help you combat pests and aid in pollination. Plants such as alyssum, campanula, geranium, gypsophila and salvia are ideal.

Get rid of ants by placing half a squeezed orange where the ants will find it. Soon the peel will be full of ants and you can then dispose of them suitably. Placing the peel where the birds will find the ants and eat them is a good idea.

Place banana skins around plants and rose bushes outside the house to stop ants from coming in.

If you have an infestation of ants in your wall-grown fruit, make a small trench under the wall and pour in a mixture of brine and soot.

To clear areas infested with red ants, try a sprinkling of whole cloves or oil of cloves.

To keep ants away, scatter spearmint leaves.

Prevent ants from coming into the house by planting mint beside the kitchen door.

Wherever you see ants, sprinkle equal parts of borax and icing sugar.

To destroy ants' eggs pour boiling water on the nest.

If you want to treat mildew without resorting to modern fungicides, try a simple solution of soapy water instead.

Don't want your garden used as a cat's loo? Keep the soil moist and use a moisture retentive mulch to keep the cats away.

Alternatively, burying prickly leaves just under the surface of the soil will deter a cat when it starts to dig.

Prevent cats from climbing over a fence by spraying the wood with surgical spirit.

Keep dogs away from fence posts by spraying the posts with unwanted perfume or aftershave.

If your dog has peed on the lawn, pour a couple of buckets of water over the spot straight away. This will dilute the urine, making it harmless, and avoid unsightly brown patches of grass.

A prickly hedge such as pyracanthus will stop a neighbour's dog from digging through into your garden.

If your dog likes rummaging around rubbish bins, sprinkle the area with pepper to deter him.

Tree stumps can encourage fungus if left, so always try to remove them.

If your lawn is suffering from a rash of toadstools, sweep them away with a stiff brush before the caps open and release the spores.

If your hedge is prone to silver leaf disease, only give it its annual trim during the summer months.

Keep your garden tidy to reduce the risk of pests and diseases. Remove any rubbish, old plants and bits and bobs – these are the natural habitats for many of your garden's enemies.

Do a regular spot check for pests and diseased leaves. If you find any, pick them off and dispose of them carefully.

No fly spray? Try hair-spray instead. Flies hate it because it sticks their wings together – they'll soon get the message and leave you alone.

Always clean out seedling trays and pots. This will cut down the risk of disease.

Use plastic pots and trays for young plants and seedlings. They are easier to keep clean and free of pests and diseases.

If you live near a busy road, your plants can be affected. A laurel hedge is more able to cope with high levels of pollution than other plants.

Marrow seeds are a most effective bait in a mousetrap.

Free CDs are a part of junk mail – make use of them for scaring deer away by hanging them round your boundaries. They flash in the light and the deer won't come near (unless they want free internet access).

Sowing & Planting

You don't have to scatter seeds randomly. If you sow them in straight lines, you will be able to distinguish between them and weeds as they grow.

When planting out, make sure that the stem base isn't any deeper than it was before.

An old sieve is ideal for putting compost for seeds into trays.

Use white sand to mark out the areas where you are going to sow your seeds.

Collect seeds from flowers – it's a lot cheaper than going out and buying them in packets.

Cut up old magazines to make seed packets.

Sew vegetable seeds in the clean plastic containers from ready-cooked meals.

Before planting parsley seeds, pour boiling water into the trench. This speeds up germination.

Can't bend down to sow seeds? Use a drainpipe or hose and drop the seeds down through it.

To stop larger seedlings from wilting in the sun, make them little hats out of newspaper. Weigh down the rim with stones to stop them blowing away.

Train young plants – use a bit of exhaust putty or blu tack.

Grow house plants from the green tops of fresh pineapples and carrots. Just cut off the bit you intend to eat and push the green end into some compost. When your plant starts to grow, cover the pot with a clear plastic bag, secured by a rubber band, to give it a kick-start.

To help your carnation cutting to take root, place a grain of rice alongside the cutting when planting up.

Fast-growing climbers such as *Ipomea, Eccremocarpus scaber* and *Thunbergia alata* will cover an archway really quickly.

Alternatively, runner beans make an attractive edible arch.

If you want to cover an archway with roses, choose a rambler rather than a climber. Ramblers are more flexible.

Save money and create a stunning effect. Buy annuals in bulk and only use two or three colours.

Don't use just herbaceous and annual plants. Vegetables and fruit look attractive in flowerbeds as well. Rhubarb, runner beans, strawberries and chard, for example, all look good and produce fresh food for the table.

If your shrubs are getting too leggy, grow climbers like clematis over them.

Never plant roses in soil where other roses have previously been grown for five years or more. Roses can't thrive in poor soil.

Don't plant roses under trees – they need air to be healthy.

Before planting small alpines, wrap the roots in moist tissue, then place in a crevice. This will protect the roots and give the plant a good start in life.

Spring-flowering bulbs like narcissi are ideal to fill in the gaps in a newly planted border. They look at their most effective just at the time when all the other plants aren't doing much.

Planting a climber at an angle will encourage it to grow towards its support. It will also prevent the roots from being too sheltered from the rain.

Don't buy plants after a very cold spell – their roots may have been badly affected.

Annuals, perennials and bulbs are great for filling gaps in borders.

Grow fragrant flowers, such as honeysuckle, jasmine and roses round the area where you keep your dustbins. They'll not only make the area look more attractive but it will smell better too.

Dense planting round the bin area in the summer will help cut down any strong pong.

Bulbs should be planted at a depth of between three and five times their height.

When choosing bulbs, 'big is best'.

Most bulbs look best planted in informal groups of odd numbers.

Save yourself time and effort – plant several bulbs in one large hole rather than having lots of little holes with one bulb in each.

Plant annuals on cool days or in a shady area. Avoid extreme temperatures. The best time to plant is in early evening, as it gives the plants time to settle before the midday heat.

Autumn is the time to divide congested water plants. Remove any weak or damaged sections before replanting.

Split the contents of a grow bag into four pots rather than using the three holes. This will give you room for one extra plant and they will all be much healthier because the soil is looser.

Plants with a blue, silver or grey leaf generally like to go in the warm part of the garden.

Don't plant plants that are in flower. No one wants to move while they're making love… and it's the same for a plant!

Acidic plants can be grown in alkaline soil. Collect leaves from your garden and place them in plastic bags. In the spring, dig a large hole, line with the dead leaves and place the plant (now cocooned by the leaves) into the hole. Fill and water as normal.

Prune climbing roses in September – they bend more easily.

If a climber has grown in too symmetrical a fashion, trim it back unevenly to give it a more informal outline.

Prune a pyracanthus in stages and you will have berries in the autumn. Cut some stems in early spring and others after flowering.

Always handle plants by the soil or leaves, never by the stems.

If you suffer from hay fever, try avoiding pollen-rich flowers and go for something else – hostas are a good alternative.

The best support for clematis is nylon wire wrapped around sheds, posts and tree trunks.

Moved into a new house and don't know what to put in the garden? Have a peek over the fence and see what's thriving next door.

Feeding

Perk up your plants by feeding them with half a can of non-diet Coca-Cola.

Rake up the moss from your lawn and keep it in a damp place to use in hanging baskets.

Make your own fertiliser – boil nettle leaves and leave to steep for 24 hours.

Horse manure, cow dung and compost make good fertilisers.

Wood ash is also a useful fertiliser and a good way of getting rid of what's left of a bonfire. It also deters beetles and other insects if spread around your plants.

Comfrey leaves are potassium-rich. You can harvest the leaves, put them to soak in some water or let them rot down before putting them on the garden.

Keep grass cuttings. Throw them on to the compost heap (or into a black bag) and cover with a piece of carpet until they've mulched down.

Make your own mini compost heap – use plastic bin bags (heavy duty ones if possible) and put all your kitchen waste, garden trimmings and old newspapers in them. Make a few holes in the side and turn the contents over every now and again. Use when everything has rotted down.

Alternatively, bury small amounts of rubbish and clippings around the garden. The worms will then take over and do the composting for you.

Accelerate your compost by mixing green manure into it.

Leaf mould rots down faster if you wee on it.

To bring out really deep colours in your roses, scatter crushed eggshells around their roots.

To get a strong blue colour in your hydrangeas, plant something made from iron underneath.

Lawns

If the edge of your lawn starts to look a bit tired, cut the edge of the turf off, turn it over and place it back on the ground where it came from.

Gaps in the lawn? If you can't be bothered to start all over again, simply fill in the gaps with tea-bags.

During a drought, use bath water to water the grass. Avoid using the water though if it has bath foam or oil in it.

Water the lawn in the evening so that the moisture has time to soak in overnight and not get burnt off by the sun.

Autumn and spring are the best times to lay a new lawn because the grass will re-establish itself quickly. Always water a new lawn regularly.

For lawns that suffer from heavy use, add finely chopped car tyres to the top dressing.

If your lawn has too many dips and hollows, it might be due to poor drainage (check for moss; this is a good indicator of poor drainage). Use a lot of grit in the soil you use to fill in the hollows.

Uneven areas can also be caused by buried tree roots or lumps of debris. Dig out whatever is causing the problem and replace it with topsoil.

Don't have the blades of your mower set too low. If you do, you could weaken the grass and make it more vulnerable to weeds and moss.

Tools of the Trade

When tying canes, secure them temporarily with an elastic band. Now your hands are free to tie the canes in position.

Make planting holes for small bulbs with an apple corer.

Cut up old margarine tubs and use them to label plants.

The bottom of an old washing-up-liquid bottle makes a very effective scoop.

Use the black plastic bases of drinks bottles as seed trays – they already have drainage holes cut in them and are ideal for the task.

Digging a new bed? Use your hosepipe as a guide to give you a great curve.

Make a kneeling mat out of an old hot-water bottle stuffed with bits of material.

Put a used gun cartridge over the ends of your canes to avoid blinding yourself!

Alternatively, cover the ends of canes with ping-pong balls.

Don't throw away your old tights – use them as hanging baskets.

Put plastic pots in the legs of old tights, hang them in the shed and cut off the toes. The pots are then easily accessible and can be taken out (rather like cups from a vending machine).

Pick fruit using an old sieve attached to a broom handle.

Twigs make good supports for multi-stemmed plants.

Put your tools in a bucket and carry it around the garden with you; you'll have everything to hand.

Never leave tools standing on soil. If you can't hang them up, rest them on a wooden board wrapped in a bin bag.

Always keep your tools clean; use an old kitchen knife to scrape lumps of soil away.

Alternatively, use any left-over engine oil. Leave the bottle to drain into a jar, then brush the oil on to your garden tools or furniture to keep them in good condition. Wipe off before using.

Don't throw away broken terracotta pots – they can still be planted up. Plants such as sempervivum grow well in dry conditions.

Conceal broken or chipped edges on containers by growing trailing plants such as lobelia or aubretia.

Keep drainpipes clear – stick a ball of galvanised wire wool into the opening of the drainpipe. This acts as a filter and stops debris from bunging up the pipe.

Protect plants from overnight frost by covering with old net curtains.

Alternatively, cover plants with a couple of sheets of newspaper held in place by some stones.

Garden Furniture & Structures

Stop cast-iron furniture rusting by wiping with olive oil or sunflower oil.

To restore a saggy cane or wicker chair seat scrub with soapy water and then rinse. Leave the chair outside in the sun to dry.

Put each leg of wooden furniture on a brick to stop any rot setting in over winter.

If you are worried about staining your wooden table, put some cling film across the wood before placing a cloth over it. If you are concerned about hot dishes burning the wood, put a blanket underneath the tablecloth.

Save the rainforest! Avoid buying hardwoods such as mahogany.

When painting wood, make sure you get rid of any algae and other growth. Scrub it down, allow it to dry and then paint it with preservative.

Clean the upper and roof sections of your greenhouse using a long-handled floor mop.

To remove stubborn marks from greenhouse glass, put some methylated spirits on a cloth and rub hard.

Buff up the windows of a greenhouse with newspaper and a mixture of water and vinegar.

Always build a barbecue a little larger than you think you'll need. You'll be glad you did when you hold a big party.

Don't build a barbecue too near the house – you want to cook food, not smoke out your home.

Don't put it too near your neighbour's fence either – you want to remain on good terms with them!

When building your own barbecue, make sure you can fit standard-sized metal grilling racks so that they can be easily replaced.

Avoid placing a barbecue under trees – they may be badly scorched by the heat.

Make your barbecue double up as an incinerator in the winter. Just lift off the metal grilling rack and secure it to the front of the barbecue so that it will hold in the leaves and rubbish you're going to burn.

If you want to create a garden on a balcony or roof, always check that it can take the added weight.

On a balcony or roof garden, use large containers that can take as many plants as lots of small pots but won't dry out as quickly.

If you live in a high-rise flat, only put low-growing plants in your window box. Make sure they are anchored firmly in the soil to protect them from the wind.

A newly planted pond will invariably turn bright green with algae at first. Be patient. Allow the natural balance to establish itself before you rush in with drastic solutions.

If you want fish in your pond, introduce them to the idea gently. Float the plastic bag that they've been transported in on the surface of the pond water for an hour. Once the water temperature in the bag has equalised, you can release the fish into their new home.

Watering

Remember to water plants ten minutes before you dig the holes for them.

Get a water butt. Rain water is soft and much better for your plants. It will save water as well.

Old bin bags surrounding a plant will help retain moisture. Just cover with soil to disguise it.

Before planting a shrub, soak the roots in tap water. This way they get a really good drink and it's easier for you to unravel any knotted roots.

During a drought, use bath water to water the garden. Try not to use the water though if it has bath foam or oil in it.

Water from a dishwasher or washing machine isn't suitable for the garden.

During drought, leave grass clippings on the lawn to act as mulch.

Choose drought-tolerant plants such as yarrow, cotoneaster, broom, euonymous, lavender and lamb's ears.

Water plants in the evening so that the moisture has time to soak in overnight and does not get burnt off by the sun.

Prevent bacteria from building up in your garden hose – don't leave it lying around in the sun. The bacteria can breed really quickly in those conditions.

To ensure water gets to the roots of plants in a grow bag, plant a plastic bottle. Cut the bottom off the bottle, make sure the cap is off and put the top end into the compost. Water through the bottle.

If you're planting a shrub in a dry spot, make sure there's a bit of a depression in the soil round the shrub so that the water soaks down through the soil rather than running off.

Alternatively, if your soil is wet and heavy, don't put anything round the plant that might retain moisture. Too much water will damage the roots.

Regular watering will prevent fruit from cracking and developing any disorders.

Water plants under a cloche with a leaky hose. Block one end of a section of hose and make some small holes along its length. Lay the hose along a row of plants and attach the other end to a tap. Turn on the tap very gently when you need to water.

Certain plants need a lot of water: house plants that are actively growing, have budding leaves and flowers, have delicate thin leaves, are housed in fairly small pots, live in a fairly dry atmosphere (like a centrally heated house) or come from marshy areas.

To water house plants, use tepid water. Fill your watering can the night before so you don't give your plants a nasty cold shock.

If you are going away for a short time and are worried about your house plants, water them thoroughly, leave them to drain and then seal them in large plastic bags. Put some small canes or twigs in the compost to stop the plastic from touching the leaves if necessary.

Fruit

A good choice for fan-training a fruit tree against a shady wall is a morello cherry tree.

Fruit can be grown in containers – try strawberries, apples, pears, plums, nectarines and any tree fruit on developing rootstock.

Make sure your strawberries get enough water. Put some holes in a length of hose and place this in your strawberry pot before planting up. Then just water through the hose.

Putting your strawberries under cloches will bring the crop on earlier.

Edging a bed with neat plants such as alpine strawberries gives a sense of unity.

Once you've picked your strawberries, don't get them near water – they'll turn soggy and tasteless.

Strawberries are a good way to clean your teeth – they remove plaque and leave your mouth feeling fresh.

For a reviving face mask, mash some strawberries and spread them over your face.

Never pull stalks out of fruit – infection may spread in the resulting wound.

Always store different varieties of fruit separately.

To store apples, put a dozen in old shopping bags; punch a few holes for ventilation.

Alternatively, use a cabbage leaf in the bottom of the fruit bowl.

Pears should be stored individually on slatted trays. An old wooden shoe rack or plate rack is ideal as long as it's thoroughly scrubbed.

A dab of sealing wax on the end of a pear stalk will help to keep the fruit fresh while you're storing it.

Don't throw away old fruit. Pop any fruit that's gone too soft into the blender. Use the mixture as an all-over body mask and nutrient. Once you shower it off, your skin will feel really soft and you'll smell good enough to eat.

Vegetables

Sunflowers, with runner beans growing up their stems, make an attractive and effective screen.

Mix runner beans with sweet peas on the same support. Pollinating insects will be attracted to the sweet peas, which will help your runner beans.

Vegetables can be grown in containers – try French beans, beetroot, radishes, tomatoes, aubergines, peppers, spring onions, lettuce and carrots.

If growing vegetables in containers, make sure you choose large pots. They're easier to look after and water than small ones.

Tomatoes will grow well in a window box.

Plant African marigolds alongside your tomatoes to keep greenfly away.

Try planting vegetables for effect as well as food. Oak-leafed lettuce next to purple basil, or spring onions between curly, red-leafed lettuce look stunning.

Plant flowers like poppies and love-in-a-mist between vegetable beds. They can survive in fairly poor soil so won't mind if the vegetables get most of the nutrients and the flowers will look pretty between the foliage.

If you are bothered by slugs, but don't want to use slug pellets, plant a ring of cheap lettuce around your more prized varieties. Once the slugs have found some food, they won't bother looking elsewhere.

If you want easy-care vegetables, stick to dwarf varieties.

LITERARY AGENTS & PUBLISHERS

Susanna Wadeson

Take the trouble to ring a prospective publisher, and find out which editor you should address your manuscript to. Make sure you spell their name right too.

Writing fiction? Send an outline of the plot and up to 100 pages of your manuscript. For non-fiction, send an outline and the first chapter.

Include a biography of yourself with your submission.

Visit your local bookshop, and find the book most like yours in subject. The publisher will know the market, and contrary to what you might think, that's the one you should approach with your book.

In your submission letter, acknowledge the competition, then go on to explain how your book is an improvement on theirs.

Publishers are like sheep, so try to get something in print already. Write for a local magazine or newspaper, then include that in your biography.

When submitting your manuscript, make sure lines are double-spaced, on single sides of paper, with a decent margin.

Whatever you do, don't submit the only copy of your manuscript. Lots of people do!

When writing fiction or non-fiction, think hard about the title – a bad one will put people off. A sales rep will have only 30 seconds to sell the idea of your book to a bookseller, so a good title and a concise concept will be more effective. If you can't sum up your book neatly, who can?

There's no such thing as an original idea to publishers. In fact they are suspicious of it. If you say it's an original concept, they'll wonder why it hasn't been done before.

MAKE-UP ARTISTS

Skin

Nyki Collins;
Shannon Keogh;
Françoise de Pigny

If the weather's very hot and you have a tendency to become 'shiny', make it look deliberate! Wear lip gloss and sheen on your eyelids.

Keep your make-up fresh however hot the conditions – use a quick spray of water every so often.

Loose powder often looks too heavy because it sticks to moisturisers and cleansers. Blot your face with a tissue before you put any powder on.

Apply loose powder with throw-away cotton-wool pads. The puff provided with the powder will quickly build up dirt and won't do your skin any favours.

If you've got a reddish complexion, use a foundation with a greenish tinge. Applied under normal make-up, this will help to neutralise the red.

If you've got a really, really bad spot, you'll never be able to cover it up. Instead, turn it into a trendy beauty spot with a dark eyeliner pencil.

The oil from your skin can affect the powder in your compact. Store the powder puff or sponge face upwards towards the mirror.

Get better coverage from your foundation by tapping it into place instead of blending it.

To make blusher look more natural, tilt your head downwards till you naturally blush and use the blush areas as guide lines.

Luscious Lips

To get the deepest, longest-lasting effect from lipstick, powder your lips before applying the lipstick.

To mend a broken lipstick, carefully melt the broken edges with a lighted match and press them together. Smooth down the join with a toothpick and then leave the lipstick in the fridge for a couple of hours.

When applying lipstick, do it with a brush following the contours of your lips, then define with a lip pencil in the same shade and blot with a tissue.

Minimalist make-up bag: rather than spending a fortune on cosmetics, invest in just a pale glossy lip colour to use on eyes and lips, then touch up lashes with mascara.

For long-lasting matt lip colour, line the entire lips with lip liner. Add a coat of lip balm to moisturise the lips.

To get a perfect line with lip liner, place the pencil (with the lid on) in a glass of water for about five minutes then apply as usual.

Apply lipstick, dust with powder, then apply another layer and it will last longer.

A thin layer of Vaseline will moisturise very dry lips under lipstick.

Test if you've overdone the lipstick by putting your finger gently into your mouth and pulling it out again. If there's any trace on your finger you've applied too much.

Making Eyes

Eyeliners need to be really sharp. Try chilling eye pencils in the fridge before sharpening them to get a really pointy point.

Avoid smudgy eyeliner by dipping a wet brush in dark eye shadow and using this to line the eyes instead. It will stay on all day.

When applying mascara, look down directly into a mirror. It makes it impossible to get mascara into the eyes.

After applying mascara, spray a little hair-spray on to the brush and apply a layer to the lashes (avoid this if you have very sensitive eyes).

When you run out of mascara, stand the tube in a cup of hot water for a minute. This will loosen the last bit of mascara and allow you to use it for at least two more coats.

Run out of eye make-up remover? Use petroleum jelly or Vaseline instead. This even works for waterproof mascara.

You can change the colour of a lipstick by adding face toner with an eye-shadow brush.

Replace your mascara every three months – it'll become clumpy as well as full of bacteria.

When applying moisturiser, avoid the eye area. Not only is the skin more delicate but you will coat the lashes with oil and your mascara will smudge.

If your mascara is too runny, leave the lid off overnight to dry it out a bit.

To lighten the colour of cream eye-shadow, cream blusher and lipstick – mix with some concealer.

Before you do anything radical when colouring eyebrows, apply some coloured mascara to see the effect. Eyebrow pencil works well too.

Thick eyebrows? Clear mascara will keep brows neatly in place.

MASSAGE THERAPISTS

Clare Maxwell-Hudson,
www.cmhmassage.co.uk

A massage is much more enjoyable if both the giver and receiver are feeling calm and comfortable, and both will benefit from the relaxing atmosphere created.

Have a supply of folded towels to cover up the recipient and to use for support.

When giving massage to someone lying on their back, they may be more comfortable with a small folded towel under their head, and a small pillow under their knees.

When giving massage to someone lying on their front, a folded towel under the chest, a small pillow under the abdomen and one under the ankles makes for a more relaxed position.

Whatever position you are working from, keep your back straight and use your body weight rather than just your arms to apply pressure.

Stack your folded towels on a hot water bottle for the ultimate in luxury. Remember to use the ones from the bottom of the pile first.

Once you start giving a massage, neither you nor your partner will want any interruptions so make sure you have everything close at hand, and put the answerphone on.

Consciously slow down your breathing when giving a massage. When you're learning it's very easy to hold your breath, and your tension will communicate itself to your partner.

To strengthen you hands, practise drumming your fingers up and down your forearm, varying the speed and depth of movement, but without tensing your hands.

Also helpful for hand strength is squeezing a rubber ball – children's foam 'tennis' balls are about the right size and firmness. Squeeze and release repeatedly for about 30 seconds, then swap hands.

For flexible arms and wrists, place the backs of the wrists together with your elbows out to the sides. Rotate the wrists against each other, moving them in opposite directions and stretching the fingers, then twist them back to the starting position.

Try developing your sensitivity by holding your hands with the palms facing each other but not touching. Slowly draw them apart then move them close together again. Continue for a while and you should feel a slight tingle and perhaps a sensation rather like compressing a soft balloon between your palms.

For ticklish recipients, flatten your hand, reduce the tempo and increase the depth of the massage. Ticklishness can often be a sign of tension and it may disappear as the massage progresses. If not, leave that part for another time.

When blending oils for an oil massage, the normal dilution is 2 per cent, which works out at four drops of essential oil to every two teaspoons of carrier oil. For babies, children, those who are ill and those with sensitive skins use a dilution of 0.5 per cent, or one drop of essential oil to every two teaspoons of carrier oil.

Keep your massage mix in a dark glass bottle. Label it clearly with a note of the oils used, the dilution and the date. Blends are best used within a few weeks.

When giving an oil massage, never pour oil directly on to the skin. Warm it first between your hands before applying at the start of the massage.

To add more oil in the course of the massage, drizzle a little oil on to the back of one hand, then stroke it on with the other. In this way you can keep one hand in contact with your partner at all times.

When massaging the abdomen – yours or someone else's – always work clockwise stroking round in a circle. This follows the workings of the intestines and can help regulate digestion.

If you only have a few minutes for a massage, try working on the hands. They can get surprisingly tense and a few minutes' work can relax the whole body.

At the very beginning of a massage, just place your hands on your partner – typically on the shoulders if they're sitting up, or on the ankles if they are lying down – and keep them quite still for about ten seconds while you breathe calmly and deeply. It makes a wonderful stabilising start.

For a quick back massage at work, ask the recipient to sit backwards on an office chair. You can easily work on the head, neck, shoulders, back and arms.

If your under-eye area looks puffy or discoloured, place two fingers on top of the cheekbones, starting next to the nose and make small, gentle stationary circles (not dragging on the skin) using the pads of your fingers. Repeat, moving the hands gradually outwards to the sides of the face, then make stationary circles down each side of the face.

For a facial massage, try this gentle oil blend: two drops each of camomile and geranium oil in two teaspoons of sweet almond oil.

If your partner wears contact lenses, make sure he or she removes them before a facial massage with oil.

For a gentle toning treatment for the face, either for yourself or a partner, tap the fingertips of both hands all over the face and forehead, varying the speed and depth of the movement.

Babies and children love to be gently massaged and stroked, but make sure the room is warm as they feel the cold more than adults. Don't massage a baby too close to feed time. Use a light, unscented oil, such as cold-pressed sunflower oil.

For aching feet, roll your foot on a ball to massage the underside, or try picking up pencils with your toes for a great – if unusual – workout.

For a headache, first massage the back of the neck and head, then the forehead, around the eyes and the temples. Finish with gentle stroking on the forehead.

If arthritic hands are causing pain, gently stroke up between each tendon from the knuckles to the wrist.

MIDWIVES

Conception

Chris Warren; Su Down, Derby General Hospital; Association of Radical Midwives; Midwife Information and Resource Service; Independent Midwives Association; Glynis Fletcher, NCT

If you want a girl, make love a couple of days before ovulation – female sperm survive for much longer than male sperm.

For a female baby, make love a lot! This will lower the proportion of male to female sperm in your partner's semen.

Eat lots of bananas if you want a girl – apparently, a potassium-rich diet will increase the chances of a daughter.

If all else fails, go and train as a fighter pilot. They seem to father a greater number of girls!

If you want a boy, only make love on the day of or immediately after ovulation because male sperm swim faster than female sperm and will reach the ovum first.

For a son, make love infrequently as this increases the proportion of male sperm.

Before the Baby Comes

Eat sensibly… three-quarters of mums remain at least 2 lb/1 kg heavier after the birth! However, you do need to increase your intake by 500 calories a day.

Little and often is best. Try five or six small snacks instead of one or two blow-outs.

To accommodate your bump without splashing out on lots of special clothes, wear your usual leggings back to front.

Don't buy dungarees. You'll want to go to the loo a lot more often when pregnant so skirts and dresses are much less fiddly.

If you can't face eating anything, wear travel-sickness bangles on both wrists.

Sick or nauseous? Try sucking on some ginger. If that doesn't work, vitamin B6 is good, so tuck into some Marmite.

Travel sickness is a common complaint during pregnancy. Driving yourself, rather than being the passenger, will help.

Have some glucose tablets to hand if you suffer from travel sickness, as it is often caused by low blood sugar.

If you are laid low by morning sickness, cut out caffeine which triggers nausea.

Backache is common in pregnancy. When washing up, rest the bowl on another inverted bowl to make it higher – it will be much more comfortable for your back.

Cramp in your legs, especially first thing in the morning, can be another pregnancy ailment. It is caused by calcium deficiency, so drink a large glass of milk before bedtime or eat more yoghurt.

Thrush can often irritate mums-to-be. If you haven't eaten all the yoghurt to help your cramps, try spreading it on the infected area to soothe and heal.

Constipated? It's very common in pregnancy. Prevent it by doubling your intake of water.

If you are suffering from heartburn, a glass of milk will help to neutralise stomach acid.

To tone up your uterus for labour, drink lots of raspberry-leaf tea in the later stages of pregnancy (but never in the first six months because it might bring on premature labour).

Most heavily pregnant women get insomnia. Make sure you get a good night's sleep. First, try a long, relaxing, warm bath. Then enjoy a warm, milky drink and a plain biscuit. Finally, put a couple of drops of lavender oil on your pillow – it's wonderfully relaxing and will ensure sweet dreams.

If you simply can't get comfortable, lie curled up on your side around a soft pillow. Put the pillow between your knees and rest your bump against it.

If you have given birth prematurely in the past, eating oil-rich fish, such as mackerel and sardines, will help reduce the risk of pre-term birth.

If you've gone past your due date, you'll be desperate for the baby to come. To avoid a hospital induction, try nipple stimulation to help the uterus to contract. Sex also helps to bring on contractions.

Kick-start a late baby by eating certain foods. Curry, chilli and other strong foods are believed to trigger things off.

Bring on labour by rubbing a little jasmine oil on to your abdomen or adding a couple of drops of clary sage oil to your bath.

To get your baby into a good position for delivery, try cleaning the skirting boards – being on all fours will shift things about.

The Labour

Avoid being in hospital too early. Once contractions begin, try setting yourself a little task to finish before you leave. Tidying a drawer or writing a letter not only kills time but will also help to distract you from the discomfort of early labour.

To help you relax and prepare you for labour, try running a warm bath. You'll enjoy it far more at home than in a hospital bathroom.

Labour has been compared to running a marathon. Prepare yourself for the big event by eating lots of carbohydrates – potatoes, pasta, bread and vegetables.

Many women can't face eating or drinking during labour. Your mouth gets very dry so take a damp sponge to suck on when you get dry.

Back pain can be a real problem in labour. Try making a simple back rub by filling a sock with some uncooked rice mixed in with a little massage oil, and knotting the open end. When you need it, ask the midwife to pop the sock in the microwave (most hospitals have them) and then get your partner or anyone else who's with you to rub it over the painful part of your back.

To help ease back pain, take the weight off your spine – kneel on all fours with your bottom in the air and your head on a pillow.

For sheer reassurance and comfort, take a hot-water bottle with you into hospital.

Women in labour often get very hot – ask your partner or someone else with you to have a plant spray filled with cool water to hand so you can have a quick burst of cool spray when things start to heat up.

If you have long hair, take a hair band. There's nothing worse when you're hot and sticky than having your hair flop all over your face.

Women often feel a burning sensation in labour. Try holding a hot or cold pad against the skin to ease the pain.

To ease back pain during labour, pop two tennis balls in an old sock and tie the top to keep them together. Lean against a wall with the gadget against your lower back and you can move around and press against it so that it soothes any discomfort in your lower back.

Take a pair of thick woolly socks with you – it's amazing how cold your feet get when the blood supply is busy round the uterus!

Labour rooms are always hot because babies can't regulate their body temperature. To help you regulate yours, take a travel-size spray dispenser filled with mineral water and mist your face with it at sweaty moments.

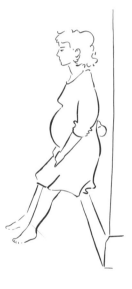

After the Birth

You are likely to be starving. Be prepared and have some high-energy food ready, such as a chocolate bar or a banana.

If you're left sore after stitches, try holding a bag of finely crushed ice wrapped in a soft cloth against the painful area.

Soothe sore stitches with a bag of frozen peas or sweetcorn.

To speed up healing after stitches, add some salt to the bath or, even better, some good-quality lavender oil.

Drying with a towel can be painful, but it's important to keep stitches clean and dry. Try a quick blast with the hair-dryer.

Weeing can really sting if you've had stitches. When nature calls, try standing up in a cool shower – the running water will dilute the acid that causes the burning sensation.

Having stitches makes it painful to sit down. Try sitting on a child's rubber ring – you may feel a little silly but it's a great way to reduce painful pressure on the sore area.

To stop your breasts feeling sore, pop a couple of cabbage leaves inside your bra.

If your nipples become sore, try sleeping topless at night (put a towel under you to stop any leaks). It will help if you can let air circulate around your boobs.

Go to the doctor if you get sudden pains, a rash or feel as if you're coming down with flu. It could be mastitis, which must be treated straight away.

Feed your baby last thing at night before you go to bed so you can get as much sleep as possible before it's time for the next feed. Prepare a thermos so that you can have a nice warm drink while you do the feed in the middle of the night.

Lots of new mums suffer hair loss. Add some powdered gelatine to your shampoo and leave it on for ten minutes to encourage the return of glossy locks.

Start building up a mental map of where all the mother-and-baby rooms are in your area so that you won't panic if you get caught short.

Try to make some time for yourself. When the baby is asleep or someone is looking after it for you, try to do something that you enjoy – read a magazine, have a hot soak, listen to some music.

Be kind to yourself after the birth. Don't go on a strict diet – you will be tired and need all the energy you can get. There isn't a prize for getting back into your jeans within a fortnight.

Your New Bundle of Joy

... will cry more than you think. Don't worry. The average baby will cry for at least two hours a day, and up to four is not unusual. If you accept it's normal, you'll find it less stressful.

New-born babies may appear to be very fragile but will be much happier if you handle them firmly – they're used to being contained in a very confined space so try wrapping them quite tightly in a blanket.

Babies are born without any bacteria in their mouths. Nearly all children under three catch tooth-decaying germs from their mother's saliva, so avoid 'cleaning' your baby's dummy or teething ring by sucking on it yourself.

Reassure your child. While you are out of the room, play them a tape of familiar sounds, such as the vacuum cleaner or the hair-dryer, so that they don't feel isolated.

If your baby gets colic, try lying him face down across your lap with his tummy resting on a hot-water bottle filled with warm water.

Babies hate having tight things pulled over their heads so choose clothes with wide, envelope necks.

However pretty they may be (the clothes, not the baby!), don't choose knitwear with lacy patterns. Babies will only get their fingers caught up in them.

Jaundice is common in babies. Lying in natural sunlight for a short time, while adequately dressed to avoid either cold or sunburn, clears it up quickly.

When bottle-feeding your baby, you must keep the bottle at such an angle that the teat is always full of milk. Swallowing air while feeding is the most common cause of colic.

You can get pregnant when breast-feeding – most accidental pregnancies happen within nine months of giving birth! So perhaps we should learn from the women of Papua New Guinea who avoid resuming sex until their first-born can walk, or the African Masai who abstain until the little one has cut its teeth!

To remember to take your contraceptive pill, put the packet in your knicker drawer.

MILLINERS

Just the Hat for You

Geoff Bates; Paul Pleass; Locks the Hatters; Katherine Franklin–Adams

To measure the size of a head correctly, take your tape-measure around from the centre of the forehead, behind the ear, over the bump at the back of the head, behind the other ear and back to the front.

If the final hat is going to be made from a thick fabric such as velvet, add 1 in/2.5 cm to the measurements.

If you're making your first hat, a lightweight fabric is easier to work with.

Don't be tempted to buy a hat that's slightly tight. It'll give you an awful headache and you'll be too embarrassed to remove it because it will leave a red mark on your forehead.

To avoid a lop-sided look, the front brim of a hat should always be wider than the back.

If you have a long neck, a wide-brimmed hat will suit you best.

Big shoulders can be made to look smaller by wearing smaller, neater hats.

The best hat for heart-shaped faces is one with a medium brim worn at an angle.

For those with square faces, choose a wide-brimmed hat.

For those with long faces, hats that have curved brims with some decoration look best.

Those with round faces should choose hats that are deep-crowned and worn low on the head. If you can't find this sort of hat, tilt any other sort of hat at an angle.

Always try a hat on standing up and walking about so that you can assess the whole outline and not just the 'head and shoulders'.

Hat Care

Never iron a hat backward and forward because this will stretch the fabric. Instead, place an iron straight down on the fabric and lift it off.

To avoid marking a hat when ironing it, always use a chromium-plated iron.

When steaming a hat, use a kettle with a short spout, not a jug kettle. You'll have more control over the direction of the steam.

To prevent your hats becoming discoloured, use acid-free tissue paper to store them.

To clean a Panama hat, wipe it with a mixture of water and lemon juice, and use a soft, clean cloth.

To get marks off your Panama hat, rub them with stale bread.

Store your Panama hat in the bathroom – they love the humidity.

Only real Panama hats should be rolled so don't be tempted to try it on your cheap holiday bargain. The best way to carry a Panama is to hold it gently by the brim and not the crown.

To pack crushable hats in a suitcase, fill them with underwear.

Straw hat gone floppy? Brush over the inside with a thin layer of cellulose varnish, which will dry quickly, but stay flexible enough for you to manipulate the brim.

If you want a straw hat to remain completely rigid, brush it with a thin layer of clear varnish or picture varnish and leave it to dry. This also gives a glossy look.

For a quick new look for a straw hat, spray with oil- or acrylic-based paint.

Light-coloured straw hats can be stencilled using wax stencil crayons applied with a brush. Apply one colour, then leave for three to four hours before applying the next.

Create your own hat stand – use a bottle of champagne.

Before using a hat block, cover it with cling film to prevent any dye leaching on to the block and possibly staining the next hat you block.

If you're making a bobble hat (do people still do that?), crochet it rather than knit it. This will give it more body and shape.

Felt

After wearing your felt hat, brush it gently with a soft brush. Do this each time you take it off. Keep it in a plastic bag.

Remove hairs, fluff and dust from felt hats with the sticky side of masking tape.

To check for weak spots in a length of felt, hold it up to the light to see if there are any uneven or thin patches.

You can mould a felt hat by steaming, but be very careful not to burn your fingers. For a crease in the crown, hold over the steam for just a few seconds, then mould the crease with your fingers and leave to dry. A light spray with fabric spray will help to hold it place.

If you get caught in the rain wearing a felt hat, use tissue paper to blot the raindrops away and then get a handful of tissue paper and run it over the hat with a smooth, circular action.

If your felt hat has become droopy, steam it for a few seconds and then brush it gently, making sure you are brushing in the direction of the nap.

To brush felt, use a stiff clothes brush to get rid of any dust, then hold it over the steam from a kettle but only for a few seconds. Once it's dry, you can repeat the brushing.

A felt hat that's really beyond repair can be cut up and used to trim another in better repair.

Update a classic beret by making holes with a hole-punch and adding eyelets.

Take great care when storing a peach-bloom felt hat to avoid marking the delicate finish. Pad with tissue paper and always store on its own, upright in a box.

To bring up the colour on a white or cream felt hat, sprinkle with talcum powder.

Sprinkle a white or cream felt hat with bran. Leave it overnight, then brush it off in the morning. This works like an exfoliator.

If you get your beret wet, slip it over a plate that is the same size to stop it from shrinking.

Remove stubborn stains from a felt hat by brushing with sandpaper. If that fails, colour in the mark with an appropriately coloured felt-tip pen.

Store your felt hats upside down, particularly if they have a wide brim, otherwise the weight of the crown will push it out of shape. For perfect storage, pack the crown with tissue paper, inside and out.

Don't store hats one inside the other – you'll ruin them.

Gents

Always buy a flat cap one size too large. You're most likely to be wearing it in damp or really wet weather and it will probably end up shrinking.

To clean a flat cap, wash it in mild soapy liquid.

To change the size and fitting of a top hat, heat it up on top of an Aga or in front of a fire then put it on your head. It should mould to the shape of your head while it is still warm and give you a perfect fit.

Make sure you are wearing your hat the right way round. A woman should wear the bow or feather to her right, the man to his left.

All the Trimmings

To revive flowers on a hat, shake them over a steaming kettle and they'll blossom back into life.

For attaching small, fairly light decorations to a hat, a glue gun is the fastest thing around.

For perfectly matched feathers, you don't have to hunt round for the right coloured bird. You can spray them with paint (before you attach them to the hat, of course).

After the glorious 12th, ask around at butchers that specialise in game to get pheasant or partridge feathers for an elegant trim. Bind feathers together with fuse wire before inserting them into your hat band.

When searching for millinery trimmings, don't restrict yourself to the haberdashers' department – look among stationery, gift wrap, Christmas decorations and (for braid and tassels) upholstery departments too.

Restore a floppy brim to perky splendour by wiring the edge then covering with a strip of petersham ribbon, folded in half.

Give a new lease of life to a felt hat by adding a leather belt with a good-looking buckle around the crown. You can change the belt to match other accessories.

Fabric stiffener works wonders with floppy trimmings in fabrics like organdie.

You can freshen the head ribbon by removing it – simply unpick the stitches – and giving it a quick press with an iron before you sew it on again.

Don't mess up expensive ribbon by practising how to tie it. Play around with some muslin instead until you are sure where and how you want the bow.

If you need to replace a head ribbon, choose petersham in cotton or a cotton mix. To be on the safe side, never buy less than 2 1/2 ft75 cm. If the old ribbon was a good fit, simply cut the new one to the same length.

Trimmings are usually the first thing to fade on a hat, so change them to give the hat a fresh look.

Keep a small hat firmly in place by adding a comb. Snap a small, curved comb in half, then cover the base in petersham and stitch firmly in place at either end and between the teeth. You can stitch it by the corners to the inside of the crown in the position you need, but make sure the teeth are pointing towards the centre of the crown.

When sewing a fur fabric hat, make sure the pile lies away from the line of stitching. If you do trap any fur in the stitches, simply tease it out using a pin.

To make sure your hat goes on straight every time, make a mark on the head ribbon inside the hat at the centre front. Just make sure it's lined up with your nose.

MODELS

Caitlin Powell; June Macdougall

Make sure you give the agent the best shots of you. Take in holiday pictures of you looking relaxed and natural and, no doubt, wearing a swimming costume.

When visiting an agent for the first time, let them judge how you really look. Don't wear make-up, high heels or do your hair in an elaborate style.

Keep your portfolio up to date by asking for test Polaroids at a shoot. They may be as good as the finished product and you won't have to wait months for them to be ready.

To improve your portfolio, include pictures of any special skills you may have, such as horse riding, wind surfing or skiing.

For a child's portfolio, don't pay more than £60.

When placing your child with an agency, find out as much information as possible before parting with any money.

Don't let an amateur photographer take shots for your portfolio – they may just 'click' six times for six photos.

Accentuate your cheekbones – say the word 'poor', while keeping your lips soft, and hold for a couple of seconds.

Perfect your catwalk technique – practise walking towards a mirror, keeping your toes directly ahead, brushing your knees together and taking steps no longer than 12 in/30 cm.

To test whether you need to wear a bra or not, place a pencil underneath your breast. If the pencil falls, you don't need to wear one!

Avoid blemishes – always have your body waxed a couple of days in advance of a shoot.

To be prepared for a shoot, you should take a pair of black shoes, and your own make-up and beauty products, just in case the stylists and make-up artists don't have anything suitable for you.

Create a good impression on a shoot. Write down the names and job descriptions of each member of the crew. You never know when you'll meet them again.

For free information on what to look for in a modelling agency contact the Model Information Bureau (Body's House, 25–27 Queens Road, Southend, Essex, SS1 1LT, tel: 01702 435328).

MUSICIANS

Playing

Nicholas Korth, Birmingham Royal Ballet Orchestra; Rosie & Luca Clementi; E Harfleet; Ed Barnes

Keep ahead of the game when playing. Check what's over the page!

To avoid having to turn the pages of a music book, photocopy the relevant pages and stick them edge to edge in a concertina shape, so you can lay them open on your music stand.

If you get stuck on a particular passage, divide it into two. Play up to the bit where you go wrong, then stop. Do this a couple of times, then start from the place where you get stuck and repeat that. When you play straight through, you often find the problem has gone.

To play any instrument effectively (apart from the guitar), you should keep your nails relatively short. If you can see the ends of your fingers above your nails, then so much the better.

To avoid making too much noise when moving between your percussion instruments, don't wear shoes. Put on some thick slipper socks.

If you want to be a pianist and get the best out of your fingers, don't play racket games.

To start playing the piano after the age of 16 is not a good idea. Go for something a little easier.

To play the piano effectively during a concert, avoid wearing long sleeves, and take off your bangles.

To play your horn well for a long period of time, pace yourself. Don't use all your strength up in the first few pages of music.

When performing, don't try to pretend the audience aren't there. Look straight at them as you come on stage.

Try getting to the auditorium early and taking a look from the audience side. It shouldn't seem so scary after that.

If you have any say in the matter, ask the stage manager not to turn the light down too low. It'll make the auditorium seem enormous.

The performance starts as soon as you walk on stage. Walk up to your instrument or your place gracefully and stylishly, just as you want to perform – with grace and style. This can win you easy marks in an audition or competition.

If you play a wind instrument, never chew gum, suck sweets or drink fizzy drinks immediately before or while playing. Your sugary saliva will damage the inside of the instrument.

If you (as a teacher) haven't enjoyed the lesson, you can bet your pupil won't have either. Remember that if a pupil doesn't enjoy a particular lesson, it may be their last.

Encourage children to practise their instruments by getting them into a routine. They should play at the same time every day. It sounds simple but it's very effective.

Keyboard skills and the ability to read music will always be helpful, whatever you want to do in music.

Looking after an Instrument

To clean the inside of your guitar, fill it with uncooked rice, give it a really good shake and then empty.

You'll know when it's time to change the strings on your guitar when the sound goes.

Keep an eye on the strings of your violin bow – if little hairs are beginning to come off the bow then it's time for a change.

Make sure you get a good sound from your piano – once it is in the room, leave it where it is.

To polish your piano keys properly, never spray directly on to them. Spray on to a cloth and work from the top of the key to the bottom. Don't polish sideways.

You can clean your brass instrument cheaply and effectively with warm, soapy water.

Avoid valve problems during a concert – keep a small bottle of valve oil with you at all times.

To get a good strong sound out of your horn you should not clean it on the inside. All the dirt and bacteria add to the beautiful sound. If you clean the horn, it sounds too clinical.

Get the most out of your wind instrument by cleaning it as soon as you have finished with it.

Clean your clarinet properly by attaching a piece of flannelette sheet to a knitting needle and pushing that down your instrument.

Ensure that your clarinet produces a good tone – change the reeds quite often.

Make a halter for your saxophone from an old silk scarf.

For a slipping peg on stringed instruments, alternate applications of chalk and soap until you get the right degree of stick.

Woodwind drip? Never be without cigarette papers to blot under the keys and a soft duster as a pull through.

If a string breaks and you don't have a spare, you can knot it below the bridge for an emergency repair that will let you go on playing.

Store gut strings straight. Only synthetic strings can be kept rolled up.

Before plane travel and in very cold weather, loosen your strings by about a semitone.

For flights, check in with just your instrument as hand luggage – you can't run the risk of having to consign it to the hold.

To help your music books last just that bit longer, laminate them and store them flat in a box.

Singing

If you are a singer with a sore throat, never take throat sweets or pastilles, as you may strain your voice without noticing because of their anaesthetic effect.

If something affects your body, it will also affect your voice. Lack of sleep and tiredness particularly will affect your voice and throat as much as it affects the rest of you. A singer should take their health as seriously as an athlete does.

Women's voices seem to be more quickly and noticeably affected by smoking than men's.

Dairy products have a big impact on singers' voices. Giving them up or massively cutting down clears the passages and reduces the amount of phlegm and mucus in the throat, making the voice sound clearer.

Don't trip over your microphone wire – it doesn't look too cool. Tuck it into your belt at the back.

NAIL TECHNICIANS
Hand & Nail Care

Midge A Killen, Amazing Nails, USA; Lynn Shaw at Nailtiques; Mandy Rouse, Beautique, Stratford-upon-Avon

Always protect your hands – try to wear gloves for washing-up, cleaning round the house and gardening.

Before starting a dirty job, such as gardening or decorating, scrape your nails over some soft soap. This prevents the dirt getting in. When you wash your hands afterwards, use a nailbrush to remove the soap.

To get rid of gardening grime, apply washing-up liquid to your hands with a generous pinch of salt and rub in before rinsing.

If you get ink stains on your hands, rub the stains with a nail-brush that you have dipped in vinegar and salt. You could also try rubbing the ink stains with the inside of a banana skin.

Don't wash your hands in very hot water because it strips the skin of natural oils. Warm water and a gentle soap is just as effective. Always apply hand cream after you've got your hands wet.

For a home-made exfoliator, mix one teaspoon of olive oil with enough salt to make a paste. Massage over your hands and then rinse off under warm to hot water. This leaves hands feeling like silk, and is ideal for gardeners as the salt removes the dirt and the oil rehydrates skin.

Clean grubby nails – especially if you're a smoker – with minty toothpaste.

Avoid nail fungus by cleaning your manicuring tools in antibacterial soap.

Nail fungal infections can be treated using tea tree oil. This is a great, natural treatment.

Hand creams can be expensive. Soften up rough skin on hands and feet (especially at night) with aqueous cream (available from the chemist) and cover hands and feet with cotton gloves and socks.

For heavy-duty hand cream, mix virgin olive oil and petroleum jelly together. Rub the mixture into your hands and then put them into freezer bags. Sit and have a cuppa or read the paper while your hands absorb the benefits of this perfect conditioner.

Always style nails with hand cream on as this protects the nails. Remember nails are most vulnerable when filing.

Don't wipe away excess hand cream – rub it into the cuticles and let it soak in.

Dipping your nails in warm olive oil will moisturise them, soften the cuticles and help to stop them splitting.

Push back cuticles with lollipop sticks.

When filing nails, keep going in one direction. Sawing backwards and forwards weakens the edges.

The 'stiletto' (square nail to a point) will be the latest trend in nail shape. The other popular shape is the 'small oval' almond, which is ideal for red and dark polishes. It's like the button Coco Chanel shape.

Nail-polish

To make short nails look longer, use darker shades of nail varnish, and don't paint the edges of your nails.

Metallic nail colours make small nails look bigger.

File nails when you are wearing polish to avoid splitting or breaking them.

Shaping nails for a home manicure is always easier with your nail-polish on, as you can see the shape you are creating.

Colour the tip of the nail first with nail-polish. It will help it to last longer.

To help nail-varnish dry quickly – run newly polished nails under cold water or dip them in iced water.

Dipping them in baby oil works well too.

Stop nails discolouring by using a colourless base coat first.

Clear nail-varnish applied on top of colour will help it to last longer.

The new fast-drying nail-varnishes can make your nails go yellow if used constantly. Once in a while give your nails a break from polish altogether, just rub in some almond oil and give them a really good buffing.

Keep nail-varnish in the fridge – it lasts for much longer and dries much more quickly when applied.

Try a classic French polish. The white tipped-manicure works just as well on toes, creating a clean, well-maintained look.

Stop the top of the nail-varnish bottle from sticking – rub some petroleum jelly on to the top of the bottle.

Avoid bubbles in your nail-varnish by gently rolling the bottle to mix it, rather than shaking it (as we all do).

Remove any stains left by nail-varnish by dipping your nails into fresh lemon juice.

When applying nail-varnish at bedtime, coat nails with oil as this will help to prevent indentations.

NANNIES

Marianne Bell;
Catherine Wilson;
Linda Elderkin; Alison
Tweedale

Babies

Don't be too fastidious about constantly washing and changing the cot sheets – babies like the smell of familiar surroundings.

To reassure the baby and encourage good sleeping habits, place something in the cot that the baby's mum has worn during the day.

Leave a babysitter some extra pieces of a parent's clothing to wrap the baby in if they wake up fretful.

Leave a babysitter a tape of a parent either singing or, for older children, telling a story.

Don't hush everything up when you put the baby to sleep. Teach your child to sleep through normal noise levels.

Young babies don't need expensive toys. They will love to watch a washing machine going round or listen to a vacuum cleaner. Many new mothers try to keep all noises down – but babies find them fascinating and it's good to get them used to normal domestic surroundings.

Make your own changing table from the top of a chest of drawers. Place the chest against a wall and add a 4-in/10-cm high lip to the front to stop the baby rolling off. Never leave the baby unattended though.

Bathing tiny babies can be a bit tricky. You may find it easier to bathe them in a sink rather than bending down over a large tub.

If your baby dislikes having a bath, it may be because the bathroom is too cold. Make sure the room is warm before you start the bath, or bathe the baby in another, warmer room.

Babies can be bathed every day or every other day. You can 'top and tail' them – wipe their faces and bottoms – at least twice a day.

New babies (up to a month old) can be washed in a washing-up bowl. Cover the taps with a towel so that you don't bang the baby's head against them. Remove dirty pots and pans first!

To prevent babies from slipping in a big bath, use a terry nappy as a non-slip mat.

Never leave a baby or child alone in the bath. It only takes a few inches of water to drown a child so always supervise them.

Babies quickly get cold after a bath. Make sure you have everything you'll need before you put the baby in the water.

Feed babies after their bath and not before. Babies often decide to throw up if they've been jiggled around, so wait until after they've been cleaned before feeding.

Keep all your equipment together – use a hanging shoe container which you can fill with cotton wool, ointment, creams, terry towels… in fact, anything that you need for changing or cleaning your baby. It can be hung on a wall or door for easy access.

Use plastic stacking boxes from DIY stores for storage. They are cheaper than specially designed baby equipment.

When babies are young, put them in nighties rather than playsuits at night. It will make night changes easier and less disruptive, and begin to teach them the difference between night and day.

Lay out a clean set of night clothes before you go to bed so that you're not stumbling around in the gloom if you have to do a complete change in the wee small hours.

Make your own baby wipes – they're cheaper and less synthetic. Simply soak some cotton-wool roll in an old ice-cream carton filled with water and a little baby oil. Tear off strips as you need it.

Make your own nappy-rash cream. Whip up an egg white until it has soft peaks. Apply it to the affected area with cotton wool.

Treat nappy rash with a soft paste of fuller's earth and water. Gently apply to the affected area.

Cradle cap looks horrid – a little almond oil should clear it up in no time.

Teething can be a major problem. Cut some slightly stale bread into fingers, dip into milk and then bake for a couple of minutes until brown for excellent teething strips.

To soothe hot, painful gums, put some fresh fruit flesh into the middle of a muslin square and twist the cloth into a tight sausage. Chill it in the fridge for a couple of hours then let your baby gnash away at it.

Always have lots of muslin squares around – they have lots of uses. Try placing one over a pillow to save laundry if your baby keeps posseting; or use one tied to the cot with a little vapour rub on it to help a sniffly baby. Take the chill off a baby-changing mat by laying a muslin square across it first.

Cleaning first milk teeth is a fiddly job and many babies hate toothbrushes. Instead, wrap a little muslin around your finger – it makes it much easier to get at little gnashers.

To wind a baby, try holding him or her over your shoulder and walk up and down the stairs – the natural up-and-down movement works much better than trying to bounce the baby and the rhythm is relaxing, too.

When you first wean a baby on to solids, you will only need a bit each time. Avoid waste and make life more convenient by making up large batches of fresh vegetables or fruit then puréeing them into ice trays to use as needed.

Be patient when introducing solids. Start off with one or two teaspoons of food a day. If your baby isn't interested, go back to milk for a day or so and then try again.

Introduce new foods one after the other. You can then detect more easily if your child is allergic to anything.

Save time by cooking for the whole family at once. Cook the 'grown-up' food without seasoning, put a little to one side for your baby and purée it. Then season your own food the way you like it.

Don't use baby talk. It doesn't help children to pick up anything useful. Use simple, short sentences and look at children when you speak to them.

Turn learning new words into a game. Point at things and get the child to repeat the words.

Use body language to reinforce what you are saying: for example, when waving goodbye to people.

Expand on what your child says. Always try to add new words for your child to learn. If they point out a fire engine in the street, you can say 'Yes, it's a red fire engine'.

Toddlers

When you wash children's hair, draw a thin line of petroleum jelly above their eyes; it will stop the shampoo running down into their eyes and stinging them.

To keep shampoo out of children's eyes, get them to wear a golf visor.

To cure an early riser, try setting an alarm clock! It may sound mad, but children love gimmicks and your toddler will start to wait for the bell to go off, often falling asleep again before that time comes. Eventually, their body clock will change, teaching them to sleep until your chosen time of waking.

Keep the route from nursery to your room clear of obstacles. If your child comes looking for you at night, you don't want them tripping over things in the dark. Put up a safety gate at the top of the stairs.

If your child is suffering from nightmares, make a point of turning the pillow over to 'turn the bad dreams away'. Leave a night-light or soft light on in the room.

Encourage toddlers to dress themselves by laying out their clothes so they can see the whole outfit. Then make the task a game by setting a clock and challenging them to a race against time.

To get your toddler to wear a coat, put the garment inside out on the floor. Teach him to push his arms in and pull the coat over his head; the coat will then be the correct way round.

Teach little ones their left and right by putting stickers on their wellies.

To teach tying shoelaces, get some liquorice laces and practise making edible butterflies.

Feeding Time

When children want to start feeding themselves, dress them in a painting bib rather than a normal feeding bib – it will cover much more of their clothing and is waterproof so can be wiped clean.

Faddy eaters may be encouraged to eat if you make mealtimes fun. Arrange food to create patterns or to spell out their name.

Involve toddlers in buying food and cooking – they'll feel much more inclined to taste something they have helped to prepare.

Arrange finger foods in the different compartments of an ice tray – children love 'little things'.

A fun way to encourage children to eat their dinner is to give them chopsticks instead of knives and forks (not for the faint-hearted or anyone with a new carpet).

To get the kids cooking, but without giving them sharp kitchen implements, allow them to use plastic knives and forks.

To make cooking fun for kids, let them press all the buttons (on the blender, oven and so on) while you do the boring job of removing all the hot food.

For a healthy and tasty pizza with a difference, spread some Marmite on to a pizza base before adding favourite toppings.

To create fun-shaped sandwiches for children, use metal pastry cutters.

Children thrive on routine in their daily activities. Try to serve meals at the same time each day.

Eating is a new experience for small children. Don't be surprised if at first a child is cautious and curious, plays with food, is reluctant to try new foods and rebels when forced to eat. Try to be patient, relaxed and maintain a sense of humour – even if they appear to be eating nothing, you'll be surprised how much actually goes in during a day.

Snacks are not always bad for children. Nutritious snack foods can help children to obtain required nutrients. Since children have smaller stomachs than adults, they are natural grazers – so serving three small meals with a nourishing snack in between each meal may be more appropriate than serving three large meals.

But frequent snacking may contribute to tooth decay. Clean children's teeth each day and check with a dentist about the need for fluoride.

Children often want to eat one particular food at every opportunity. This is called a 'food jag' and typically occurs among toddlers. As long as the preferred food is nutritious and the jag does not last long, there is nothing to worry about. If you go along with it, the child will probably get bored of the food soon enough.

Children's appetites may suddenly decrease around the age of two due to a decrease in their growth rate. As growth slows, energy requirements are also reduced. So don't worry if a previously hungry hippo turns into a nibbling mouse.

Don't present children with huge helpings – they'll eat much better if confronted with an obviously manageable portion and, if they then manage a second helping, they'll feel a real sense of achievement.

Slice frankfurters into four strips length-wise and then cut into small pieces that can't block the windpipe and cause the child to choke.

Cook meat at a low temperature (150–160° C/300–325° F/Gas Mark 2–3) to keep it tender and juicy. We all remember chewing on a mouthful of meat that just wouldn't go away.

When children are first learning to feed themselves, cut meat into small julienne strips that can be picked up and eaten by hand. Older children who are using tableware still need to have their meat cut into bite-size pieces with the fat and gristle trimmed to prevent choking.

Children usually enjoy brightly coloured fruits and vegetables.

Children like their vegetables crunchy, not soft. Vegetables steamed in a small amount of water, microwaved or stir-fried are not only crisp, but retain most of their colour, flavour and nutrients far better than boiled ones.

Many strongly flavoured vegetables such as cabbage, turnip, cauliflower, spinach, broccoli and asparagus are very acceptable to children when served with grated cheese or a cheese sauce.

To prevent choking, avoid giving raw carrots and whole peas, corn and grapes to children under four years old. Cook and mash carrots, corn and peas, and cut grapes into quarters.

Many older children enjoy raw vegetables served with their own individual bowl of dip.

When shopping with children, encourage them to help select fruits and vegetables, especially ones they have never tried before.

Taste food before adding butter, margarine, dressing, jellies and jams. Since children follow the example of adults, limit your own use of fats and sugars, and use only moderate amounts of these foods in meal preparation.

Seat children at a table for meals and snacks, and discourage them from eating while walking or standing.

Cover the floor directly beneath a child's seat with paper, vinyl or plastic.

Purchase a spoon or fork with a short, straight, broad, solid handle. The spoon should have a wide mouth and the fork should have blunt prongs. Children will begin to feed themselves with a spoon and will learn to use a fork later.

Place food at the level of a child's stomach, where it is less tiring for a child to reach.

Children playing with food should be allowed to leave the table rather than disturb others. This usually indicates that a child has had enough to eat. Don't encourage children to clean their plates when they're no longer hungry. This may lead to overeating or the development of an aversion to food.

Sometimes children behave better and enjoy mealtimes more when they sit down to a meal with the family at a nicely set table. Allowing older children to have candles makes a meal into a special occasion, and little ones can help to blow them out when everyone's eaten well.

Encourage children to try at least one bite of a new food. If, after one bite, children reject it, reintroduce the food later.

Allow children to eat at their friends' homes. These visits offer an excellent opportunity for them to try new foods. Try incorporating these new foods in meals you prepare.

Start nutrition education early by explaining the function of nutrients found in common foods (for example that milk makes bones and teeth strong).

Meal preparation should not be a burden. Salads, raw vegetables, fruits and ready-to-serve meats, fish and cheese are nutritious and easy to prepare.

Breakfasts don't have to be traditional. Any nutritious combination of foods from all food groups is recommended. Incorporate left-overs when preparing breakfast.

Encourage children to participate in quiet activities before mealtimes. It's difficult to get an excited child to settle down to eat.

Feed children before guests arrive. Children require a lot of attention at mealtimes and it may be impossible to give it to them while entertaining guests.

Children's blood sugar levels often run low quite quickly. If your toddler suddenly seems irritable for no apparent reason, try giving him a little bit of fruit or cheese.

Boring bites can be transformed into magical meals with a few drops of food colouring and a little imagination. Mashed potato can become green grass or blue sea, pasta can be colourful snakes, and rice can be any colour of the rainbow. Even the humble egg boiled in its shell can become jewel red or sunshine yellow. Choose your child's favourite colour and they'll soon start eating up.

Whenever they eat, children should be sitting upright, not lying down or running around. Always supervise at snack and mealtimes, because a child who is choking cannot make a noise to attract your attention. Coughing, on the other hand, is a sign that the child is removing the obstacle naturally. Before intervening, give the child the chance to cough out the food.

The grinding action of a child's teeth is not very effective until at least four years of age. Because of this, foods that are hard or tough to chew, small and round or sticky are most often choked on. These include: frankfurters, raw apples, crunchy or hard-boiled sweets, raw carrots, nuts, corn, grapes, peas, popcorn, chunks of meat, raisins, and peanut butter spread too thickly.

When travelling by car, bus or train with young children, consider their special needs. Pack snacks when taking a trip that will last longer than one hour.

Be sure to keep hot foods hot and cold foods cold. A cooler, which can be stored in a car or below the seat of a bus or train, will allow you to pack a variety of foods that must remain cold.

Raw vegetables, fruits, cheese, crackers and tubs of yoghurt are easily eaten in a car, and store well. Pack cheese, cold cuts, peanut butter, jelly and a loaf of bread to make sandwiches on an extra long trip.

Pack tableware, napkins, moist towelettes or a washcloth that has been moistened and stored in a plastic bag.

When travelling by plane, don't expect the airlines to cater for the needs of children, although sometimes they do. Today many airlines are limiting their meal service in order to reduce air fares. It's usually a good idea to bring along sandwiches, fruit, cheese, crackers and raw vegetables, which can be kept for a short period of time without refrigeration. Even though airlines usually provide beverages during a flight, you may want to bring a thermos of milk or cans of juice. There will be so much new going on around them, but at least the food and drink can be familiar.

Pay attention to the special needs of children when dining with them at restaurants. If you must wait before being seated, take children for a walk outside the restaurant to prevent them from becoming impatient.

Some children expect to eat as soon as they sit at a dinner table and will fill up on appetisers and bread, leaving no room for their main meal. Try to prevent this by asking the restaurant not to put out the bread in advance of the meal and, when you order, inquire about children's portions.

Young children will feel more at home in a restaurant if you bring along their cup and tableware.

Children involved in meal preparation develop a more active interest in food. They can accomplish many different tasks when working one-on-one with an adult in the kitchen. A number of activities children can do successfully at various ages are listed below. Having patience and time to spend with children when involving them in meal preparation is the key to success.

Two- and three-year-olds need to learn about personal hygiene – encourage them to wash their hands before handling any food or eating.

But they love having 'jobs' to do. Try asking them to wash vegetables, wipe the table, tear lettuce, help to shape burgers and meatballs, peel bananas (if the top is started) and clear their own place setting.

Three- and four-year-olds like to feel challenged. Let them break eggs into a bowl, measure and mix ingredients, knead and shape dough, pour their own cereal out and toss salads.

Five-year-olds can make cakes and cookies using baking mixes, help make pancakes, French toast, scrambled eggs, hot cereal and rice (with close supervision), set and clear the table and load the dishwasher.

Encourage teenagers to help out in the kitchen. Put up a notice each day saying what's for dinner. If they get home before you they will know which vegetables to start chopping or to preheat the oven. You may even find dinner waiting for you – but don't bank on it!

For healthy ice-lollies that will still please little ones, top and tail a pineapple and cut downwards into six to eight chunky wedges, then freeze.

Give the kids a treat with home-made creamy banana ice-lollies. Blend a banana with some milk, then pour into moulds, add a stick and freeze.

When making your own ice-lollies, put any piece of real fruit in to pep up the taste and make them healthy.

To remove home-made ice-lollies from their mould, place the mould under running warm water.

Keep insects out of the children's drinks when having a picnic. Cover the tops of beakers with cling film and push a straw through.

Children will love bananas if you coat them in melted chocolate and roll them in coconut.

Dilute pure fruit juice with sparkling mineral water when serving to children.

Do your kids' hands get messy when eating ice-lollies? Just take a disc of card, put the stick of the lolly through the card and, as the lolly melts, the juices will just drip on to the card and not on to the children's hands.

Give kids small cups to drink from – they're easier to carry and so less likely to be dropped. If they do get dropped, there's less to clean up.

For fun cup cakes, top them with a marshmallow a couple of minutes before removing from the oven.

Children don't usually like ice-cold milk – try pouring it a short time before serving to take off the chill.

Serve milk in plastic cups with covers that fit or unbreakable cups with weighted bottoms. Fill cups halfway to make milk more difficult to spill; this will also make the task of drinking milk seem less awesome.

Only offer flavoured milk on special occasions. Children should develop a taste for plain milk, which has fewer calories than flavoured.

If children refuse to drink milk, try to include milk-based soups, cottage cheese, yoghurt, cheese, custard or cereal with milk in their diets.

If a child is over the age of two, serve low-fat milk rather than whole milk.

Young children often prefer the taste of bland, sweet fruits over tart fruits. Serve tart fruits from time to time to develop a child's taste for all fruits.

Peel, core and seed fruits for very young children.

Fresh, dried, canned and frozen fruits and juices make nutritious snacks and desserts.

To reduce the chance of cavities, clean children's teeth with a moistened washcloth or gauze, especially after they have eaten dried fruits.

Do not offer sweets as a bribe or withhold them as punishment.

Since children know that sweets exist, serving sweets on special occasions may be a more sensible approach than excluding them completely. By sometimes including them in your child's diet, you avoid making them into a big deal.

While you should avoid feeding gumdrops, jelly beans, hard-boiled sweets, nuts and popcorn to very young children, many other childhood favourites can still be enjoyed.

Milk and fruit juices are more nutritious than soft drinks and can be stored in a cooler or thermos. Juice will remain cold if you slightly freeze individual cans before packing.

Children love sweets but to keep things under control put the sweets in the freezer for a couple of hours. The paper should peel off easily and the sweets won't be too sticky for little fingers.

Behaviour

Tantrums and the 'terrible twos' needn't be the end of your sanity. They are just a cry for attention. If you ignore them, the toddler will realise they don't work. If your child is really stubborn, try leaving the room yourself and say 'I don't want to be with you while you do that' – young children hate to be ignored and will soon come and say sorry!

It's never too early to start learning good manners. Make sure you say 'please' and 'thank you' as well. You want to set a good example!

Dressing up can be great therapy for shyness and can be used to overcome fears. Superman wouldn't be scared of the dentist and Cinderella would always have clean teeth and hair!

When children are cleaning their teeth, use an egg timer in the bathroom so they know how long they should clean their teeth for.

To wean a toddler off a dummy, have a special box that is home for the offending soother. At night, after the child falls asleep, put the dummy in the box – letting the child know it is there if it is needed. At some stage, send the box off to Father Christmas or the fairies, then return it to the child with a small toy in it instead of the dummy.

Start potty training when your child can stay dry for a few hours at a time and can understand some simple instructions. Let your child see other children or parents using the loo. Make a star chart – one star for every time they successfully use the potty. And be prepared for it to take time!

Get Creative

Children love magic and surprises. Make special paper by writing messages or the children's names in white crayon on white paper. When they colour the paper in, they'll reveal your message.

Make modelling dough out of flour, water and some food colouring. Children enjoy the process of making it as much as the modelling that follows and it's much cheaper than buying it ready-made. If your child makes something really good, this home-made recipe can be baked hard and kept afterwards.

Use old offcuts of wallpaper and get your child to lie down on the plain side. Draw around them to make a silhouette and then pin it up and get them to colour it in with whatever they fancy.

To make a fun place-mat for your child, take one of their paintings and stick it on to a cork table mat. Then cover the mat with some clear sticky-back plastic.

Use sponges and vegetables as stamps. Cut out a simple design for them and then leave them to make patterns on paper by dipping the stamp in paint.

If your children have made thickly daubed finger paintings, a quick blast of hairspray will stop the bits of paint falling off once it's dried.

Keep a box of odds and ends that you can use for drawing, sticking things together or modelling. Old toothbrushes, old office stationery, large buttons, yoghurt pots, cereal packets and that old stand-by, the washing-up bottle! Keep everything in shoe-boxes for a rainy day.

Children's parties needn't be a nightmare for parents. Don't do too much food: children are often too excited to eat a lot. Make sure you've moved all your precious objects out of harm's way. If all the children are under four, they'll need one-to-one supervision. If children are four or five years old, it's best to have one adult for every five children.

If you are going out somewhere busy, like a crowded park or fun fair, tie a brightly coloured balloon to the pushchair. If your toddler runs off and gets lost, he'll be able to find you again more easily.

Encourage your children to tidy their rooms with an egg timer or clock. Make it a race with prizes for the tidiest competitor.

Teach young children to count by marking the back of a jigsaw in numerical order. The little ones can enjoy piecing the jigsaw together using the numbers as a guide and then turn it over to see the finished picture. The numbers will also help you to quickly check if you have all the pieces.

It's important to calm children down at the end of the day. Read them stories and let them know that the quieter they are, the longer you'll read. If they start being noisy, it's end of story.

Children's tattoos don't always come off easily – use a tiny drop of nail-polish remover on a cotton bud.

If the kids are left with orange moustaches after drinking cordial, rub on some toothpaste and rinse. Lovely clean smiles!

Take a big tub of talc with you when you go to the beach. Sprinkle generously on to sandy skin and the sand just rubs off.

Finally, enjoy your children. The early years will go far too quickly.

NATURISTS

Mike Berridge,
Press Officer,
British Naturism,
www.british-naturism.org

There are bits of you that may never have seen the sun. Make sure you use the highest protection factor sun-block available.

Carry a towel with you on nudist sites. It's a matter of courtesy to use them to sit on.

Carry your keys by looping a broad rubber band through the key-ring, passing one end through the loop and wearing it round your wrist.

You can carry loose change in a neck purse.

Take a mobile phone with you, particularly when not using designated naturist beaches. You may come across inappropriate behaviour, and it helps if you can threaten to phone the police.

On non-designated beaches, have a long T-shirt or a pair of loose shorts handy to slip on in case a hoard of people suddenly arrive.

You don't have to be nude all the time to be a naturist. Dress appropriately for the weather conditions.

You may find that your tolerance of cold improves. Most naturists are healthy specimens and don't seem to suffer with cold.

Wear sensible footwear for whatever you are doing, even if you're wearing nothing else. You can't do the garden in flip-flops.

If out hill walking, avoid well-frequented paths, particularly at weekends.

If there are people coming your way, you will probably spot them in their bright rambling gear well before they spot you, and even if they do see you, at a distance, they won't be able to tell for sure that you're nude. Slip on a T-shirt or a pair of shorts, and you won't upset anyone.

If you do meet someone unexpectedly, step off the path to diffuse any perceived threat from your sudden appearance.

When out hill walking, make sure you take plenty of clothes with you. As you get higher, the temperature drops and the wind increases.

PAINTERS & DECORATORS
Prepare to Decorate

Colin Philips; Cyril Cohen;
Ray Mansell & Mark
Vince, Cain Decorators;
Paul Pavlo; Robert Smith;
Dave Jenkins; Keith Myles;
Scott Warroll

Sometimes, when a house gets really grubby, for instance if it has been empty for some time, it can be cheaper and more effective simply to redecorate.

Always clear and prepare the area you are going to decorate – remove as much as you can from the room and cover the furniture and floor with old sheets.

Always buy paint and wallpaper with the same batch number – there can be a slight variation in colour from one batch to the next.

If you have to buy a tin of paint or roll of paper with a different batch number, use it in places where it won't be too obvious (behind furniture, for example).

Don't wear slippy shoes up a ladder – an obvious tip but a sensible one.

Keep any left-over paint or wallpaper in case you need to do the odd bit of repair work later on.

Painting

Before you start decorating, rub your hands in petroleum jelly. You'll save time at the end of the day when the paint washes out easily.

Don't get paint in your hair – wear a shower cap.

To prevent drips on your head when painting a ceiling, cut a slit right through the middle of a large sponge and slip the handle of your paint-brush through it.

Cover your spectacles with cling film so that if you get paint on them, you can just peel the cling film away.

Avoid paint drips all over your hand, wind a rubber band round the thick end of the brush to catch any drips.

An old fish slice makes a good paint scraper and because the edges aren't too sharp, you can let the kids help scrape the paint off.

You don't need a roller or expensive brush to paint a wall. A sponge works just as well.

When mixing up filler to repair cracks in walls you are going to paint, mix in a little of the emulsion to colour the filler, so the repair won't show through when you paint.

To touch up a small chipped area of paint, use a cotton bud instead of a paint-brush and simply throw it away afterwards.

If you paint steps or stairs, paint alternate ones and let the paint dry, then paint the ones in between. That way you'll still be able to use them.

When painting skirting boards, hold a piece of cardboard between the skirting and the floor under the area you are painting.

When painting from a ladder, always paint from the outside in so you don't stretch away from yourself and overbalance.

It's difficult to work up a ladder while carrying a pot of paint and a brush. Make life easier by placing a small tin of paint inside a larger empty tin. Tuck the brush in the gap between the two and you can carry everything you need and still have one hand free.

Don't spoil your newly painted wall with ugly ladder marks. Pop a pair of clean socks over the ends of the ladder.

The smell of new paint can linger for ages. Stir in a couple of drops of vanilla essence to disguise nasty fumes.

To get rid of the smell of new paint, leave a cut onion in a recently painted room.

Paint perfect straight lines by putting a rubber band round the bristles of your brush. This keeps them together in a stiff shape making it much easier to control where you paint.

Protect your walls when painting close-resting pipes by sliding a sheet of cardboard down behind the pipes as you work.

Painting railings can take hours. You can finish really quickly if you dip a flannel mitt in the paint and then run your hand up and down the railing a few times to coat it.

Keep paint off window glass – put masking tape around the edge of the glass. Be sure to leave a tiny gap between the tape and the frame; this will allow the paint to seal the join between the glass and the putty. Remove the tape as the paint starts to dry; if you leave it too long the adhesive will stick to the window.

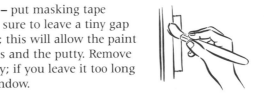

Keep paint off odd shapes such as taps, hooks or doorknobs by covering them with kitchen foil.

Never paint from a large tin of paint, pour a small amount into a paint kettle. This keeps the majority of the paint free from dust.

Intricate mouldings are fiddly to rub down with sandpaper – use a small pumice stone instead to get into all the corners.

When rubbing down window-frames, try using wire wool instead of sandpaper; it won't scratch the glass.

If a window sticks after painting, run a thin knife around the window and frame to release it.

To prevent your windows sticking, start painting early in the morning and leave the windows open all day until evening.

Keep a pair of shoes or slippers outside the room you are decorating. You'll have something to change into and you won't walk paint all over the rest of the house.

If you find your paint has got grit in it, stretch the leg of an old pair of tights across a clean paint kettle and pour the paint through it.

If your paint-brushes have hardened, soften them by dipping them in a pan of boiling vinegar for a few minutes.

Roller trays are a pain to clean. Pop the whole thing inside a plastic bag, press the bag well into the corners and then fill with paint. When you've finished, simply remove the tray and throw the bag away.

When you want a lunch break, wrap your paint-brush in cling film or aluminium foil – it saves on cleaning it.

When storing brushes, wrap an elastic band round the tip, so the bristles don't splay out.

Don't waste turps by throwing it out each time. Pour any used liquid into a screw-top bottle. After a few days the sediment will settle leaving you with lots of clean turps at the top.

If you are switching paint colours regularly, and you don't want to keep washing out your paint kettle, just line it with kitchen foil. When you've finished with one colour, just throw the used foil away and replace with a clean sheet.

Never stand brushes in water when you take a break – it can swell the wooden handle and rust the metal ferrule.

To soak a brush without leaving it in the bottom of a jar, drill a hole halfway down the handle and push a pencil through it, then balance the brush across the opening of a jar.

To clean brushes, put the paint cleaner in a plastic bag along with the paint-brush. You can then rub the bristles with your fingers to get all the paint out.

Don't spend hours washing out rollers each night, just rinse out and place in a plastic bag and they will be ready to go in the morning.

If you've only got a small amount of paint left, don't leave it in a large tin. Put it into a screw-top jar, label it, and it will keep for years.

Store paint tins upside down to prevent a skin from forming.

Always keep white spirit in a jam jar with a lid to stop any evaporation.

Wear surgeons' gloves to keep your hands clean when painting.

To clean your palette, use a mixture of white spirit and soap.

Wallpapering

When stripping wallpaper, thoroughly soak all the paper at once with a 7-in/18-cm brush to make the paper easier to remove. Or use a paint roller dipped in hot water and washing-up liquid to wet the paper.

Add a tablespoon of bicarbonate of soda to warm water to make stripping wallpaper easier.

Write the number of rolls of paper used in that room next to the light switch before you finish decorating. It will save the calculations next time.

Keep left-over wallpaper paste into a screw-top jar to use on edges that haven't stuck down properly.

Shiny patches on wallpaper usually mean they have been rubbed too hard. Rubbing the area with a ball of white bread may help to remove the shine.

When wallpapering a ceiling get a friend to help, but bear in mind that you probably won't be friends afterwards.

Mix a small amount of paste even when you are hanging ready-pasted paper. The paste may have begun to dry before you have finished hanging a strip.

Use a matchstick to mark where fittings have been removed when hanging wallpaper. Push the matchstick into the screw hole just proud of the wall, and ease the matchstick through the paper when you smooth it over the wall.

If a ceiling is very uneven, don't cut the paper in advance of hanging it. Hang one piece and then match the next to it on the wall.

Use a left-over roll of wallpaper to measure how much paper you will need to paper a new room.

If you are going to wallpaper a room, paint a ½ inch/1 cm area around doors and windows. It is sometimes hard to line up paper completely flush with a door or window edge without leaving a gap.

Support your pasting brush by tying a piece of string across the rim of the bucket. You can rest your brush on the string when not using it and it's useful for wiping off excess paste too.

Even the pros get small blisters under wallpaper. They get rid of them by making a tiny clean cut with a sharp knife and then pressing down with a little extra paste.

When you have finished with your pasting brush, rinse it in salted water before washing. This gets rid of the paste and leaves the brush nice and soft.

To stick down a corner of wallpaper, damp the back with egg white. Let it go a bit sticky and then press down.

If you have to repair a bit of damaged wallpaper, tear a piece of matching wallpaper into an irregular shape (don't cut it because the regular straight lines will show up). Paste the patch and stick over the damaged area, making sure the pattern matches.

PERFUMIERS

Floris;
Caroline Samuels

Make sure your perfume is working for you – always apply it to your pulse points (behind the ears, nape of the neck, inside the wrists, the temples, the crook of the elbow, behind the knees and on the ankles). Perfume rises, so putting it on your lower body works well.

To create a 'voile' or veil of perfume, spray one or more fragrances into the air and walk through. It creates a subtle layer of fragrance all over your body, hair and clothes.

The higher the concentration of perfume, the longer the scent lasts – extrait or perfume has the highest concentration, followed by parfum de toilette and eau de parfum, then eau de toilette, eau de Cologne and, lowest of all, splash Cologne.

Perfumes should not be stored and kept for long periods of time as the fragrance and colour will begin to change. They will last up to three years if kept in a cool, dark environment.

Perfumes should be kept out of direct sunlight.

Keep perfumes away from heat too. They will not enjoy being stored over a radiator for example.

Store fragrance in a cool area as this best preserves the balance of the ingredients for longer. A cool, dark drawer or cupboard is the ideal longer term storage solution. (A fridge is not recommended as it may make the product go cloudy.)

The eau de parfum is more expensive because it contains a greater percentage of essential fragrance oils than an eau de toilette.

However, because the eau de parfum fragrance content is that much stronger you do not need so much of it to obtain the same effect. It will also be longer lasting on the skin.

What makes perfume last? This is determined by the blend of base note essential oils and fixatives used. Lighter fragrances, by their very nature, do not contain the base note essential oils that create more lasting power on the skin.

Each fragrant blend combines essential oils as top notes that evaporate on application to the skin, middle notes that evaporate less quickly and base notes that last many hours. The base notes also bind the more volatile essential oils together to increase their lasting power.

If you find your favourite fragrance has changed, it could because the formula has changed. The chemical reaction that a fragrance and the wearer's skin generate can also change. If you have been wearing a fragrance constantly for more than seven years, you may find that through the natural ageing process and the changes to your skin, the chemical reaction is different and so the fragrance smells different. The acidity level of the skin changes with the ageing process and this can easily react with a fragrance to present a differing fragrance on use.

Your sense of smell can change too – the olfactory system can deteriorate with age, which can lead to the loss of sensitivity to some fragrance notes.

When testing fragrances in a laboratory, all new products are tested at 39.2 °F/4 °C, room temperature and at 98.6 °F/37 °C for a minimum of three months. During this time, products are also tested on the skin, for light stability and for component compatibility.

Samples of each batch are kept and monitored for three years.

PERSONAL SHOPPERS

Catherine Fenwick;
Dickins & Jones,
London; Sally Fabian

Look the part – if you are going out to shop for an evening dress, wear the right underwear and take favourite necklaces and/or earrings with you to get the full effect.

The right underwear should be a flesh-coloured thong and flesh-coloured bra.

Ask to take the garment to the door. Shop lights can distort colour and you should see it in daylight. This is especially important if you are buying black.

Remember that buying shoes is affected by the time of day as your feet swell as the day wears on.

And when buying shoes, wear tights.

Shopping for skirts or trousers after a big lunch is a bad idea. Your stomach will have swollen.

It's a disaster to impulse buy.

Neither is it a good idea to be driven by trends. One high fashion item will be enough each season, especially if you are of a 'certain age'.

Try to remember what you have in your wardrobe at home and don't duplicate it when you're out shopping. You can also buy to complement what you already have.

Have a good wardrobe clear-out before you sally forth – be ruthless about getting rid of stuff that you know doesn't suit you.

But do hold on to classic pieces. They'll come back into fashion. Some clothes of your mother's can be really 'now'.

Take off your pop socks when trying on skirts and dresses. They look awful!

Don't wear too many clothes when you go out shopping. You'll get hot and bothered in over-heated shops and it will be too much to take off each time you try something on.

Try things on – don't guess!

Leave the children behind at home.

In fact don't take anyone with you – unless you are incapable of making decisions. You'll get a lot more done on your own and it's important to make it a time for yourself.

Don't shop till you drop. Take time out when shopping. It's surprisingly tiring, and stopping every hour or so for a break will keep your energy levels up.

Ask for the help of a personal shopper. They'll know what's in the store and what will suit you, and once they have your details on file, you can ring in advance even if it's just a pair of jeans you're looking for.

PERSONAL TRAINERS

Lynne Robinson, www.bodycontrol.co. uk; Harriet Morgan

When you go jogging on holiday or in a strange city, always take some identification on your person.

Climb stairs two at a time for a great bum toner.

Start each workout with a few minutes' relaxation.

The best time to exercise is in the late afternoon or evening when muscles are already warmed up. If you exercise in the morning, you'll have to spend longer warming up.

Clear your mind and focus on your body as you exercise. Concentrate on each movement and on relaxing the parts of your body that aren't involved.

Clear a space before you start – you don't want to have to keep stopping to move furniture.

Having strong pelvic floor muscles is *so* important. Some people have trouble isolating them but if you suck your thumb as you squeeze, concentrating on drawing the muscles up inside, you should have no problem!

Cross patterns in exercise are good for your brain as well as your body. Any kind of movement where the left arm is moved at the same time as the right leg, and vice versa, will do.

Exercise instructions can be complicated. Try taping yourself reading them out and work along with the tape. Be careful not to read too fast!

When using arm weights, start with half-kilo weights and work up gradually to two-kilos. You can improvise weights with a bag of rice or dried beans.

Small cans are fine for starting resistance work, but don't use big ones in an effort to increase the weight. If they're too big your hands will strain to keep hold of them.

Add sneaky exercises to your daily routine – do pliés while you make the packed lunches, leg raises while cleaning your teeth, clench and release your buttocks while on the phone and squeeze your pelvic floor at traffic lights.

You can do standing push-ups against a door-frame. Stand in the doorway, then take a step back. Place your hands against the door-frame at shoulder height then bend your elbows and smoothly straighten again. Start with five reps and work up from there.

Step-ups on the stairs are not quite as effective as a step class, because you can't vary the direction of stepping, but they can help to raise your heart rate. Be careful not to wear a hole in the carpet.

PEST CONTROLLERS

Small Pests

Pauline Pears, Ryton Organic Gardens, Warwick; Peter Bateman, East Grinsted; David Jones, London; Paul Hoyes, Foreward Environmental, Bristol; Clive Evers, Southend on Sea; Tony Stephens, Lingfield, Surrey

The most effective weapon against unwelcome creepy crawlies is the vacuum cleaner. Use it regularly and make sure you always clean under the furniture.

Woodlice like the damp. Sprinkle talcum powder around the kitchen and bathroom floors to create dry surfaces. The woodlice will soon look for alternative accommodation.

Woodlice are fond of house plants so don't put plants on window-sills and ledges; it will only encourage the woodlice to come into the house.

Get rid of booklice – give them a good blast with a hair-dryer on its hottest setting.

Bedbugs love a cosy bed so, contrary to everything your mother told you, don't make the bed! Simply leave the bedclothes folded back and the bugs will leave in search of a warmer home.

Sleep with your window open at night – this will keep the temperature too low for the bedbugs.

If you suffer from asthma, pop your pillow in the tumble dryer for 20 minutes on a hot setting to kill off any bedbugs that might be lurking there.

Beetles and small flies often lay their eggs in flour and sugar. Defy them by removing food substances from their paper packets and sealing them in airtight containers.

Moth eggs won't survive intense heat. If your clothes can stand it, give them a quick tumble dry on a high setting.

Little spiders grow up... into much bigger spiders. Plug up any holes in outside walls, however tiny, to stop the little ones crawling in.

Ants avoid any surface that has been treated, so keep them out by drawing a chalk line around the area you want protected.

Ants hate salt and pepper, so sprinkle a liberal dose wherever you need it to get rid of them.

To get rid of ants, sprinkle curry powder.

Aphids can wreck plants in hanging baskets. Spray the baskets with soapy water to kill off the aphids.

Worms on a golf putting green needn't be a handicap – try spraying soapy water on to the turf. All the worms will come to the surface and you can simply remove them to a more convenient place.

Entice slugs from your drain – pour turpentine down the drain. The slugs will come out and you can get rid of them permanently.

Or try putting a piece of board or hardboard down on the ground. The slugs will hide underneath it to get out of the sun. When you've got a fair crop, lift the board up and wreak vengeance!

To make a slug trap, bury an empty tuna can up to its neck in the garden. Put some beer in the bottom and leave it for the slugs to drop into.

Stop slugs coming into the house – lay a line of salt across the doorway. The slugs won't cross the line.

Keep flies away – hang up bunches of elderflower.

If bees have taken up residence in your chimney, light the fire. They'll soon leave and won't risk coming back – well, would you?

Never swat a wasp. Many species give off a distress signal when swiped and, before you know it, you could be surrounded by its family and friends!

When a wasp lands on you, he's looking for something to eat. Keep very still and he'll soon realise that there is no lunch laid on, and he'll fly off.

Attract wasps with a jar filled with jam. Add a splash of detergent and they'll drown more easily.

Mosquitoes hate vitamin B, so you could try eating copious amounts of vegetable extract (like Marmite) to stop them nibbling you.

For a useful mosquito deterrent set out a pint of stout – it's a pleasant way to keep them at bay.

Drive annoying insects away from you on a summer's day by drinking some tonic with a slice of lemon. The combination of quinine and citrus will put off most pests.

Catch lots of fleas in one go – fill a hot-water bottle with hot water, cover with double-sided sticky tape and then drag the bottle round the infected area. The fleas will jump on to the warm bottle and get stuck on the sticky tape.

Mice

You think you've got mice but you're not sure? Sprinkle flour where you believe them to be and next morning check it for footprints. If you're lucky, you can then track them to their hole.

Block up small holes to keep mice out. Mice can squeeze through the tiniest hole – if you can fit a pen through a space then it's big enough for a mouse.

Deter mice from entering your home by attaching a bristle strip to doorways.

Attract mice with their favourite titbits. Mice prefer fruit-and-nut chocolate to cheese… unless they live in Birmingham where the local rodent population have a yen for tuna (we kid you not; an earnest postgraduate student spent two years studying the phenomenon).

A humane way to catch a mouse is to use a wide-necked jar. Fill the bottom with broken chocolate biscuits (unless you're in Birmingham) and lean a ramp against the jar. The mouse will climb in but won't be able to get out. You can then release him outside.

A refreshing way to evict a mouse is to squirt minty toothpaste around the edges of its hole. Mice don't like the smell.

Double your chances of catching a mouse by placing the trap at right angles to the wall. Mice feel insecure in the middle of a room and are more likely to skirt the edges.

Other Wildlife

Keep squirrels and birds out of roof eaves and rafters by screwing chicken wire into tight balls and pushing it into any awkward holes or crannies.

Squirrels hate loud noise so try playing heavy-metal music at full volume. The neighbours will hate it but, more importantly, so will the squirrels.

Human hair deters the most determined rabbit from nibbling garden plants. If you're a bit thin on top due to the stress of your unwelcome visitors, ask a barber or hairdresser for cuttings to sprinkle around the base of the plants.

Moles hate any foul-smelling liquid – try pouring cleaning fluid or old flower water around the entrance to mole holes.

Alarm moles into leaving. Set an alarm clock and push it down the mole hole. Once it goes off, the moles should leave home.

Keep foxes out of the garden by spreading lion dung around the edges. You don't have to gather it yourself: just ask at the local zoo.

PHARMACISTS

Jane Meier

Prescription drugs may sometimes be cheaper and available to buy over the counter – ask when you hand in your prescription.

If you pay for your prescriptions and have more than a couple of items each month, it might work out cheaper to buy a prepayment certificate at quarterly or yearly intervals.

Ask your pharmacist if there is a cheaper, non-branded version of what you want to buy – the obvious example is Ibuprofen instead of Nurofen, but there are plenty of others.

There are some cooking ingredients that you can buy cheaply from a pharmacy, for example, citric acid for making home-made lemonade or liquid glucose for adding to cake icing.

You can buy oral syringes (which are very useful for measuring out small quantities of liquid, particularly if you have shaky hands), specimen bottles, dropper bottles and small ointment jars (ideal for taking cleanser away when travelling) – just ask what's available.

Local papers list rota chemists on a weekly basis, and list opening hours for bank holidays – very useful in a panic.

Most chemists carry catalogues featuring items that could be useful for special needs – walking sticks, bath rails, bottle openers and other implements for those with limited use of their hands, and more.

Don't forget that chemists carry information on many aspects of general health, from holiday health to care of the elderly and will have contact numbers for associated organisations.

PHOTOGRAPHERS

Camera Care

Maddie Attenborough, The Portrait Studio; Justin Quinnell; Nick Mather; Ray Lowe; Duncan Elson

When you're travelling, don't attract thieves by carrying your camera in its expensive carrying case. Put it in a normal canvas bag.

Make your camera batteries last longer – warm them underneath your armpit before use.

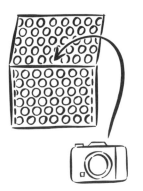

If you do drop your camera in the water, keep it submerged in a plastic bag full of water to stop the film from drying out and getting stains on the negatives. Take it to a developer as soon as possible.

Protect equipment from sand and water on holiday; take a large piece of bubble wrap, fold one-third back on itself and staple the two sides together to create an envelope for cameras and lenses.

When going through X-ray machines at the airport, make sure your films are wrapped in cooking foil to stop them getting foggy when they are being passed through the machine.

If you want to get biro marks off a photograph, rub the mark with some silver polish wadding. Then rub the same spot with some cotton wool… and the mark vanishes!

Taking Better Photos

Learn from your mistakes and from your successes. Make notes on photos you've taken.

Don't 'snatch' at a picture – when you're squeezing the shutter button, press it gently. If you do it too quickly, you can end up shaking the camera and getting a blurry picture.

A lens hood stops stray light coming into your lens so stick black tape around the edge of a lens on a compact camera to stop some of that reflective light.

You can make a lens hood from a washing-up liquid bottle, painted black and cut out to fit around the lens.

A margarine tub lid is good for DIY vignettes. Cut a hole in the middle of the lid, hold it over the lens, and your pictures will have hazy edges.

To create a soft edge to your shots, put sticky tape around the edge of your lens.

Add a new look to photos – stand on a wall. Getting up high changes the perspective and the nature of the shot completely – a trick that works wonders.

If you are taking photos with a timer, don't place the camera precariously on a wall. Half-fill a plastic bag with pasta, shells, sand, scrunched-up newspaper or beans and put the camera on that. It makes a soft and manoeuvrable base for the camera to rest on.

If you have an important set of photos that you are afraid might get lost during the developing process, take a photo of your name and address on the first frame so that there is a record of who the photos belong to. Also, stick a label with your name and address on the film canister.

Portraits & People

Shoot from the hip – literally – to capture spontaneous shots. People quickly become self-conscious if they see you holding up a camera.

To get the best portrait shots, focus on the eyes.

Ask people to take off their sunglasses so you don't get any reflections and you can see their eyes.

At weddings, don't tell everyone to smile because the end result is bound to look forced. Instead, ask everyone to blow a raspberry. They'll feel so silly they'll end up laughing and you can then take a lovely natural shot.

Once you've tried the raspberry technique, try pulling out a pair of frilly knickers to make everyone laugh for a second fun shot.

Get your subject to close their eyes and blow a raspberry before you take a shot of them. This helps to relax their jaw and mouth where tension and nervousness can show most.

To get a good portrait shot use the automatic wind-on. Take two portraits in quick succession (keep your finger on the shutter button); the second shot is usually the more relaxed… and therefore a better picture.

When taking a picture of a large group, it's a good idea to get yourself into an elevated position so that you can include the people hiding in the back.

To soften the image, put a cigarette paper, cling film or stocking over the lens. Or just breathe on the lens.

'Red eye' can spoil a shot. Avoid the problem by putting tracing paper over the flash. Or you could increase the light in the room.

If your subject is wearing glasses, check for any reflections in the viewfinder.

When taking a photograph of someone with a receding hair line, shoot from lower than eye-level.

If your subject is an older woman, don't use a flash because this shows up the wrinkles… and she won't thank you for that!

Try shooting towards the sun but use a flash to fill in the face so you can see the features. Shooting at this angle means that your subject is nicely backlit.

If there's not enough light, ask someone wearing a white or pale shirt to stand close by so that you can bounce some light off them. Or you could ask someone to hold up a white handkerchief.

To take a shot of people on a sofa, put a telephone directory on the sofa for the person in the middle to sit on. Sofas tend to dip in the middle, leaving one person looking a lot shorter than everybody else.

When taking pictures of children, get down on their level so that they fill the frame.

To keep a small child happy while you take a photo, give them a piece of sticky tape to play with. They'll be amused for ages while you concentrate on getting great shots.

To take a picture of a group of children, you want all of them looking at the camera at the same time… which can be difficult. Blow a whistle to get their attention and quickly take the picture.

If you are in a foreign country and you want to take a photo of one of the locals without being too intrusive or rude, take a Polaroid of them first and give it to them as a memento. It's a good way to get the ball rolling.

When in a photo booth, put an A4 sheet of white paper on your lap to reflect light under your chin, thus avoiding double chins. This is also flattering for people with fuller faces.

To show off your cheekbones in a photo booth, place black paper or card on either side of your face (out of shot) for the Dietrich look.

Landscapes & Still Life

When in the great outdoors, take only photographs and leave only footprints.

To keep a camera still, get a piece of string and attach one end to your camera. Make a loop at the other end and hook it under your foot. This creates tension, which will help to steady the camera.

For a muted effect, shoot through a magnifying glass.

Place Polaroid sunglasses over the lens to give landscape pictures a dramatic effect.

Early morning or late afternoon light creates a wonderful mood. The long shadows can make startling effects.

Taking a picture at an awkward or low angle can be made easier by resting the camera on a small bean bag. You can make your own bean bag by sewing 2 oz/50 g of dried beans into a cotton bag.

Don't be put off by shooting in the rain – you can get some wonderful results. Just pop your camera inside a clear plastic bag and when you're ready to take your shots, tear a hole in the bag for the lens to poke through.

Alternatively, snip the corners off a freezer bag and thread the camera straps through so you can cover the camera in the rain. Just raise the bag when you need to take a photo.

If you're going to be in really damp conditions, wrap your camera in cling film until you're ready to shoot.

PIANO TUNERS

Nigel Brown,
The Music Studios

Caring for a Piano

Putting a piano into storage is the quickest way either to ruin it completely, or to have to spend thousands getting it restored when it comes out. Lend it to a friend instead.

Never let anything spill into your piano. Once water gets into a piano, it is ruined.

Never keep things on top of your piano, as they will vibrate and alter the sound of the notes. Similarly, check that nothing in the room is likely to vibrate when the piano is played.

Before you stack pot plants and photographs on your piano, remember that there is already 15 to 20 tons of tension on the works in the piano, and a down-pressure on the soundboard of about 1 to 2 tons.

Covering the keys does not in fact protect them, as it allows moisture to build up under the fall (the lid which covers the keys). Keeping the fall up also exposes the keys to sunlight which stops them from discolouring.

On the other hand, keep the lid down on a grand piano, as at night the dust particles in a room cool down and attract moisture, and leaving the lid open allows moisture to collect in the works of the piano.

On pianos with a French polish finish, use turpentine or Brasso to maintain the polish.

For regular maintenance of a piano with a plain finish, use furniture polish.

For pianos with a plastic finish, use car-polishing materials, or the black polish for removing the scratches from black cars. These give a great finish and are anti-static.

Never use yellow dusters to polish your piano, as they are made from synthetic fibres, which can scratch the piano. Use the paper used for polishing cars.

Keep pianos away from radiators, as the dry heat they give out heats up the whole piano, which will put it out of tune.

Also keep pianos away from fires – either gas or wood, as the heat from these contains a lot of moisture, which damages the piano.

Older pianos were made using traditional scotch or hide glues, which are melted down and stick when they are liquid. Although this glue lasts for centuries, it also means that the piano will fall apart if it gets hot or wet.

Use methylated spirit to clean piano keys – or better still, wash your hands before playing!

Never touch the strings of a piano with your hands, as the oils on your skin will corrode them.

Felt is used under the pedals, under the keys, and in the workings of pianos. Good quality felt used on old pianos can last for the lifetime of the piano, but if the piano gets too dry, the felt dries and shrinks, which makes it loose and makes the piano rattle.

If the atmosphere is humid, the wood swells and won't ever return to its normal state. This can cost thousands of pounds to mend, and sometimes the damage is irreparable.

Because so much of the piano is made of wood and felt, it is important to keep the piano in a constant atmosphere. The atmosphere can either be damp and hot, or cold and dry. On average, a piano should be kept between 45 and 65 per cent relative humidity. If the temperature is 95 °F/35 °C, the piano can survive 90 per cent humidity, but if the temperature is only 50 °F/10 °C, the piano can probably only survive 35 to 45 per cent humidity (these figures are all relatively normal atmospheres anyway).

Lots of pianos were made in times before houses had central heating, and have been known to fall apart when they come into contact with a centrally heated atmosphere.

When cleaning ivory piano keys, use toothpaste on a damp cloth. Rub gently, rinse with milk, then buff.

If you're moving house, phone your nearest concert hall and ask if they can recommend a specialist remover.

These days it can be cheaper to buy a new piano than mend or restore an old one; restorations can cost between £4,000 and £6,000, but you can buy a good new piano for around £2,500.

Tuning

The piano wires have to be so tight that they are nearly at breaking point; a piano tuner is likely to get hit by a breaking wire at least once in their career. The wires are vicious and can cause deep gashes, so carry a first-aid kit.

In Britain, pianos are tuned to A440 hertz, which means that the pitch for the 'A' note is 440 vibrations per minute. The US pitch is 442 hertz. To change the pitch is arduous, and as pianos are the only instrument, other than the oboe, whose pitch is not easily tuned, the orchestra tunes either to the piano or the oboe.

Never let your piano get out of tune. The longer you leave it out of tune, the harder it will be to tune it, as the piano strings will settle in their out of tune state, and will always eventually pull back to that position, almost as if they have a 'memory'.

A piano needs regular play to keep it tuned. It goes out of tune very quickly when not played.

Tuning a piano is not about having a perfect pitch – what you are actually listening to are very high harmonics, as each note has three strings to it which must all be tuned relative to each other to reach the same pitch.

Piano tuners have such highly developed hearing that eventually all they can hear are high frequencies, and noises such as brakes squealing and cutlery scraping become excruciating.

In a group of 30 children, at least one is likely to be pitch sensitive. If the pianos at home, at school and at the music teacher's house are not tuned correctly to the same pitch, they will sound different to the child, which will confuse them, and their musical ability will probably be hindered.

PICTURE FRAMERS

Kitty Anderson

If you tear the paper when framing a picture, stick the torn edges together with some flour and water for an invisible join.

To mend a hole in paper, mash some of the same paper type with a little flour and water and fill in the hole. Allow the repair to dry.

Never use transparent masking tape to hold a picture in place because, in time, the tape will exude a damaging rubber solution.

To mount delicate items, use stamp hinges.

To draw the eye towards a picture, use a dark mount.

A grey mount is best for bright pictures because it doesn't distort the colours.

The correct size for a mount should be, on average, one-fifth of the picture size.

To cut an oval or round mount, draw around a bowl or dish.

You can pull a group of different pictures together by using the same colour mount for all of them.

When hanging two pictures next to each other, the gap between the two should be the same width as the mounts.

When framing pastels, always use a mount to separate the glass from the picture. Otherwise, your beautiful picture will smudge.

Wet backing paper before sticking it down – this way it will firm up as it dries and remain taut.

To give paper an authentic distressed look, gently wipe over with a used tea-bag.

For an attractive effect on plain frames, apply one colour and allow to dry. Then add a contrasting colour and gently rub the frame with wire wool so that a little of the first coat shows through.

To add lustre to old master reproductions, use a suede or leather mount.

Clean gilt picture frames with a mixture made from one egg and a teaspoon of bicarbonate of soda.

To stop a picture slipping sideways, wrap sticky tape around the centre of the wire.

To hang a very heavy mirror or picture, brass chain is stronger than picture wire.

If you're hanging a picture above a seat, make sure there's enough space for someone to lean back without knocking the picture.

Don't hang a lone picture against a bold wallpaper pattern because it tends to disappear into the pattern. Group it with other pictures if possible.

Nails will take more weight from a hanging picture if driven pointing down into the wall.

Don't damage your pictures. They should never be hung in direct sunlight or above radiators or heaters.

Hold panel pins in place using an old comb.

To remove a dent from a canvas, gently dab the back with some damp cotton wool. As the canvas dries, it will contract and flatten out the dent.

To judge whether insect holes in a wooden frame are fresh, check for fine dust on the floor and surfaces below the picture.

PIGEON FANCIERS

Mr Francis

To help make your pigeons go faster, put them on the train when transporting them. They prefer it to modern-day transporters.

For faster flight, try something called 'widowhood'. Separate the hen from the cock, then put them back together for a short time during the night. Then separate them again and the cock should fly home faster to be reunited with his mate!

To help get a ring on a pigeon, smear it – the ring, not the pigeon – with petroleum jelly.

To buy food at the best price, get it directly from the farmer at harvest time.

To stop your birds' food getting wet, place an old jam jar at an angle in a ball of cement and leave it to set. This makes a good, sturdy feeder and the food will stay dry.

To help the birds when they are moulting, feed them linseed as well as regular corn.

Look out for your hen bird – watch that the cock bird doesn't punish the hen too much.

To keep the peace over the winter, separate the sexes.

To cut down on fighting, make sure that the number of nesting boxes corresponds to the number of pairs. If there are too many boxes, some pairs will use more than one and this can start fights.

PLAYGROUP LEADERS

Diana Cockerton, RSC
Nursery; Helen Cox

Before you throw away empty cereal packets or washing-powder boxes, cut out the large letters individually, and keep them in a box for spelling games.

Don't overwhelm small children with choices. Structure their environment by putting out a selection of toys and activities, and changing them round after a few days.

A completely new environment is very confusing for a child. Give them time to explore a new location in their own time.

Having 'news time' at the start of every playgroup session helps children learn to listen, speak and take turns, and can give valuable cues about how the child is feeling that day.

You can make absolutely anything fun – especially the routine clearing up jobs – if you let the children join in and feel they're taking responsibility.

Before you try to teach anything to a child, find out what they can do and build on that. It will make them feel far more valued and involved.

Pencils with a triangular profile are easiest to hold for small hands, and encourage a good pencil grip.

Children need to be able to control big movements before they can move on to small ones. Practise drawing shapes in the air, or 'painting' on a wall or fence using an emulsion brush and clear water.

Big chalks are great fun for pavement drawing.

Try not to limit children's creativity by channelling their ideas too strictly. Listen to what they say and take your cue from them.

If it's getting too rowdy, try talking more and more softly – even whispering – so the children have to be quiet to hear what you're saying. If you shout, they'll shout.

Clapping games are fun and encourage careful listening. Clap the rhythm of each child's name and see if they can guess who it is.

Get a good supply of reward stickers and make liberal use of them. Try to make a note of who you've given them to – it can be crushing for a child not to get one when everyone else has.

Try to ignore the use of rude words. If it's clear that you're not shocked, the children won't derive so much fun from saying them.

If you need a nice, quiet game, ask the children to shut their eyes and listen while you make a noise, such as shaking a bunch of keys, or tapping a spoon against a glass of water. See if they can guess what it is.

Have a set of simple commands that you use regularly, such as 'Busy fingers!' to get all the children to put down what they're playing with and wiggle their fingers in the air, or 'Ears up!' to get them all standing up and cupping their ears.

Make discipline an interesting part of other activities as in: 'See how quietly you can close the door', or 'See if you can sit on your chair all through the meal'.

Try to resist helping a child just to speed things up. If they can do up their buttons – let them, unless you're in a great rush to go out.

Games that can help with early writing skills include: transferring rice or sand from one bowl to another using a teaspoon, putting clothes pegs around the outside of a plate, screwing nuts and bolts together.

A child with a floppy pencil grip will be encouraged if you let them use a softer pencil, such as a 2B, because it will make a good dark mark without much pressure.

Let children draw on window-panes with felt-tips, for an interesting change. They can try tracing the shapes they see outside, then help with cleaning once they have finished.

To encourage early letter formation, don't do a dot-to-dot shape for your child – they won't get a smooth action. Instead, draw the letters and shapes with a highlighter pen and let them draw over your line.

PLUMBERS

George Wingfield;
Andy Greenfield;
Simon Mitchell; The
Institute of Plumbing;
National Association
of Plumbing; Peter
Baker

Always know where the main stopcock is. If you have an emergency, like a burst pipe, you will need to get to the stopcock quickly. If you don't know where it is, put this book down and go and find your stopcock – try looking under the kitchen sink.

Make sure your stopcock is in good working order. When you have found it, make sure you can turn it on and off. To turn it off, go clockwise; you will have done it properly if no water comes out of the kitchen tap when it's turned on. If you can get water from the tap, the washer probably needs replacing.

Ensure that your stopcock doesn't jam. Open and close it several times a year. When you have opened it, give it a quarter turn clockwise. This should stop it jamming without interrupting the flow of water.

To make sure your main stop valve opens and closes freely, avoid painting it as this can make it inoperable.

When changing the washer on a tap, start the job in the morning. That way, if you have the wrong size or you need some other equipment, the shops will still be open.

Always put the plug in the sink when you are taking a tap to pieces just in case you drop anything – you don't want it disappearing down the plug-hole.

To prevent scarring on chrome and gold tap fittings, use a thick cloth between the jaws of a wrench whilst carrying out any maintenance.

To prevent limescale build-up, clean your shower heads at least every three months.

To lubricate new O-ring seals, use petroleum jelly, not oil.

To open up a drain-cock, you don't need a special key – you can use a pair of pliers. The drain-cock is at the lowest part of the system for when you need to drain the parts that cannot be drained from the kitchen or bath taps.

Drain-cocks sometimes become clogged with debris. You can clean them out using a straightened paper clip but be prepared for some flooding!

To clean out a blocked loo pan, use an old string mop. A couple of plunges should do the trick.

To stop an overflow from your cistern, place a wooden spoon across the cistern and tie the lever arm, attached to the ball float, to the spoon. If you need to flush the loo, you will have to release the arm to fill the cistern. Tie it up again when you have finished.

If the ball float in your loo has a leaky valve and the cistern is about to overflow, you can make a temporary repair. Unscrew the float and empty it (you may have to make a hole to get the water out). Screw the float back on and wrap it in a plastic bag to keep water out. You can then replace the float with a new one later.

To clear blockages in sinks or basins, cover overflow holes with a damp cloth to build up pressure while you use a plunger.

If your pipes have frozen, you can melt the ice by putting hot-water bottles over the pipes. Or you can use a hair-dryer to blow warm air on to the pipe. Don't use a blow torch or anything similar – you may end up setting the house on fire.

If a pipe has split, wrap torn strips of fabric tightly around the break, put a bucket underneath to catch any drips and call a qualified plumber.

To avoid damaging taps, use a spanner that's the right size rather an adjustable wrench.

If a spanner is too big, you can introduce a shim to make it the right size – a feeler gauge from a car, or a 5p piece.

Bal-o-fix valves on the supply pipe to each tap, cistern or radiator mean that you can isolate each one individually.

Pipe hammer or judder (ticking noises from pipes) is usually caused by loose pipes or they may be passing through something that they are rubbing against. Can melt candlewax round the pipe to lubricate it. Try spray polish diagnostic.

Have a stop tap on the cold-water feed from a head tank, otherwise you will have to drain off the head tank or bung it.

If you take off a radiator to decorate, add a limescale-prevention product to the central heating head tank because the new water you introduce may be limey.

Bleed radiators with the return valve closed so you don't suck air back into the system, but you'll have to rebalance the system afterwards by opening the return valves again and checking to make sure the radiators are uniformly hot.

Put a cloth over the valve you're bleeding to prevent mucky water staining the walls, radiator or you.

If you're replacing a washer, take the old one with you – there are loads of different sizes.

If your loo is very slow to fill, the plumber may have fitted a high-pressure inlet nozzle to a low-pressure system. Both are supplied when new, so check to see if the correct nozzle is still attached to the ball valve. The low-pressure one will have a bigger hole.

POSTMEN

The Post Office

Address, Postcode & Stamp

Mail should always be clearly addressed and include the postcode. Customers can call 0845 7111222 (calls charged at local rates) for the postcode of any UK address, or visit the Royal Mail website at www.royalmail.com

Putting the sender's address in small print on the back of an item helps us to return any mail that we cannot deliver, without having to open it.

Sorting machinery automatically searches for the postcode on the last line of an address so make sure the postcode is there.

Commas and full stops can confuse optical character recognition machinery so don't use them when addressing an item.

Don't use 'near' or 'by' when addressing as it can confuse sorting machinery – the postcode is enough to ensure the item gets through.

Place stamps at the top right hand corner of the envelope or package because this is where our sorting machinery automatically looks for them.

If stamps or gummed labels get stuck together, cover them with a sheet of paper and press them gently with a warm iron. They should separate easily.

Use an ultra-violet marker to write your postcode on property around the house, and on laptop computers, briefcases and similar items. This can help police to identify stolen items and reunite them with their owners.

Packaging

Mail should always be well wrapped to prevent loss or damage to contents or other mail, and injury to postmen or recipients.

Envelopes should always be sealed. There is no cheaper rate for unsealed envelopes.

For larger items, use cartons that are appropriate for the weight of the item to be sent. The boxes that goods are sold in are not always suitable without extra packaging or stiffening.

Strong tape should be used to cover all openings to prevent them from catching on other items.

Any metal fastenings or staples should be flattened and covered with tape to prevent them causing injury or catching on other items.

For packing, we recommend polystyrene chips, polyethylene foam sheeting, bubble wrap, shredded paper (inland only), moulded polystyrene blocks, crushed or corrugated paper or wood wool.

Padded envelopes are perfect for paperback books but for larger books use a corrugated fibreboard book pack with 1 in/2.5 cm clearance at the ends.

CDs, cassettes and computer discs should be packed in material that will protect the item from magnetic fields. We recommend either a rigid purpose-made container or wrapping the item in at least 1 in/2.5 cm of soft packaging.

Films should be individually labelled with the sender's name and address, and packed in a string envelope.

Marking the weight of heavy items on the box helps to avoid lifting injuries.

Keys can damage sorting machinery if they get loose so they should be packed in a padded envelope with details on an attached label.

Make sure that tins or bottles containing liquids and creams, such as cosmetics, are sealed with tape, wrapped in polythene, sealed once again and then packed in absorbent material such as sawdust or newspaper in a fibreboard or polystyrene container.

Powders such as tea-leaves or instant coffee should be sealed first in a strong polythene bag and then placed in a rigid corrugated board box.

Sharp items like knives and scissors should have heavy cardboard wrapped around all sharp edges to avoid injury.

When packing framed pictures, each picture should be sandwiched between two pieces of hardboard or polystyrene slabs that overlap each side by at least 1 in/2.5 cm. At least 2 in/5 cm of soft packing should be placed between the frame and the boards.

Delivering

Please keep dogs and other animals under control. Dog bites are painful and distressing and may result in a suspension of deliveries to the address where the dog owner lives.

Some letter flaps are sprung to seal in the heat. They can really snap on your fingers and cause a lot of pain. Using both hands to post letters and flyers helps avoid this. Push the flap open with one hand and push the letters through with the other.

Keep your hands strong and supple by exercising with a strong elastic band. Place the tip of your thumb against the tips of your fingers, slide a thick rubber band round your knuckles, then spread your fingers apart against the resistance of the band. Return to the starting position and repeat ten times in all.

Post Office Counters

Make sure that you have all the relevant documents with you when you apply for your motor vehicle licence – photocopies are not acceptable at the counter.

If you have a number of bills to pay in one go, you can just write one cheque payable to Post Office Counters Ltd to pay them all.

If you are travelling to a European Economic Area country, get an E111 form (in a booklet called Health Advice for Travellers). This is available from post offices, and needs to be filled in and stamped at the counter. It's free and will help you to claim free or reduced-cost health care in those countries. It is not, however, a substitute for having travel insurance. (EEA countries are Austria, Belgium, Denmark, Finland, France, Germany, Gibraltar, Greece, Iceland, Republic of Ireland, Italy, Liechtenstein, Luxembourg, the Netherlands, Norway, Portugal, Spain and Sweden.)

If you are going on holiday, you can order foreign currency and traveller's cheques from most post office branches, and save yourself a trip into town.

If you are applying for a photocard driving licence and hold a UK passport, you can have your application checked with the passport at a main post office (for a small fee) without having to send your passport to the DVLA.

Fill in any forms that you need for services like Royal Mail Special Delivery before you get to the counter to save a little time.

When collecting pensions or allowances, make sure that you put your money safely away in a wallet or purse before leaving the post office.

POTTERS

Whichford Pottery, www.whichford pottery.com; Robin Wade, www.clayworks.co.uk

Repairs

Araldite and brick dust mixed will fill in a crack or a chip on a terracotta pot.

A clean break can be fixed (at least temporarily) with Araldite.

A large, broken pot with a rim can be fixed by wrapping a piece of strong wire round the pot under the rim, then twisting to make it tight.

Keep broken pots to use as crocks in the base of newly planted pots.

To fix a large pot, car-repair webbing and resin can be applied on the inside – it'll last for years. Get all the bits clean and dry, and remove algae and soil with a wire brush. Use car-repair chemical metal to join the pieces together and, before it dries, rub off any excess on the outside, on the inside use fibreglass tape and resin. To disguise the join, paint on resin (using a throw-away brush) and sprinkle with dust from a matching pot.

Tap a pot with your knuckle – if it rings true, it's sound.

Pots Outside

There's no point putting frost-proof pots up on little feet – it doesn't do anything and makes them unstable.

To weather a new pot, paint with a mixture of garden lime and water.

Imported pots are rarely fired to an appropriate temperature to make them frost proof – stick to British!

A rough texture round the rim of a pot will help deter slugs and snails.

Moving Pots

To transport a big pot, the back seat of the car with a seat-belt is ideal.

To transport empty pots by car, turn them upside down for greater stability. Put something soft, like a duvet, on top to stop them bouncing.

Pack pots inside each other separated by wood wool rather than bubblewrap, which allows them to bounce.

When moving a large pot on a trolley or wheelbarrow, place it on a clean, preferably non-metal surface, like a piece of wood. Even a small piece of grit on a metal surface can act as a pivot that could break the base in two.

Making Your Own Pots

Make sure your pot is at the right height before you start work – you won't want to stop and change it in the middle.

You can make pots with flat sheets of clay rolled out like pastry – use clay or modelling material.

Always roll clay on an absorbent surface. Unvarnished wood, or fabric is suitable – you could use a chopping board or tea towel. Avoid shiny wood or formica.

Roll the clay using a wooden roller.

Old bank cards are ideal for smoothing the surface of a pot before drying.

Clay sheets can be draped around or over almost any form so long as it can be lifted off with no overhang.

Make a simple vessel to use as a vase, pencil holder or utensils container. Wrap a piece of cloth around a Pringles tube, and fix it round firmly with sitcky tape. Wrap your clay around the cloth-covered tube and join down the length. Make a round base, and join this to the clay tube by smoothing around the edge.

To make it more interesting, before you wrap the clay around the tube, lay some leaves, grasses or simple flowers on the clay surface and gently roll the pin across it to leave an impression in the clay. This will make an attractive surface design on the finished work. No drawing skills needed!

PUBLICANS

Anton Paul

Save money when throwing a party by buying beer in small barrels or firkins. Your local landlord will advise you on what to buy and where to get it. It tastes much better, too.

If you haven't got time to chill beer for your guests, just chill the glasses instead.

People often say they like dry white wine best but in blind tastings medium comes out on top. Choose medium for the safest bet at a dinner party.

All wines benefit from being decanted – even if you only use a simple jug.

Don't risk your own glasses. All drinks retailers now provide free glass hire when you buy your booze from them.

If champagne starts to fizz over as you are pouring it, discreetly dip one of your fingers into the glass!

Keep the bubbles popping. Champagne bubbles go flat instantly if they come into contact with detergent so make sure your glasses are squeaky clean. Fill the glasses to the top so the bubbles last longer.

Store wine horizontally to keep the corks soft.

Get your wine ready before your guests arrive – white wine needs to be chilled for about an hour and red wine should be opened at least an hour before you intend to drink it.

Tie your tools down! When you throw a party, tie the bottle opener and cork screw on to a length of string attached to something immovable. They have a habit of disappearing just when you need them.

Remember the 'designated drivers' and non-drinkers. Always have enough soft drinks. Try mixing fruit juice with mineral water rather than just having lots of fizzy drinks.

Make drinks fun by adding food colouring.

It's difficult to judge how much people will drink so for a big event buy your drink on a use-or-return basis. Be on the safe side and order more than you think you'll need.

To avoid wax on your tablecloths, put a beer mat under the candles.

PUBLIC SPEAKERS

Miranda Powell

Practise speaking in public by going to a local lecture or public meeting where you can ask a question out loud.

Get used to the sound of your own voice. Keep practising your speech out loud.

Ask someone to video you while you practise so that you can see where you are getting things right or wrong.

Try your speech out on a friend. Ask them to eliminate any irritating habits, such as 'I mean' and 'you know'.

When you rehearse your speech, always do it standing up so that it will feel like second nature on the day.

Try to appear confident – even if you're not! Don't cross your arms or legs. Stand tall.

Avoid confusion. Find out how long you are required to speak for, you don't want to talk for too short (or too long) a time.

Keep perfecting phrases – use a thesaurus.

Don't try to learn your speech off by heart – it's hard enough to give a good speech without putting this sort of extra burden on yourself. Nobody minds if you put your speech on paper and refer to it from time to time.

Put your speech on to small cards – a phrase or point per card – so that you can speak clearly and succinctly.

Make sure your cards are stiff. You don't want your notes to wobble as your hands hold them; people might think you are trembling with nerves!

Don't be afraid to use a microphone. It's much easier once you get used to it and it's better than having people in the back rows straining to hear what you are saying.

It helps to feel that you have something in front of you. Ask for a lectern or a table.

Keep your audience interested. Try to involve them as much as possible.

Encourage a few laughs. It actually helps the audience to stay alert because people take in lots of oxygen when they chuckle!

If you get lost or forget what you should be saying, try a big smile for a moment. It will disguise any nerves and give you a moment to get back en route.

RAMBLERS

Jacquetta Fewster, Claire Madron, Charlotte Prager at The Ramblers' Association, www.ramblers.org.uk; Bernard Cheek

Getting footwear right is crucial. Whether you prefer boots, wellies (to keep dry) trainers or sandals the main thing is that you feel comfortable and that the footwear doesn't rub.

Make sure your socks and boots or shoes fit properly, and attend to any problems at the first sign of rubbing. Sheep wool in between the toes helps on longer hikes. There are lots of products available from chemist shops that can be taken with you to put on if you get rubbing.

When you sit down for lunch take off your socks and swap them over. Any places that were rubbing are relieved at once.

GORP – stands for 'good old raisins and peanuts' – the rambler's friend!

In case you have an accident – leave a note clearly visible on the dashboard inside your car, stating your route and departure time.

Suffer from sore knees? Walking sticks or poles take a huge amount of weight off your legs if you are walking regularly.

For clothing, the mantra is comfort. Don't wear anything too tight or unwieldy. Skin-tight jeans may look fabulously sexy – until you get stuck climbing over a stile or the skin on your inner thighs is sore from chafing. Denim takes a long time to dry and doesn't protect you from the wind. If it gets wet, you can get very cold.

There is no need to splash out on any high-tech gear unless you really want to. Loose layers will keep you cool, dry and allow freedom of movement.

If investing in a jacket, make sure you have one with a hood – nothing is more miserable than rain down the back of your neck.

Walking on your own can be a wonderful, enriching experience – easily as much fun as in a group. But do make sure you tell someone where you are planning to go and what time you expect to return.

If you are trying out an unfamiliar route, calculate how long you expect it to take you – then add at least half an hour. This saves stressful struggles back to catch trains, buses or last orders. Always make sure you know when the sun sets and aim to return well before nightfall (unless you are planning a night walk that is).

Always make sure there is a really good pub (or tea shop) at the end of your walk – great incentive to get to the finish and a welcome reward.

When packing your rucksack, don't put the heaviest things at the bottom. And always use your hip straps. The weight will be more evenly distributed and you will save energy if the heavier things are higher up in your rucksack and your hip belt is fastened.

Make sure you have plenty of fluids with you.

Dried fruit is better for giving you energy than chocolate bars.

Lean forwards when walking up hill.

Carry a torch with you. If you are lost in the hills, the mountain rescue will be able to detect the tiniest amount of light, much easier than the noise of a whistle.

Carry a washing-up brush with you on your walks. It's much more fun cleaning your boots in a stream at the end of the walk rather than under the tap at home when the mud is caked on hard.

The Ramblers' Association is a walking charity that was established in 1935 to promote walking for all and to campaign to protect the countryside, open footpaths and secure a freedom to roam. Today, it has 130,000 members and 400 walking clubs. It has won legal protection for all Britain's public footpaths, is on the verge of winning greater public access to some areas of mountain, moorland, heath, down and common land, and has helped millions of people start walking, whether for health or for fun. Walking is now the nation's most popular form of regular exercise.

REMOVERS

Dennis Auld; Matthew Mackay; Eric Delo, Coventry; Priscilla Chase

Before the Move

Shop around for the right price – removal firms usually give quotations free of charge. Get quotes from two or three firms before you make your final choice.

The cheapest removal company isn't necessarily the best. You get what you pay for and a more expensive firm will have enough people and boxes to move you efficiently.

Even after you have had the estimate, telephone the removal company to check the date is confirmed before sending out the deposit.

Always make sure your take out good insurance with the removal company.

Avoid being charged overtime. Don't move on a Friday, over the weekend or over a bank holiday.

You can cut the cost – some removal firms charge less if you do part of the packing or unpacking yourself. Discuss this beforehand with your removal firm.

Give your removers a clear idea of how much they're going to have to move – don't forget to show them the contents of your shed, garage, loft and cellar.

Lists, lists, lists. Long before your removals day make a note of correspondence you receive (opticians, dentist, vet, TV licence, car registration and so on) so you can inform them of your new address.

Before you move, make sure you've told the electricity, gas, water and telephone suppliers, organised the disconnection of the cooker/ washing machine, cancelled the milk and papers, sent out your change of address cards and got a bottle of champagne ready to put in the fridge of your new home.

Make sure the driveways and access are reasonable, at both the house you are moving from and to, or the lorry will not be able to get close enough.

Liaise with your neighbours about leaving enough space for the removal company's lorry.

If you have to provide your own boxes, make friends with the local supermarket. Banana boxes are ideal for moving house.

Start collecting old newspapers well before you move. You will need a lot for packing.

Ask your local electrical retailer if they have any spare boxes with polystyrene shavings that you can use for your TV, video, computer and hi-fi system.

To help the new occupiers of your home, collect all the relevant keys of the house together and clearly label them.

Packing & Transporting

Labels, labels, labels. Make sure you have bought enough labels to mark items to go in particular rooms in your new home.

Organise the packing so that boxes are packed by room. Otherwise you'll have cake tins in with your toilet brush.

Use a coding system to label boxes. This makes it easier to identify which room a box should go into for unpacking; for example, you could use a colour-coding system: red for the kitchen, blue for the dining room and so on. Label the side of the box, not just the top.

Protect china plates by packing a paper plate in between each one.

Make certain that curtains are easily accessible. You will need them to cover windows on the first night.

To protect furniture during the move, use rugs to cover anything that could be scratched or damaged.

Protect your hands while packing and unpacking – wear gloves.

Don't pack boxes full of books because you won't be able to lift them (or you'll do your back in) – only fill them half full.

Prevent creased carpets – don't fold them, just roll them.

Don't be tempted to move yourself long distance. It is often cheaper to hire professional removers rather than make a large number of long journeys in a hired van.

When moving large objects yourself (such as a freezer or cooker), check the size of van doors and try to hire one with a ramp or a hydraulic lift.

It's easy to forget the contents of the freezer. Make sure you have removed all items and defrosted it before it's moved.

To move a freezer with food still inside, ensure that it is no more than a quarter full, that it is on maximum freeze for at least 24 hours before disconnection and that you don't open the door while it is switched off.

To transport a fridge – always carry it upright.

When moving your washing machine, make sure you immobilise the revolving drum first.

If you're not sure how to move your pets safely, call an animal welfare organisation in advance for advice.

On the Day

If necessary, book a cleaner to clear up as you pack, and to follow you to your new home to clean up there before you unpack. You don't want to move into someone else's dirt.

Don't leave important bags or keys lying around. They will end up being packed in the van.

Think about farming out your children to friends for the first night. This will give you space to move in and prepare their rooms.

Keep children amused and as settled as possible – make sure that you keep their favourite toys handy and that they aren't packed away at the back of the van!

You'll get more out of your removal men if you offer them a bribe like fish and chips if they will put in a couple of extra hours.

Pack a box of essential items for the actual day of the move – kettle, tea, coffee, mugs (enough for the removal men), pens and notepaper, light bulbs, torch, string, hammer, pliers, nails, adaptors, loo paper and aspirin. You will also need cleaning equipment and lots of bin bags. Label the box clearly so that it is not packed.

Don't run out of money on the day – you may want to buy a take-away meal, make an emergency dash to the shops for supplies, buy a bottle of wine or even tip your removal men!

To make unpacking easier, put your carpets in the van last so that they can go down first before any furniture.

When you arrive at your new home, make sure the entrance hall is protected from dirty footmarks as people tramp to and fro with furniture and boxes.

RESTAURATEURS

Tables & Settings

Patricia Sedgwick, Crosby Lodge Country Hotel, Carlisle; Judy and David Green, Teviotdale Lodge Country Hotel, Hawick; Giles Hine, Corse Lawn Hotel; Nick Jefford, Lygon Arms Hotel, Broadway; Steven Morris, Grafton Manor Hotel; Richard Niazi, Sarastros, Drury Lane, London; Mini Chutrakal, Busabong Tree, London

Always set your dining room table with candles. Apart from looking pretty, they disperse strong smells.

To make candles burn brightly, soak the wicks in vinegar.

If you get candle wax on your tablecloth, heat a spoon over the candle. Then place a piece of wet newspaper over the wax and rub the hot spoon over the newspaper to melt the wax, which will then come off the tablecloth and stick to the paper.

A few grains of rice in the salt cellar will ensure it stays dry and fresh.

To keep brown sugar really fresh, put a small piece of brown bread in with the sugar.

Keep flowers fresh for longer – add a splash of lemonade to their water.

Dirty ashtrays look so ugly. Keep them clean with an old shaving brush.

Don't panic if you've forgotten to heat the plates. Just splash with hot water and pop them in the microwave for a few seconds (check that your china is microwave proof first).

To make your plates gleam like new, rinse in a weak solution of water and vinegar.

Good-quality china will really sparkle if soaked in denture-cleaning tablets.

It really is simple to impress your guests with hot cleansing towels after a dinner party. Just wet some clean flannels with water and a splash of eau de Cologne, loosely wrap in cling film and heat in the microwave for about a minute.

Inexpensive firelighters can be created from the stubs of burnt-down candles, orange peel or matchboxes filled with old matches and a bit of candle wax. Waxed milk cartons are excellent for bigger blazes.

Once your fire is going, a few digestive biscuits thrown in make it burn like fury.

For a pretty Christmas napkin ring, dry a slice of orange with the middle cut out.

Dairy Delight

Keep cartons of double cream fresher for longer by turning the carton upside down in the fridge.

To make really light whipped cream, add a dash of icy cold water just before you do the final whip.

For an instant and healthy milkshake, whisk together equal quantities of yoghurt and milk.

Make a truly de luxe creamy porridge by stirring in a scoop of quality vanilla ice-cream during cooking.

If honey is too runny, give it a ten-second blast in the microwave on the high setting. This will thicken it up slightly.

Stop the sides of cheddar cheese going hard and waxy – spread a thin layer of butter over it before you wrap it up and put it away for the night.

In the Kitchen

Always store cooked foods above uncooked food in a fridge. This avoids raw juices dripping on to cooked food, which is the quickest way to food contamination.

Eggs will stay fresher for longer if stored pointed end down.

There's nothing worse than a stale-smelling fridge. Put a few charcoal bricks at the back to keep it smelling fresh and clean.

If you've got ants in your kitchen, direct them towards something sweet in one corner and annihilate them there.

Kill off germs in kitchen cloths – heat damp cloths for several minutes in a microwave.

When freezing big bags of ice, sprinkle the cubes with some soda water to stop them all sticking together in lumps.

Don't despair if you burn a pan – boil up some sliced onions and water in the pan, and leave for several hours.

Alternatively, boil up some water and vinegar in it and leave overnight. It will be easier to clean in the morning.

If you have a discoloured aluminium pan, boil up a weak solution of rhubarb or tomatoes in it. The food acids lift the stain.

To clean baked-on food from a cooking pan, put a sheet of fabric conditioner in the pan and fill with water. Leave overnight and then next day the food will just lift off with a sponge.

Polish up cutlery using a cork, soaked in water and scouring powder. Rinse and buff with a soft cloth.

Clean a grotty roasting tin (not aluminium or non-stick) with a solution of washing soda and water boiled up in the tin. Rinse and then dry in a cool oven.

To remove barbecue fat stains from your patio, cover with cat litter, grind with your heel, leave for half a day, then sweep up.

Pep up your potted plants – put some old tea-bags in to their soil.

To clean perspex and get rid of scratches, rub with toothpaste, then buff up with a cloth.

As a rule sharp knives are safer than blunt ones.

Never store vinegar in a metal container – the acidity will affect the metal.

Never cover an entire oven rack in foil – it stops the air circulating so your food will take longer to cook.

Different types of baking dish produce different results. Dark, dull pans produce crispy crusts (so suitable for pies); shinier ones give more delicate results (so good for cakes).

To make cutting raisins and other sticky things easier, coat the blade of your knife with vegetable oil.

To keep fruit and veg in your fridge nice and fresh, place a dry sponge at the bottom of the salad drawer – it will absorb excess moisture and stop food going rotten.

Store kitchen bits and bobs such as piping bag ends in empty film canisters to save losing them.

Reuse good quality storage bags – just wash thoroughly and dry.

Plastic containers from your supermarket are great for storing herbs, left-overs or for freezing stock.

Filter coffee left-overs are excellent for removing grease from stainless steel.

Get to the Meat

If sliced ham or tongue has dried out, soak it in a little milk for five minutes to restore its flavour and texture.

Does the meat seem a bit tough? Squirt a little lemon juice on to it before carving.

Your bacon will be really crisp if you trim the rind with pinking shears before cooking it.

If you need to reduce fat, but love the taste of bacon, try using turkey rashers as a substitute – they're virtually fat free.

For a low-fat gravy, try separating the meat juices and fat by pouring them into a jug and adding ice cubes. The ice will cool down the gravy quickly, allowing you to spoon off the fat straight away.

To make top-quality meat gravy, wait until the fat has solidified and then remove it from the liquid.

Make your own marinade for pork: use a tablespoon of honey mixed with grated ginger – sweet and spicy.

For a more subtle flavour in chilli con carne use lemon or lime rind grated into the mix.

Try placing a layer of cream crackers or Pringles on top of the sauce in a shepherd's pie or cottage pie – they'll absorb the juices from the sauce and keep the mashed potato fluffy.

To tenderise meat cover it with slices of kiwi fruit for about 15 minutes.

At Christmas baste your turkey with fruit juice for that extra bit of taste.

To roast a turkey evenly, begin roasting it upside down and only turn it right side up after about 45 minutes.

To add a bit more flavour to the turkey, before cooking the bird, lift up the skin and rub olive oil and herbs on to the meat.

To stop a turkey sticking to tin foil during cooking, place a piece of celery along the breast bone.

To skim the grease off stock during cooking, drop in a cold piece of lettuce for ten seconds. The grease in the hot stock will stick to the lettuce leaf.

If you have left-over turkey, take the stuffing out before putting the bird in the fridge and refrigerate the stuffing in a separate bowl. You risk bacteria growing if you leave the stuffing inside.

To tenderise the meat in stews, add three or four wine corks to the pot. The corks release chemicals that both tenderise the meat and reduce cooking time. Just remember to remove them before serving!

To get the skin off chicken more easily, dip your hands in flour before trying to remove the skin. This will make the whole process much less slippery.

To make sure the centre of burgers get properly cooked poke holes in the centre before putting them on the grill.

For uniform hamburgers and meatballs, use an ice-cream scoop.

Keep poultry moist while roasting by placing a bowl of water in the bottom of the oven. Make sure you use a heat-proof bowl or roasting tin.

Before opening a packet of bacon, roll it up. It will make it easier to separate the slices.

To tenderise tough cuts of meat, rub both sides with a mix of vinegar, olive oil and perhaps a little salt. Then put it in the fridge for two or three hours before cooking.

Freeze meat in the coldest part of the freezer.

Save time struggling to get corned beef out of the can – pour hot water over the unopened can for a few minutes and the meat will slide out easily.

A turkey is only as good as the food it eats, so try to find free-range birds that have been fed on a variety of grains.

Roasting a chicken? Put some vegetables in a heat-proof bowl and cook in the oven at the same time to save an additional ring on the cooker.

Mince or finely chop left-over meat from your Sunday roast to make cottage pie on Monday.

Fruit

To peel an orange easily, drop it into hot water for about five minutes. Dry and peel as usual.

To get more juice out of a citrus fruit, warm it in the oven for a few minutes before squeezing it.

Alternatively, roll the fruit back and forth over a hard surface before cutting it in half.

Liquidise watermelon for a refreshing drink. You don't even need to pick out the seeds because they'll sink to the bottom.

To bring out the flavour of strawberries when cooking them in desserts, add a touch of balsamic vinegar to the recipe.

To keep strawberries fresh in the fridge for as long as a week, wash them (but don't remove the green stalks) and put in a sealed glass jar.

To slice kiwis easily, just use an egg-slicer. Remove the skin of the kiwi by edging a teaspoon around the slice, between the flesh and the skin.

To pep up pineapple chunks, sprinkle with black pepper.

Pineapple juice helps to ease a sore throat.

When you buy or pick a quantity of berries, there are often small twigs or leaves mixed in with the berries. The quickest way to get rid of the twigs and leaves without harming the fruit is to pour them from one container to another across the path of a fan.

Veg

If your roast potatoes take an age to brown, sprinkle a little flour over them as they cook.

For quick-cooking roast potatoes, remove the centre length-wise with an apple corer. For a sumptuous flavour, place rolled bacon strips in the hollow.

For crisp baked potato skins, brush the potato with a little oil before cooking.

To stop potatoes falling apart while you boil them, turn the heat right down and boil them for longer, rather than cooking them too fast.

Keep boiled potatoes firm by adding a little vinegar to the boiling water.

Buy cooking potatoes of similar size to avoid different cooking times.

For perfect mash, drop a teaspoon of sugar into the water as you boil the potatoes – it will make them more floury and they'll fluff up better.

To turn oven chips into a crispy and tasty treat, sprinkle with sea salt during cooking.

For a delicious alternative topping for shepherd's pie, add cream cheese to the mashed potato.

A good way to use left-over mashed potato is to make savoury croquettes. Try adding finely chopped onion, tomato, parsley, even tuna and grated cheese. Mix well, form croquettes, roll in flour and fry.

Freshly grated horse radish will pep up tired mashed potato.

Try putting salad dressing into a spray bottle so that you can control the amount you use – there's nothing worse than soggy drowned lettuce.

A cheap and easy alternative to using haricot beans is to drain a tin of economy baked beans and rinse off the tomato sauce. Remember that they're pre-cooked, so just adjust any recipe accordingly.

Carrots will keep fresh in the fridge for weeks if you trim the tops and bottoms and put them in a plastic container.

Spice up your sex life with a carrot! Carrots are full of beta carotene, which produces sex hormones.

Don't throw away left-over lentils – fry them in a big pan with a splash of oil until dry. It makes a great topping for toast.

Make a quick chilli sauce using left-over vegetables. Pop them in a pan with some chillies and stew them gently.

When cooking asparagus, wedge the bundles upright in the pan using potatoes.

Keep a nettle patch. Don't allow it to flower, but pick the nettle tops to use in cooking. The cooking gets rid of the sting and the taste is like spinach. Boil new shoots for two to three minutes, drain and serve with butter.

For an exciting spread for sandwiches, freeze some really good quality virgin olive oil in a plastic container and, when the olive oil is cold and thick, spread it on.

Never store apples and carrots together because the apples give off a gas that makes the carrots go bitter.

And never store potatoes and onions together either. The potatoes will spoil faster.

To make celery that bit crisper, put it in a bowl of iced water and leave it in the fridge for a few hours.

The brighter the colour of a dried bean, the fresher the bean.

The stronger broccoli smells, the less fresh it is.

A good artichoke will make a slight squeaking noise when handled.

Wrinkled green or yellow peppers aren't bad – they just have a mellower flavour.

Singe the root end of your onions – then they'll store for much longer.

Left-over Brussels sprouts and potatoes from your Sunday roast make lovely bubble-and-squeak. Just fry all the left-overs together.

Leave your bubble-and-squeak in the pan to go nice and crispy before serving. The crispy bits have more taste.

Boil cabbage with salt, pepper and butter – the strained juice makes a great drink to aid digestion.

Keep cauliflower white by adding two tablespoons of lemon juice or white wine vinegar to the cooking water.

Try cooking corn-on-the-cob in equal parts of milk and water to tenderise the kernels.

Alternatively, top with a couple of knobs of butter, a generous amount of pepper and wrap in tin foil. Roast in the oven for 20 to 30 minutes for a really intense flavour.

If you find canned vegetables taste tinny, drain them, and then blanch in boiling water for one minute and rinse in cool water.

Don't get in a muddle at the supermarket check out – put loose items that need weighing, like fruit and veg, on last to allow you time to pack your bags.

Herbs

For a subtle garlic flavour, spear a clove with a toothpick and dip it into the pan for 30 seconds every three minutes.

To preserve garlic after peeling, place it in a jar and cover with olive oil. If you store it in the fridge, it will keep for up to four months.

Don't throw away elderly garlic bulbs. Plant in a sunny spot and water. The resulting garlic shoots are excellent in salad.

Keep fresh herbs longer – grind in a food processor, add four tablespoons of vegetable oil and refrigerate.

When a recipe calls for the leaf of a fresh herb to be added during cooking, add the stem of the herb instead. The stem has a stronger taste and, because it has less chlorophyll than the leaf, it won't add a green tint to the dish.

Or just mix dried herbs with fresh parsley and no one will notice.

Save empty spice jars – the plastic bag refill packs are cheaper than buying replacement jars.

Always bruise a bouquet garni slightly with a mallet or rolling pin to release the aromatic oils before placing in your pot.

For a home-made bouquet garni, place bay leaves, thyme, parsley, cloves, allspice and black peppercorns on to a foil square. Fold and seal, then pierce with a pin to release flavours.

Alternatively, if you have a tea ball, just pop the ingredients in and hang over the rim of your pan.

Chop mint the easy way – sprinkle some sugar on it first.

Freeze chopped chives in ice cubes for convenience – it saves fiddling about when you're in a hurry.

Entertaining

Use a balloon whisk to stir your rice – you'll find it keeps the grains separated and fluffy.

To serve up pasta on heated plates, drain the pasta over the plates to warm them.

When serving soup to children, stir an ice cube into their portions to cool it down quickly.

If you can't get the last drops of salad cream out of the bottle, add some mustard powder and a little vinegar – it makes a great salad dressing.

Peanut butter will spread easily if you add half a teaspoon of sunflower oil to it and stir in well.

Like capers? Take a bottle, drain the vinegar and replace with olive oil. After a couple of weeks, the oil sweetens the taste.

Make consommé look more appetising – drop a lump of sugar into the soup before serving.

For a quick party dip, beat milk and onion powder into Philadelphia cheese until you have the desired consistency.

To make a tasty dip, mix half a packet of mushroom or onion soup with a small carton of cream and chill for a few hours.

Scoop out green or red peppers to make containers for mayonnaise, salad dressings, sauces and dips when entertaining.

For a special custard for adults pour in a small glassful of apricot or cherry brandy just before serving.

Add a measure of Bailey's Irish cream to custard for a really special flavour.

Add a touch of luxury to coffee with one teaspoon of vanilla ice-cream instead of milk.

Surprise guests? No desserts? Take two ginger biscuits and sandwich them with some gently whipped cream. Serve with coffee.

Stop last-minute panics at dinner parties. Boil your vegetables in advance, then run them under the cold water tap. Just before serving, boil the kettle and pour the boiling water over the vegetables. Leave for 30 seconds and serve.

Before serving cheese at a dinner party, warm the cheese knife in the oven. This makes it easier to cut through the cheese and spares your guests embarrassment.

Keep picnic food cool on a hot day. Put the food in a bowl. Take a larger bowl and put ice in the bottom. Then put the smaller bowl inside the larger one – a portable refrigerator.

Experimenting with new ingredients? To test ingredients before adding them to the mix, take a spoonful of the mix out of the dish and add a drop of the new ingredient. Taste this rather than risk spoiling the whole.

To keep bread rolls warm when served in a bread basket, line the basket with foil and then cover with a napkin.

You'll find party sandwiches stay fresh if you place paper napkins over them and sprinkle with cold water regularly.

You can't beat iced tea or coffee when the weather's hot. Why not freeze any leftovers from your usual brew in ice-cube trays. You'll have plenty of ice to chill your drinks without diluting them.

When serving something cold such as pâté, ice-cream or a cold soup, always add lots of flavourings because the cold will numb the palette.

A simple way to remove a frozen dessert or jelly from a mould is to loosen the edges with the point of a knife and give the mould a blast with a hair-dryer for a few seconds.

Dental floss pulled tightly will cut through cheesecake and other similar puddings with ease.

Used too much chilli or curry powder? Rescue the day by adding two tablespoons of milk.

Egg sandwiches always whiff, so try chopping the cooked egg and then storing it in the fridge in a covered container overnight. This should reduce the smell when you come to make up your sandwiches.

If you keep salt for seasoning in a small bowl instead of a shaker or grinder, you'll be less likely to over-salt a dish because you'll have total control of the amount you use.

To transform instant coffee into a more sophisticated offering, add a few cardamom seeds. Serve the coffee black… and remember to remove the seeds before serving!

To bring out the taste of fresh coffee, put a pinch of dried mustard powder into the percolator.

If you want beautiful, smooth icing on a cake, try using an artist's palette knife.

If you want perfect cheese curls, try using a potato peeler.

To make neat butter curls, freeze the butter for a few minutes first.

Cheers!

To chill beer, wine or champagne quickly add four to six tablespoons of salt to the ice and water in the ice-bucket. The bottles should chill in about 20 minutes.

Wine will chill much quicker with the cork out – ideal if you're in a hurry for a cool glass of wine.

Hold a bottle of chilled white wine by the neck rather than the body of the bottle so that your hands do not warm the wine inside.

If you're tasting wine, always make sure your glass is tulip shaped, curving inwards towards the rim, then, when you swill the wine around, it doesn't splash out all over you.

When tasting wine, remember to swill it all around the mouth as different parts of the tongue pick up different flavours.

If you're tasting lots of wine, here's an easy way to clean your glass. After each wine pour a thimbleful of the next wine into your glass, swill it around and pour out – so you're effectively cleaning the glass with the new wine, leaving no trace of the old.

Choosing between two wines? Taste the first, then the second, then back to the first – wines have lots of complex flavours and you'll notice subtle differences if you do this a few times. Keep going until you're sure.

Magnums of wine will always be of superior quality to the same wine in a regular-sized bottle as the ratio of wine to air is greater. So, if you can afford it or if you're entertaining, go for a larger bottle.

If you find a wine you like, look for the name of the producer rather than the name of the wine. Wines of the same name will often be made by many producers with varying degrees of quality. Better to stick to a producer you trust and try out their range of wines.

It is more polite to half-fill your guests' glasses with wine rather than fill them right up to the top – they'll also get the full effect of the aroma.

Twist the wine bottle when you pour to avoid messy drips.

Plain glasses are better for wine because you can't see colour and clarity through cut or patterned glass.

Impress your guests with expensive wine first – then bring out the cheaper stuff when everyone's slightly merry and they'll hardly notice the difference.

If you suspect a champagne bottle has been shaken up but you need to open it, hold it absolutely horizontal before easing the cork out.

When you're pouring champagne, put a little in the bottom of each glass before topping them up. This stops them from overflowing and wasting all the bubbly!

Don't worry if you have to decant a bottle of wine or port at very short notice. Just pour it out very quickly to get lots of air into it.

If your decanter looks stained or dull, fill with vinegar and crushed eggshells. Replace the stopper and give it a good hard swill around. Once rinsed with warm water, it will look as good as new.

To clean your decanter, half-fill it with warm soapy water and two tablespoons of rice. Swish the mixture around and leave for half an hour before pouring out. Rinse the decanter and stand upside down to dry.

If the stopper gets stuck in a decanter, put a few drops of cooking oil around the neck and leave in a warm place for a while before loosening the stopper.

It's messy when fizzy drinks overflow. To avoid this, pour fizzy drinks into warmed glasses and then put in lots of ice to chill the drink.

Rejuvenate fizzy drinks that have gone flat – add a dash of bicarbonate of soda.

Keep your mineral water fizzy – give the plastic bottle a good squeeze before screwing the top back on.

If you don't have a cocktail shaker, use a smaller glass inverted inside a pint glass.

To separate glasses that are stuck together, put cold water inside the inner one and place the outer one in warm water. Gently increase the temperature of the warm water until the outer glass expands and the inner glass can be lifted off. Easy!

There is no actual evidence to suggest that combining 'grape and grain' makes for worse hangovers – except that those who mix their drinks are probably drinking more.

Feeling hungover? Vitamin C is the most important ingredient in any hangover cure – soluble, flavoured vitamin tablets are virtually designed for hangovers.

Finally

If you turn up at a restaurant having booked a table to be told they haven't actually got one for you, the restaurant is in breach of contract and you're entitled to compensation.

And there is such a thing as a free lunch – a restaurant is actually obliged to ask you if you enjoyed your meal. If they fail to do this and you didn't really enjoy the food, you are not liable to pay the bill.

RUNNERS

Caroline Armstrong &
Dave Scott, Nike

Buy decent shoes. Go to a specialist running shop and have your feet properly measured. Don't skimp on the price either. You'll never regret it.

Avoid running in cotton T-shirts, which get wet, cold and heavy. Get yourself into moisture-wicking fabrics and you will be a whole lot more comfortable.

People with bigger legs should wear cycling shorts or running tights to stop their legs chafing together as they run.

Warm up before you set out running. Not only will it stretch your muscles. It means you won't have to wear a sweatshirt or other top, which you won't want to have with you once you have been running for a while.

Run with a Walkman or Discman. It has been scientifically proven that music can affect sporting performance. Listen to music you like whilst you are running and you will not only feel better, you will achieve more and exert less energy. The reverse applies with music you don't like.

But be aware that running in headphones will mean you won't be able to hear traffic or someone coming up behind you.

If you're prone to getting a stitch, avoiding eating or drinking fluids for up to an hour before you run.

Run with a partner, especially if you are female and especially in the winter when it gets dark earlier.

Just starting running? Don't try to be too ambitious. Try to run several laps that pass your original starting point. That way you won't have such a distance to go back if you become tired.

Stop running if you injure yourself, become dizzy or very tired.

However, don't stop if you are only a bit tired. You need to push yourself to improve. Just stop and walk for a bit until you get your breath back.

You need to run for 15 or 20 minutes before you even begin to burn off calories!

If you do have an injury, have it treated by a professional. It won't get better just by ignoring it – it will get worse.

Attempting a marathon or half-marathon? Boost your carbohydrate levels by eating pasta and rice three or four times a week for three or four weeks before the run.

Take plenty of fluids on board – even if you don't think you need them. By the time you think you do, it will be too late – you'll have started to dehydrate.

Try to train for a big run with a group. It will keep you motivated, even when you're not in the mood.

If you are running a marathon, buy a copy of the newspaper before you go to the start. It has many uses:

> It's something to read when you are sitting for hours at the start – Sunday papers are the best for this.

> You can sit on the sections you are not reading while you wait to start.

> It provides an extra layer of insulation when you are hanging about.

> It has good listings of things to do, restaurants to eat in and bars to drink in when you've finished the marathon.

In any marathon a bin liner is also well worth taking for warmth.

SAILORS

Simon Purchon,
Second Officer
Merchant Navy; Pete
Goss, Yachtsman

Eat out of a plastic dog bowl on a boat. They are nice and deep and you can get gallons of food in. The very wide base also means that it won't tip over, but...

The plastic must be milk quality. Test it by putting water in the plastic bowl overnight. If there is a plastic taint to the water in the morning, then it's not suitable.

Always carry a knife with multi attachments, and always pin or tie it to you in case you drop it.

A head-torch, like those worn by orienteerers, is always useful, and leaves two hands free for working.

If you need to relieve yourself when at sea, make sure you face down wind. Ladies – bucket and chuck it.

On large ships, to know how much anchor chain has been let out, the chain is marked every fathom with rings of wire. Do the same on your boat by marking the chain every set number of feet with string. That way you'll know how much you've let out.

String on the anchor rope will also help you to know how deep you are if you haven't got an echo sounder.

Jif or Cif is ideal for cleaning fibreglass boats because it's abrasive without being too strong.

If you are starting to feel sea sick, an old Merchant Navy trick is to eat oranges.

Arm bands for morning sickness in pregnancy work well for sea sickness too.

An ideal method of stopping a can or mug spilling on deck is to construct a ring out of a wire coat-hanger wound around the guard rail and the can or mug. It makes a perfect gimbal.

On yachts where rope comes through jam cleats, use white electrical tape and permanent marker pen to label up your ropes. It's especially useful if you have guests on board crewing for you.

When you have a new boat, test that, when going astern, the boat will paddle in one direction. Use that to your advantage, because if you put a bow rope on first then put engine astern, you can walk the stern due to the paddle effect of the propeller along the side of the quay.

Always fix your life raft on the outside of your railings. It makes releasing it in a crisis far easier than having to lift it over.

The easiest way to fix a Danbuoy to the stern of a boat is to sit it in a short piece of white drain pipe, attached with cable ties. Conservatory pipe, which is square, looks even better and is easier to attach.

In a marina it's sensible and courteous to put fenders on the outside of your boat because, if the marina fills up, other boats will be moored close alongside yours.

Use a plank, suspended at each end by a rope, from your guard rails between the fenders on your boat and the quay wall. This will ensure that your fenders protect your boat from damage.

Always carry as mask and a pair of flippers on board in case you pick up a rope around your prop.

Remember to remove the loo roll when using the shower on board – especially when the shower is the whole cubicle!

The correct way to go down the steep companion ways on a ship, is to have one hand behind you on the rail and one in front of you, so you don't slip.

Never slide down handrails with just your hands.

In rough weather, place a bulky object, like a lifejacket, under the mattress to tilt it towards the wall to stop you falling out.

If you need to untangle a piece of rope or twisted fishing line, pass the end over one side of the boat and put it back out to sea again on the other side. By the time you have put it all out, the motion of the water will have untangled the rope or line.

In heavy seas, to slow down a boat and stop it surfing, tow a rope. The longer and thicker the rope, the more control you will have. It will keep you straight and prevent capsize.

In a tidal estuary, at anchor, hold yourself in line with the tide not the wind, by streaming a bucket or droge to the stern of the boat.

Keep a lipsalve in the pocket of your waterproofs to protect your lips.

Remember that the sun is much stronger when it is reflected from water.

SCOUT LEADERS

Gareth Robers, The Scout Association, Birmingham; birminghamscouts@demon.co.uk

If you have a long coach trip, don't allow youngsters to eat or drink on the coach, especially fizzy drinks or chocolate. Once one youngster starts feeling ill, the effect will spread like wild fire.

If you are going to an event with lots of other children, think of some way of identifying yours, such as a fluorescent label, arm band or baseball cap. They will then stand out in a crowd.

Always have a plan B, just in case of bad weather, or the attraction being closed.

Appoint a home contact, who has a list of everyone going on the trip. This person can then contact everyone back at home if the coach breaks down or you are delayed.

Link youngsters together in small 'buddy groups', who will keep an eye on each other. This will act as a double check when it comes to ensuring that everyone has been accounted for.

Take a supply of large plastic bags, they can be used for everything from collecting rubbish, to keeping dry.

SCULPTORS

Paul Astbury; John Mills, Chairman of the Royal Society of Sculptors; Hilary Brock

To make interesting hair for figures, squeeze clay through a fine sieve.

If you're making an ambitious piece of sculpture, make sure you can get it out through the door when you've finished!

To keep clean when you are working, wear an old dustbin liner. It's much easier to throw these away each day; rather than washing out aprons covered in clay all the time.

You don't need expensive tools. Try experimenting with hair rollers, straws or tea strainers for interesting effects.

To prevent your tools sticking to the clay, keep a jar of cool water handy and dip the tools into it regularly.

To seal up a clay model that has cracked, wait for it to dry totally, then use a very sharp knife to cut away the clay from inside the crack. Mix that clay with some vinegar, then replace it in the gap. It will seal perfectly.

If you are in a hurry, you can speed up the clay-drying process with a heat gun... but be careful!

Create an interesting and lighter effect with your clay. Before you fire it up, mix the liquid clay with some polystyrene balls. When it comes out of the kiln, it will be a totally different texture.

Experiment by brushing some oil paint on to your clay before you fire it. You can get some amazing effects. Red oil paint leaves an iron residue and blue leaves traces of cobalt.

SECOND-HAND CAR SALESMEN

Gary Redman; J M
Littleton; Gerry
Silverman

Inside the Car

To judge whether a car might have done more miles than the clock claims, look at the gear stick and the steering wheel. If either is very well worn, it indicates that lots of miles have been clocked up.

To check a car's true mileage, look at the driver's seat and foot pedals. Wear and tear on these can signal heavy use.

It's a good move to buy a car that has genuinely been on the road in recent months. Take a look at the tax disc; one that was bought two or three months ago is ideal. But, be suspicious of brand new ones. It might be a clue that this is a trade car that has been recently 'tarted' up.

Look under the carpet in the boot. If the floor has ridges in it, the car has been shunted from behind at some point and should be avoided.

When buying at an auction, always check the oil and water levels. Occasionally, dealers put a car that has a smoky engine into an auction. They will have drained all the oil out first so that the car will appear to run perfectly at the sale... but it will quickly get into trouble when you drive it away.

When you open the bonnet, check to see whether the wings have been beaten out. This indicates a previous crash of some sort and the car is best avoided.

Check all the gaps on a car, such as spaces around the tops of the doors. If any are wider than another, there's a good chance that the car has been rolled at some point. So don't touch it with a barge pole!

Outside the Car

Never buy a car in the dark – you are bound to miss something.

Try to judge what sort of owner a car has had by its stickers. AA or RAC stickers show a caring previous owner. Greenpeace or charity stickers show that the owner has cared as well. However, avoid any boy-racer stickers, which might mean that the car has been put through its paces!

If you're choosing a metallic car, give it a good rub to check that no one has smeared oil on to it to disguise faded paintwork.

'Buy dirty, sell clean.' Never buy an immaculate car at an auction. It is a sure sign that someone from the trade has got hold of it and is now trying to get rid of it.

Be cautious of cars with black shiny tyres. Why have they been tarted up? All revamps should alert you to possible cover-ups and possible problems.

Are the number plates the original ones with the supplier's name on them? If not, they may have been replaced after a crash.

Tap along the bodywork. If filler has been used at some point, you will hear a duller sound there than everywhere else.

To see if the car has had an easy life, crouch down a few feet in front of the bonnet and look down the sides of the vehicle. Any little bumps or ripples will show up a treat and, a bit like human wrinkles, you can decide what kind of life the car has led so far!

Another mileage tip: look for little stone chips on the bonnet. They indicate that the car's likely to have done plenty of motorway driving, which clocks up lots of miles but causes less wear and tear than hundreds of short journeys.

If you can only afford a high-mileage car, go for the newest car that has done all the miles in a short time.

Test-Driving a Car

Does the needle on the speedometer go round smoothly? It's a delicate instrument and one of the first things to react to a bad knock or two.

Take the car for a really good spin. Just around the block a couple of times is no good. Many faults won't show up until the car is truly warmed up.

Don't test-drive with the radio on or the windows open. You must eliminate as much noise as possible so that you can hear any unusual sounds.

Beware of the loud-mouthed salesman who talks non-stop while you're driving. He's probably trying to distract you.

Looking After Your Car

When washing your car, don't use washing-up liquid because it contains salt, which can cause rust to form.

Remove rust spots from chrome bumpers. Dip kitchen foil in Coca-Cola and rub off the rust spots.

Always keep a supply of hand wipes from fast-food outlets and plastic gloves from petrol stations to keep your hands clean when you have to do any minor repairs.

When you've got your new car, put the registration number on a post-it sticker on the dashboard until you remember it.

Doing the Deal

Never buy a car for the advertised price. Haggle down. A typical dealer's margin is ten per cent, but with foreign imports increasingly threatening their business, most should be willing to cut the price further. If they are not, go elsewhere.

If you can't negotiate down as far as you would like, ask for goodies to be included in the price. These tend to include floor mats and mudflaps, but it's worth asking for 12 months' road tax and/or a full tank of petrol.

Before agreeing to a finance deal from a dealer, see if you can get a more competitive APR from a personal loan at a bank or building society.

Breakdown and motoring organisations are worth joining but shop around. Some insurance companies offer better deals than the two big names, the AA and RAC.

New cars lose their value as soon as they are driven out of the showroom. Save money by purchasing a nearly new or ex-demonstrator model with a few thousand on the clock.

'Ringing' is the name given to the practice of stealing a car and giving it the identity of a similar car. Look out for signs of tampering with the vehicle identification number on the body in the engine compartment when looking at a second-hand car.

Before taking your car to a dealer to get a part-exchange price, get a good idea of its value by looking it up in car guides like *Parkers* or motor magazines, then you'll have a good idea as to whether you are being offered a competitive price.

Before signing on the dotted line for a second-hand car, always check that it has no outstanding payments on it, and that it hasn't been stolen or been an insurance write-off. The AA has a car data check for this.

SECRETARIES

Leigh Thomson, BT; Sue Blake; Sharon Hinds, Birmingham TEC

Every good secretary has an emergency survival kit with spare birthday cards, a blank card or two, some peppermints (in case your boss had a heavy lunch), some aspirin, a pair of tights and a sewing kit.

If you can't get the plastic hub out of the centre of the sticky tape, push two or three £1 coins through the middle to shift it.

For meetings, always order one or two extra teas and coffees in case someone changes their mind or an extra person turns up late.

When setting the table for a meeting, turn the cups upside down so that afterwards you'll know which ones have been used and which are still clean.

If the photocopier is broken, send the document through the fax machine on 'copy'.

If you are photocopying a long document, jot the page numbers in pencil on the back. At least if there's a jam you will be able to sort the sheets out afterwards.

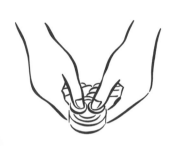

Leave jobs like photocopying until a lunch hour so that the phone won't go unanswered.

Photocopy the boss's diary schedule for the day for easy reference and to make notes on.

Write down the ten most used numbers and stick them to the phone. Many secretaries speed-dial them into their phone and are then lost when someone asks for the number.

Every time you answer the phone, jot the person's name and company down. Once they've rambled on and asked to be put through to the boss, it's easy to have forgotten their personal details.

Always let the phone ring twice before you answer it so that people think the office is busy.

If you know you have something vitally important to remember for the next day, ring your own answering machine at home and leave a message to remind yourself.

If you want to sound confident and authoritative on the phone – stand up. It really does work!

To make a good impression, learn the names of your boss's kids. Even if your boss is in a foul mood, you can ask how little Tom or Jane is.

When someone calls to complain, don't pass them around the phone system to different people. Tell them your name and then say you will make sure someone gets back to them immediately.

Tie a pen around your neck so you'll have one handy at all times.

Clean an eraser by rubbing it on blotting paper.

If you need to take a long lunch, leave early rather than return late. It's much less noticeable.

Wear blue and gain everyone's trust.

SECURITY GUARDS

Ben Thompson

Stop a thief from sneaking up in the night by putting gravel down on your pathway or drive. The thief will go for a house with a quieter approach.

A dog is the best deterrent of all.

If you haven't got a dog, borrow a friend's and make a tape of occasional barks to play when you're away from home.

Trick thieves into thinking you have a dog by leaving a dog bowl outside, hanging a lead near a window or leaving the odd dog toy or chew around.

To stop thieves walking off with your planters and tubs, put several stones in the bottom of each tub before filling and planting. They will then be too heavy to lift.

Prickly plants and cacti make a great deterrent. Line your window ledges with them.

Use a baby alarm for extra security. Plug one half into your home and give a neighbour the other half so they can listen out for intruders while you're away.

Burglar alarms cost a lot of money but a dummy box stuck on the outside wall will put off most intruders.

Make sure you can find your keys in the dark – stick fluorescent tape on them.

If you've lost your own keys but have managed to break into your own home then it simply isn't secure enough.

SELF-DEFENCE TEACHERS

Chris Philips
Travel Safely

Avoid wearing a personal stereo – it deprives you of your hearing, which is one of your most valuable self-defence assets.

Using a mobile phone can also distract you from paying attention to what is going on around you.

If you go jogging, try to vary your route and to go at different times.

Inform someone where you are going and when you expect to be back. Make sure you update them if your plans change.

Make sure your mobile phone is all charged up before you go out, particularly if your job involves travelling, either by car or on public transport.

Walk confidently and briskly, in the middle of the pavement, even if you're not sure where you are going.

Don't take short cuts away from lighted areas and public places. It's not worth the risk, no matter how much time it saves.

Walk facing on-coming traffic. This prevents drivers approaching you from behind.

Hold any bags close to your body. Shoulder bags should be carried across your body.

Don't carry more money or credit cards than you realistically need. If you are mugged, at least your losses will be minimised.

Think about the way you are dressed. Can you move easily? Could you run in your shoes, if you had to?

Be aware of how much your jewellery is on display. Turn flashy rings so that the jewels are facing inwards and only a plain band is on display. Tuck necklaces inside you clothes until you reach your destination.

If a mugger demands your bag, money or jewellery, for goodness sake hand it over. Possessions can be replaced – you can't.

Car Sense

Make sure your vehicle is well maintained.

Be sure you have at least enough fuel for your journey.

Plan your route.

Join a motoring organisation.

Carry a mobile phone, in case of emergencies, but keep it out of sight. Make sure the battery is well charged and programme essential numbers (including that of the motoring organisation) into the memory to save time.

Never place your handbag on the passenger seat. Smash and grab robbers take advantage of this kind of opportunity. Keep other valuables out of sight too.

If you place valuable items in the boot, be aware that you may be vulnerable when retrieving them, particularly if you have reversed into a parking bay.

Try to avoid parking in unlit areas. If parking during the day, give some thought to what the surroundings will be like at night.

Reverse into parking spaces. This makes exiting in a hurry much easier.

If using a multi-storey car park, try to park as close as possible to the attendant's booth.

Keep your doors locked when driving.

Never leave your car unlocked, and always check behind the front seats before you get in.

Have your keys ready in your hand when returning to your car.

Mark your car key, and your house key, with luminous paint so you can pick it out easily in the dark.

If your car has electronic locking, don't unlock the doors until you are close to it. This reduces the opportunity for someone else to get in before you do.

Remember that central locking is also central unlocking, so watch out for anyone near your car as you get in.

Women drivers – remove anything that advertises your car as a woman's car – soft toys, tissues, umbrellas and any window stickers that carry witticisms about men!

Public Thinking

Try to use well-lit bus stops and railway stations. If your regular station is poorly lit – complain to the managing company.

Check timetables to reduce the time you'll have to spend hanging around.

On buses, sit close to the driver.

On trains, try to sit near the guard's van or in carriages that are carrying mixed gender groups.

Only use taxis registered as licensed hackney carriages. These are regulated by strict rules, and can be identified by a license plate.

When travelling alone by taxi, or if you are the last of a group to be dropped off, always sit in the nearside rear seat. This protects you from the driver and will allow you to get out fast if you need to.

Try to book a taxi in advance. Take precautions, such as asking for the name of the driver and the colour, make and model of the vehicle.

Phone Safety

List only your initials in the phone book.

Consider being ex-directory if you live alone.

Answer your phone with a simple 'Hello'. Don't give out your name or number.

Women living alone – ask a male friend to record the message on your answer phone.

Make sure your message implies that you can't come to the phone, and not that you aren't there.

A phone in your bedroom will allow you to make emergency calls in the middle of the night.

If you get a nuisance call, try not to respond in an emotional way and don't get involved in talking to the caller. Just hang up. If you receive unwanted or abusive calls frequently, British Telecom can help. They have specialist advisors to help you deal with the problem.

SKI INSTRUCTORS

Vanessa Haines, Ski Club of Great Britain, www.skiclub.co.uk; Bernard Cheek

In white-out weather, goggles are better than sunglasses.

Save weight in your main bag and protect your skis, by packing clothes around the skis in your ski bag.

Tie a bright strip of ribbon or tape around your boot bag in order to recognise it when travelling. Hundreds of skiers and boarders at airports have similar boot bags.

Take a roll from breakfast and make a sandwich for lunch – this will save you money at lunchtime.

If wearing an all-in-one, tie the arms together when going to loo so they don't drag on floor.

Wear lots of thin layers as opposed to one thick layer under your ski jacket.

Take a few boiled sweets up the mountain with you – they are excellent for a sugar rush when tired.

Always wear high-factor sun-cream – even when cloudy, sun reflects off snow and can burn your face.

Never ski without sunglasses or goggles – they prevent snow-blindness.

At the end of a ski holiday make sure your skis are dry before you pack them away. Damp skis will rust along the edges.

Try to do some pre-ski exercises or, if this fails, have a quick stretch before you head down the slopes. Also try to remember to stretch again before going to bed to ease aching muscles.

Ease off on the alcohol on some nights. Altitude dehydrates anyway, so drink plenty of water before hitting the sack. Two Nurofen will help first thing in morning.

Don't sit down on a button lift – let the poma gradually pull you up the hill.

Make sure you don't poke your poles out behind you when walking up stairs.

Always carry skis on your shoulder with the front end of the skis pointing forwards.

Many owners will not be happy if you start eating your own picnic at their mountain restaurants.

Restaurants on the continent sometimes charge a small amount for toilet entry – check you have small change before heading to the loos.

Undo back and or side clips on your ski boots to ease walking.

Beginners should take at least one dry slope lesson before heading to the mountains.

If you fall and your skis come off, always put the skis across the slope and put the lower one on first.

If heading off piste, make sure you are wearing an avalanche transceiver and that it is switched to the 'transmit' mode.

Mittens can keep your hands warmer than gloves.

Hand and boot warmers make life more pleasant on cold, snowy days.

Girls – a sports bra is an essential item for negotiating a mogul field.

Buy a double ski bag to save money carrying two pairs of skis – and you get extra room for stuffing socks and undies in.

Remember to take spare camera films with you – they can be expensive and difficult to get hold of in small resorts.

Don't go off piste without a guide – it just isn't worth it.

If you're skiing with a guide, always stay behind – if he or she stops make sure you stop behind.

If you're inexperienced at off-piste skiing, rent 'fat boys' (broad skis) to make life easier.

Never ski with a baby in a back-pack baby carrier – they can get chilled and you won't even notice.

Woollen socks are far more comfortable than synthetic.

Become a Ski Club member – huge savings and benefits for skiers and boarders.

SMALL-ANIMAL BREEDERS

Pamela Milward;
Belinda Francis

Cleanliness

During the summer months, drinking bottles for small animals often get covered in green algae. To get rid of it, fill the bottle with sand and water, shake it vigorously and rinse it out thoroughly. The sand scours the algae off the glass.

To clean a small-necked water bottle, fill the bottle with a little water and a chain from a plug. Rattle it round for a bit to remove the stains.

Stop water bottles from freezing by adding a few drops of glycerine to the water.

To get into awkward nooks and crannies when cleaning a cage, use an old toothbrush. It's a great tool.

Keep flies out of cages – hang old net curtains over the cage.

If you've just laid a new lawn, give it a chance to settle before introducing your pets on to it. New grass is often treated with weed-killer, which can harm animals.

Hamsters

Rats, mice, hamsters and gerbils are ideal for the novice 'keeper'.

Hamsters are very active at night. If you want a good night's sleep, don't keep their cage in your bedroom.

When waking a hamster, make soft noises, talk to it gently, and move the cage to and fro so that it's not rudely awakened and frightened.

To clean a hamster's cage, fill a jam jar with sawdust, put it on its side and encourage the hamster to explore it while you do housework on the cage. This also works if you want

to create a hamster loo in one corner of the cage.

If a hamster escapes, put some of its food in the bottom of a bucket and lean a small, hamster-sized ramp up the side. The hamster will smell the food, go and investigate and drop to the bottom of the bucket with no means of getting out again.

Hamsters are great swingers. Hang a cardboard tube from the top of their cage to make a fun swing for them.

Baby hamsters love porridge and similar cereals.

Teach a baby hamster to enjoy being handled by always feeding it straight after play-time.

To prevent a hamster from going into a state of hibernation, warm it up gently in your hands – not by the fire.

To stop hamsters biting, scoop them up from below when you want to pick them up. If you pick them up from above, they think they're being attacked and become aggressive.

If a hamster does bite you, put it back in the cage and leave it for a couple of hours to calm down.

If a hamster bites, use a small fishing net to catch it and save your fingers from nips.

To groom your long-haired hamster, use an old comb or toothbrush.

Give a hamster something to play with – cotton reels, jars… anything as long as it hasn't got sharp edges and isn't toxic.

Give your hamster something to chew on – attach some white wood to the side of the cage. Alternatively, use a clothes peg.

To help hamsters get over a cold, feed them a mixture of lukewarm milk, water and a drop of honey.

When buying a hamster, try to do so in the evening because they will be more active.

A healthy hamster should have a smooth, well-rounded body, with no bald patches on the coat. The eyes should be bright and clear. The ears should be clean and, if you're buying a young hamster, should have hair on the outside.

Male and female hamsters are equally good tempered.

You can keep two hamsters in one cage depending on what kind you want to get. Short dwarf hamsters and Russian hamsters are sociable souls and will go together. But it's best if they've been together since birth and are of the same sex. All other hamsters should be kept separately because they are territorial.

Feed your hamster once a day in the late afternoon or evening.

An adult hamster eats only a tablespoon of food or less a day.

Avoid iceberg lettuce and citrus fruits. Give small amounts of juicy fruits, such as tomatoes, strawberries or pears.

Hamsters are rather partial to yoghurt, but don't give them a rich variety like choco-late or caramel. They should have no more than a teaspoon two or three times a week as a treat.

Don't use cotton wool or anything similar as bedding because it can be dangerous if eaten.

If your hamster escapes, try leaving some sunflower seeds in each room of the house. Shut all the doors and go to bed. The next morning, you'll be able to tell which room he's ended up in by the absence of seeds. Once you know which rooms he's in, get his cage and leave it with the door open and food inside.

Alternatively, put a pile of food in the centre of the floor and surround it with a ring of flour. Then just follow the footprints till you find the escapee.

Guinea Pigs

Guinea pigs are partial to left-over cooked peas.

Treat your guinea pig – give it some toast.

Recycle a guinea pig's droppings and left-over food. Sprinkle them on the garden to grow sprouted oats which, when peeled, can be fed back to the hamster.

Don't leave uneaten food in the cage because it will quickly go off.

Stop males from fighting. Put a few drops of lavender oil on their bottoms. It confuses their sense of smell.

Get your guinea pig used to being handled – support the whole body when you lift it up and hold on to it with the other hand so it doesn't make a dash for freedom and end up injuring itself.

You can keep a guinea pig in with a rabbit – they seem to get on rather well.

Give your guinea pigs hay all year round. The floor of the cage should be covered in it.

Guinea pigs' mouths are right underneath their heads, which means they have to feed from the floor, so don't leave their food where they can't reach it.

Guinea pigs can't 'make' vitamin C, so you must ensure that their diet includes vitamin C-rich food (broccoli, carrots, swede or any dark green, leafy vegetable).

Spinach leaves drive guinea pigs wild.

Avoid rhubarb and beetroot leaves because these are poisonous.

Lettuce leaves have a high water content, so aren't very nutritious.

Guinea pigs love melon, tomato and weeds.

If you like the grunts and squeals that guinea pigs make, start to make a regular noise just before you feed your pets. Like Pavlov's dog, they'll start squeaking themselves into a frenzy.

If your guinea pig starts to rumble, it means that it's not happy.

Guinea pigs can be very chatty and have a full range of sounds. Try not to alarm them (by picking them up unexpectedly, for example) because they tend to shriek at full volume.

A happy guinea pig is a leaping guinea pig.

You can keep male (buck) guinea pigs together as long as they are introduced to the cage at the same time.

Guinea pig females are pregnant for around 63 days. Avoid handling a pregnant female because you could damage her unborn babies.

When guinea pigs are born, they are the spitting image of their parents – a full coat and eyes open.

When trimming a guinea pig's toenails, put it on a tennis racket. The toenails will poke down through the gaps of the strings, making them easier to clip. Avoid cutting into the quick.

One way to avoid clipping toenails is to give your guinea pigs a hard, abrasive surface to walk on so that their nails wear down naturally. Bricks (without holes in them) are the cheapest and easiest option.

It's not a good idea to give guinea pigs the run of the house because it's all too easy to lose them behind the furniture. If you really want to have guinea pigs indoors, build an indoor run.

Not too hot, not too cold. Guinea pigs can cope with cold more than heat, so don't put their cages too near radiators or pipes.

Make sure the cage is sheltered from the sun.

While guinea pigs aren't rocket scientists, they're not stupid either. They can be trained to use a litter tray when out of the cage and will come when called. Training takes time, but the potential is there.

Guinea pigs have been farmed for fur and food for over 2,500 years in South America.

Another name for a guinea pig is a cavie.

Rabbits

Cool your rabbit down in summer. Chill a ceramic tile in the fridge and then place it in the hutch.

Use sawdust on the floor of the cage rather than wood shavings or straw. Sawdust is softer and more comfortable.

Hang a carrot on the cage using a metal skewer. It will stay fresh longer and remain free from sawdust so your rabbit will enjoy it more.

Amuse a house rabbit – put its food in a washing ball from a washing machine. This will keep your rabbit happy for hours.

Prepare a crunchy snack by baking left-over bits of bread.

Rabbits need bulk so make sure they get hay as well as root vegetables, green food and mixed cereals.

Don't let rabbits graze where dogs have been. They could pick up tapeworm.

Always make sure your pet has enough water. If you keep the hutch outside, remember that the water in its bottle can freeze in the winter, so don't fill it right to the top because the water will expand as it turns to ice and crack the glass.

Hay is an essential part of a rabbit's diet because it provides roughage. Apple tree twigs are also a good source of roughage.

Don't suddenly change your rabbit's diet – the bacteria in its stomach, which break down its food, need time to adapt to any changes.

Rabbits produce two kinds of droppings – the good and the bad. The first sort is made up of partially digested food and is usually passed at night. These droppings are full of nutrients, which the rabbit eats so that they are absorbed into its small intestine. The other kind are large, round and stay on the ground.

If your rabbit develops diarrhoea, give it a weed called shepherd's purse, which should help its condition.

Rabbits are able to suck in their cheeks when they eat, which stops sharp, tough things like twigs from getting into their mouths.

You can put your rabbit's hutch on an overgrown patch of vegetable garden. They'll help to keep the weeds down and their droppings will fertilise the earth.

Make nail clipping easy. Rabbits are pushovers when it comes to putting them in a trance. Simply lie your rabbit on its back and gently stroke its tummy until it drifts off. You can then clip the nails without fuss before snapping your fingers and bringing it back to the real world!

Handle your rabbit frequently so that it gets used to it. Always be gentle. Pick the rabbit up with both hands, placed just behind the front legs. Don't pick a rabbit up by the ears or the scruff of its neck.

If a rabbit panics while you are holding it, put it down on the floor. Rabbits have powerful hind legs and you could get badly scratched trying to restrain it.

Rabbits like to climb. Put shelves in their hutch.

If the hutch is to be kept outside make sure it's in a sheltered, draught-free area.

The bigger the cage the better – it should be at least four times the size of the rabbit and a lot more if he's going to be confined for most of the day.

Rabbits come in different sizes – for example, Netherland dwarf rabbits are tiny (weighing in at 2¼ lb/1 kg), while the Belgian hare (which isn't a hare, but a rabbit, just to be confusing!) can weigh up to 9 lb/4 kg.

Paper bags and cardboard boxes make great places to hide. Rabbits also have fun playing with cardboard loo rolls, bits of paper to shred, small towels, things to jump on and hide under.

Keep an eye on a rabbit when it's loose in the house. Rabbits are great chewers and think nothing of sinking their teeth into electric cables, rugs, plants and so on.

But rabbits can be house-trained – you can teach them to use a litter tray. Unlike cats, they don't damage the furniture, but can scratch the carpet.

You can train a house rabbit to walk on a harness and lead – but don't take them for long walks in unfamiliar territory. Stick to the familiar.

Placing your hand round its ears will help calm a struggling rabbit. But never pick up a rabbit by its ears because this will cause it a lot of pain and distress.

Don't pick up a rabbit with your bare arms because you could get badly scratched.

If your rabbit starts circling your feet and biting your ankles, it could be sexually frustrated. Neutering can reduce aggressive behaviour.

Rabbits are territorial. When you open the cage, let them come out on their own; don't reach in and drag them out, because they could bite you.

If your rabbit gives you a nip, let out a sudden high-pitched, loud screech to let him know he hurt you. Keep on squealing every time you are nipped; soon your rabbit will get the message and be more gentle.

Put ice on the spot where your rabbit has nipped you to ease the pain.

Netherland dwarf rabbits can be martyrs to their teeth, which sometimes don't fit together properly, making eating difficult.

Give your rabbit something to gnaw on like a log or piece of hard-baked bread. It's better they chew away on something like this than on their cage.

Lop rabbits have extremely long ears, which can grow over 2 ft/60 cm long. The dwarf lop makes a good pet because it doesn't need any special care and has a nice, friendly nature.

Angora rabbits are one of the oldest breeds and can look spectacular, but they do need a lot of grooming and special housing.

Don't keep buck rabbits together in a cage because they will probably fight each other all the time.

If you keep doe rabbits together, they will often experience false pregnancies.

A pregnant rabbit pulls at its fur to make a soft nest for its young.

If you want to breed from your rabbits, put a doe and buck together. Obvious really, isn't it? The female rabbit will immediately start to produce eggs once she is placed with a male. Rabbits are pregnant for around 31 days.

Clean litter boxes often to encourage a rabbit to use them. Rabbit wee is really smelly so you won't want to leave used litter hanging around.

If your rabbit has an accident on the carpet, clean the stain with white vinegar or soda water.

If you let your rabbit in the house, don't encourage it to climb the stairs. If it falls, it could damage its back badly.

Gerbils

When buying a gerbil, look for an animal that is bright-eyed, alert and inquisitive. If it's dozy and disinterested, it could be ill.

If you want to restrain a gerbil – hold it firmly by the base of the tail. Try to avoid grabbing the tail any further along because you could damage it.

Wooden cages are hard to keep clean. Gerbils also tend to chew large bits off, so stick to a metal cage.

A gerbil's idea of a des res is an old coconut shell. It may not be much to you or me but it's a palace to a gerbil. Place it in the cage.

Stop sawdust from getting everywhere. Stand the cage in a cardboard box with the sides cut down. The sawdust collects in the bottom of the box and can be shaken out every few days.

Gerbils are very gregarious and hate to be kept on their own. A same-sex pair will bond as closely as a mated pair and be as happy as Larry.

Gerbils make ideal pets because they are desert animals. This means that they make very efficient use of food and water and hardly wee at all. That means you don't have to clean their cages as much as other rodent pets.

Give a gerbil a bit of wood to gnaw. It will help the cage look attractive and will also serve as a look-out post for an inquisitive gerbil.

As desert creatures, gerbils are used to dry conditions and like to dig. Give them plenty of wood shavings (about 2 in/5 cm deep) to burrow in.

Put a dish full of sand in your gerbil's cage – they love to have sandbaths. It helps to keep their fur in good condition. Change the sand every few days.

Hay is much appreciated as a nest-building material.

Don't get your gerbil a hamster wheel to play with – it might catch its tail in the open spaces.

Unlike many animals, gerbils practise a form of birth control. If you have a breeding pair that produces a litter or two then they won't have any more. If, however, you remove the litter, the parents become fertile again.

Gerbils are sexually mature at 60 to 80 days.

Gerbils are unusual in that they generally mate for life in pairs (or sometimes as a threesome, the kinky devils).

Rats & Mice

When choosing a pet, look for a healthy animal. There shouldn't be any bald patches on their fur and they should be alert and agile. Small scars on ears and tails are not necessarily signs of illness but are probably from old fights.

Always try to choose a young rodent as a pet because these animals tend to have quite a short life span. A young mouse or rat can be taken from its mother when it's four weeks of age.

Rats don't fight as much as mice so you can keep them together more easily. Adult male mice tend to be argumentative with each other so are best kept apart.

Pick up rats by their shoulders with your thumb held under their chin to stop them from biting. Don't pick a rat up by the scruff of its neck – it'll take a lump out of your finger.

To pick up a mouse, grasp the base of its tail firmly and lift its hindquarters. Slide your other hand under its bottom and then lift your hand with the mouse sitting on it.

A mouse can be picked up by the scruff of its neck.

When picking up a rodent, try not to swoop down from above in case you frighten your pet. Allow them to sniff your hand before you pick them up.

Place the cage in a slightly raised position. Mice and rats react strongly to danger from above, even if it's only you coming to feed them. Eye-level is about right.

Try to put the cage in a busy area. Rats and mice love to see, smell and hear what's going on.

Rats can be kept in guinea-pig cages because they can't slip through the bars.

If you're worried about your pet mice escaping from a wire cage, see whether you can get your finger through the wire. If you can, a young mouse can get out.

The advantage of wire cages is that mice love to climb and the wire gives them ample opportunity to do this.

Don't keep rats and mice together.

Wood shavings are ideal as litter. They are very absorbent and cheap to buy. Spread them around the cage, about 1½ in/4 cm thick. Don't use cedar or pine, though, because they contain toxins.

Rats and mice tend to use the corners of the cage as their toilet. You could try adding a layer of cat litter in their favourite spots. It will help keep the smell down too.

Female mice don't have the same musky odour as male mice.

Mice like their cages to smell familiar. Try changing only half the litter at a time so that a familiar smell remains.

Equally, put back a little bit of old bedding each time you clean the cage, so that there is a familiar smell where the mice sleep too.

Rats like sleeping in old shoeboxes, or 3-litre wine boxes – with the wine bag removed, of course!

If your mouse or rat gets out, put a cardboard tube on the floor with some food inside it. Once it runs inside, close both ends with your hands and return the escapee to its cage.

To lure a rat out from under the furniture, entice him or her by holding a rat of the opposite sex a short distance away.

Try to avoid feeding your pets too many berries because this can cause rodents to wee more often and make their litter really damp.

Avoid windy pets – don't give them cabbage and onions.

Give mice a challenge – don't make life too easy for them. If you're about to feed them, put the food on a different level so they have to climb up to it. Make ladders steeper or give them ropes as bridges.

Avocado goes down a treat with a rat.

Mice adore sunflower seeds, but don't give a fat mouse this kind of treat.

A cheap alternative to rat food is out-of-date baby food.

Rat delicacies also include titbits like biscuits (both human and dog varieties), apples and tomatoes. But remember to keep them on a balanced diet.

To help a mouse lose weight, cut out oily seeds (like sunflower seeds or peanuts) and fatty treats. Give it soaked stale bread or plain boiled wholegrain rice with fruit and vegetables.

Cheese is not an ideal treat for a mouse because mice don't feed on dairy products in the wild. Cheese is, however, a convenient way to bait mousetraps.

Rats and mice can be fed a few treats now and again. Dry, healthy, low-sugar cereals, plain popcorn, dry oatmeal, spaghetti or wild bird seed all add variety to their diet.

You can keep mice and rats on their own as individuals, but you will have to give them a lot of love and attention to make up for lack of rodent companions.

Keep mice and rats amused – fill their cages with cardboard tubes, climbing frames, ladders and exercise wheels.

You should allow at least half an hour each day for your pet, even more if you only have one animal.

Rats can be taught to come when you call their names.

Mice love empty egg boxes – they're great to chew to pieces.

Rats love to gnaw on things. Try rawhide chew sticks or dog biscuits.

Alternatively, cooked soup bones are a particular ratty favourite.

A rat will require a wheel that is at least 12–14 in/30–35 cm in diameter.

A cheap but effective toy for mice is a section of branch with holes bored into it. Your mice can use it as a climbing frame and ladder.

Alternatively, an upside-down terracotta flowerpot with holes in the edge makes an ideal place to hide.

Add a few small branches from a birch, beech tree or hazel bush – it will give your rat or mouse something to clamber up and down and explore from.

Mice are sexually mature at 30 to 49 days old, while rats wait a little longer – 30 to 79 days.

Reptiles

If you're going to buy a snake, take a pillow case with you to the shop or breeder. You can then wrap the snake up so that it won't become too stressed on the way home with you.

If your reptile gets a cold, put a jar of vapour rub in its cage and turn up the heating in the cage.

To handle a lizard properly, pick it up by holding it firmly around the body and forelegs – never by the tail.

To help a lizard adapt to its surroundings, cover the floor with enough sand and gravel for it to bury itself.

To create a perfect basking area, place a rock inside the vivarium.

Margarine pots are excellent wet boxes for geckos.

When feeding a snake defrosted mice, put the food under the hair-dryer for a while. This will make it look and smell more like the real thing.

Never put frozen rats or mice in the microwave because this will build up the bacteria. Always allow them to defrost naturally.

If a snake is having problems eating, feed it at night or when all the lights are turned off. This will make it feel more secure and it should go back to the normal routine. If the problem persists, take the snake to the vet.

When feeding a snake, ensure that you wrap rubber bands around the end of your tweezers so you don't damage his teeth or mouth.

If your snake has difficulty shedding his skin, get a good dollop of vegetable oil on your hands and stroke the snake from head to tail. You should find that the skin will come off more easily then.

If there's a problem shedding skin from around the eye area, wrap a bit of masking tape around your finger and gently remove the skin with this.

If your snake is laying eggs, she'll appreciate a good hide. Drape a towel over two pieces of wood and she'll curl up underneath. Spray the towel regularly to maintain humidity.

Use old egg boxes for your snake's favourite dish – crickets – to jump around in.

To house an aquatic amphibian, you need the water to be at least 6 in/15 cm deep for the animal to swim in. So make sure you've got a good water-filtration system.

To distinguish toads from frogs, check their skin. A toad has a dry, warty skin, shorter hind legs and a flatter appearance.

To keep your frogs happy, collect moss from trees, wash it and put in with the frogs. Then spray it regularly to keep it damp.

To feed your newts a nutritious diet, give them earthworms, tadpoles and insect larvae – and nothing that moves too quickly.

Snakes don't require a lot of space. A cage one half to two-thirds of its body length is sufficient for most adult snakes.

Snakes are shy creatures, so give them somewhere to hide: a cardboard box turned upside down with a hole cut in the side is perfectly adequate.

Don't feed your new snake when you get it home. Give it a few days to settle down and get used to its surroundings.

Temperature is extremely important – the cage should be kept at a temperature of between 80 °F/26.6 °C and 86 °F/ 30 °C with an incandescent red light (red bulbs cause less stress to snakes). Don't guess at the temperature – use a thermometer.

Proper lighting is important for reptiles because it aids in calcium metabolism. You need a light source that provides the full spectrum of light (including UVA and UVB rays).

Most reptiles and amphibians become less active when they are cold. This makes them easier to handle. Put them in the fridge for a short while (in a container, of course). On no account try to speed up the process by using the freezer. Don't leave them in the fridge for longer than a few minutes. If ice crystals form on their bodies, it can cause a lot of pain and distress.

To create a perfect basking area, place a rock inside the vivarium.

Snakes eat other animals – when thinking about buying a snake as a pet, it's worth investigating whether you can get a ready supply of rats and mice.

Young snakes will need to eat about once a week. Adult snakes can be fed twice a month. For really large snakes, such as boas and pythons, you need only feed them once a month.

Don't leave live food animals in with your snake – mice and rats can give a nasty bite that can seriously injure a reptile.

Don't handle a snake immediately after feeding. It will be sick. Leave it for a day or two.

Bearded dragons make good pets – they can be extremely tame, but have high energy levels and big appetites with personalities to match.

The more you handle a bearded dragon, the tamer it will become. Soon you will have it eating out of your hand (literally) and perching on your shoulder quite happily.

Bearded dragons need a light source for basking and the daily heating of their bodies. You will also need to provide places to hide, so that they can regulate their body temperature.

If you don't want a large lizard, don't get a green iguana. Properly cared for, they can reach 5–6 ft/1.5–1.8 m within four to five years.

Green iguanas can live for up to 20 years in captivity and weigh up to 18 lb/8 kg.

In the wild, iguanas feel more comfortable in trees. Make sure you have enough height in their tank to allow them to climb.

Iguanas love to climb, so provide them with branches, ropes or towels to climb up and bask on. Make sure they are securely placed to prevent your pet from falling.

Choosing a suitable flooring (or substrate) for your iguana's cage is important. Artificial grass, carpet or paper towels are ideal. Always have a few pieces in reserve so that, while a soiled piece is being washed and disinfected, you can put the spare piece in the tank. The clean piece must be completely dry before you put it into the cage.

Newspaper does not make suitable flooring for iguanas because the ink can get into their skin.

Iguanas don't need to eat meat – they can be raised on a strictly plant-based diet, and can get their protein from plant materials. Alfalfa is an excellent source of plant protein.

Chop your iguana's food carefully. Although they have a sharp set of teeth, iguanas don't chew their food – they gulp it down, so don't give them big pieces.

You can make up a week's worth of basic salad for your lizard and keep it in an air-tight container in the fridge. Just spoon in the required amount when you need to. A good mix would consist of green beans, alfalfa, parsnip and fruit.

Add a little extra to your iguana's salad with some left-overs. A bit of rice or bread will add calcium to their diet.

Frogs eat slugs and snails – they make up about 25 per cent of their diet.

You can't get warts from a frog – that's just an old wives' tale.

A group of frogs is called an 'army' of frogs. And a group of toads is called a 'knot' of toads.

When a frog swallows, his eyeballs close and go down into his head. This is because the eyeballs apply pressure and help push the food down the frog's throat.

Toads are partial to ants, beetles and woodlice. Earthworms always go down well.

If you have to handle an amphibian (such as a frog, toad, newt or salamander), make sure your hands are slightly damp. They have very sensitive skin.

Never mix different species together – many amphibians secrete toxins that can be deadly to other species.

Always wash your hands after handling your pet.

Grass snakes are harmless to humans – their only form of defence is to play dead.

Slow worms are not snakes – they are lizards, so don't handle them by the tail. They are usually extremely friendly and happy to be handled.

A slow worm will eat in the late afternoon and early evening. Give it snails, slugs, worms and insects.

Pot-Bellied Pigs

Pot-bellied pigs can be kept indoors or out. Give them some shelter if they are kept outside.

In hot spells they will need a pool of water to keep cool.

Even domesticated pigs need to root around, so make sure they have an area of soft dirt or soil to stick their snouts in.

Puberty occurs at around six to seven months of age. If you don't plan to breed from your pigs, you can have them spayed or neutered at around three to four months old.

If your pig does have a litter, the piglets' needle teeth should be trimmed, so that the sow and other piglets don't get nipped by the sharp teeth.

Pot-bellied pigs aren't aggressive, but they can give a nasty nip if their canine teeth aren't removed. You can have this done when the pig is around four months old.

These pigs don't raise a stink. In fact, they hardly pong at all.

Grooming is important. Brush them down with a soft bristle brush each day. Hooves and tusks will need trimming regularly.

Why get a dog? Pot-bellied pigs are intelligent and can be trained as you would a dog. They respond to litter training, can do simple tricks and walk on a lead.

SOFT FURNISHERS

Curtains

Ben Butterworth, Cheshire; Courtney Spence, Jamieson Furnishings, London; Juliette Bardon, London; Val Adams, Totnes; David Pugh, Birmingham; Ruth Hyde, London

Emphasise natural daylight in a room by using curtain fabrics with a dark background.

To dress a window for decorative reasons only (when you'll never need to draw the curtains) use half as much fabric. No one will know the difference and it will save you a lot of money.

For really cheap curtains, muslin is ideal. Create dramatic effects by swagging and draping metres of the stuff. You can leave it as a plain white fabric or dye it to match your colour scheme.

For a toddler's room, try shower curtains instead of fabric ones. However grubby the little fingers that tug at them, the curtains will always wipe clean and they come in lots of fun designs.

To hang curtains effectively, use the wall space, not the window space. Measure 8 in/20 cm above and 12 in/30 cm either side of the window and hang your curtains in this space.

If you are drilling a hole for a curtain pole, vacuum up the dust at the same time to prevent it from getting everywhere.

Make cheap curtain poles from wooden broom handles. Stain them to suit your decor.

Instead of an expensive metal rod in the bottom of your blind, simply sew in a bamboo stick.

To calculate the length of a pelmet, divide the drop of the curtain by five or six.

Experiment with pelmet shapes – cut out trial shapes in newspaper and blu tack them to the wall. Adjust them until you're satisfied.

To make your window look taller, position the bottom of the pelmet at the top of the window.

Make cheap curtain liners from sheets or old blankets.

Place curtain hooks no closer than 5 in/13 cm apart as it improves pleating and draping characteristics.

When taking curtains down to wash, mark where the curtain hooks go with nail varnish so you know where to replace the hooks for the correct spacing.

To keep curtains hanging straight, put old or foreign coins inside the hems.

If a blind curls up at the bottom, put matched magnets on either side to weight it down.

Measuring high windows for curtains is much easier if you fix the end of your tape measure to the end of a bamboo cane using a drawing pin.

Stick curtain hooks into a bar of soap and you'll be able to slip them into your fabric with a lot less hassle.

Once dirty, it's impossible to get net curtains really clean, so wash them regularly.

Make invisible repairs in your net curtains – dab colourless nail-varnish on the torn edges and hold them together until the varnish is dry.

Vacuum your curtains every few weeks and you won't need to have them dry-cleaned so often.

To avoid taking down curtains when washing windows, drape them through a coat-hanger and hang them from the curtain rod.

Floors

See if that small-patterned carpet is really going to work. Place a mirror on the carpet so that it stretches out in front of you and gives you a better idea of how it would look on your floor.

Make an inexpensive floor covering by painting a piece of canvas with dyes and acrylics. When dry, coat with tough floor varnish.

Cushions & Pillows

Make stuffing from old pairs of tights. Place a bit of dried lavender inside for a lovely smell.

Wash your feather pillows while imagining you're in the vineyards of France. Dissolve a handful of soap flakes in a bath of warm water. Place pillows in and tread with bare feet to remove the dirt. Repeat and rinse, spin in the washing machine and hang up to dry.

Tired looking pillows can be brought back to life by making an opening in the seam and pumping air in with a bicycle pump. Remember to stitch the seam back up.

Fabrics

Felt is a cheap alternative to velvet – it's very effective and is half the price.

The arm rests of a chair quickly get mucky so clean them up by rubbing with a loaf of bread.

Create your own designer fabrics – tie-dye gingham or muslin.

A simple way to create a circular tablecloth is to fold the material in half. Take a piece of string and attach a pencil to one end and a drawing pin to the other. Stick the drawing pin on the edge of the fold, draw a semi-circle over the fabric, and cut out.

If your old sheets have worn away, don't throw them out. Cut around the edges and sew them up into pillow cases.

Change the look of your room – simply throw a white sheet over a piece of furniture. It works rather like correcting fluid, blanking an object out so you can start all over again.

The secret of great-looking throws is to measure generously.

Keep a throw on the sofa by sewing Velcro on the back of it.

Make soft furnishings last longer – simply spray them with Scotchguard or any water-proofing spray of the kind that you would use on suede shoes.

Delicate tapestries or needlepoint coverings can be safely cleaned with a baby's soft hairbrush.

Don't ruin beautiful chintz – always iron the wrong side out to protect the special glaze.

Clean velour upholstery with a solution of warm water and washing-up liquid. Dip some muslin into the mixture and wipe over the fabric.

Lighting Up

Don't throw old lampshades away – give them a quick wash and create a new effect with a different-coloured light bulb.

Blast the dust off a pleated lampshade with a hair-dryer.

Or use an old toothbrush.

Wash fabric lampshades in warm water, then dry them with a hair-dryer on cool. This tightens up the material so the shade looks like new.

Tools of the Trade

Make a 'third hand' – cover bricks with material and use them to hold down fabric while you work on it.

Clean scissors and needles with surgical spirit. It's a great way to remove fabric glue.

Transparent thread on a sewing machine can be extremely static – to prevent static from building up, place a piece of sponge on the last hook so it cleans the thread as it is pulled through.

For an instant spot-remover, use shaving cream. Apply, blot into the stain, wash up with water and blot dry.

Leather sofas should be buffed up with a mixture of linseed oil and vinegar. Simply heat equal amounts of each, then allow to cool to room temperature and apply with a clean duster. Your sofa will gleam.

SPECIAL NEEDS CARERS
Hearing Impaired

Judith Eaton; Pauline Haller, Guide Dogs for the Blind; Denise Smith; Ray Hill, RNID; Disabled Living Foundation; Elaine White; Martin Hughes; Peter & Maggie Baker

When you are doing sign language, try not to wear multi-coloured clothing because it's very difficult to follow what you are saying against such a busy background.

If a deaf person is trying to read your lips, don't stand with your back to the light.

For the hard of hearing, there are phones with variable volume.

For the whole family to enjoy watching a video, get one with subtitles that go along the bottom of the screen. The RNID (19–23 Featherstone Street, London, EC1Y 8SL, tel: 020 7296 8000) have a list of companies that do this.

Blind or Partially Sighted

If you visit a house where a blind person lives, remember to put everything back in the same place.

To thread a needle if you are partially sighted, stick a bit of sponge on to a block of wood. Place the needle in the sponge and then use the needle threader. This method allows you to use both hands.

Store all your buttons, needles or whatever, in a screw and nail box with transparent drawers. Everything can be found much more easily.

Fastening a shirt can be made easier if you substitute press studs for buttons.

To identify appliances easily if you're partially sighted, buy different-coloured plugs or mark each one with a large initial of the relevant appliance – a large K for kettle, for example.

To help your guide dog settle in and get to know its new owner, keep the family away to start with so that the owner is the only person to deal with the dog for the first couple of months.

Elderly and Living at Home

Elderly people living on their own should have a panic button – they're not very expensive and give tremendous peace of mind.

If you don't have a gadget for removing lids, try putting a rubber glove on – it'll give you more grip.

Have a walking stick about the house, but get advice on how to use it properly from the district nurse or occupational therapist. It's easy to get in a tangle if you are not used to using one.

Have a list of your most important numbers written in black ink in large letters by the phone.

It's a good idea to have a phone by your bed, just in case.

To help you remember to take your medication, use containers with the days printed on them. Get a relative to lay out a month's supply to keep you going. Or ask if the medication is available in a blister pack.

Oral syringes can be helpful if your hands are shaky.

Anti-inflammatories can be hard on the stomach lining, and may make you more prone to indigestion.

Ask your pharmacist for a catalogue of equipment to make independent living easier – and ask an occupational therapist for advice.

The Red Cross can sometimes rent out equipment from their medical loan department.

Mats are a danger and should be removed – they can cause accidents.

Buy a small step ladder, just two or three steps with a rail across the top can prevent accidents – elderly people are devils for climbing on chairs!

Elderly people often have a better appetite than you think – they just don't bother when they're on their own.

Isolation is a huge problem for the elderly – it can bring on depression and sometimes confusion. Don't forget that prolonged solitary confinement is used as a form of torture. In extreme cases, individuals may start to neglect their care, medication and not bother with eating. The situation can be improved by regular social contact – but it may be time to consider a move once such a stage has been reached. Often people seem much better – even years younger – after such a move.

The belief that it's better to stay in your home at all costs is a dangerous fallacy.

In the Bathroom

Try to avoid having a bath when you're on your own.

If you do get stuck in the bath, let the water out first – you won't get so cold and it's usually easier to get out.

Bath mitts can make washing easier, and loofahs can allow you to reach awkward places.

Make sure you have a non-slip mat in the bottom of the bath.

Mixer taps with the hot water controlled by a fail-safe thermostatic control avoid the possibility of scalds.

Getting into a scalding bath is a great danger. A baby's bath thermometer can help to avoid this.

Don't use bath oil – it can make the bath very slippery.

Run cold water first, then add hot. But don't put in too much cold.

Having a shower needn't be difficult – fix a grab rail to the side of the wall, but make sure that the wall is sturdy enough to take the weight.

Clothing

A lot of elderly people find heavy clothes uncomfortable, especially if they are rheumatic. Thermal underwear is ideal for keeping them warm and comfy.

Knitted silk underwear is very warm and light and can be found in ski shops.

A fleece jacket is warm without being heavy and doesn't look daft worn indoors. Better quality ones will keep you warmer. Get one that unzips all the way, rather than one you pull over your head.

Keep the extremities warm, as circulation gets slower with age.

Electric blankets are fantastic, but not advisable for anyone who has a problem with incontinence.

Some incontinence supplies – pads and knickers – can be obtained free from the district nurse.

Pulling things over your head is very awkward. Go for front fastening with Velcro, big buttons or chunky zips.

Back-fastening skirts – do up at the front then twist round.

Bras can be a problem. Do them up at the front and then turn them around, or get front fasteners.

Shoes with Velcro fittings are much easier to manage than laces.

Make sure shoes are in good repair and that soles aren't worn. They can cause accidents.

Turning over in bed needn't be a struggle – treat yourself and buy satin pyjamas... or go the whole hog and get satin sheets as well!

Alternatives to Living at Home

Plan ahead – don't wait for an emergency before making plans for the future. Move into sheltered housing or care earlier rather than later.

Before making a choice of care beyond one's home, look at all the options – and visit different types of establishment. It's not always easy or desirable to move on when you need to.

You can admit yourself to a private nursing home, sheltered housing or residential home. You don't need a doctor's letter or assessment.

In retirement flats, the accommodation is usually specially designed for elderly people and will be physically appropriate to their needs but may not have any supervision.

Sheltered or warden-controlled accommodation is appropriate to a variety of physical needs and additionally there is supervision on a daily basis. These often have an emergency alert system built in. They often also have communal dining and social facilities, and will often provide lunch if required.

Residential care homes provide assistance on a regular basis with, say, washing and dressing. All meals are provided, but medical care is not available.

Nursing homes have, in addition, medically qualified nursing and other qualified care staff. They must have passenger lifts and must be equipped to deal with most physical disabilities.

EMI units are specialist units for patients suffering from dementia, Alzheimer's and disruptive behaviour. They will have psychiatric nurses in attendance.

SPIRITUAL GURUS

Barefoot Doctor,
www.barefoot
doctorglobal.com

To experience chi, life-force, the ultimate energy (call it what you will) in your own body, sit comfortably, close your eyes and imagine you're holding something about the size and shape of a rugby ball between your hands. With palms facing, raise and lower the 'ball' about nine times and you'll become aware of a tingling sensation in your palms – that's chi.

To allow your vital energy to move freely round your body, think of extending your vertical support (spine), lengthening it both upwards and downwards, while also visualising your horizontal axes (shoulders and pelvic girdle) widening. Everything else can hang from this structure.

Stick to any agreements that you make. Breaking them is as bad (if not worse) for you as for the person you've let down, and weakens the free flow of chi between you and the rest of the world.

Possessions and chattels beyond your immediate needs drain your energy and slow you down, keeping you tied to the past. Have a good clear out and try to travel light.

Receiving and being open and ready to receive is as important as giving – and that's pretty important. To help keep your heart centre open and receptive, visualise yourself breathing in through an opening in the very centre of your chest. As you breathe in, imagine drawing towards you all that you need; as you breathe out, imagine giving to those in need.

Keep everything you need for the practice of your trade (including yourself), clean, organised and in working order. Visualise all these things surrounded by a soft pink glow – it will afford a special quality to them so that they serve you even better.

Go barefoot (like the doctor) as often as practically possible to massage reflex points in your soles, and treat your feet with love and respect at all times. They deserve it.

For yucky between-toe areas, direct application of lavender oil after thorough cleansing does the trick.

Why try to eradicate fear? You just can't. Make it your friend instead and let it push you in the right direction, but override it when you want to move on, and turn it into excitement instead. It's there to serve you, not rule you.

You have a centre of energy about 1¼ in/3 cm down from your navel and extending right through your body from front to back, called the tan tien (pronounced more like 'dandyen'). When you breathe, feel yourself filling it up with energy, and if you get all hot and bothered as you rush around, pull your energy back down into it – the energy has probably all gone up to your head.

Make your footsteps light as you walk around, and you automatically feel lighter yourself. To help you focus on this, imagine a full cup of tea in your tan tien and try not to spill any as you go on your way.

As yin and yang ebb and flow, so it is with everything. What's full becomes empty, what's empty becomes full. By emptying your mind, for example, you create a space for new knowledge, understanding and visions to enter. The same applies to the heart, belly and pockets (and a nice cup of tea).

When you give, do so freely without any thought of what you'll get back in return. Actually, if you do this, the return is likely to be far greater, but try not to think about that when you're doing the giving!

Enhance your creativity by imagining a channel from the inside centre of your forehead back over your brain to the inside centre of the base of your skull. Breathe in and imagine your breath entering your forehead and passing through the channel to the back of your neck, breathe out and visualise it returning to the front again. As you continue, feel your mind becoming more and more receptive to new and wonderful ideas.

Do everything you have to do (even the unpleasant things) with conviction and grace, and you'll transform it all (especially the unpleasant things) into a heroic performance that you and everyone else can enjoy.

Start to learn t'ai chi or chi kung to be simultaneously humbled and uplifted, and for instant access to unlimited chi. Cheers!

STRESS COUNSELLORS

Sarah Henshall

Make sure that your goals in life are realistic, whether they involve writing a project or simply tackling the ironing. Collapsing into bed at night with a sense of failure that tasks have not been achieved is a recipe for stress.

Make a list, arranged in order of priority: what needs doing urgently and what can realistically wait.

Know when to stop? Give yourself time off. Shut down the computer at a set time, and go for a walk or put your feet up in front of the television. It's a temptation to bring your work home, whereas you need to set parameters for work time and relaxation time.

If your time is short, rationalise the tasks that are too demanding. Do you really need to grow your own plants from seed when low-maintenance shrubs will do? Can you do your supermarket shopping on the internet and have it delivered? Do you need to change the bed sheets completely or will clean pillowcases do for the next few days? Can you delegate a time-consuming job to someone in your work team?

Have a good quality hair cut that needs little after-care. Time is wasted by having to add mousse or blow dry it.

Eat energy foods, especially at breakfast. Stressed people often skip meals, which leads to low blood sugar and then a feeling of fatigue and depression. Time taken out to eat properly will make you more efficient in the end.

Money causes more stress than any other subject. Spend an evening going through your finances, and work our ways you can cut spending and make your life more organised. Throw away leaflets that come through the post claiming to be able to save you pounds, and consult an independent financial adviser about ways to maximise your income and your savings.

Allocate a time to organise your week: perhaps a Sunday evening. Look through your diary and be ruthless about meetings or jobs that are unnecessary and are a drain on your time. Make a shopping list too of goods and menus that will see you through the week (ensuring there is enough in the freezer for last-minute meals), so that you have the week sorted without the need for frantic dashes to the shops for items you have forgotten. You will wake up on Monday morning armed and ready for the week ahead.

Ask yourself if you are being burdened by other people's problems. Friends or work colleagues may be leaning too hard on you and exploiting your sympathy. Be supportive, but don't add other people's problems to your own. Let them fight their own battles.

However, if you are feeling anxious, unburden your thoughts on a good friend or your partner. Their comments may help to put your problems into perspective.

Take time out to enjoy your children, friends or hobby. A little time spent with fun and laughter is a great way to unwind and will enhance your feeling of self-esteem.

Get enough sleep. Most adults need between six and seven hours of good quality sleep to function properly. Wind down slowly for bed, have a warm (but not too hot) bath and curl up under the sheets with a good book.

Be kind to yourself.

SUPERMARKET BAG PACKERS

Leonard Goode,
Safeways

Open those pesky plastic bags by placing them between your hands, held together in a prayer position, then rubbing your hands back and forth against each other – the bag should open easily.

If you're packing heavy or sharp items, such as bacon in plastic trays, take the precaution of popping one bag inside another before you start to put the items in.

If a bag does split while you're packing, put it down, open another bag and pop the whole thing inside, keeping the handles together at the top.

Pack household-cleaning products separately. Even if they don't leak, they can still have a strongly perfumed smell that may taint food.

Always pack cooked and uncooked food separately, and keep them apart in the fridge too.

When packing a trolley, bag or plastic box, make a foundation of heavy items, such as spuds, at the bottom and lay lighter things on top.

The most crushable items go right on top – flowers, bread, eggs, grapes, berries and light veg, so put them to one side and pack them last.

Pizzas get crushed if laid flat. Try standing them on their edge, alongside other items.

Bottles are amazingly heavy – so no more than two to a bag. Double up the bag if you take a third bottle.

Keep bottles upright in trolleys and in bags. They are then much less likely to break if put down with a bump than if they are on their sides.

Bottles are best put upright on the conveyor belt at the checkout. If you put them on their sides, be sure to wedge them in place, or they're likely to roll.

Baguettes are a real nightmare. To keep them in one piece, stand them up in the corner of a deep trolley. In a shallow trolley, buy them last and lay them across the top of the other shopping.

Plastic boxes call for a different technique. Loaded, they can be really heavy. Try to distribute heavy and light things evenly between boxes to keep the weight about equal.

Make sure you've got the right trolley for the plastic boxes before you start.

Iced cakes must stay on top. Even a light item on top will cause the plastic to stick to the icing and ruin the whole thing.

Stray trolleys in the car park can cause accidents – please return them!

Check you haven't left anything behind on the till. Wrapped deli snacks are easy to miss among the spare bags.

If your trolley has a wobbly wheel, don't suffer in silence. It'll only get worse as you add more shopping, so ask an assistant to get you a better one. If you use a faulty one, inform the bag packers at the end – they'll arrange to send it for repair.

SURVEYORS

James Burne; Graham Dickenson

Don't just book your surveyor over the phone. You are entitled to meet your surveyor without cost or obligation to make sure you have chosen the right one for you.

Help your surveyor. Write out a specific list of things that worry you before the survey.

A survey should be done in the morning to make the most of natural light.

Good surveyors always take a double look at new extensions and alterations. They are often signs of a past problem or a cover up.

Check out general problems such as flooding in the vicinity with a building inspector at the local council offices. They are generally very helpful.

Encourage natural ventilation and avoid condensation in the loft – don't seal the eaves with insulation.

Cure condensation by cleaning the affected area with bleach, then drying out with lots of warmth and ventilation.

To check whether the roof has had slipping tiles, look for pieces of foam placed underneath the roof slates.

Take a pair of binoculars with you – you want to get a really good look at gutters and roofs.

Be wary of a house that has very large trees close by. The roots can cause havoc with foundations. A good general rule is that no tree should be closer than one and a half times its own height to any building.

If you are checking a property yourself, have a probe around with a screwdriver. If the walls feel a bit soggy, then the house probably has rot.

To find rising damp, tap the wall with the handle of a screwdriver. If it produces a dull sound, there could be a problem. Compare the sound by tapping the wall at a higher level where damp is unlikely to be.

Test out the upstairs floorboards by bouncing on your heels in different parts of the rooms. The boards may give a little in the corners but should be solid and silent in the middle of each room.

Test the open fire too. Burn a piece of paper in the hearth and ask a friend to see how quickly smoke appears from the chimney. If it's drawing well, it should be almost immediate. If not, call a chimney sweep in.

SWIMMING TEACHERS

Louisa Laughlan

Very Small Children

When introducing children to a swimming pool for the first time, let them sit on the side of the pool for the first few visits and watch the other children. They'll soon be dying to have a go themselves.

When small children first go swimming, let them take a favourite bath toy into the water with them.

To boost your child's confidence, gradually reduce the amount of air in the water wings.

To help children under six months become comfortable in the water, encourage them to play in the bath.

When your child has had a bath, let most of the water out and let her lie on her tummy and kick her legs. Tell your child that she's swimming so that she gets used to the idea.

Teach a child of over six months to breathe correctly in the water by getting him to put his mouth slightly underwater and blow bubbles.

Encourage children's arm movements when in the water. Hold them under the armpits and put a ball just out of their reach; then let them try and grab it.

Get your children used to going underwater by playing 'Ring a ring o' roses' in the shallow end of the pool. On 'we all fall down', everyone has to bob under the water.

When teaching front crawl, ask the children to make sure their eyebrows are in the water. If you say eyes, they freak out!

Children quickly get cold once they've come out of the water so take a towelling bath robe to the pool edge to pop on as soon as they leave the pool.

To stop little ones catching cold, dry their hair under the hand-dryers in the changing rooms.

Older Children and Advanced Swimmers

Keep your diving mask clear and unfogged by rubbing spit (preferably yours) on the inside before you put them on.

To put goggles on correctly and stop water seeping in, put the eye-pieces on first and then adjust the strap at the back of your head.

To increase the power in your leg movements, wear flippers – but always check at the swimming pool that you are allowed to wear them.

Put your flippers on before getting in the water but stay in the water to take them off.

Stop your swimming cap from sticking together by sprinkling it with talcum powder after use.

Avoid see-through swimsuits – stick to dark colours.

An easy way to practise a particular leg movement is to hold on to a float so you can concentrate on what your legs are doing.

To hold your head correctly during backstroke, don't look up at the ceiling – look at a point on the wall you are swimming away from.

Check you are moving as quickly as possible during backstroke – try to do six to eight kicks for every arm stroke.

During front crawl, you can get the most movement from your arms by trying to touch your bottom or thigh before bringing your arm out of the water.

Teach yourself front crawl turns by practising somersaults underwater.

To give yourself confidence when you start to dive, imagine a hole in the water and aim for that.

Avoid slipping when taking a dive by curling your toes over the edge of the pool or board.

Keep your legs together during a dive – place a coin between your feet… and keep it there!

To judge whether a pool is suitable for synchronised swimming, check that the depth is 10 ft/3 m and the width and length are both at least 40 ft/12 m.

In order for synchronised swimmers to hear the music at all times, make sure you have a good quality, battery-controlled cassette player and underwater speakers.

Appropriate music can make a big difference in synchronised swimming – select something with a dramatic beginning and end to grab the audience's attention.

To increase the overall style of a synchronised swimming performance, all swimmers should act with confidence and poise even before they get into the water.

Keep your hair in place during synchronised swimming – apply gelatine at least one hour before the performance. This will wash out later in a warm shower.

Wetsuits can smell if not looked after – keep yours in top condition by always rinsing inside and out with fresh water after use.

Get rid of wetsuit smells by rinsing the suit with disinfectant solution on a regular basis.

Dry your lifejacket quickly – inflate it first.

TEA & COFFEE MERCHANTS

Making the Perfect Cuppa

Whittard of Chelsea;
The Roast and Post
Coffee Company

Always keep tea (loose leaf or bagged) in an airtight container.

To get the best flavour out of the tea, the water must contain oxygen. This is reduced if the water is boiled more than once. Use freshly drawn and boiled water.

When your grandmother warmed the pot, she was right. Tea will brew better in hotter water.

Pour the boiling water into the pot as soon as it boils. It puts effervescence into the brew.

Vary the amount of tea depending on the leaf size. The old adage 'one teaspoon per person and one for the pot' makes very strong tea. Small-leaf teas need one spoon per person and infusion for four to five minutes. Larger-leaf teas need treating more delicately. One or two spoons per pot and infuse for the same time.

Quick brewing never works. It doesn't get the full flavour from the tea.

If the tea is too strong after four or five minutes, you've been too heavy handed with the tea.

Milk first, tea second. Milk dissolves better in hotter liquid.

Never bleach a teapot. In fact wash it out only occasionally.

The Perfect Cup of Coffee

Left-over residues or grounds will taint the coffee. Ideally clean out your coffee maker thoroughly at least once a week with a mixture of vinegar and water to remove the oils.

Make sure coffee is fresher than fresh. No matter how good the coffee is, if it is stale it will be flat.

Keep coffee beans in the freezer and remove enough to grind each time you want a coffee.

Ninety-eight per cent of a good cup of coffee is the water. Bad water makes bad coffee. Always use fresh clear water.

How much to use? A rule of thumb is two level tablespoons of ground coffee for each 6 fl oz/175 ml cup. This is strong for people unused to coffee, but is a good starting point to discover the strength you prefer.

If coffee is brewed with boiling water, it will lose delicate flavours. Too cool and you won't extract all the flavours and end up with a thin cup. Use water that is just off the boil.

Warm your cup before pouring in the coffee.

Coffee left in a coffee warmer will slowly be robbed of flavour. Keep it in a thermos if you have made too much.

No wonder office coffee left in the jug tastes so foul. If it sits for more than 20 minutes it will become bitter and acrid.

Buy a variety of ground coffees to suit your mood, and keep them in the freezer. Simply scoop out the amount you need (it won't be rock hard because it is ground) put it into the filter paper or cafetière and pour on boiling water. The water will release all the flavours!

TEACHERS

Nursery School

Susan Cawthorne, Heaton Nursery; Broad Oak Nursery School; Leap Frogs Nursery School; Rocking Horse Nursery; Acorn Kindergarten; Susan Woodroff; Mary Lapworth

To get a child to sleep, stroke its forehead between the eyes.

You can make dinner more interesting by putting food colouring in milk or mashed potato.

To lure a child into eating boring (familiar) food, put it in a different container to disguise it.

To make children eat more, give them lots of tiny portions.

To keep children entertained during a meal, don't use a tablecloth. Put a sheet of wallpaper face down on the table and leave some pens or crayons lying around. Then they feel as though they are scribbling on the table – very naughty!

Make a pretend cooking hob – take a square, silver cake board and draw four rings on it.

To teach left and right, put little 'l's and 'r's on cutlery and door-frames. Paint 'l' and 'r' on the inside or bottom of shoes with some nail-varnish.

Make a game out of everyday things to help educate your child. For example, they can learn the difference between heavier and lighter by helping you to unpack the shopping.

If you want to encourage children to put things away in the right place, put different-coloured stickers on toys, which correspond to stickers on or in different cupboards, shelves, boxes or other items of furniture.

Make your own curtains. Find some plain white fabric and get children to walk all over it with paint on their feet, or cover it with hand prints.

To show children which tap is the cold one, cut a soft, foam tennis ball in half and place it over the cold tap. They will know which one is safe to use, and it's easier for them to grip.

To make non-dribbly paint, mix it with wallpaper paste (not one that has an anti-fungus agent in it).

For easy hand painting, fill a bathroom spray with paint and use it to spray the children's hands.

For a novel paint effect, trail some bits of string through a paint pot and then pull them across a piece of paper.

Dip marbles in different coloured paints. Put some paper in the bottom of a washing-up bowl and roll the marbles around for wonderful 'snail tracks'.

To blow your own paint bubbles, make up a solution of paint, water and washing-up liquid in a large margarine tub. Take a straw and blow into the mixture, creating a froth of bubbles. You can then place a piece of paper on top for a bubbly, coloured print.

An alternative paint-brush can be made by filling a used, roll-on deodorant bottle with paint.

To make textured paint, add sand, tea, rice – pretty much anything really.

Do your own rubbings. Stick cereal, lentils, rice and/or spaghetti on to some paper. Put a clean sheet on top and rub over with a crayon.

Rub a wax candle over some paper. Paint over the top and then lay a clean piece of paper over the picture to blot the extra wetness. Remove and leave to dry.

Make your own balls of gunk – extremely popular with small children! Mix cornflour with water in a tray and leave the children to do what they will with it!

More gungy gunk! Mix soap flakes with white paint – great for playing with. As it gets dirty, you can start to add colour to it. Begin with light colours and get darker as it gets dirtier. You can make it bright red or green and call it blood or snot – children love it!

Create a grass ball. Get an old, plastic washing-powder ball and poke some holes in it. Fill it with earth and grass seed. Water it regularly.

To make some funky fabric, take two layers of bubble wrap and sandwich confetti, glitter, dried leaves, old sweet papers (whatever you like) between them. Then, place the bubble wrap between two sheets of greaseproof paper and fuse them together with an iron. Use your new 'fabric' to create bags, ties, tabards and so on.

Fill balloons with coloured water and then freeze them. You can then burst the balloon to create an enormous round ice ball!

To make your own DIY musical instrument, use an empty Pringles box and fill it with rice or pasta shells.

Make your own mobiles from coat-hangers. Hang or stick pictures, old cards and bits of ribbon on the hanger.

To make a skittle alley, take old washing-up liquid bottles, juice bottles and even cans, and line them up as your skittles.

To make puppets, use old socks with buttons sewn on for the features.

A good game for children is to cut up a picture and hide the pieces around the house. The children have to find all the bits and, in a set time limit, complete the jigsaw picture.

On rainy days, cut up old birthday and Christmas cards that have photos on the front. These can be used to make cards to play with.

Primary School

Make sure you've got plenty of stickers and give them out liberally, whenever you spot any good behaviour!

To find the end of the sticky tape quickly, put a button on the end.

Stop powder paints from cracking when drying – put a drop of washing-up liquid in with the water when you mix up the paint.

Hair-spray makes a good fixative for models and collages (but don't let the children spray it on themselves).

When teaching children left and right, make sure you stand with your back to the class; otherwise they'll be seeing a mirror image and this will only muddle them up.

Children often get confused by the difference between 'b' and 'd'. The word 'bed' is a brilliant way to show them the difference between the two.

Teach young children to listen to you. Keep your voice quiet. As you raise it, the sound level of the class will just go up and up.

Keep control of a lively class – use a few simple, key words (such as 'stop') sparingly. The children will then know that they must respond immediately.

When you begin to teach children to write, let them make letters in sand.

When children move on to writing with pencils, give them the chunky, triangular-shaped type because they are easier for little fingers to grasp.

If you are using water to measure different amounts, colour it first with a little food dye so that it shows up clearly.

When teaching the alphabet, create a physical action to go with each of the letters so that they become easier to remember.

In winter, ask the children to put their gloves and woolly hats inside the sleeves of their coats when they come back inside. Everything will be easier to find at home-time.

Secondary Education

Take time to talk to your children when they come home. You'd hate it if no one asked you about your day at the office.

If your son or daughter isn't concentrating in class, make sure they don't need glasses. Short-sighted children often get frustrated because they simply can't see the blackboard.

If you think your child has more of a problem, make an immediate appointment to see a teacher. There's nothing worse than waiting until parent's evening and then saying 'I've been worried all term'. It's frustrating for the teacher and it won't have helped your child.

Don't be intimidated by bullies. Just think of them naked or suffering a severe attack of the squits. Suddenly you'll find they don't look so terrible!

Exams & Revision

Never revise on an empty stomach. You simply won't be able to concentrate.

Be quiet! Wherever you choose to revise, make sure it's not noisy.

You need to be comfortable when you revise. Lie on the floor or on the bed, sit in a chair with your feet up… if you fall asleep, that's fine. You obviously needed to.

Surround yourself with cups and trophies while you revise to remind yourself that you can succeed.

Good tip for parents: it's a good idea to forget the state of the bedroom when children are revising!

Allow twice as much time to revise as you think you'll need. There are always distractions.

Be selfish. Ignore that phone call from your panicky friend. They'll be okay – they're usually the ones who end up getting the best grades!

Stick key phrases, dates or words round the house. Put them in prominent positions where you know you'll see them – the back of the loo door, the lid of the biscuit tin, the fridge door.

Don't drink coffee every time you take a break. It will make you jittery. Instead, sip long, cool drinks.

If you're getting really angry with a text, take a photocopy of the author's picture, stick it to a football and kick the ball around for half an hour!

It's really important to keep up your physical exercise whilst you revise. Give yourself an hour's break a day to do your favourite activity. It helps you to process what you've learnt and reduces stress levels.

To relieve stress, try alternate nostril breathing. Cover your left nostril with your finger, breathe in through your right nostril, then breath out of your left nostril with the right one covered, and so on. Carry on doing this for five minutes and it will help you to relax. Best done in the privacy of your own room!

It helps to feel business-like when revising. Don't dress in sloppy leggings or track suits. You are working after all.

Read your revision notes into a tape recorder so that you can utilise wasted time. You can play the tapes while you're travelling, cooking or just lying in the bath, soaking up the information.

Play your recorded revision notes while you're asleep. It is one of the best ways to really digest facts and figures.

Prevent eye strain while you're revising. Sit at a desk or table that has a view out of the window. Each time you look up, you will automatically focus on the distant images. In this way, you'll relax and rest the muscles you've been using for close-up revision work.

Help your concentration. Stare at an orange spot on the wall.

If you are finding it hard to concentrate, stand on your head for a few seconds. The rush of blood allows you to think more clearly.

Make up rhymes to help you remember key facts – 'In fourteen hundred and ninety two, Columbus sailed the ocean blue!'

Practise writing in two- or three-hour bursts to prevent an aching hand on the big day. Many marks can be lost because of an illegible scrawl.

When you're feeling completely overloaded or think you might explode if you revise one more fact, try focusing on something really simple – an orange dot on a piece of paper – and think positive thoughts.

If you need music on while you revise, make it classical music (or easy listening) so that you don't get distracted by the lyrics and end up singing along.

Burn essential oil while you're revising. Put some on a tissue before you go into an exam and hopefully the smell will help you to remember.

Take time out – there's nothing more relaxing than stroking a dog or a cat for a few minutes.

Don't be too ambitious. It's better to revise several subjects thoroughly than cover everything superficially. On the day, you will only get to show a fraction of your knowledge anyway.

Organise your research into sections. Keep scaling them down until you end up with some block headlines and a few key facts.

On the morning of the exam, even if you wake up at the crack of dawn, don't keep revising. Just glance through the headlines and key facts.

Double-check the time and place of the exam. Then double-check the number of questions you're meant to answer.

Get to the exam in time and check that you will be comfortable. Is the desk wobbly? Is there direct sunlight in your eyes? Can you see the clock? And so on…

But don't arrive too early. You'll only get more and more nervous.

Take a lucky mascot with you. If nothing else, a little bit of home is reassuring!

Just before you go into an exam, clench and unclench your hands. It helps to get you psyched up and gets rid of any excess adrenalin.

If it's a long exam, it's good to take a few nibbles along with you but avoid anything noisy or distracting. Break up a chocolate bar into little pieces or take some glucose tablets in with you.

Try to quote from texts that aren't on the obligatory reading list. It makes you look passionate and well-read.

If you feel tired in the exam, rub your hands together, then place them over your forehead and eyes for a minute or two. You will quickly feel revitalised.

Inspections

Prepare to let inspectors see your pupils learning and doing – not just you teaching. Provide lesson notes with follow-on activities.

Teaching should not just consist of chalk and talk but should involve worksheets, film and video.

Pupils' attention spans are short – so divide the lesson up. The aim is to show that you are pursuing a variety of activities.

Show awareness of differing abilities by setting tasks to suit varying levels. You should have clear aims and expectations.

Keep records of finished work and know about assessment recording and reporting. Your pupils should progress in knowledge, understanding and skills.

Make sure you can show off your classroom control – have a question and answer session, activities in groups or individual work. Are you giving your pupils a chance to hypothesise? Are there links being made with other subjects?

Be organised – store your resources and equipment neatly and make sure it's all labelled so that pupils can select things, use them and then tidy them away.

'Work' noise can be productive so don't be afraid of making it!

How does your classroom look? It should be a stimulating and colourful place with children's work mounted on the walls as well as themed displays.

And remember... the inspectors will always miss your best lesson!

TELEVISION PRODUCERS

Alex Fraser

Don't film somebody directly in front of a window – it may look fine through the eye piece but you'll probably end up with a silhouette that looks more like an identity parade for axe murderers than Auntie Maud at her birthday party.

People never think enough about sound. If you're going to edit your home video rushes, sound is as important as pictures. If a phone is ringing or birds are singing, get what's called a 'wild track' – that is a minute or so of recorded sound that you can then put over one or two successive shots. Otherwise the phone will suddenly cut in and then out, or a bird will burst into song from nowhere and then seemingly drop dead.

If you ever find yourself filming under water, condoms are the best thing to put over a microphone.

Want to achieve that professional look when a shot is 'tracking' – that is, the camera seems to be moving to keep up with the action? Just use a supermarket trolley - rest the camera on the child seat for a steady effect. Try not to get one with a wobbly wheel.

Invest in a tripod. Hand-held shots never look really steady.

If you're low on batteries, avoid flip-out monitors – use the eye piece instead. Flip-out monitors eat up power.

Sand is the camera's worst enemy. Next time you take your video on the family beach holiday, put the camera bag inside an extra carrier bag.

Different temperatures can affect your camera. If you come in from the cold to the heat always allow your camera a few minutes to 'acclimatise'.

Home videos often look amateur because we shoot everything we see. Be selective. Professional cameramen take time to choose the right shot, the best backdrop and the right framing.

If you're filming children, come down to their eye level. You'll get a more attractive shot and probably a better 'performance'.

Vary your height of shooting. Stand on a chair, get down on your knees or change the actual angle of the camera. It will all make for a much more interesting final video.

The laziest shot is the 'mid shot' – that is from the head to the tummy bottom and usually lots of empty space around the person. Experiment with very tight close ups on faces for dramatic or personal moments – or, for a bit of fun, allow your subject to move around rather than being fixed to the spot.

Recording the bride and groom opening their wedding presents is much easier and less prone to mistakes than lists after the event. It also makes thank you's much easier. Alternatively they could say thank you to camera after opening each pressie and send off short tapes instead of letters – people will love to see the happy couple opening their gifts.

When shooting a wedding video, think about the background. The outline of a white dress won't show up unless you shoot the bride against some nice darkish foliage or similar. Likewise, a groom in his morning suit splendour needs a bit of light background.

TENNIS PLAYERS

Charles Applewaite, Tennis Wales; Jonathan Markson Centre; Steve Daly

Serving

Get your timing and co-ordination right – throw one ball up with your left hand and then, rather than hit it with your racket, throw another ball at it with your right hand. The aim is to get the second ball to hit the first.

Also, try saying '1, 2, 3' out loud as you serve to get the timing right. 1 – throw, 2 – racket back, 3 – hit ball.

Make sure you are throwing the ball up to the correct height for serving by standing next to a fence and raising your racket up to your 'serving height'. Tie some string to the fence at the correct height. Practise throwing the ball up to that mark.

Placing the ball for a serve is like placing a plate on a top shelf. Don't throw the ball from waist height.

To help improve your serve, pretend you are throwing your racket over the net. Even better, practise throwing a stick for the dog – it's exactly the same action.

Throwing the ball over-arm without using a racket will also improve your serve – it's very much the same action as the one above.

To practise your serve indoors, throw crumpled newspaper at the wall.

To encourage players to serve up over the net, get them to serve kneeling down.

To make sure you are standing in the right position every time you serve, chalk around your feet and hold that position.

Stand with one foot on the other to get your balance right when you are serving.

To help children serve, get them to serve from the service line rather than back on the base line. When they get three out of four serves in, they move back 3 ft/1 m and start serving again from there. This prevents them becoming disillusioned if the serves don't go in at first.

Different Strokes

Improve your dexterity – practise with your racket in your other hand.

Practise with two balls going at the same time.

Bending your knees is important in tennis so pretend that you are playing in a room with a low ceiling and that you aren't able to stand upright.

Improve your reaction time and learn to bend your knees – get someone to roll the ball along the ground to you so that you have to move all over the court, and bend down to return the ball.

The best volleys come from a flat, punching movement so stand with your back to a wall to volley shots back. This will prevent you bringing your racket back behind you.

Hold a ball in your armpit to keep your arm close to your body for forehand volleys.

For a more defensive shot, rather than a harder, more aggressive shot, put your left hand (or right hand for left-handers) in your pocket.

The basic stance for a smash is to have your left hand (or right) up towards the ball as it drops with the racket behind your head. To practise this, try catching the ball rather than hitting it. After a while, you can substitute the action with hitting the ball.

The double-handed backhand is principally done with the left (or right) hand. To practise the shot, stand in the backhand position with both hands on the racket and them remove your right (left) hand and practise the shot with just your left (right) hand placed halfway up the handle.

The forehand ground stroke action is just like throwing a bucket of water.

After hitting a shot, get used to taking one step forward.

To practise your top spin, colour one half of the ball so you can see it spin. Practise adding spin by hitting the ball against a wall and not over the net; it becomes psychologically frustrating if you do a great spin shot that ends up in the net.

To put spin on a ball, imagine a clock face – you are hitting from 6 o'clock to 12 o'clock. Or imagine the ball is a face – you want to hit him on the chin.

Sharpen your reactions by getting someone to throw the ball between your legs from behind you. You'll have to run forward and play the shot.

Don't think about your next move too much – if you do, you could mess it up. Shout 'bounce' and 'hit' as the ball bounces and you hit it; this stops your mind from wandering.

To make tennis a bit more fun, get four players to play with two rackets or, like a three-legged race, tie their legs together.

Improve young player's hand-and-eye co-ordination – get them to keep a balloon up in the air with their hands.

To cheat at tennis, when you are running after the ball, get in a position that prevents your opponent from seeing it when it hits the court and you can call it out.

If you are playing on concrete, put two pairs of socks on your feet for support.

If your tennis balls are wet, dry them in the tumble dryer.

TRAVELLERS

While You're Away

Alison Keeling, Cox and Kings Travel; Jane Breeden, Virgin Atlantic Airways; Charlie Hopkinson; Fiona Seton, Imaginative Travel; Sarah-Lou Reekie, www.alfresco.uk.com

Before going off on holiday, leave half a lemon in each of your rooms at home to keep them smelling sweet.

Get a neighbour to keep an eye on your house while you are away. They can push post through the door, mow the lawn, take the rubbish out and so on. It will give you peace of mind and help you to enjoy your holiday more.

Leave photocopies of passports with a friend at home. If your passports are lost or stolen, the photocopies can be faxed to your hotel.

Packing

Lost passports and documents? Avoid the stress by photocopying the relevant pages and keeping them in your luggage. At least you'll have something to show the authorities if things do go missing.

Credit cards get a better rate of exchange than cash or cheques.

Hotel phones are expensive. Use a calling card from companies such as BT, AT&T or Cable and Wireless.

Pack an empty pillow case to pop all your dirty clothes in whilst you're away – it saves time sorting the clean from the dirty when you unpack.

Seal all bottles and jars with clear nail-varnish to avoid messy spillages whilst travelling.

A snappy idea to save space when packing for short trips is to fill empty film canisters with shampoos and conditioners rather than taking a huge bottle.

If space is tight, pack a sarong. It can be a skirt, towel, throw, shawl or useful shield for changing on the beach.

Use two cases when packing – one smaller than the other. Put your clothes and belongings in the smaller case and then pack this in the larger one. You then have a spare case to fill with all your holiday souvenirs.

Make space in your luggage – take the cardboard tube out of your loo roll and flatten the paper. If you can't get the tube out, stuff it with your smalls so that you use all available space.

Keep luggage more secure – thread a key-ring through all the zip pulls.

If you are taking a torch in your luggage, make sure you have put some sticky tape over the switch so that it doesn't get turned on by accident.

When packing your camera, put all your films in a clear plastic bag and keep them in your hand luggage. In most airports, you'll be able to hand over the bag while the rest of your stuff passes through the X-ray machine.

An old spectacle case is ideal for carrying little bits and bobs – nail clippers, safety pins, needle and thread.

Minimise laundry on holiday – stick to dark colours.

Many hotels in Eastern Europe still don't run to bath and sink plugs. Either take one yourself, or take a squash ball, which works just as well.

Most hotels now offer shampoo and bath gel in rooms (unless you're going to Outer Mongolia), so that's one less thing to pack in your bag.

If you have to pack glass bottles (such as medicine), wrap them in towels or pack them in old margarine tubs.

It's a good idea to have wheels on your suitcase because some airport concourses involve long walks.

Make sure the suitcase is squashy enough to pack away in a locker.

Never put your home address on luggage labels. When you arrive at the airport, it only advertises the fact that you are away on holiday for a while and that your house is unoccupied. Put your address inside your suitcase.

Mark your luggage with a ribbon or cord (or a funny sticker if you have children) so that you can spot it easily as it comes around on the carousel.

Put suitcases in bin liners before strapping them to the roof rack of the car. It will protect them from the rain and anything else that's flying around.

Medical Considerations

Check with your GP six weeks before leaving about relevant vaccinations.

No insect repellent? Eat plenty of garlic to keep the bugs away – we can't promise a successful holiday romance though!

If you get bitten by mosquitoes, lemon juice is a natural astringent and acts as an antiseptic.

Make sure you apply insect repellent under your sun-block.

If you use a natural insect repellent, re-apply after bathing, and don't forget your feet and ankles – a tasty treat for mosquitoes.

Make yourself less appealing to biting insects by taking brewer's yeast or garlic for several weeks before going abroad.

Reduce irritation from bites with ice cubes.

Snap an aloe vera leaf in half and apply the soothing sap to bites or sunburn.

Water is generally clean now in most countries – though there are some exceptions such as China and India. In the Western-style hotels bottled water is always available. Check the seal is still intact.

When buying bottled water, turn the bottle upside down. If it drips, don't buy it, it may be filled with untreated water.

If you ask for a Coca-Cola in a restaurant, don't be surprised if they bring you a can, unopened and put it on the table. This is so that you can see that it's 'safe'.

Try to steer clear of anything with ice cubes in it.

Avoid salad and fruit in Third World countries because they are often washed in untreated water.

Beware of watermelons! They may look wonderful but the really plump, juicy ones have usually been left in local rivers to soak up more water. Avoid them if you don't want an upset tummy.

On the Beach

To encourage a good and rapid tan, eat plenty of carrots and apricots for a month or so before going on holiday.

Get really comfy on the beach. Half-fill a carrier bag with some sand and lay it under the end of your towel as a pillow.

Firmly sew some fabric pockets to the inside of your windbreaker so you can safely store keys, sunglasses, cans of drink and so on while you're on the beach.

If you get sunburnt and you've run out of cream, dab on some neat vinegar to ease the pain.

Business Trip

If you are on a long business trip to several destinations, try to work in a two-night stay at a hotel about every four days. That way you can have your laundry done and you won't need to pack so much in the first place.

When you do pack, work out what you need to wear to each meeting, and put a couple of shirts and a suit on a hanger in a suit bag. Pack two more shirts folded inside the bag – they can be pressed when you arrive.

Check the dress code before you go. More and more, especially in the USA, casual dress is quite acceptable for meetings, so no need to pack a suit and tie.

When booking in to hotels, specify a room on a non-smoking floor, not on the ground floor (too noisy) and not near the lift shaft.

Chains like Hilton, Sheraton and so on have points systems, so, as with booking on airlines, try to arrange a business trip so that you stay in the same hotel chain in different cities.

Minibars are notoriously expensive, so steer clear of them unless you're desperate. If you're on your own go down to the bar and talk to someone. Make a friend!

If your clothes are creased on arrival, hang them in the bathroom while you take a shower. By the time you're dry the creases will have dropped out.

Take a coat-hanger with you because in many hotels you can't take the hangers out of the wardrobes. You'll find it useful to be able to hang clothes in the bathroom.

Flying

Avoid puffy eyes when flying. Place a couple of slices of cucumber over your closed eyes.

Combat jet lag on long plane journeys with a ball-point pen. Take the blunt end of the pen and press it into the ball of your big toe several times; this massages a pressure point and relieves tiredness and nausea.

Prevent swollen feet on long flights by rolling a golf ball under your feet while you watch the movie. It feels great and stops the swelling.

To stop your feet swelling, try a Chinese remedy: put your feet in brown paper bags and then put your flight socks over the top.

If you feel tired during the flight, a quick blast of Cologne is a great pick-me-up.

Avoid dehydration by drinking lots of fizzy drinks and keeping your salt levels high with some salted nuts or crisps.

Reduce jet lag – don't wear sunglasses. Try not to put on your shades as soon as you reach your destination. Instead, give your eyes a couple of days to adjust to the new brightness.

To stop babies' ears from popping when flying, give them a dummy or bottle to suck when landing.

To help children overcome varying pressure when taking off and landing, tell them to 'be like a crocodile (or a hippo)' – it encourages them to open their mouths really wide so that the pressure rebalances.

You can carry disposable nappies as hand luggage – although most countries do sell them they are often more expensive than at home.

Spread your children's possessions around the family's luggage – if a case does go missing, you will still have some of the things that they need.

If you're flying with children, you can always ask if they can visit the flight deck. Not everyone says 'yes' but it's worth asking.

When taking young children on long flights, take your own snacks. Food on planes is very salty and never comes at the right time for kids.

If your flight is long-haul, consider homeopathic remedies to keep children calm and to combat jet lag.

If you're worried about your children getting jet lag, make sure they drink fruit juice or water, and try to book a flight that arrives at your destination in the early evening. Then they can start adjusting to 'sleep' time immediately.

Take a bottle of water on to the plane with you. If you are sitting in cattle class on a full plane, you may have to wait a long time for the flight attendant to reach you.

Although travel agents may say to the contrary, don't expect airlines to provide anything for your baby. If there are lots of children on a flight or they are busy, they may well run out of 'baby-packs', so make sure you take snacks, nappies and things to keep them amused.

It is actually easier to travel with smaller children (under two) than with older ones. You pay hardly anything, and babies are more adaptable than older children.

If you are going long-haul, pre-book a bulkhead seat.

Holidays with Children

Dress your children in a similar fashion for the journey so that if one gets lost, you can give an accurate idea of what they look like by showing what their sibling is wearing.

Pick a venue that is semi self-catering. Restaurants for three meals a day with fractious little ones can be very wearing, but it's good to get a break from cooking occasionally.

Take medications (like paracetamol) in sachets not bottles.

A high factor sun-cream is essential with children, but take one that goes on easily and that the sand won't stick to.

Pack hats – don't rely on being able to buy them at your destination.

Whatever your destination, pack a medical kit. Not only is it essential in an emergency, but medical costs can be high in foreign countries even for minor complaints. Include plasters and bandages, sterilising tablets for drinks, sunscreen, insect repellent, bite-soothing cream, formula for dehydration, and infant paracetamol.

Take supplies of raisins, dried apple and bread sticks for the journey and as snacks for the first couple of days of your holiday.

Pack a survival bag with essentials in it (nappies, toys, food and so on) and keep it with you at all times. You may be hugely delayed or your luggage may end up getting lost.

Take a goody bag of toys, books, sweets and cuddly toys to keep children amused, and include old favourites and a few new ones to interest them. Save the presentation until children are well and truly bored or you'll have blown it too early!

Invest in a good backpack (either for a baby or for essentials) so your hands are free and you don't have to fight with a buggy. Get the baby used to this form of travel by practising at home before you depart.

Don't over pack for a journey. You'll only have to bring it all back.

Expect two or three unsettled nights when you first arrive. Children need to get used to a different bed and temperature… but they will in the end!

Being intrepid? If you are planning to visit a developing country, take your own supply of nappies and your baby's favourite formula milk (if you are not breastfeeding).

Try to keep breastfeeding for as long as possible. It is free, on demand and sterile.

Be scrupulous about good travel insurance.

Relax! Travelling with children can be fun as they absorb new experiences – but if you are tense they will sense it and become tense or naughty.

Attach a balloon to your deckchair to help your children find you on the beach.

Caravanners

Prevent your caravan screen from being splattered by flies – just cover the screen with cling film when travelling and peel it away when you stop. All the flies will come away with the cling film.

If travelling during the winter, always wash your caravan down to avoid salt from the road corroding the surface.

To get your loading right, carry heavy items over the axle, followed by the medium weights, and ending with the light weights at the edge.

Stop the car after about 20 minutes of journey time and have a good look around your caravan to check that everything is intact.

To avoid any problems with the refrigeration unit attached to the LPG (liquefied petroleum gas), turn it off before you stop at a garage.

Protect yourself from greasy stains off tow hitches – place a tennis ball over the tow ball. Or just pop a sock over the top of the hitch when you've parked.

Check that your caravan is level. Put a packet of digestive biscuits on the floor; when they no longer roll, you'll know the caravan is level and then you can treat yourself to a cup of tea and a biscuit.

To keep your caravan level, take large blocks of wood with you. It's a lot cheaper than buying a leveller from the shops.

If you want to keep your table level while you're having a picnic outside, use a couple of rubber door stops. They're waterproof and long-lasting – and come in very handy!

To stop your tablecloth from flying away, use some office bulldog clips.

If you take a large umbrella with you to keep the sun off you while you eat, make sure you don't damage it when trying to push it into hard ground. Take a steel rod, about 6–9 in/15–23 cm long and bash that into the ground first.

If you're a light sleeper, don't park the front of your caravan so that it is facing east – you'll be woken by the rising sun.

To avoid getting stuck in the ground during a wet weekend, park opposite a gate or exit downhill from the site.

Take a jack with you just in case – they don't come as part of the equipment in a caravan.

Always remember to take a spare tyre with you. If you have a flat and need to call someone out to help you replace it, they will charge you.

To check your tyres, look between the treads and on the inner side walls.

To make your own water-waste container for half the price, get an old 5-gal/23-l drum, fit it with a sink outlet and away you go!

For easy cooking in a caravan, always take your wok.

To liven up your peas and potatoes, keep some fresh mint in a brown paper bag in the fridge. It should last for about a week and you can add it to the vegetables when you cook them.

To cook delicious potatoes on the barbecue, slice them, add seasoning, then wrap in foil and place on the barbecue for about half an hour.

To save money on gas, buy the large canisters of 29–31 lb/13–14 kg because you generally have to pay to have the bottle cleaned. Go for one big one and you'll only have to pay for one to be cleaned. Or, alternatively, you could put your coffee percolator or kettle straight on to the barbecue after you've cooked the meat.

To cook food in tins without using any gas, open them up and place on the barbecue – it saves on washing up, too.

To keep batteries charged up, take a lead with you. If your caravan battery fails, you can run the electrics off the car battery.

To make more space in your cupboards, see if you can divide them into shelves.

To avoid any breakages, go for plastic crockery and not china.

To stop the contents of your shelves from falling off, place two hooks on either side of each shelf and attach a stretchy net curtain rod across the front of the shelf.

Save money – don't buy a caravan toilet brush – just get a washing-up brush and place it in a plastic beaker.

When not in use, store your caravan cushions in a dry attic.

To ensure that your caravanning is trouble-free, try to have the caravan serviced every year.

To get a good idea of what you want from a caravan, try hiring one first for a couple of days before making the decision to buy one.

TREE SURGEONS & ARBORICULTURALISTS

Planting Trees

Nigel Finn; Archie Miles; Andrew Poppy

Try to plant only hardy species in areas of prolonged exposure.

Trees can reduce your heating bills! Strategically placed trees around your house can create a windbreak design that will reduce the effect of wind chill. (Even if temperatures are not low, wind chill can take them way below freezing point.)

In warm weather, mature shade trees can block up to 90 per cent of solar radiation, helping to keep your home cool.

Don't plant a cherry, willow or sycamore tree too close to the house, as their roots can interfere with the drainage system.

Gingko biloba is a good choice for planting in towns as it is very resistant to pollution and seems unaffected by fungal disease or insect attack. Choose a male form, because the females produce smelly fruit!

If your trees are constantly attacked by goats or deer, try growing Syrian juniper – the spiny leaves will resist anything.

Silver maples are less attractive to grey squirrels than other forms.

Tree Maintenance

Dead wood should always be pruned from a tree as it can be a point of entry for insects and disease. You can do this at any time of year.

In winter, check to see if your trees have cracked forks or tight 'V' forks that can hold water. The water may freeze, expand and cause splits in the wood.

After heavy snowfall, it's worth trying to knock the snow off branches, particularly on trees like cedar of Lebanon, which can crack under the weight of snow.

The best time to prune trees is in winter, when they are dormant. When there are no leaves on a tree, it is easier to evaluate its shape and spot dead and diseased branches. In addition, the under-planting will suffer minimal damage at this time.

Stop fertilising trees in early autumn to allow them to prepare for winter. Too rich a diet makes them produce soft growth that is easily damaged by frost.

To treat a tree wound, first clean it by removing ragged bark or splintered wood, and the bark surrounding the injury, using a knife, saw or garden shears, keeping the edge as even and straight as possible. Remove any broken limbs close, but not flush, to the trunk.

If you want to fill a hollow cavity in a tree, remove as much of the rotten wood as possible from inside with a chisel. Use foam insulation instead of cement to fill the cavity, as if you ever have to cut the tree down, insulation is much easier to cut through than concrete.

Never put your weight on a branch to make it easier to saw. If it snaps off, you, the branch and the saw will all fall in a heap.

Tree surgeons wear kevlar trousers, steel-capped boots, goggles, ear defenders and hard hats – and we know what we're doing! Don't take risks when using saws.

To remove tree sap from your hands, use mineral spirits, paint thinner or baby oil on a rag or paper towel. Hold it against the sap for a moment, then dab and rub it gently. Repeat until all the sap is removed, then wash your hands thoroughly with soap and warm water.

Covering pruning cuts by painting over them doesn't really provide any benefits. Paints don't do anything to prevent the invasion of decay organisms, and in some cases they may actually speed decay. If you want to cover up a large cut, it's better just to rub it with soil to darken it.

Get decayed matter cut out of a tree as soon as you see it, or you could lose the whole tree.

Deciduous trees and shrubs are dormant over the winter and are best pruned at this time, as there is no chance of shocking them, although the flowering time of shrubs often has a bearing on when they should be pruned.

Dead, diseased or injured wood should be removed from trees before pruning. Branches that are different in colour from the main body of the plant are suspect. Any marks that look like splits or blisters are probably injuries. Black patches along the branch are probably disease.

Before pruning, cut into the tip of the branch to check that it is dead. If it is green on the inside, it is still alive; if it is brown on the inside, it is probably dead. Cut back from the tip until you reach green wood.

Branches that cross the centre of the plant should be removed, as they interfere with air circulation and encourage fungal growth.

A tree should only have one main trunk. You should cut out any upright growing limbs that are competing as leaders.

Remember that different trees are meant to be different shapes. Before you start pruning, know the basic shape of the plant. Prune fruit trees with their branches low so that you can reach the fruit; maples usually have a rounded crown.

The wood on fruit trees should be very dark and crooked. Water sprouts, which are light in colour and grow vertically, should be removed.

Don't leave prunings and fallen leaves around the base of the plant, as insects can survive the winter in the debris.

People usually lop trees to control the upwards growth of the tree, but it actually has the opposite effect. The new sprouts are far more numerous than normal growth, and grow more rapidly, which means that the tree is soon back to its original height and with a far denser crown.

Some trees are more tolerant to lopping than others. After severe pruning, beeches do not sprout very readily, and the reduced foliage will almost certainly mean the tree will not survive.

If the leaves on your apple tree wither and die during summer but don't fall off the tree, it's a sign of fireblight, a bacterial disease with no cure. The tree will almost certainly die in the next couple of years.

Watering

You do not need to water if there has been adequate rainfall. Over-watering can be just as bad as under-watering. The soil should be allowed to dry out somewhat between watering to avoid 'drowning' the tree.

Help trees, especially newly planted ones, during hot dry periods by applying 2–4 in/5–10 cm of mulch around the base of the trees. This conserves soil moisture and keeps the soil temperature cool. Lower temperatures result in less evaporation and better conservation of water. Make sure you water really well before mulching.

In times of drought, some trees may lose their leaves. It is important to remember that although these trees are weakened, they are not dead. Many defoliated trees will survive and recover. They drop their leaves in an attempt to retain water and save themselves.

In hot weather, a light sprinkle of water may only settle the dust, and in some cases can actually do more harm than good. If you water only the upper surface of the soil, the tree's roots could start to grow upwards in search of water. When the soil dries, the new shallow roots will be killed more easily.

Trees rarely need watering after the first two years of their life.

Cutting Down Trees

Make sure you really do want major trees removing – they can't be replaced.

Move cars and other items clear of the working area, and make sure passing drivers are warned, if necessary.

Make sure you and your tree surgeon are clear about what is to be done with the debris. Who is going to remove it? Will the logs be cut and stacked? Will the branches be chipped?

Try to be at home when your tree surgeon is there – if he cuts off more than you wanted, it takes a long time to grow back.

Always check that your tree surgeon has at least £2 million Public Liability Insurance, or you could be facing a huge fine if any damage is caused to your house or car.

If a branch overhangs your garden, you are permitted by law to cut it down, but you must either return the branch to the owners or ask them if you can dispose of it.

You can avoid major tree surgery by regular maintenance; conifers should be trimmed yearly.

Before cutting down a tree, check with your local authority that the tree has not got a Tree Preservation Order on it, or you may be facing a £20,000 fine. If you live in a Conservation Area, you should assume trees are protected, although fruit trees are usually exempt.

Oak and beech trees, which are native to Britain, are protected under conservation orders in many areas.

You should be qualified to use a chainsaw. Most fatalities involving trees occur during tree surgery and involve a chainsaw.

UNDERTAKERS

Natural Death Centre; Martha's Funerals; Barbara Butler; British Humanist Association

You don't have to relinquish the body of someone you love. It is perfectly legal to ask to keep the body at home until the funeral.

Remember to register the death within five days. You have to be a relative of the deceased, someone who lived in the same house or have been present at the death.

You may need several copies of the death certificate so make sure you ask the registrar if you can have some. You will have to pay a small sum of money.

Make sure your funeral is just as you want it to be. You can leave clear instructions in your will. It saves family and friends a lot of worry if they know what you wanted.

If cremation is your choice, avoid complications. Remember to state if you have any medical implants. Pacemakers have a tendency to explode in extreme heat.

The most eco-friendly way to bury someone is in a cotton body bag or cardboard box, not a coffin.

Lessen the amount of pollution in the atmosphere – opt for burial rather than cremation.

You can be buried on your own land but you have to get permission from the local planning department and you must inform the environmental health officer.

If you are planning a traditional service, with family members carrying the coffin a fair way, it is worth ordering the box to be made from a light-weight wood, such as willow. People struggling to carry a heavy coffin robs a service of any dignity.

Customising coffins is increasingly popular. Try jazzing it up with some paint or use découpage to stick on lots of pictures and articles about things the deceased liked.

Decorating the coffin is a wonderful way to get the family involved. Doing this can be a great catharsis.

For an alternative non-religious funeral, call the British Humanist Association (47 Theobalds Road, London, WC1X 8SP, tel: 0207 430 0908) or the Natural Death Centre (20 Herber Road, London, NW2 6AA, tel: 0208 208 2853) for information and advice.

To help you record details of loved ones forever – put them on the internet. Contact Meadow Rest Ltd & Information Net UK (tel: 01275 341111).

VETS

Nick Horniman BVSc MRCVS, Pets Barn Animal Hospitals, Gloucestershire

Getting a dog? Read about the breed, know the commitment required, and know the costs. Get your pets insured – it isn't *if* they ever have a medical or surgical condition requiring veterinary treatment, it's *when*. It will happen, so let the insurance company pay.

Most fleas – even on dogs – are cat fleas, so you will need to treat all pets in the household. Use spot-on vials from your vet once a month, 12 months of the year. Spray with an environmental household spray once a year, and vacuum regularly. Don't wait until you see fleas. Prevention is better than cure, and cheaper.

Having just one dog or cat should not be a problem – they won't get lonely. Although two dogs can play together, they can also hate each other – not unlike children.

Two dogs will work out a social order of who's in charge. Support this order rather than treating them both equally.

A male and a female rabbit live well together – but have them neutered!

If you lose a favourite pet, don't immediately replace it unless you feel that is right. It was probably an important part of your family so mourn it and explain what has happened to your children. It's all part of learning about mortality.

Giving pills is always tricky. There's an excellent little device called a 'pill-giver' that's available from vets and pet shops. Otherwise, you could hide pills in cheese, ham or another treat – people have even been known to drill holes in dog biscuits to hide tablets.

Keep cats in at night – more cats get killed on the roads and get into fights at night. Get the cats in by bribing them with treats intermittently, so they don't expect them every time.

More dogs get put to sleep annually due to bad behaviour than for any other reason, such as disease. This bad behaviour can be due to poor socialisation as a puppy. Socialisation in dogs is very important and can be helped by vaccinating earlier than ever before, that is at eight and ten weeks. Get your vaccinated dog to meet other dogs, children, ice-cream vans, horses and so on.

Don't let your dog come upstairs or in bed with you. Your dog needs you as leader, not for him to dominate you.

Get a cat. You'll live longer.

Dogs are generally okay with children but be careful, mainly when a child is at the same eye level as the dog.

Cats suit elderly people and people out of the house at work for the day.

Find a good vet – one that just does cats and dogs, a tidy clean practice with lovely staff who love your pet.

Feed your dog twice daily. Bones are okay so long as they are part of a balanced diet – seek professional advice from your vet. Avoid all canned foods – you would if you knew what was in them!

Wipe the feet of your dog before coming into the house to reduce foot problems.

Don't clip a Westie's hair too short – it makes skin allergies worse during summer months.

Vaccinate your dog – the fatal diseases are still out there on the streets of our towns and cities – despite what the dog press might say.

Canine prostate cancer has quadrupled in the last five years, so castration is recommended once the dog has reached maturity.

Bitches do not naturally benefit from having a litter of puppies – either plan to breed or get her neutered

If your bitch is to have pups – contact your vet in advance so the practice knows. Contact the vet if she is straining to have the pups but nothing happens for half an hour.

VICARS, PRIESTS & MINISTERS

Fr John Arnold, Catholic Canon Lawyer; Mark Emerson; Sonia Clarke

Ministers don't expect you to be familiar with the appropriate readings – just ask, we've usually got a list as long as your arm.

It's quite normal to feel unable to organise a service if you've just been bereaved. Any distance on your part won't be interpreted as a lack of faith or care.

Check with the usual flower arrangers before you get stuck in – they'll appreciate it and may be able to help with equipment, watering and so on.

Check the arrangements for using confetti – and make sure everyone knows.

At funerals, you don't have to give a potted biography of the person whose died – the people at the funeral know who it is they're remembering. It's more important to emphasise thanksgiving and hope.

Don't worry if your baby yells blue murder at its baptism – the baby only actually has to be there for the anointing and pouring of water. The parents and godparents can stay put and the baby can go outside until it's needed, if necessary.

Don't get in flap about putting on wedding rings – it's easier to put them on when the ring finger is slightly bent, not straight.

Always include the words of any hymns to be sung at a wedding in the printed order of service – it saves people scrabbling around for hymn books.

There's no right or wrong about who's present at signing the register, or who walks out of the church with whom at the end of the service – just make sure you've decided in advance what you want at your wedding.

You can choose a godparent who cannot be present. He or she can be a godparent by proxy.

In Catholic Canon Law, at least one godparent must be practising. The rest should at least be interested in the spiritual well-being of the child.

Save the order of service from any wedding that you go to – they may come in handy for planning.

If you're thinking of getting married, you should let your minister know well in advance – at least six months.

You may find it easier to book a church than somewhere for your reception, so book early.

Videos are welcome in most churches nowadays, but most ministers would prefer the cameraman to remain in one position once the service has begun. Please ask first.

Most ministers would welcome guest clergy to celebrate baptisms, weddings or funerals. Better to extend the courtesy of asking, rather than just assuming.

Brides often worry about whether they have to wear white or should wear a veil. Very little is absolutely essential in the rite of marriage, and certainly nothing to do with clothing!

You do not have to 'obey' in any rite!

You can marry in a registry office, in premises licensed for marriage or in a church or place of worship.

In an emergency, you can baptise someone – and you don't even have to be a Christian to do so. Using a little water on the head, simply say the words 'I baptise you in the name of the Father, and of the Son and of the Holy Spirit', and it's done. If the person recovers after the emergency, they can't be baptised again, but there can be an appropriate church service.

Captains on board ships can perform marriages and funeral services.

Churches are only locked because of security – we much prefer to leave them open.

Anointing the sick is intended for those who are seriously ill, but you don't have to wait until they're at death's door. You can request it more than once.

Most hospitals and nursing homes have contact with priests and ministers, and will arrange for communion if requested – it's a right for all those in good standing with their church.

Priests and ministers are not just ministers of sacraments and religious services – they are pleased to assist in whatever way they can with personal problems.

Priests and ministers welcome social contact and regard it as part of forming close contact with their community.

VOICE COACHES

Joanna Crosse at MetaMedia, meta.media@virgin. net; Andrew Wade, Head of Voice, Royal Shakespeare Company

Everyone has a right to be heard. More importantly, everyone wants to be heard. Our voices represent who we are.

There are no great myths to using your voice well. Many people imagine public speaking or broadcasting to be a select job for the few who can do it. Not true. All of us have the potential to use our voices well and be heard.

Imagine your voice is a palette of many colours and the more you use the richer and more resonant you sound.

Try this breathing exercise. Close your eyes. Sit up straight with your feet flat on the floor. Take some good, deep breaths and you will be begin to feel more relaxed and at ease. Imagine there are roots going through the bottom of your feet into the ground. This will help you to feel connected. Also imagine where your stomach is. Just connecting in this way makes you centred and it helps you to use your voice from that central part of yourself, rather than your upper body.

If you try speaking when you're feeling tense and not breathing properly it will make your voice go higher and you will sound strangulated!

The secret is you just have to be real. You have to sound interested in what you are saying. If you sound bored and disinterested then everyone else is going to switch off. Put meaning into your words. If you're talking about a tragedy, sound tragic. If it's business news you're delivering then sound businesslike. If you want to sound like you care then sound compassionate.

Whether you're talking on a one-to-one basis or to an audience of thousands remember you are really only talking to one person. You need to sound conversational, and that means using conversational language. The written word can often sound stilted.

Don't let messages of self doubt run around your head when you're in the middle of a speech. If you're not thinking about what you're saying, you can guarantee no one else will be. You can't afford the luxury of self criticism.

You have to stay connected to every word. If you switch off (because you're worrying about your delivery or presentation) it's exactly the same as putting the telephone down in the middle of a conversation. You cut the line dead. You need to bring the words to life with feeling.

Most of us don't use our voices properly so remember if you're broadcasting or making a presentation, in order to sound natural you have to be a caricature of yourself. It's like a cartoon exaggeration of who you are. So go for it, put lots of feeling and energy into your words. You might feel ridiculous but you'll sound great!

Vocalising is a physical activity and the voice is linked to how we relate to our body.

The less we feel able to express ourselves successfully, the more insecure we can feel and less capable of verbally communicating.

Sore throats and voice loss can result from a loss of confidence in our ability to communicate. Voice problems further undermine our self-image, and a vicious circle can be established. Regular practice can resolve such difficulties.

Breath is the energy of communication.

To relieve tension or anxiety before an important event, take conscious deep breaths. Anxiety, fear and panic can cause us to hold our breath, breathe more shallowly or even attempt to speak without taking a relaxed full breath.

Practise consciously speaking on the active outgoing breath so that this sensation will become habit and happen unconsciously as well.

If you are feeling tense, consciously breathe out – expel all your breath 'FFF' – then enjoy the sensation, freedom and relief of the breath replacing automatically!

If the atmosphere is dry where you are working, drink more water.

Your body needs six to eight glasses of water per day to get it fully lubricated. Unfortunately coffee, tea and alcohol all dehydrate!

Inhalation of dry air may result in a general lack of lubrication and, consequently, problems with the voice. Steam inhalation is the best way to alleviate this situation and the only way to get moisture directly on to the vocal folds.

If you have an important speech, practise it out loud, not silently in your head. Your mouth is your 'thought muscle' and your mouth needs to keep up with your brain!

Three little sounds that get lost more than any others, in public speaking, in a theatre space or in a classroom, are m, v and f. Make them *active*!

Pause for thought! The listening ear can take in approximately seven to nine words in any one go – so phrase what you're saying accordingly and leave a pause so your audience can process what you've just said.

Alert your listeners with a change of pitch (a different vocal note). It's far more effective than changing the volume, so let your voice have musical variety.

Final consonants should come through loud and clear. If they are voiced ones – such as b, d, g, n, l, z and particularly v and m – make sure they are vibrating with sound. To practise, put your hand on your throat, and feel for the vibrations as you say 'To*m*'.

Can't get your mouth around certain words? Try whispering your problem word or phrase a few times. By removing the voice we find the muscularity of language – the movement as it were.

WAITERS

Adam Lloyd; Oliver Woodhead

Check on the table setting before you start. If a client doesn't like the linen or cutlery, you'll just have to change it.

Start setting the table by arranging the chairs around the table. Always leave enough space between chairs that all the guests can be seated comfortably without rubbing elbows, but are near enough to allow conversation.

Use a large platter to mark the spot where each guest's dinner will be served. If the platter is large enough for all the plate sizes that will be used, it does not have to be removed until the main course is cleared – and makes it easier to keep the plate-spacing even around the table.

Clear plain glasses are preferable to cut, frosted or coloured glass as they don't distract attention from the wine. Seeing the wine gives the diner information about its taste and allows the diner to see any impurities.

A wine glass should be big enough to allow the wine to breathe, and for you to swirl the wine around in it.

When taking orders, as well as remembering and using the table numbers, number the seats at each of your tables. With your back to the kitchen door, make the first chair on the left number one, then continue clockwise. Then you can number the orders as you take them, so you can deliver them to the right people without having to ask who ordered what.

If you're taking drinks orders at the table, place the ordered drinks in the same numerical sequence round your tray as the seats at the table.

If it's the practice of the restaurant to serve the ladies first, on your pad, circle the seat numbers where the ladies are sitting.

If you are using a system like those mentioned above, make sure anyone new has it clearly explained, or the system could collapse.

When carrying a loaded-up tray, put damp towels under the lower layers, to prevent them shifting as you go.

Although a good waiter should be unobtrusive, don't be elusive. If the customers have to keep waving you over, you're not being attentive enough.

If you have to complain about the food or the service, make sure of your facts – note the time you place your order.

Customers should understand that the waiter has little to do with the length of time you have to wait for your food.

WEB DESIGNERS

Myriad Creative

Web design is a skill that is still in its infancy. The best starting point is to look at other examples – the good, the bad and the downright ugly. Browse sites that are offering similar ideas and products to yours, and look at the ones that are recognised as being very good in their field. Inspect what they have done and ask yourself what works and what doesn't. What's impressive and what's irritatingly bad? Create a favourites list of the ones you like and try to emulate them.

Poll everyone you know: what do they like and dislike about websites? How skilled are they at surfing the web? What kind of hardware, software and internet connection are they using?

Web browsers average a ten-second attention span per page, and only a minority scroll down the page. You need to grab them quickly. Select your main message and make that the 'big story'…

… but browsers are becoming more sophisticated. They won't want to be faced with pages of text to read – they buy a paper or magazine for that – they want to see pictures or graphics, touches of colour. They don't want to get bored.

They won't want to get lost either. Websites are not like magazines or books, which have an element of spatial awareness about them. They are linear. If a user feels disorientated they will click out of your site faster than you can say Bill Gates.

Good web design begins not with the designer, but with the user. Work out who you are aiming to attract, and put yourself in their shoes. What would they expect to see?

They're not readers, they are users – show them something in a format they will be familiar with – pictures, news pages, photo album. Draw people into your website, and then you can give them your message or sell your product.

Ask not what you want to say, but why would anyone want to listen?

Build a website as if you were designing a house. Bring people in to the hallway (the home page) and mark the doors off it. They can then choose which door they want to go through.

But once they are in a room, make sure they know what other rooms there are in the house by keeping a navigation index on each page of your site.

Each screen or page of your site should provide clues to which section the user is 'in'.

Keep the number of menu items per page between four and eight. Users prefer a few dense screens of choices rather than many layers of simplified menus.

Don't have more than a couple of 50K graphics to the page. Anything that takes more than a few seconds to load had better be fantastic!

Use links to other pages sparingly. If you want people to finish reading a piece of text, you don't want them following invitations to go elsewhere.

Incorporate links into text rather than interrupting text with 'Click Here to find out more' sentences.

Or make a list of relevant links at the bottom of the text, rather than confusing the text with links within it.

Buttons on the page don't need to be enormous. The browser's mouse pointer will turn into a hand as it reaches a link anyway.

Don't have more than two dominant colours per page. You won't want browsers reaching for their sun-glasses.

Use contrasting colours for the background and the text. If a light text colour is used on a light background, it will be hard to read, as will dark text on a dark background.

Blocky, square shapes tend to make the page look static and as if you lack professionalism. Rounder, soft-edged images are more inviting.

Try not to split the screen into frames – it's confusing and means you cannot bookmark the current page and return to it.

You'll turn off casual browsers by being too flashy. Useful content and good customer service is much more important than showing off what a web wizard you are.

Moving images have an overpowering effect on the human eye – give your reader a bit of peace to read the text.

Keep URLs readable and brief – people do try to decode them – but also if they have to retype them there is less chance of typos.

Link colours are standard – blue for unseen pages, red or purple for previously seen ones – so don't change them.

If you want to emphasise a point, use bold, italics or different colours, but don't underline it. Underlining makes words more difficult to read and it also confuses the browser, because text that links visitors to alternate locations is underlined.

WHITE WITCHES

Tony & Aileen Grist

If you can't get to work outside, create a link with the natural world by keeping house plants in your temple space.

Place symbols of the elements at the four quarters in your temple. For example: feathers in the east to represent air, decorative candles in the south to represent fire, sea shells in the west to represent water, fir cones and acorns in the north to represent earth.

If you work with a group, let each member leave an object representing themselves on the high altar.

Put candles out using a snuffer or your fingers. Blow them out and you blow away your luck.

Watch out for floaty robes around lit candles. This is one good reason why many witches work in the nude.

Make a pentacle out of a circular breadboard with symbols painted on it.

Gods and spirits tend to hang around places where they've been made welcome. Never invoke any god or spirit you wouldn't want as a house guest.

Imprecisely focused spells bring unforeseen results. Make sure your intention is completely clear.

Write spells and prayers on strips of cloth or paper. Tie them to a tree and let the wind and rain take them.

Always remember the *Wiccan Rede*: 'An it harm none, do what you will'.

The sacred is all in the mind. No site is intrinsically more sacred than any other. Your own street or back garden will be sacred space if you want it to be.

You don't need expensive tools. Every tool of witchcraft can be found in the kitchen or in the garden shed.

Actually you don't need tools at all. As one old witch put it, 'who needs tools, when you've got fingers'.

Don't take yourself too seriously. The best ritual is often the one where things go wrong and everyone falls about laughing.

A prayer is when you ask the divine to do something for you. A spell is when you draw on divine energy so you can do it yourself.

WILDLIFE ENTHUSIASTS

Paul Wallace;
Gerry Silverman

Squirrels

Unlike many wild animals, a squirrel does not like being enclosed in a box. So, if you have caught an injured one and intend taking it to a vet, use a cage instead. Make sure it's made from metal – squirrels have sharp teeth.

If you are tending to an injured red squirrel, you will have to contact your local Nature Conservancy Council. Red squirrels are a protected species and you will need a licence to care for one.

Foxes

Keep foxes out of the garden by spreading lion dung around the edges. You don't have to gather your own lion poo, just ask at the local zoo for a batch.

If you are looking after an injured fox, give some thought to its water container. Foxes love peeing in them so you will have to come up with a more suitable solution.

To feed a fox cub, don't use cow's milk. Feed them goat's milk every three or four hours. You'll need to use a bottle if the cubs are less than four weeks old. They can go on to solids when they are about a month old.

Hedgehogs

If you have to catch a hedgehog, but don't want to handle it, wait until it's rolled into a ball and then gently roll it on to a handkerchief or piece of newspaper, which you can use to transport it.

If you want a hedgehog to unroll so you can examine it, hold it in the palm of your hand and gently rock it backwards and forwards. The theory is that the animal will get a bit giddy and unroll to see what on earth's going on.

Alternatively, try to work out where the head is and hold it pointing downwards over a table. The hedgehog should start to unroll and try to reach the surface below. You can then hold it gently by its hind legs.

Hedgehogs are nocturnal animals so, if you find one during the day, there must be something wrong with it.

Hedgehogs drink a lot of water – they need up to 4 fl oz/120 ml at a time.

Don't give milk to hedgehogs – water is best.

Hedgehogs are the gardener's friends. They will quite happily keep down the slug and beetle populations for you.

If you're keen to leave food out for a hedgehog, try pet foods and baby foods, not milk and water.

If you need to force feed a sick hedgehog, dribble a solution of warm water and glucose into its mouth with a syringe.

Baby hedgehogs with their eyes closed need to be fed every two to three hours – they will need about ½ tsp/3 ml milk and water with a dash of glucose.

If you don't have a pipette for feeding, you could try a paint-brush or small spoon.

After each feed, a baby hedgehog must be cleaned and gently massaged with baby oil or kitchen wipes. You have to imitate the licking action of the mother, which stimulates circulation.

Equally, you need to encourage a baby to empty its bowels. Dip a cotton bud in warm water and gently tickle the baby's bottom. Do this before and after each feed.

You must keep baby or injured hedgehogs warm. Wrap a hot-water bottle in an old jumper and put in the bottom of a cardboard box.

Don't release a hedgehog into the wild until it weighs 1 lb 6 oz/623 g. Wait until warm weather (around April time) because there will be plenty of insects around to be eaten.

Try to release a hedgehog where there are other hedgehogs. This means that there is enough food and shelter for them to survive.

Hedgehogs love garden bonfire heaps – they make ideal places to hibernate. Always turn your bonfire over to check for guests before setting it alight.

Secure a piece of chicken wire so that it dangles into your garden pond or swimming pool. Hedgehogs can swim, but might need some help getting out of the water.

Always check grass and weeds before using a strimmer because these are ideal places to nest if you're a hedgehog.

The gap underneath a raised shed provides excellent shelter for hedgehogs and keeps them out of the clutches of any cats.

Deer

If you accidentally corner a female deer, watch out for its front feet. They are great boxers when they need to be, and often use their feet first rather than their horns.

Avoid deer during the rutting season, especially male deer. A fully antlered red stag in rut is quite capable of disembowelling a person.

When caring for an injured deer that doesn't want to eat, it's worth persevering with force feeding. Make up some baby cereal so that it's very thick, and squeeze or dribble it into the deer's mouth. For a large deer, 1 pint/600 ml, two or three times a day will do the trick.

When feeding a fawn, give it goat's milk in a baby's feeding bottle. You could mix in some cod liver oil or egg as well.

Bats

If you have to handle a bat, be careful not to hold its wings because they are extremely fragile. Support its body. Better still, offer it a vertical surface and it will instinctively turn itself upside down and hang downwards, gripping with its hind feet.

During the day, bats become torpid, so won't react if you go near them. After resting, they have to raise their body temperature, which they do by shivering for around half an hour before they can fly.

If you find a bat crawling around the house or garden in the summer, it's likely to be a baby. Pop it in a ventilated box until dusk and then hang the box outside near the roost, where its mother can get at it.

An injured bat will need water as soon as possible – use an eye-dropper or syringe.

If you are looking after a baby bat, feed it some skimmed milk through a pipette.

Ferrets

Ferrets have a nasty bite. If you're unfortunate enough to be on the receiving end of its teeth, try to let the animal's feet rest on the ground (even though your instinct will be to pull away from the source of pain). Once it feels its feet on solid ground, it will probably be so pleased that it will let you go.

If the ferret still hangs on grimly, try pinching its forehead or a foot to distract it.

Most ferrets are easy to handle, however. Just support its body with your hand. Putting your thumb under its chin means it won't be tempted to bite you.

If you want to catch a ferret, try using a tube. They are incredibly curious and love exploring dark holes. A piece of drainpipe with the cage at the other end is one way to catch them.

Wild Birds

To make your own instant bird feeder, take the cardboard tube from a loo roll or kitchen paper roll and cover it in honey. Then roll it over some birdseed until it's completely covered. You can then hang it outside and enjoy watching the birds as they eat.

To transport a bird such as a swan or goose, chop the corner off an old sack and pop it over the bird. They can put their head through the hole, but their wings and body are kept secure.

When handling birds such as ravens or herons, keep an eye on their beaks, which are formidable weapons. If you have to examine them, slip a rubber band over the end of the beak for your safety. Don't leave it there for very long.

When handling birds of prey, wear heavy-duty gloves. Their beaks and claws are designed for ripping and tearing. They should be handled by experts but if you're in a position where you have to catch one, don't handle it more than necessary. Put it in a warm, dark, ventilated box (not a cage) until you can hand it over to an expert.

A hooded bird of prey is a quiet bird. An old sock with a hole for the beak will be an effective hood. Don't try hooding an owl, however – it won't work.

Don't bind the beak of a bird while transporting it because it may want to throw up due to the stress of capture.

When feeding birds of prey that might not be used to dead food, try cutting up a day-old chick so that its innards are exposed.

First Aid

In the spring you may come across a baby animal. Don't assume it's been abandoned – just leave it alone. Unless it's obviously hurt or in danger, retreat to a discreet distance and keep an eye on it if you're not sure whether the parents are around.

When out camping or walking, use an inverted frisbee as a water or food dish for your pet.

If an animal has suffered a burn, you must try to take the heat out of the affected area. Plunge the area into cold water for 10–15 minutes. Once the area is cool, you can cover it with a clean, dry bandage or cloth. Don't use oil or lotion.

Alternatively, soak the cloth in very strong tea. The tannin encourages the wound to coagulate quickly and protect the sensitive spot.

If an animal has suffered burns caused by acid or alkaline, remember that an acid substance will neutralise an alkaline one and vice versa. Milk or bicarbonate of soda (2 parts bicarbonate to 98 of water) to neutralise acids; weak vinegar (5 parts to 95 of water) will neutralise alkalis such as caustic soda and ammonia.

When an animal has swallowed something acidic, neutralise the acid with alkaline substances such as bicarbonate of soda or chalk (mixed in barley water or milk). If you don't have anything alkaline to hand, dilute the acid as much as possible with water.

If you suspect an animal has eaten barbiturates, give it an emetic and keep it warm. Even strong coffee will help.

Lead can be extremely dangerous to animals – two pieces of lead shot can kill a pigeon. The best immediate treatment for mammals is a large dose of Epsom salts, milk, egg whites or strong tea. Send for the vet immediately and keep the animal warm and quiet.

Heatstroke is a killer, so you must do everything to cool down the animal as quickly as possible. Reduce body heat rapidly by showering with cold water, applying wet sheets and towels, putting paws in cold water and trying to get cold air into the lungs. Get the animal to a vet as soon as possible.

If an animal has eaten poison, you need to give it an emetic to cause vomiting or a purgative to empty the bowels. Useful emetics are: salt with water (around two tablespoons to a cup), washing soda (about the size of a hazelnut for a dog or cat), Epsom salts or mustard in water (one dessert spoon in a cupful of water for a pig).

Animals can suffer from bee and wasp stings as well as humans. If you can, remove the sting carefully. Apply a paste of bicarbonate of soda to the afflicted area.

Alternatively, rub half a freshly cut onion over the sting spot.

Tar can be difficult to get off fur (or skin, for that matter). Try margarine, melted butter or eucalyptus oil.

If creosote is the problem, wash it off as soon as possible using warm, soapy water or warm castor oil. Make sure you clean the skin as well as the fur.

If you are involved in a road traffic accident with horses, dogs or cattle, you have a legal obligation to report it to the police.

WINDOW CLEANERS

Cleaning

Harry Dixon; Peter Lewis; Beryl Murray, National Federation of Master Window & General Cleaners; Crystal Clear, Sheffield; Mr Robinson, Premier Window Cleaning, Sheffield; Mr Baxter, Intake Window Cleaning, Sheffield

Prevent smeary windows by adding a drop of vinegar to the water and rubbing with a chamois leather or old newspaper.

Remove bird droppings and dried paint from windows with a rag dipped in hot vinegar.

Use warm water with a little fabric conditioner to wipe over glass-topped tables, computer and television screens and so on. Then rub dry with a lint-free cloth.

Use spray air freshener to clean glass – it doesn't smear and it smells delicious.

Use pure alcohol, like methylated spirit, to clean it until it sparkles.

Professional window cleaners use scrim, a lint-free cloth made of Irish linen. It is very hard-wearing and absorbent, and won't leave tiny threads on your windows. Scrim is available from window-cleaning suppliers.

Mirror, mirror... if you find the bathroom mirror steams up in the morning when you are trying to shave, rub on some shaving foam and wipe until the foam disappears. The mirror won't steam up for about two weeks.

Soap has the same effect. Rub a dry bar of soap on to the mirror and rub off.

To remove dried paint splashes from glass, don't use a Stanley knife or scalpel. Buy a proper flat-edged safety knife to get the right angle on the paint marks.

Use a paste of baking soda to remove masking tape residue left on windows and woodwork after painting.

There is no magical ingredient in a window cleaner's water – it's usually just a bit of washing-up liquid, or sometimes the juice of some over-ripe lemons.

Other window cleaning solutions: ½ cup vinegar to 1 gallon/4.5 litres water; or ½ cup sudsy ammonia to 1 gallon/4.5 litres water; or in freezing weather, ½ cup sudsy ammonia, 2 cups rubbing alcohol, 1 teaspoon washing-up liquid to 1 gallon/4.5 litres water.

Use as little soap as possible in your solution to prevent streaking.

To clean the perfect window, dip your sponge in the solution to absorb just enough water to cover the window without flooding it. Wet the surface of the window with the sponge, paying special attention to the sides and corners. Dip a squeegee into the solution, press it lightly on to the surface of the window, starting at the top, and pulling down vertically, stopping a few inches from the bottom of the window. Wipe off the squeegee with a paper towel, then repeat all the way across the window. Then pull the squeegee horizontally across the bottom of the window before wiping the bottom of the window-frame with a paper towel.

For hard-to-reach windows, you can buy squeegee extension poles from most hardware stores.

Try to clean windows when they are in the shade. Not only can you see the glass properly when there is least reflection from the sun, but when windows are in full sunlight the sun dries the glass quicker than it can be polished, so it becomes streaky.

To clean Venetian blinds, tilt the slats of the blind so they are closed. Place one hand on the blind to hold it steady to prevent it from banging against woodwork and chipping paint. Starting at the top, use the brush attachment on your vacuum cleaner, a soft, dry cloth, or clean, soft, cotton gloves on your hands. Brush from the centre to the right support, and the centre to the left support, and then from the supports to the edge of each slat, about 8 in/20 cm at a time. Repeat in 8 in/20 cm sections down to the bottom, then repeat on the other side of slats by reversing the tilt.

You can get two types of squeegee blade: use hard blades in the summer, as they will soften in the heat, and soft blades in the winter, as they will harden in the cold.

UPVC window-frames have a smooth join between the window and the frame. To get close in to the edge, nick the ends of the rubber blade on your squeegee.

Small cracks in the window-pane? Add a drop or two of superglue to the centre of the crack. Capillary action should pull the thin liquid along the length of the crack and may be enough to make the crack disappear.

To touch up light scratches on the glass, rub them lightly with mildly abrasive tooth-paste, using cotton-gloved finger or soft flannel cloth. Also works on mirrors.

Safety

All reputable window cleaners should hold a current certificate of Public Liability Insurance, or if they are employees, Employers Liability Insurance.

Check that sash lines or balances are in good condition and not liable to break while cleaning.

Check for locks that operate when the window is closed, and check that the window is not liable to jam shut. Use a folded cloth to prop the window open.

Do not stand on wooden window boxes or lean your ladder against them, as they rot with age.

If possible, clean windows from the inside, but remember that leaning out of a win-dow is just as dangerous as being on the outside.

If you are outside, make sure you are properly secured. Don't hold on to fittings, as you can't rely on their strength.

Don't stand on polished sills or ledges, and remember that sitting on an outside window-sill is no safer than standing on it.

Cracked or broken glass is not safe to clean, as it may smash or splinter.

Check that the rubber feet on your ladder are not loose, and never use a ladder with a broken or bent rung, as not only might you miss your footing, but the strength of the whole ladder might be affected.

Ladders that come apart should not be made to mix-and-match a new ladder – only use parts from the same ladder.

Always use the right length ladder for the job. A useful guide is: the ladder should extend at least four rungs above the highest rung you are going to stand on, and still leave an overlap of three to five rungs on a two- or three-part ladder.

A good guide on how to rest your ladder at a safe angle is: 3 ft/ 1 m out for every 12 ft/4 m up.

Always stand your ladder on a firm base, but on wet or highly polished floors, stand your ladder on a damp swab.

Only use pointed ladders into corners or angles, so they can't slip sideways. You can buy spreaders to convert pointed ladders for use on flat surfaces.

Never paint a ladder, as you will not be able to see any cracks in the structure under-neath the paint. Use clear varnish instead.

Frames

Clean the woodwork around the window first, as it is difficult to do it afterwards without dirtying your clean windows.

To clean painted window-frames, use a solution of mild detergent and water, or if you use a commercial cleaner, check that it is safe for painted surfaces. Always rinse off the solution. Wipe off the excess water with a dry cloth. Do not use strong cleaners as they will damage the paint.

To clean wood or varnished frames, vacuum or dust regularly. Only clean when really necessary. Use a wood-cleaning product or wax.

Putty can be kept for ages by putting it in a plastic bag in the freezer. Squeeze all the air out of the bag and secure it with an elastic band. It only takes a few minutes to defrost.

When painting wooden window-frames, remove loose or flaky paint – all the way down to the wood if necessary. You may need to replace the putty between the frame and the window if it's cracked or crumbling. Remove or tape over locks, handles and hinges, and lay masking tape around the edges of the glass. Remove the tape slowly as soon as the paint is dry to the touch. Scrape off any paint on the glass with a razor blade as soon as the paint is tacky.

To paint sash windows, paint each window separately, allowing one to dry before painting the other, and leave them slightly open while drying so they don't stick together. Never paint the vertical grooves on the side where the window is actually hung, as this gums up the works.

WINE MERCHANTS

Berry Bros & Rudd

Staying for more than one night at a hotel? Don't order half bottles of wine, which are expensive. Order a full bottle and ask the maitre d' to keep it for you until the next evening.

Spray labels on wine bottles with hairspray before consigning them to a damp cellar. It keeps them readable for years.

To remove a stubborn cork, dip woollen cloth into boiling water, wrap tightly round the bottle neck and the cork will loosen.

Remember when buying wine that between £1.80 and £2.00 of the retail price is accounted for by the cost of the bottle, label, cork, capsule and VAT. It's worth forking out a bit more – you'll get a better bottle of wine.

When selecting a wine to drink with food, take into account the way the food is prepared and in particular any sauces that will be served.

Red wine too young? Decant it and pass the wine from the bottle to the decanter and back again (using a funnel) to get as much air into the wine as possible. This will prematurely age it and soften out the wine.

Taking a cork out of a bottle of red wine only gets air into the very top of the bottle. If you want to let the wine 'breathe' then it must be decanted into another vessel.

In fact you can mask the poor quality of most wines by decanting it – it also means knowledgeable guests won't be able to read the label.

But it is easy to destroy an old bottle of wine by decanting it. Too much air and the wine will be over the hill. Better instead to pour the wine carefully from the bottle so as not to disturb any sediment.

Don't scrimp with a good meal by using plonk to make a sauce. The better the wine, the better the sauce. A full-bodied red over a watery one is preferable.

Your guests shouldn't be guinea pigs: a dinner party is not the best venue to try out an exciting new wine from Estonia you found at the off-licence. Test it out on your own first. A bottle of acid rain will ruin the party.

Spirits should be stored upright. Prolonged contact with 40 per cent alcohol may make the screw cap deteriorate.

The larger the bottle, the longer the wine will keep, and the more slowly it will mature, owing to the fact that there is less surface area of wine in contact with air in the bottle.

'A glass of wine without some cheese, is like a kiss without a squeeze.'

The words 'Fine Champagne' on a bottle of Cognac refer to a blend of wines from two of the authorised Cognac making areas, Grande Champagne and Petite Champagne.

It is better to open one bottle in a case too early, than all of them too late!

Wine merchants don't bite (well, only when provoked). Talk to your wine merchant who will be happy to give you advice. They're a godsend in moments of panic and indecision.

LIST OF INGREDIENTS

It's surprising how many common, household items can be utilised in these *Trade Secrets*. If you've got these in your cupboards, you should be able to deal with any eventuality!

Bicarbonate of soda

Petroleum jelly

Methylated spirits

Vinegar (white, cider ... all sorts)

Washing-up liquid

Kitchen foil

Cling film

Chamois leather

Sticky tape

Oil (olive, vegetable ... all sorts)

Cornflour

Lemons

Bread

Sugar lumps

Tea bags

Denture-cleaning tablets

Coca-Cola

Toothpaste

Milk

Salt

Eggs

Cotton wool

Talcum powder

Elastic bands

Safety pins

Old tights & stockings

Old corks

Bin liners

Cat litter

Empty yoghurt pots

Empty two-litre plastic bottles

Cardboard tubes

Empty film canisters

Bottle of wine – not really anything to do with *Trade Secrets* but it's always nice to have one lurking in the cupboard!

INDEX